CHRISTIANIZING CRIMEA

NORTHERN ILLINOIS UNIVERSITY PRESS *DeKalb*

Christianizing
CRIMEA

SHAPING SACRED SPACE
IN THE RUSSIAN EMPIRE
AND BEYOND

Mara Kozelsky

© 2010 by Northern Illinois University Press

Published by the Northern Illinois University Press, DeKalb, Illinois   60115

Manufactured in the United States using postconsumer-recycled, acid-free paper.

All Rights Reserved

Design by Julia Fauci

Library of Congress Cataloging-in-Publication Data

Kozelsky, Mara.

Christianizing Crimea : shaping sacred space in the Russian Empire and beyond / Mara Kozelsky.

   p.   cm.

Includes bibliographical references (p.   ) and index.

ISBN 978-0-87580-412-5 (clothbound : alk. paper)

1. Russkaia pravoslavnaia tserkov'—Ukraine—Crimea—History. 2. Crimea (Ukraine)—Church history. I. Title.

BX494.C75K69 2009

281.9'4771—dc22

2009032476

Contents

List of Tables   vii

Acknowledgments   ix

Note on Transliteration, Names, and Toponyms   xiii

Introduction   3

1—Challenges of the Confessional Empire and the Limitations of Conversion   15

2—From the Temple of Diana to the Cradle of Christianity   41

3—Athos in Crimea—*A Local Response to the Eastern Question*   62

4—Monasticism Takes Root   103

5—War—*The Crucible of a Holy Place*   125

6—The Legacy of War for Crimean Christianity   150

Epilogue   175

Notes   197

Bibliography   239

Index   265

Tables

TABLE ONE—Number of Non-Orthodox in Tauride   23

TABLE TWO—Colonies in New Russia and Bessarabia   36

TABLE THREE—Numbers of Colonists by Type   37

TABLE FOUR—Population Shift in Tatar Villages after the Crimean War   154–155

Christ Resurrection Church at Foros

Acknowledgments

I began to think about the role of religion and Russian identity after my first extended stay in a small village in the Moscow region as part of a peace exchange program in 1994. A crumbling palace that had once belonged to the Vorontsov family housed the children's sanatorium where I volunteered. The Vorontsovs gave the palace to the state for use as a military hospital in 1812. Later it became a health facility for sufferers from tuberculosis, and finally the children's sanatorium. A decrepit, old church sat opposite the palace, separated by an overgrown courtyard. The church was half in ruins, covered in scaffolding, a restoration begun after the Soviet collapse but halted by the severe economic depression that gripped Russia in the 1990s. Every so often workmen appeared with tools in their hands. In small increments, these workmen—many of them believers who donated their time—budged the restoration forward.

Travels that season and subsequent visits to Russia and Ukraine revealed numerous cases of similar religious reclamations. The revival of Orthodoxy in the post-Soviet period caused me, and many others in the field of Russian history, to question not only the conventional depictions of a weak Russian Orthodox Church, but also the broader assumption that faith declined in the modern era. Grand gestures such as the rebuilding of the Christ the Savior Cathedral in Moscow impressed upon me, moreover, the centrality of monuments for religious identity. Thus, I became increasingly interested in religious landscapes, the relationship between sacred structures and the surrounding environment. Even today, I remember being struck by the image of the restored church in the small Russian village. It stood as a reminder of what once was, a representation of continuity between past and present. Few places demonstrate the importance of religious monuments more than Crimea, an autonomous republic attached to Ukraine. Crimea was home to the independent Crimean Khanate and has been an outpost of the Roman, Byzantine, Russian, and Ottoman Empires. Hallowed histories of sacred ruins and overlapping sacred landscapes dominate the territory. Memories of Islam, Christianity, and Judaism linger in the foundations of old buildings long destroyed or under reconstruction. Believers are locked in a struggle to protect these symbols of faith from the abuse of nationalists who exploit religious sentiment for dubious purposes.

Acknowledgments

This book began as a dissertation in 1998 at the University of Rochester, where I had the opportunity to study with Brenda Meehan. Professor Meehan shared her deep appreciation of Russian Orthodox spirituality with me, and provided constant encouragement through the early stages of the project. The faculty's diverse interests at the University of Rochester inspired me to understand religious monuments in the context of empire and nationalism, while Celia Applegate especially helped me when Professor Meehan could not. Kathleen Parthé gave generously of her time as a member of my dissertation committee. The book in its earliest form, then, owes much to their patient oversight.

Countless other people have helped me along the way. Philip L. Kohl and Heidi Sherman shared their knowledge of archaeology with me, and I discovered Crimean *kraevedenie* with Victoria Klein. Stephen M. Norris taught me about *lubki* and allowed me to use Crimean War images he discovered. I had the great fortune to meet and travel with Idil Izmirli in Crimea in 2006. Continuous conversation with Idil in the summer of 2006 added much more nuance to my understanding of current issues in Crimea than I could have achieved on my own. Inci Bowman introduced me to important contemporary debates, as has Kemal Gafarov. Collegial comments and criticism at the following conferences has made my work stronger: the American Association for the Advancement of Slavic Studies, the American Historical Association, and the Association for the Study of Eastern Christianity. I would like especially to recognize Nathaniel Knight, Theophilus Prousis, Barbara Skinner, and David Goldfrank, who have led me to consider the project in new ways and whose cautions helped me to find the right balance.

Archivists at the Russian State Historical Archive, the Manuscripts Division of the Russian National Library, the Odessa Regional Archive, and the Archive of the Autonomous Republic of Crimea facilitated my discovery of new material, while the staff at the Gorky Library in Odessa and the Ismail bey Gaspirali Library in Crimea guided me through their rich collections. I am grateful for the kindness and attention shown me by everyone at TAURICA museum and library.

In the United States, staff connected with the interlibrary loan departments at the University of Rochester and the University of South Alabama diligently searched for rare published material; this book could not have been written without their assistance. Thanks to the Davis Center for Russian and Eurasian Studies at Harvard, I have also had access to indispensable Widener Library collections. Inter-library loan and associate programs such as that sponsored by the Davis Center are critical to the democratization of research. Several grants funded the research for this book, primarily from the American Councils for International Education, the History Department at the University of Rochester, the University of South Alabama College of Arts and Sciences, and the University of South Alabama Research Council.

Research that I have published elsewhere is interspersed in varying degrees throughout the book: "Casualties of Conflict: Crimean Tatars during the Crimean War," *Slavic Review*, 67, no. 4 (2008): 862–91; "Ruins into Relics: The Monument to St. Vladimir on the Excavations of Chersonesos, 1827–1857," *Russian Review*, 63, no. 4 (2004): 655–72 (© 2004 Board of Trustees for *The Russian Review*); and "The Challenges of Church Archaeology in Post-Soviet Crimea," edited by Philip L. Kohl, Mara Kozelsky, and Nachman Ben-Yehuda, in *Selective Remembrances: Archaeology in the Construction, Commemoration, and Consecration of National Pasts* (Chicago, 2008), 71–98.

Colleagues in the History Department at the University of South Alabama have thoughtfully encouraged me through the completion of this book. Although the entire faculty deserves my appreciation, I would like to particularly thank the chair of the department, Clarence L. Mohr, who has indefatigably protected our time for research, as well as Marsha Hamilton and Martha Jane Brazy, who have graciously mentored me these last few years, and Harry Miller, who has read my introduction. Others have contributed to this project directly or indirectly by reading bits and pieces or simply providing support: Ewa Hauser, Melanie May, Lisa Szefel, John Summers, Tanya Bakhmetyeva, Jackie Eddy, Brian Campbell, Nicholas Waddy, James K. Bryant II, Jean-Paul Vivian, and Jeanne Rose.

My largest debt of gratitude is owed my family. Joe Kozelsky, Antoinette Till, Linda Kozelsky, Harvey Brower, Holly Kozelsky, Kristin Kozelsky, Michael Kozelsky, and Richard Hunter have provided unyielding comfort and the wisest counsel. They have celebrated each step forward and supported me through the challenges. With deepest appreciation, I dedicate this book to them.

Note on Transliteration, Names, and Toponyms

Generally, I follow the Library of Congress system of transliteration. Transliterating place and personal names has presented something of a challenge, because like many territories of the former Soviet Union toponyms in Crimea continue to evolve. The official language is Ukrainian; Russian, and Kirimtatar are recognized languages; Greek and Ottoman Turkish are only two of the many historical languages. Thus, the city of Bakhchisarai might otherwise be rendered as Bakhchisaray, Bağçasaray, or Bahçesaray. Because this book primarily focuses on the Russian period of Crimean history, however, I typically employ Russian transliteration of place names. Yet, there are numerous exceptions to this rule. Nineteenth-century bureaucrats often provided several different spellings of the same place. In those cases, I chose the most consistently used form. Common usage also demands flexibility. For example, I employ the toponym 'Chersonesos' rather than the other versions (Chersonesus, Korsun, Khersones, Cherson, Chersonese) principally because this is preferred by the archaeological preserve, and I have adopted Kyiv rather than Kiev. I have also deleted the soft sign at the end of cities (Simferopol, Mariupol, Nikol, and others) for the ease of western readers.

Establishing consistent spellings among personal names follows similar principles. For the most part, I transliterate names as they appear in the documents, thus Innokentii rather than Innocent, Polikarp rather than Polycarp, or Vladimir rather than Volodymyr. Exceptions include Russian and Byzantine rulers (Alexander, Nicholas, Constantine, Basil, etc.) who are familiar to western readers by their western names. Greek and Bulgarian émigrés in New Russia and Crimea presented themselves differently for different audiences. In such cases, I either adopted the spelling most commonly employed in the historiographic literature or the most consistent usage in the primary documents. Such choices do not reflect political preferences.

CHRISTIANIZING CRIMEA

Introduction

Few places in the Russian Empire rivaled Crimea's diversity. Prince and scholar Anatolii Demidov, who traveled through the region in the 1830s, likened the capital of the Tauride province, Simferopol, to the Tower of Babel, remarking: "People of every nation are gathered here talking every known language under the sun. . . . Greeks, Tatars, Armenians, Jews, and Russians" thronged the streets.[1] More than a decade later, the Ukrainian sugar magnate Artemii Tereshchenko echoed Demidov's sentiments, observing that "various tribes mixed" in Simferopol. Apart from the "dominant Russian, or to be more exact Ukrainian [*Malorussian*] population," who lived in the "beautiful, clean city," Tereshchenko identified "French, Germans, Italians, Armenians, Greeks, Tatars and Jews." It was "not for nothing," he concluded, that Simferopol took its name after the Greek word for "gather."[2]

Smells in the bazaars, conversations on the roads, even the architecture along the skyline reflected this historically rich ethnic and religious diversity. Hellenes and Jews settled in Crimea before the first century and witnessed the entrance of Christianity under Roman influence. By the beginning of the fourth century, several dioceses networked the peninsula.[3] The rise of Byzantium further consolidated Christianity on the peninsula, as did new settlements of Greeks, Armenians, and other Europeans. The Christian period came to an end as Mongols fanned out across the Eurasian plain in the thirteenth and fourteenth centuries. Eski Kirim, the capital of the Mongolian provincial administration in Crimea, became a center of Islam, with "mosques, dervish monasteries, and schools."[4] Ottoman and Tatar successor states replaced the Mongols in Crimea. In the eighteenth century, Tatars composed the majority population, Islam was the official religion, and there were 1,600 mosques located on the peninsula, spread among six cities and nearly 1,500 villages.[5] The remaining Greek and Armenian Christian populations had dwindled to 50,000.[6] Throughout Crimea, ruins etched the memory of early Greek colonization, ancient Judaism, Byzantine Christianity, and the Crimean Khanate into the landscape. One Soviet scholar who managed to conduct a small survey of Tatar monuments before they were destroyed during World War II noted that "it was difficult to concretely establish where Seljuk influence began, where Byzantine ended, and where the Armenian enters."[7]

Population exchanges, exile, and resettlement accompanied Russia's conquest of the Black Sea region. Scholars estimate that during the Russo-Turkish

War (1768–1774), 80,000–100,000 Tatars, approximately one third of Crimea's population, left the peninsula for Anatolia.[8] The majority of Crimea's Christian populations, approximately 18,000 Greeks and 12,500 Armenians, also left en masse.[9] European immigrants replaced these peoples after Catherine II provided settlement incentives to populate the vast territory that Russia had wrestled from the Ottoman Empire. The territory consisted of the Kherson, Tauride, Bessarabia, and Ekaterinoslav provinces, collectively called *Novorossiia* or New Russia.[10] Russian Christians who fell outside the official Orthodox Church settled in New Russia as well. Islam remained the dominant faith, and the combination of all groups rendered Crimea the most confessionally diverse region in the empire.

As opposed to Russian travelers who rarely addressed the shortcomings of Russian administration openly, foreign subjects pointedly discussed the challenges of empire.[11] Victor Amanton commented that "sometimes, just to cross the street, you believe you are passing from Europe to Asia."[12] Unlike in the Americas, Europe, and Asia, where "diverse peoples exist, but they mix in the same quarter, and strive ... to assimilate," this French official noted that in Crimea "there is nothing similar; at the minimum is one race, who lives in the village inhabited only by its own, or within a separate quarter in the village that becomes two in which the religion, the manners, the dress, the houses are all very different from one to the other." Amanton was most struck by the isolation of these groups from each other. He noted that the peoples of Crimea—Tatars, Jews, Eastern Europeans, Greeks, Germans, Roma, and Russians—lived in their own colonies, divided largely by their confession.[13]

Amanton's observations, published in 1854, reveal the complex nature of religion and empire in Crimea on the eve of the Crimean War.[14] From the era of Catherine II (1762–1796), the Russian Empire promoted cultural autonomy and religious toleration among subject populations, yet recognized Orthodoxy as the state religion and based juridical status upon religious affiliation. These policies left a legacy of mixed rights and privileges that divided populations for decades. Rather than assimilating immigrants into the empire, imperial policies often reinforced or created new boundaries around native identities. Borderland politics amplified the contradictions of Russian confessional policies in Crimea, which for centuries prior to Russian annexation served as an outpost of Roman, Byzantine, and Ottoman Empires.

As Amanton ruminated over religious tension in Crimea, the Russian Orthodox Church crafted a massive Christianizing program.[15] Apart from a brief interlude (1787–1799) when the church temporarily created a diocese for the eastern region of the peninsula, Crimea had only one monastery, few active churches, and no official Orthodox hierarchy. Even after decades of internal Russian migration and foreign settlement, Christians remained less than half of the Crimean population. In the years leading to the Crimean War, however, priests reopened ancient Byzantine churches and reestablished abandoned monasteries. The consistory based in Odessa campaigned for the creation of a separate diocese in Crimea with appropriate institutional resources. The church won the war that Russia lost in Crimea. It opened new parishes, assigned a clerical hierarchy to Crimea, and developed a network of monasteries and convents with over 500 inhabitants. Russians across the empire recognized Crimea as an ancient holy place, the cradle of Russian Christianity.

This book describes the Christianizing of Crimea, a term I use to signify a set of cultural and institutional practices designed to transform a territory irrespective of group or individual conversion.[16] It spans the history of Christianity in Crimea from Russian annexation (1783) through the post-Soviet period, but chiefly focuses on the era of Nicholas I (1825–1855), when borderland politics thrust Crimea into the center of nationalist discourse and religion became synonymous with identity. During this time, the church campaigned to transform Crimea into "Russian Athos," a decision influenced by Crimea's many Christian antiquities, the revival of Athonite spirituality, and religious tensions along the Black Sea border. Although Crimea's Christianizing was *fait accompli* by 1853, the Crimean War (1853–1856) fixed the Christian advance. War exploded local religious tensions, the Muslim population went into sharp decline, and efforts to spread Christianity accelerated.

Science, migration, and war set the backdrop for Crimea's Christianizing. A devout Orthodox Christian, Nicholas I believed that "the state was to serve God, not God the State."[17] This religious interpretation of state power infused the Nicolaevin period, demonstrated in the official nationality platform, "Orthodoxy, autocracy, nationality," formulated by the minister of education, Count Sergei Uvarov, in April 1833. Uvarov viewed the "advent of Christianity" as the "turning point of civilization,"[18] and along with the tsar, understood Russia "within a Christian framework."[19] This conviction translated into a Christianizing of Russian history and, by extension, Crimean history.

For decades, Uvarov urged scholars working in nascent disciplines of history and archaeology to discover evidence of Russian origins, and to focus especially on Russia's conversion to Christianity. Due to its impressive array of Byzantine era ruins, Crimea became a magnet for imperial archaeologists. Scholars like Aleksei Uvarov, son of the minister of education, became preoccupied with locating the precise spot where Byzantium transmitted Christianity to the Slavs. According to legend this occurred in the ancient Crimean coastal city, Chersonesos, where the Kyivan prince, Vladimir, was baptized in 988. Finding evidence to substantiate the Vladimir legend occupied scholars for decades and became a disciplinary subfield termed the "archaeology of the Korsun legend."

Together, church and secular scholars—such divisions were far from rigid—produced a sacred history for Crimea that emphasized divine revelation in the narrative of the peninsula's past. In addition to substantiating the Korsun legend, scholars looked for evidence to support the hypothesis that Andrew the Apostle visited Crimea as part of his mission field. Church and secular archaeologists tried to identify where other saints, including two Roman popes, Clement and Martin, might have lived, and they searched for early Christian artifacts in Crimea's network of cave cities. Armed with archaeological studies, church publicists argued that Crimea was a holy place for the empire, the cradle of Russian Christianity with a first-century pedigree. Because sacred monuments deserved preservation and sanctification, the church entreated scholars from imperial historical and archaeological societies to help restore antiquities for active use. *Kraevedenie* (regional studies) scholars based in Odessa and Crimea played particularly active roles in the peninsula's Christian renewal by generating plans and recreating facades.[20] The journal affiliated with the Odessa Society for History and Antiquities (founded 1839), *Novorossiiskii kalendar'* (1832), and *Odesskii vestnik* (1827) regularly published reports on Christian antiquities and their restoration.

As church and secular scholars renovated Christian antiquities, Balkan immigrants revived ancient religious traditions. The Black Sea provinces of New Russia became a safe haven for Orthodox refugees seeking shelter from the Ottoman Empire during the era of Catherine II and beyond. In lieu of the sparsely populated Russian laity, Balkan Christian refugees reestablished ancient religious traditions and opened long abandoned churches. They visited holy sites and held religious processions. Following the 1821 Greek revolt through the end of the Crimean War in 1856, the local Russian Orthodox Church increasingly perceived the pan-Orthodox communities as the key to shoring up the Orthodox faith in the former Ottoman territory.

Taking inspiration from Mt. Athos in Greece, church leaders campaigned to restore the network of Christian sites as a new monastic community they called "Russian Athos." Church authorities argued that the two peninsulas shared similar topography, climate, and histories touched by miracles and saints. Russian Athos denoted Crimea's shared heritage with the Balkan Orthodox populations and reflected the peninsula's connection to the political affairs along the Russo-Ottoman border. The first proposal for Russian Athos received approval from Russia's Holy Synod in 1849, and the ancient Dormition monastery reopened the following year. A series of articles in *Odesskii vestnik* announced each stage in the development of the monastic community, while the archbishop, who traveled regularly to St. Petersburg to fulfill his responsibilities as a member of the synod, actively promoted Athos in Crimea. Before the war, three other sketes opened: the St. Vladimir skete in Chersonesos, the Inkerman skete in the cave city near Sevastopol, and the community at the Cosmas and Damian spring, a location that attracted Christians and Tatars alike.

The sudden eruption of the Crimean War forever altered the peninsula, and when the war concluded, contemporaries realized that Crimea would never be the same. Describing a traveler's account of Crimea composed in 1853 but published in 1856, the editor of *Russkaia beseda* commented: "We suggest that ... from now, this should be read as an historical document."[21] War ruined Crimea's economy, scarred its landscapes, and displaced native populations. It also created new conditions for Crimea's Christianizing. As all eyes in Russia turned toward the southern front, widely disseminated newspaper articles, broadsides, and sermons communicated the religious nature of the conflict and Crimea's special sacrifice for the empire. Sermons emphasized that a battle between Christianity and Islam, Orthodoxy and heresies of the West, was being fought in the birthplace of Slavic Christianity. Crimea's Muslims, meanwhile, fell under suspicion as internal enemies because they professed Islam. By the end of the Crimean War, observers noted that the Black Sea region in general had become "more and more Russian and more and more Orthodox," a comment that reflected the *perception* of Crimea's Christian identity as much as actual growth of Christian institutions.[22]

Crimea's transformation would not have been possible without the inspiration of Archbishop Innokentii (Borisov, 1848–1857), who according to one parish priest, "prepared for and hastened the establishment of Christianity here," due to his "russification of the Crimean mountains and administration during the Crimean War."[23] A prelate whose reputation rivaled that of Metropolitan Filaret (Drozdov, 1783–1867), Innokentii today is regarded as one of Russia's first preachers, and a father of Russian moral and pastoral theology.[24] Innokentii administered Crimean religious affairs in the twilight of his career, from 1848 through his death the year following the end of the Crimean War. From the diocesan seat in Odessa, he gathered information about Crimean antiquities, and drummed up support for the transformation of abandoned, Byzantine-era churches into living monastic communities. His sermons, which interpreted the

Crimean struggle as a holy war, secured further sympathy and support for his Christianizing project. Yet, the archbishop was not alone in changing Crimea. Instead, Orthodox believers throughout the empire committed private resources to help spread Christianity on the peninsula; their donations made the first stage of Christianizing possible.[25]

The Crimean laity little resembled Orthodox communities of the empire's interior. Orthodox believers constituted fewer than half the peninsula's population during the Nicolaevin era, and of that group, an unknown number were Greek. Before the Crimean War, most Russians living on the peninsula were associated either with the imperial bureaucracy or coastal defense. Because relatively few Russians lived in Crimea before the reign of Nicholas I, lay support quite often came from Christians based in Odessa. Other resources came from the St. Petersburg and Moscow elite who held estates in Crimea. These wealthy landowners sent the consistory in Odessa thousands of rubles to renovate Crimean churches, and gave over to the church plots with ancient ruins.

First- and second-generation Greek immigrants who lived in Crimea and elsewhere along the Black Sea coast actively contributed to Crimea's Christianizing. Some of these Greeks, such as those in the Greek battalion in Balaklava, revived ancient Greek grassroots traditions. Others, like the lobbyist Alexandru Sturdza, the admiral Nikolaos Arkas, and the scholar Zacharias Arkas, assisted church expansion through financial donations, scholarly activities, and by mobilizing the powerful Greek-Russian community in Crimea and Odessa. Hermits and pilgrims also assisted in Crimea's transformation by breathing life into renovated Christian monuments. They too represented the external influences upon Crimea's Christianizing, for many of the first-generation Crimean monks were either of Balkan extraction, or had traveled to Mt. Athos.

Borderland identity politics renders Crimea's case unique, but the Christianizing of Crimea nonetheless reflects certain contours of Russia's confessional empire. To borrow the words of Robert Geraci and Michael Khodarkovsky, in Russia "religion was far from a hermetic, bounded realm of personal or even communal spirituality." Instead, it "transcended the distinctions between public-private and spiritual-secular."[26] Terms range widely, from "religious politics," "ecclesiastic politics," "confessional politics," and "confessional empire," to describe the ordering of Russian society and its international behavior.[27] Legislation designed to preserve cultural autonomy prohibited the Russian Orthodox Church from openly proselytizing to adherents of traditional religions officially recognized by the Russian Empire, including Jews, Muslims, and Buddhists.[28] Similarly, it was illegal under Russian law to reject Orthodoxy. Individuals or groups could adopt Orthodoxy, but could not leave it. During the nineteenth century, Tatars who had been converted to Orthodoxy following the conquest of Kazan apostatized in waves: especially in the years 1802–1803, 1827–1830, 1865–1870, and 1905. The state allowed, even encouraged, the church to convert those it perceived as being formerly Orthodox, whether apostatized Tatars or Russian sectarians. As it expanded into new regions, the church had to be sensitive to the various distinctions between Russia's religious groups.[29]

In Crimea, priests and prelates carefully investigated non-Orthodox communities before determining how or whether to approach them, and they shaped the borderland in ways the state could not. Clergymen also entered into discussions over citizenship and assimilation, and acted as an influential lobby for Christian interests at home and abroad. Mainly, however, the church applied its energies to encoding the peninsula within an Orthodox identity. The Christianizing of Crimea did not require native inhabitants to adopt Orthodoxy, although priests and prelates occasionally expressed this goal. Instead, the church concerned itself with consolidating its authority and reconsecrating sacred landscapes.[30]

Church authorities reopened abandoned Byzantine churches and reclaimed holy sites, such as sacred springs and grottos, revered by Crimeans before Christianity arrived on the peninsula. Rather than transforming belief systems of native inhabitants, then, the Christianizing of Crimea involved refashioning the region's identity as an Orthodox holy place for Russians and other Orthodox believers. In this manner, the Christian mission in Crimea—if the term "mission" even applies in the years before the Great Reforms—depended upon deepening the region's historic connection to Orthodoxy.[31]

As the church influenced imperial developments in Crimea, Orthodox print culture contributed to the discourse on Russian national identity. Traditionally, theorists of nationalism have associated religious articulations of national identity with the Old Regime and not with the vast sweeping empires of the nineteenth and twentieth centuries.[32] Because Orthodoxy has featured so vitally in Russian identity discourse, scholars of Russia have more freely acknowledged the importance of religion. Nicholas Riasanovsky's classic study of official nationality opens with a discussion of Tsar Nicholas's personal piety and devotes a significant portion of the book to an examination of the Orthodox element in the platform's trinity "Orthodoxy, autocracy, nationality." Similarly, few studies of unofficial nationalism, whether detailing the thought of early Slavophiles or later Pan-Slavists, fail to register the central position of Orthodoxy.[33] Despite the ubiquitous role of religion in Russian identity discourse, the clerical contribution to the conversation has received very little comment in the vast body of literature. This investigation of Crimea's Christianizing will show that, as much as the writings of the non-clerical intelligentsia, the sermons, pamphlets, and books composed by members of the clerical estate shaped Russian identity.[34] What is more, clerical rhetoric existed independently from state prescriptions and had real consequences for Russian borderland policies.

Works that emphasize the Greco-Russian axis in the Eastern Question have described religion and politics in ways that are especially useful for studying the Black Sea region.[35] The "Eastern Question" is a term used to describe the international crisis that revolved around the gradual disintegration of the Ottoman Empire in the nineteenth century. Britain feared Russian expansion into Ottoman territory and the subsequent threat to British interests in the East. Russian rulers vacillated between dreams of a restored Orthodox commonwealth under Russian protection, and their commitment to uphold Ottoman authority in concert with the major powers of Europe. Nicholas I's policy in the Near East, which balanced an Orthodox nationalism with pragmatic diplomacy, combined elements of both projects.

While the Eastern Question generated tense diplomacy between Russia and the West, it brought the Russian and Ottoman empires into war several times in the nineteenth century, twice during the reign of Nicholas I. These wars had dramatic results for the administration of both empires. Borders shifted, land was lost and gained, peoples were colonized, exchanged, or relocated.[36] Religious identities, like those within Crimea, were forged. The Christianizing process was intricately bound up in Greek independence, Balkan nationalism, the Crimean War, and population exchanges between the empires. After Russian annexation, Crimea convulsed with each new phase of the Eastern Question; it became a constant harbor for refugees and a site of festering ethnic and confessional rivalries that broiled across the Black Sea. Thus, this book understands Christian renewal in Crimea as an expression of confessional politics and the Eastern Question, a local response to the international crises unfolding off its shores.

The Christianizing of Crimea demonstrates that the policies of the Russian Orthodox Church adapted to the modern era and made good use of new tools. Recently, Mark Steinberg and Heather Coleman have asserted that innovations of the modern era transformed belief. "Quite tangibly," they write, "urbanization, modern rail transport, and the rapid expansion of popular literacy and the press worked together with other new social and economic realities to cause many people to experience their faith in novel ways."[37] The church was no less a part of this transition than believers or other institutions of faith. It entered the public sphere by engaging in debates over identity and imperial affairs, and transcended the secular by appropriating methods of scientific inquiry. The church also made exemplary use of mass publications to promote its activities in Crimea, and it invested in new stock certificates to fund restoration of Christian sites. "Blurred boundaries" between modern and traditional, official and popular spirituality, religion and science, or any religious and secular spheres constitute a central theme that runs through the entire book.[38]

To gather material for this book, I worked in archival collections in Odessa, Simferopol, and St. Petersburg that remain hitherto untapped by western scholars. Consistory collections and the files of the Holy Synod, the governing body of the Russian Orthodox Church, offer insight into the debates over church expansion, the church's attitude toward other faith groups, and the church's position between government and society. Archbishop Innokentii's personal papers stored in the Russian National Library in St. Petersburg proved indispensable. A collection of more than 3,000 pieces of correspondence, it contains Innokentii's exchanges with the governor general of New Russia, Prince Mikhail Vorontsov (1823–1856), with influential émigrés, including Alexandru Sturdza, with Bulgarians seeking support for the creation of a national church, and with parish priests struggling to contain heresies. Archbishop Innokentii's papers hold hundreds of letters from Russian scholars concerned about Christian antiquities and from lay men and women offering support for the mission.

Typically, consistories submitted annual reports to the Holy Synod that summarized yearly activities of the diocese. Such reports describe seminary programs, track the movement of priests through the diocese, and carefully detail missionary activities to the number of converts.[39] The consistory of the Kherson-Tauride diocese as a habit, however, did not generate annual reviews. Through 1860, the diocese joined initially three provinces (Ekaterinoslav, Kherson, Tauride, 1787–1837) and then two separate provinces (Kherson, Tauride, 1837–1859) with very different features and needs. The sorely stretched, understaffed consistory marginalized Crimea as an exotic, distant periphery of Odessa and never succeeded in centralizing affairs, nor did it produce a diocesan journal until after Tauride received its own bishop in 1860.[40] Consequently, I worked from the bottom up, letter by letter, file by file, to create an overview of church activities for the main period covered in this book.

Published period sources reveal the rich complexity of Orthodox print culture and are central to this study. Because the creation of Crimea's sacred history occurred in the pages of scholarly publications, an analysis of imperial journals, nineteenth-century archaeological and historical research, and local newspapers proved crucial to understanding the full scope of the Christianizing process. Similarly, religious and tourist pamphlets promoted pilgrimage to Russian Athos, while memoirs reveal the depth of change in Crimea. When possible, I captured the response of indigenous populations to church expansion, some of which can also be gleaned from the more voluminous scholarship describing the history of Crimean Tatars.[41] Finally, I relied upon *kraevedenie* collections in Odessa and St. Petersburg libraries, the Taurica collection of the Crimean Ethnographic Museum and the Ismail bey Gaspirali Library in Simferopol to deepen my knowledge about natives, Russians, and refugees who made New Russia their home.

Research in church collections turned up few interchanges with Tatars; these derived from atypical cases of apostasy. A recent study grounded in Muftiate archives before the Crimean War suggests a reason for this: Tatars were more concerned with encroachment by Russian landowners than with the expansion of the church.[42] After the war, Tatars did respond to religious tensions, but they spoke with their feet by leaving Crimea en masse. Given the depth and breadth of Orthodox archival and print material, of various archaeological studies, and of the mountain of war-related sources that have yet to be fully exploited, working in Muftiate archives and Tatar national literature proved beyond the scope of this study. Capturing voices and experiences of the native Greeks, Armenians, Jews, and various immigrant populations proved equally challenging. Although each of Crimea's major ethnic groups has its own historians, much of the published history was either composed during the Soviet period or written by those with limited access to archival material. Alternatively, scholars have bypassed the Nicolaevan era to focus on the eighteenth-century exodus of Christians, or their deportations during World War II.[43] Other subjects that provide the backdrop for this book are relatively under-researched as well, whether the role of religion and the Crimean War or the fluctuation of immigration patterns before, during, and after the war. Such topics suggest books in themselves. Thus, I have charted a course that focuses on Russian Orthodox expansion and on perceptions of Christianity in Crimea, while addressing questions pertaining to nationality as much as space and time have permitted.

Chapter 1 describes the history of the New Russian diocese and Orthodox perceptions of the diverse populations in the diocese. It further explores diverging views among church and state officials about the role of religion in empire, and it examines the strategies of church expansion that varied according to faith group. The importance of Byzantine history and the Greek population to Crimea's Christianizing is the subject of chapter 2. Greeks played an actual and a symbolic role in the peninsula's Christianizing; before Russians fanned across the peninsula, Greek settlers revived ancient Christian traditions and opened abandoned Christian churches. While chapter 2 examines the Greek revival of Christianity in Crimea in the context of Russian Graecophilia, chapter 3 describes the growing influence of Greek, Bulgarian, and other Orthodox refugees in Crimea, and the adoption of Mt. Athos as a model for Crimea's Christian renewal. The selection of Mt. Athos, as chapter 3 demonstrates, had political as well as religious significance, for it reflected a localized response to the borderland conflicts and the holy places controversy. Chapter 4 analyzes the creation of a monastic community in Crimea. It discusses the sacred legends associated with each site and the assimilation of local pagan and Tatar traditions into sacred narratives. Whereas earlier chapters examined the limitations and contexts of Crimea's Christianizing, chapter 4 shows how Christianizing unfolded, and emphasizes the public ceremonies, community building, and promotion that accompanied the opening of the new monasteries.

The fifth chapter shows that the Christianizing process reached a peak during the Crimean War, as war-time propaganda highlighted the peninsula as the cradle of Russian Christianity. More than any other chapter, chapter 5 offers the most salient examples of how Orthodox print culture crafted Russian identity. The war introduced a new era of migration. Tatars left and Bulgarians took their place. Crimea received its own bishop and institutional growth began to reflect Christian rhetoric. Chapter 6 thus surveys further developments relating to the Russian Orthodox Church in Crimea, especially Russian interiorization of Crimean holiness. Lastly, the epilogue describes the re-Christianizing of Crimea in the post-Soviet period. It demonstrates that the legacy of Crimea's nineteenth-century Christianizing informs debates over Crimean identity today.

Crimea's diverse past, like that of other borderland regions along the Black Sea region, remains caught between the East and the West, forever etched in the landscape. Its abundant monuments and ruins are at once captivating, and vulnerable to abuse by nationalist and religious groups wishing to stake claims to the land. This was the case in the nineteenth century, and this is the case today as we see Christians and Muslims sparring over small areas of land that appear entirely unremarkable to the outside observer, but carry immense meaning to interested parties. My goal is to show how the Russian Orthodox Church Christianized Crimea by appropriating sacred landscapes, a process that had political as well as spiritual implications. As it revived Christianity on the peninsula, the church functioned as a critical lobby, pressuring officials to execute religiously motivated policy. Changing the focus from the state to the church in the investigation of empire-related topics reveals that state policy was subject to a diverse set of pressures and a very large cast of characters. Despite the political orientation of my investigation, however, this book does not take a purely political approach. Instead, I also desire to elucidate those elements that devout Christians believe make Crimea holy. Thus, as this book moves through the following chapters it will consider the religious experience as well as the political.

The Christianizing of Crimea presents an unusual case, but one that is deeply rooted in the imperial experience. It is unusual because the Christian transformation of Crimea occurred on a disputed borderland during war; the very scenes of battle set a painful backdrop for church expansion. The Christianizing process also depended upon Crimea's unique Byzantine ruins and holy pedigree, which dated to the first century and included the baptism of Prince Vladimir. Balkan Christian contributions past and present are central to this story. At the same time, the complex issues surrounding religion and identity evident in Crimea resonated in other provinces, and many strategies for church expansion had been tested elsewhere. Finally, as the cradle of Russian Christianity and the primary theater of war, Crimea's Christianizing took on mythical meanings that seeped into the bloodstream of the larger imperial body.

Chapter One

CHALLENGES OF THE CONFESSIONAL EMPIRE AND THE LIMITATIONS OF CONVERSION

Throughout the 1830s, Metropolitan Filaret repeatedly urged the establishment of a mission in Crimea. When the then archbishop of Kherson-Tauride Gavriil (Rozanov, 1827–1848) responded that Russian policies of toleration prohibited church expansion into Muslim regions, Filaret insisted that restrictions against proselytizing applied to Jews, not Tatars, and asked "how have these two different peoples become mixed up in your consistory?" "The law," he insisted, was "made only for Jews. The Christianizing of Tatars is much easier." Filaret then pressed Gavriil to send more priests to Crimea, arguing that "there are Muslims, whose fathers, many grandfathers, were Christians." He pressed, "find these priests, who might help you and do not avoid the affairs of God" because of "bureaucratic obstacles."[1] He chastised Gavriil for not making better use of a priest in Feodosia rumored to speak Tatar, and asked: "Why are you not using his help?"[2]

Gavriil ignored Filaret's advice, and focused instead upon buttressing Orthodoxy in the boomtown diocesan seat of Odessa. He established and staffed a consistory in Odessa, built a new home for the archbishop, opened a vestry, improved the choir, and founded a seminary.[3] In 1844, he established an orphan's home and created a women's monastery. He also doubled parish churches, bringing the total to 439 in Kherson and 101 in Tauride by 1848.[4] In terms of mission, Gavriil concentrated upon attracting Old Believers back to the church and combated the proliferation of heresies. After his departure in 1848, the Greek lobbyist Alexandru Sturdza advised the incoming archbishop, Innokentii (Borisov, 1848–1857), that the church's mission had barely begun. "Conversions of the Old Believers and the sectarians," he wrote, "are significant. The question of converting Crimean Tatars remains hitherto untouched, nothing has been done." He advocated that the seminary in Odessa teach Kirimtatar for "the door of faith remains closed without the key of language."[5] Both regional authorities in Odessa and Tauride shared Sturdza's desire for a stronger Orthodox church, but not so the governor general, Prince Mikhail Vorontsov, who steadfastly adhered to Catherinian policies of toleration.

As it contemplated expansion into Crimea, the church remained caught in the contradictions of Russia's confessional empire, in which Orthodoxy was the official religion in a state that professed religious toleration. In awkward, heavy-handed ways, the state attempted to chart a compromise between Orthodoxy and other confessions of the empire. It encouraged the church to provide a mission to those groups that shared a connection to the Russian Orthodox Church, whether they be Old Believers, Russian sectarians, or apostate Tatars, but discouraged active proselytizing to the Buddhist, Islamic, Judaic, Protestant, or Catholic groups properly registered with the state. Due to ambiguities surrounding religious identities, the Holy Synod did not enforce a consistent stance toward missions across the empire during the Nicolaevin period.[6] On few occasions, aggression and violence accompanied conversion, such as with the Greek Catholics in the western provinces or with Old Believer and sectarian populations.[7] Elsewhere in the empire, the church enticed populations toward Orthodoxy with material rewards, as it did with Tatar apostates and Mari populations in the Volga-Kama district.[8] Later in the nineteenth century, the church professionalized missiology. Strategies included developing greater awareness of Orthodoxy's historical and cultural ties to regions of the Russian Empire and using Nikolai Il'minskii's innovations in the study of native languages.[9] For the most part, bishops eschewed coercive methods and instead turned toward what Gregory Freeze has called "positive knowledge" to attract adherents. By "positive knowledge," Freeze means sermons, religious education, or dissemination of ecclesiastic pamphlets and books.[10] This approach encouraged deepening existing affinities to Orthodoxy, and enticing new adherents by displaying Orthodoxy in its best possible light, rather than aggressive conversion.

Many of these different strategies are evident in Crimea, where diversity elicited a complex response from local bishops, who approached each faith group differently. Bishops targeted the Old Believers, the Dukhobors, and the Molokan for assimilation into the official church, while largely disregarding local Jews. The church took very small steps toward the Tatars, whose divisions inspired different conversations. Unlike the Turkic Nogai, who lived in the Tauride steppe, coastal Crimean Tatars more closely resembled Caucasian Tatars, a mixed European population converted from Christianity to Islam.[11] Because of their Christian ancestry, Filaret argued to Gavriil that the church had an obligation to bring Crimean Tatars back to Orthodoxy. Although Gavriil expended little energy in this direction, Archbishop Innokentii established Kirimtatar as a language of the seminary in Odessa. Still, by 1859, only seven students graduated with knowledge of Kirimtatar, half the number who studied Modern Greek, and a very small percentage of students studying Tatar languages elsewhere in the empire.[12]

Although Crimean bishops employed aggressive measures to bring the Old Believers and sectarians into the church in the Kherson-Tauride diocese, they never contemplated coercive missions toward Tatars.[13] Only a handful of Tatars in Crimea turned toward Christianity during the Nicolaevin era, and these most likely assumed their new faith through intermarriage with Christians.[14] Even after the church professionalized missions in the late nineteenth century, it rarely turned toward the Tatars of the Black Sea region, partly due to the influence of Ismail bey Gaspirali and partly due to Il'minskii's disinterest in this group.[15]

In the years surrounding the Crimean War, the church primarily struggled to consolidate its position among the small Orthodox population, to expand institutionally, and as later chapters will show, to attract the multinational Orthodox immigrants streaming across imperial borders. This is not to say that the church was unconcerned about the other faiths inhabiting the diocese. Rather, apprehension over the multi-confessional population and the limitations of conversion provided the backdrop to Christian refashioning of Crimean landscapes.

Archbishop Innokentii: A New Bishop in the Borderland

Born to an impoverished parish family in the year 1800, Innokentii rose from an obscure background to become one of the most influential Russian thinkers of the nineteenth century. In a career that coincided with the reign of Nicholas I, Innokentii became an archimandrite in 1826 while a doctoral student at the St. Petersburg Spiritual Academy and served the church until his death in 1857. He earned a reputation for being an exceptional student and a powerful orator even as he was still earning his degree. With G. P. Pavskii and V. B. Bazhanov, Innokentii co-founded the widely distributed journal, *Khristianskoe chtenie*. He filled it with his own writings, including the controversial *Last Days of the Earthly Life of Our Lord Jesus Christ*.[16] As an interpretative account of the Gospels designed to guide the faithful through their lives, *Last Days* introduced a radical, evangelical element into Russian Orthodox study and worship. *Last Days* went through numerous editions after it cleared the censors following the Great Reforms, and it is undergoing revival today.[17]

After Innokentii received his doctoral degree, the Holy Synod rewarded his stellar performance at the St. Petersburg Spiritual Academy with a prestigious post at the Kyiv Spiritual Academy in 1830. In the Kyivan Academy, where he served as rector for ten years (1830–1840), Innokentii introduced three different theological sciences into the curriculum: Foundations of Theology, Theological Exposition, and Practical Theology.[18] Innokentii influenced the development of moral theology in Russian Orthodoxy, and contributed to the transformation of Russia's religious education.[19] In early phases of his career, Innokentii's innovations drew heavy criticism from the more conservative hierarchs, including Metropolitan Filaret and Metropolitan Ambrose.[20] Still, the synod continued to reward him. In 1836, the synod raised him to bishop of Chigirin, then he became bishop of Vologod in 1838, and shortly thereafter, bishop of Kharkov, where he established the monastery in the Holy Mountains. In 1847, Innokentii became a member of the Holy Synod. The next year the synod transferred him to Kherson-Tauride.[21]

As Innokentii rose through administrative ranks, he developed a reputation for his persuasive, pastoral speaking, and is considered by many church historians to be Russian Orthodoxy's first modern preacher.[22] His collected sermons, catechisms, acathists, and political and philosophical treatises compose eleven volumes.[23] His work, moreover, attracted attention outside the church and was frequently reviewed in secular journals.[24] Even during his lifetime, Innokentii became one of the first Russian theologians to be published abroad, translated into French, German, Polish, and English. In the introduction to his 1859 ecumenical publication *Voices from the East*, the celebrated Anglican hymnist J. M. Neale described the archbishop as "one of the most pious and laborious of Russian prelates," "one of the first preachers of his time," whose acathists "completely fuse the Western system of separate devotion to our Lord's individual Wounds into an Eastern mould."[25] The prolific church historian-theologian Nikolai Barsov described Filaret and Innokentii as the "two colossuses" of the church in the first half of the nineteenth-century, "Moses and Aaron" whose diametrical approaches to Orthodox theology provided perfect complements: "If Filaret belongs to the . . . sphere of theoretical activity ruling our church, in the sphere of dogmatics, canonical and hierarchical questions, then Innokentii must be given the palm branch in the sphere of practical influence in guiding the church for the religious-moral life of Orthodox Russian society and people."[26] Fifty years after Innokentii's death, the theologian Nikander Levitskii wrote, "even now his work could be heard in the most remote corners of the empire."[27]

Innokentii also earned a reputation as an influential voice among Russia's nationalists. His interest in religion and national identity comes as no real surprise; he arrived in Kyiv at a time when Christianity became the currency of nationalism in Russia's western borderlands. As rector of the Kyiv Theological Academy in the 1830s, he witnessed religious and ethnic strife in Ukraine and nearby Poland as well as the birth of the nationality platform and its erratic implementation. Innokentii published extensively on the significance of religion for national identity, and advocated a pan-Orthodox unity. One of his most influential pieces, *On the Beginnings of Christianity in Poland* (1842), argued that Orthodoxy united the Slavs in an organic community as much as language or folk customs. He countered the notion of a separate Catholic Poland, proposing instead that Russians and Poles belonged to one large Slavic family during the ninth and tenth centuries, bound together by Orthodoxy.[28] He maintained lively correspondence with nationalists of his era, including Sergei Uvarov, Nikolai Gogol, Mikhail Pogodin, and Alexandru Sturdza.[29] Through Sturdza, Archbishop Innokentii made the acquaintance of Porfirii Uspenskii, the head of Russia's ecclesiastic mission to Jerusalem.[30]

At the time of Innokentii's death, Metropolitan Makarii (then the Bishop of Tambov) declared that Innokentii was "one of the greatest people of our epoch, one of the most worthy sons of Russia, one of the most valorous hierarchs of the church and one of the most famous members of the Academy."[31] Similarly panegyric, the secretary of the Imperial Society of Agriculture and editor of the society's journal, Ivan Palimpsestov, described Innokentii as a "deep and holy thinker, an unrivaled orator whose words live eternally in the Academy of Science."[32] For these reasons and for his work in New Russia, the Russian Orthodox Church canonized Innokentii in 1997.[33] By the time the synod appointed Innokentii to the Black Sea region, his position in the church had been well established. His appointment can be viewed as an indication of the growing significance of New Russia in the eyes of the church and the empire as a whole.

During his ten years as archbishop, Innokentii overhauled the newly created diocese, in some respects continuing Gavriil's reforms and in others embarking on his own agenda. Throughout both provinces, he pursued traditional means of institutional expansion by augmenting the number of churches in Kherson-Tauride from 570 to 600 and enforcing stricter adherence to centralized practices and procedures.[34] He managed to elevate the status of the diocesan consistory on par with standards set in the 1842 code for the Western Provinces, which for Kherson and Tauride entailed doubling the servitors and the annual operating budget.[35] He also obtained a new space for the archbishop's home in Odessa, expanded the seminary's curriculum, and enlarged the libraries of both places. Above all, Innokentii attempted to elevate the status of the Orthodox Church vis-à-vis other faiths of the diocese. Because the empire's system of laws encoded each of the faiths differently, this meant that diocesan authorities approached each group with different sets of strategies. In these cases, church expansion was neither a clear nor a foregone conclusion.

The Russian Minority

At the time of the Russian conquest at the end of the eighteenth century, Odessa was a small Turkish port with a population numbering fewer than 5,000. The Frenchman Alexander Langueron, New Russia's governor after the Napoleonic wars, poetically observed that, "Odessa, still in its cradle, is already a flowering city."[36] Having fewer than 2,500 people in 1795, Odessa's population reached more than 90,000 in 1848.[37] Fifty-five years after its founding, it had become the third largest city of the empire and Russia's southern capital. Odessa's acclaimed theater was as famous as its stock exchange. Regional publications, including the newspaper *Odesskii vestnik* (1827) and the almanac *Novorossiiskii kalendar'* (1832), circulated information of local and imperial interest to the entire territory, the Near East, and southern Europe. The Odessa Society for History and Antiquities (1839) emerged as the leading scholarly organization in southern Russia and constituted the first provincial organization of its kind.

Other regions of the diocese reflected Odessa's growth and importance to the empire. The first Turkish wars and Russia's ambition to control Black Sea waterways produced the cities of Kherson and Nikolaev. Both cities were imperial hubs located on rivers that flowed into the Black Sea—Nikolaev had been Russia's chief naval base since 1789, while Kherson housed the provincial bureaucracy.[38] These cities became especially important to the empire during the late 1840s and 1850s, as the state relocated troops and expanded the navy in the Dnepr and Bug estuaries.[39] By mid-century, Kherson was one of the fastest growing provinces of the empire with nearly a million people.

In contrast, Tauride grew much more slowly, with fewer than 500,000 inhabitants by the middle of the nineteenth century.[40] Still, it too experienced fairly rapid development, along Crimea's southern coast especially. Known as the "pearl in the crown of Catherine the Great" and the "garden of the empire," the Crimean coast attracted the wealthy elite from Russia's largest imperial cities. Formerly a small Turkish port, Sevastopol became a naval center with six active bays and nearly 45,000 people in less than sixty years.[41] Few doubted that Tauride would catch up with Kherson, for in both provinces, Prince Vorontsov heavily invested government resources in public works; he built gardens, paved roads, and dredged rivers. He also developed the region's industry and agriculture. By mid-century, the area of New Russia, and Odessa in particular, became one of the most productive regions in the entire empire.[42]

New Russia's phenomenal growth and vulnerability to foreign influences invoked feelings of anxiety among some Russians. In 1848, the region closely observed a series of international crises, from the wave of revolution that overwhelmed Europe, to the nationalist uprisings on the Balkan Peninsula. In a letter to the archbishop, Odessa's city council complained that the city had "ceaseless relations" with "all the European ports, which were boiling with spiritual turmoil." In addition to worrying about external foreign influence coming from outside of the port, officials also feared the uncertain status of foreign colonies inside the borders. "In the heart of the city itself," the Odessa council remarked, live "numerous foreigners of various nations."[43] City representatives consistently revealed a heightened awareness of those who were foreign and those who were not. A strong representation of the Russian Orthodox Church, city officials maintained, would help ensure peace.

In Tauride, local authorities complained quite vigorously about the weakness of Orthodoxy and in 1840 criticized the church's failure to reach out to the region's diverse population. Tauride, their report pointed out, had few Russians and was mainly populated by "masses of immigrants" consisting of "runaways from landlords, those associated with war businesses, foreign immigrants, and even criminals." It was not surprising, the report continued, that "such a riff-raff of peoples, not having any links between them, preserve their former habits and faiths. The immigrants here of various sides and sects, although brought together as neighbors, cannot acquire any ties or any similar mentality." The bureaucrats argued that "instead of going to church, the people spend their free time in taverns and games." The beautiful climate and fertile soil created a poor environment for morality, because "fruitful land required very little work." Worse still, sectarians and foreign settlers often hired entire Russian families to till the land or herd flocks, and these Russians became easy prey for seduction into alien faiths.[44]

Innokentii shared the concerns of officials in Odessa and Simferopol, the administrative center of Tauride, that New Russia's foreign populations had a deleterious influence on the empire. The problem, as Innokentii more pointedly stated in a letter to Grand Duke Konstantin Nikolaevich, was the "unfortunate religious-characteristic of the region." The Orthodox populations were surrounded by "non-orthodox believers [*inovertsy*] and foreigners [*inostrantsy*]," inside regional borders and were subject to the "continuously pernicious influence of the sea." He cast his diocese in the bleakest of terms, writing that "I wish I could say something to you that is happy about the spirit of our Kherson-Tauride flock, but the hour of happiness still has not arrived for us. [The diocese] requires detailed and tireless work to cultivate a removal of thorns and weeds; to sow and water with both hands."[45] The metaphor was a sharp one that laid bare Innokentii's approach: nurture those who were Orthodox and weed out those who were not.

Apollon Skal'kovskii, the director of the New Russian Statistical Committee who generated population statistics in the region for decades, argued in 1849 that despite the unusual demographic composition of New Russia (including Ekaterinoslav, Bessarabia, Kherson, and Tauride), "Christians themselves consisted in large quantity of Orthodox; in comparison with other faiths, Orthodox [numbered] twenty-two to one." Tauride, however, presented the exception. There, "non-Christians composed the largest quantity, where up to 276,000 Tatars, together with Karaim and Talmudic Jews, composed more than half of the population."[46] Skal'kovskii's comments reveal only a partial picture. Table 1 shows slightly higher numbers for the Tatar, Jewish, and Karaim population, as well as the variety of non-Orthodox Christian groups inhabiting Tauride. Statisticians regularly reported the number of *inovertsy* but rarely took similar care to identify the number of Crimea's approximately 230,000 Orthodox believers. Many Orthodox Christians, especially along the Crimean coast, were of Balkan extraction. On the eve of the Crimean War, military authorities reported that the population of Tauride grew to 635,000, but it remains unclear to what degree the proportion of Russians to non-Russians changed.[47]

The number of recognized religious buildings further illustrates the minority of Christians and the limitations of the data. Reports for 1856 listed 104 Orthodox churches, 1,700 Tatar mosques, 6 Lutheran churches, 4 Catholic churches, and 5 Armenian-Gregorian churches (synagogues or Old Believer and sectarian churches were not listed).[48] Clearly, Muslims had a much stronger institutional presence in Crimea than Christians. The number given for churches, 104, does not, moreover, necessarily correlate to active parishes. Consistorial statistics clarify that at least fifteen of these included prayer houses, chapels, and churches without clergy. Others may have included buildings abandoned by the Greek population that fled Crimea in the years before annexation, but could still be used for special services on holidays.[49]

TABLE 1   Number of Non-Orthodox in Tauride

Type	Tauride
Catholic	4,514
Lutheran	9,154
Armenian Gri.	3,244
Armenian Ca.	1,612
Menonnite	11,306
Pietist	1,378
Jewish	3,387
Karaite	3,510
Muslim	288,699
Total	**326,804**

Source: Adapted from Table 2, "O chisle inovertsev' v novorossiiskom Krae i Bessarabii," *Novorossiiskii Kalendar'na 1848*, 78.

Tatars, Jews, Armenians, Greeks, and foreign colonists occupied the majority of smaller Crimean towns and villages. In the 1840s, for example, Yuri Bartenev described the population of Evpatoria as consisting of 3,000 Karaim, 7,000 Tatars, "Greeks, Moldavians, Gypsies, and Armenians, Gregorian and Catholic, who can not stand one another due to divisions over faith."[50] Ten years later Tereshchenko noted that of Bakhchisarai's 14,000 people, only 1,200 were Russian.[51] Similarly lacking a Russian population, Yalta consisted of "Greeks, Karaim, foreigners, and Jews."[52]

An enlightened bureaucrat, Prince Vorontsov opposed serfdom, and so he restricted the transfer of serfs to New Russia and the enslavement of native inhabitants. Thus, a small number of estates held serfs, but most Russians of the lower estates were free, runaways whose freedom had been guaranteed in 1827.[53] In general, Russians tended to concentrate in Crimean towns and cities, principally the administrative capital, Simferopol, the Black Sea naval base, Sevastopol, and Crimea's secondary defensive port, Kerch-Enikale. A disproportionate number of Russians in these cities worked closely with the state, whether as imperial bureaucrats, soldiers, or sailors and officers in the Black Sea navy. Even in the major cities, the Orthodox Christian populations hardly constituted a traditional lay community.

Few Russians, according to an anonymous contributor to *Dukhovnaia beseda* who spent a year in Crimea (1852–1853), considered the peninsula a permanent home. Instead, "they trade for a few years," or take a temporary post in Russian colonial administration, and "without fail, return to their homeland." Thus, even in the city of Simferopol, which had among the highest of Russian populations "houses belong[ed] to Jews, Karaim, Greeks, Tatars, Germans, and other foreigners."[54] During his travels through Crimea in the 1830s, the St. Petersburg scholar Stepan Kutorga noted of Sevastopol that "excluding the numerous Jews, and a few minor Greek and Russian merchants, all are sailors: Greeks, Italians, Russians, and a few German families."[55] The population of Sevastopol increased in the following decades along the same military and immigrant population patterns.[56] Here, therefore, Greeks composed a large percentage of the Orthodox population, while the most active pressure for establishing a church came not from the bottom, that is, from the sailors, but from the naval authorities. Thus, in the 1840s, the navy admiral Mikhail Lazarev initiated the building of the St. Vladimir Church in Sevastopol, obtaining 10,000 rubles from state coffers.[57]

Outside the cities, Crimean landowners often supplied the impetus for church expansion. Platon Burachkov, a wealthy landowner with extensive holdings near the Kinburn Fort on the Dnepr River petitioned the consistory to build a stone church for the "not insignificant number of Christians spread through 270,000 acres [100,000 desiatins]." The closest church for many Christians was located more than fifty kilometers away. This meant, he argued, that Christians received no religious supervision and "for a few years went with out confession and communion." The population included Burachkov's 120 serfs, approximately 250 serfs living on nearby estates, 40 Black Sea border guards, and 250 masters, shepherds, and fishermen. The consistory's slow response under Archbishop Gavriil prompted Burachkov to send another petition stating his intention to donate 150 acres for the construction of a stone church built through his own resources.[58]

Similarly, a General Lieutenant Ladinskii petitioned in 1845 to build a church in Petrovskii, a village on his estate, "at his own expense." Over the next ten years, Ladinskii built a stone church and a large home for the priest, surrounded with a fence. According to reports, this church was sanctified to the "great joy of all the surrounding Orthodox populations." Previously, Christians could not fulfill their spiritual responsibilities, because no other Orthodox church existed "for one-hundred kilometers of remote Tatar steppe between Kerch and Feodosia."[59]

Innokentii made outreach to sparsely populated Russian Orthodox laity in Crimea a key priority and often initiated the building of parish churches. In Kerch he set in motion a plan to build a church after his visit in 1850. "Kerch," he wrote to the Holy Synod, suffered from an "insignificant number of churches." For a city of 7,000 Orthodox inhabitants, "with not insignificant number of people arriving because of continuous trade," there were only two churches, "one Russian and one Greek." To support the building of the new church, the archbishop enlisted the city head, who then "opened a book for pledges and invited voluntary gifts." Three years later, the city had raised enough support for the church and identified a location.[60]

Rather than wait for petitions to arrive in Odessa, Innokentii asked parish priests and local notables to assess the needs of Christian populations in remote areas and offer recommendations.[61] A clergyman attached to the church in the town of Armenian-Bazaar submitted a revealing description of the mixed ethnic composition of neighboring towns and villages. Father Daniel Diakovskii identified approximately sixty Russians in the region, consisting of a few migrants from Kharkov and Poltava, peasants who had fled labor obligations to eke out a meager existence in Crimea's steppe. The majority of these Russians lived close to subsistence and depended upon the wealthier population of Jews, Karaim, and Armenians for work. Thus, many Russians lived among the non-Orthodox groups for "one, two, three, even five, years." They "knew Tatar language better than Russian," and when they attended services could not understand the liturgy. Most Russians in Armenian-Bazaar did not attend services, according to Diakovskii, because they followed the faith patterns of their employers. Those working with Jews and Karaim took Saturday as the holiday and kept fasts associated with the Jewish calendar, and those in Armenian households took communion at the Armenian Church (whether it was a Gregorian or Catholic church he did not say).[62]

About the nearby Perekop district, the *kraevedenie* scholar Aleksandr Zavadovskii wrote the consistory that in the outskirts of the northern Perekop district "there are no more than thirty Christians of the male sex and there is not one church or place to hold services." The closest "Christian estates," belonging to "G. G. Bulgakov, Count Dmitri Tolstoi, Moshkalovoi, Letrenka," and others were located more than eighty kilometers away. Zavadovskii suggested building a church in an unnamed "central location," and supplied the names of potential donors, including Admiral Captain Pavel Sakhnovskii and Count Tolstoi.[63] Another strategy involved moving priests into areas that had been previously neglected, but this did not always meet approval from local Christian communities. When the consistory transferred a popular priest, Grigorii Briukhovskii, from Simferopol to Yalta in 1851, Simferopol laity protested. On their behalf, the governor, Vladimir Pestel, wrote, "He is well known as a teacher and as a priest so it seems a pity to transfer him to such a city where there will be very few advantages and where the chief population consists of Tatars and Jews."[64]

Such concerns over the weakness of the Orthodox laity were not unusual in remote corners of the empire, places where the church had a smaller institutional presence than in the empire's interior.[65] The migratory nature of population in port cities and the transience of Orthodox Christians in Crimea adds, however, a different dimension. The archbishop in many cases proved more committed to building parishes than were local communities. Grassroots efforts to spread Christianity were not as evident in Tauride as they were in Kherson province, which had a more dense and established Christian population. In comparison, laity living in Kherson submitted a fair number of petitions requesting more priests, new churches, and religious processions.[66] Such petitions for Crimea in the pre-reform period are exceedingly rare. Zavadovskii recalled in a memoir published in 1880 that the people of Sudak desired a religious procession to transverse a path from Feodosia to Kiziltash on August 15, and from Kiziltash to Sudak on October 1, noting that it would be "altogether advantageous in locations primarily populated with Tatars." The onset of the Crimean War interrupted the submission of their petition.[67]

Russian Christians outside the Russian Orthodox Church

In addition to expanding the diocese institutionally to meet the needs of the Russian Orthodox community in the Black Sea region, prelates worked to attract new adherents, especially among the Old Believers. Although the policies of Catherine II and Alexander I toward the Old Believers varied according to the case, the reigns of these monarchs generally entailed a toleration of Old Belief.[68] In contrast, Nicholas I's treatment of the Old Believers tended to be more oppressive, an impulse that Robert Crummey attributes to inconsistent, insensitive policies or "heavy-handed good intentions" rather than "malice or deliberate cruelty."[69] The contradictions in the treatment of Old Believers during Nicholas's reign also resulted from conflicts between center and periphery, for even though the state issued decrees in 1827 and 1834 guaranteeing Old Believer rights, provincial officials seized Old Believer property and closed chapels and monasteries.[70]

The efforts to incorporate Old Believers in Crimea began with Gavriil, who brought 10,000 Old Believers into the church.[71] In 1836, he brought the Old Believers in the new naval city of Nikolaev into *edinoverie*, the term given to describe the official acceptance of practicing old rituals in certain Russian Orthodox churches.[72] A couple of years later, he did the same with a different community of *bespopovtsy*, or "priestless" Old Believers, living in the city of Kherson and two small villages with a combined population of over 3,500. Between 1845 and 1846, Gavriil targeted Old Believers in the villages of Klintsov, Kalinov, Elisavetograd, and Krasnyi Iara. In addition to Old Believers, he also incorporated Greek Catholics living in the villages of Snigurovka and Iavkino into the church.[73]

Following the precedent established by Gavriil, Innokentii initially devoted his energy to working with Old Believers and Russian sectarians. Data for this population is difficult to obtain, for many Russians who professed Old Belief or other Christian faiths avoided censuses. One Russian official estimated that during the mid-nineteenth century, one-sixth of the empire's Orthodox population worshiped with the old ritual.[74] Skal'kovskii admitted that "unfortunately . . . there are still significant numbers of schismatics who have settled in New Russia from distant eras." He identified fewer than 13,000 Old Believers, Molokan and Dukhobors, and Skoptsy in Kherson and Tauride. Not to worry, he implied, for "year-to-year their numbers decreased as they united with the universal Russian church."[75] Incorporating this population into the official church became a chief focus of Innokentii's administration.

These efforts covered both provinces of the diocese and included fact-gathering missions, conversion of entire parishes, and more drastically, the forceful closing of sectarian buildings and confiscation of property. Russian Christians outside the church represent an interesting case, for even though their integration into the church was technically permitted by imperial policies, it met considerable ambivalence among bureaucrats. Typically local perspectives on this issue channeled into what Nicholas Breyfogle has described as two reoccurring tropes, either "Russian colonists," or "pernicious dissenters." Some, like Vorontsov, viewed sectarians as critical agents of colonial settlement.[76] Others, such as the army's officer corps, felt that Old Believers and sectarians introduced corrosive ideas into Russia's military population. Even within these loosely divided camps, state endorsement for absorbing such groups into the church splintered further according to targeted sects. Officials appeared indifferent, for example, about the Molokan, but unanimously supported the suppression of the Skoptsy, an extreme sect known for self-mutilation.

Negotiation between state and ecclesiastic authorities is most evident in the church's relationship with Old Believers. Innokentii imported priests from Moscow who were experienced in the rites of the *edinoverie*, closed the worship houses of the Old Believers, and enjoined military and state authorities to pressure the dissenters into worshipping in the official church.[77] He even headed a "secret" commission that reported on the activities of the schism to central authorities in St. Petersburg.[78] Of the many local bureaucrats who encouraged his efforts, the military elites were most pronounced in their support.

Old Believers were particularly numerous in the military population. This developed from early settlement policies that granted them land and privileges in southern Russia in exchange for military service.[79] Military elites accepted this arrangement while the region was still a frontier. By the mid-nineteenth century military reformers began to view Old Belief as divisive and dangerous.[80] During Innokentii's administration, military officers in and around Nikolaev and Kherson actively invited religious homogenization. In 1848, for example, local priests colluded with Inspector of Reserve Cavalry Count Aleksei Nikitin to convert the local Old Believer population living in Nikol, a suburb of Nikolaev. According to diocesan reports, over 291 men and 339 women had been "won over" to *edinoverie*, a feat that despite its optimistic characterization was probably accomplished through coercion.[81] In this case, state officials were active accomplices to the church. In fact, Nikitin considered the work far from finished and expressed his hope that together, they could "perfectly eliminate the schism that permeated New Russia's military population."[82]

Elsewhere in Kherson, the church closed several prayer houses of the Old Believers, including two in Tiraspol, one in the village of Maiak, and one in Odessa. Regional and local officials, from the Odessa city council to New Russia's lieutenant governor, assisted each case. So that the closing of the "schismatic homes did not remain without fruit for Orthodoxy," Innokentii placed specially trained priests in surrounding areas to ease the suddenly displaced Christians into the Orthodox Church.[83] This collusion between state and ecclesiastic authorities was not unusual. By the end of Nicholas I's reign, Crummey notes that "a veritable army of local priests, bishops, local officials, and functionaries of the central administration had thrown their weight into the struggle against the Old Believer monasteries."[84]

Although many Russian officials supported, even assisted, the incorporation of Old Believers into the Russian Orthodox Church, others did not. Most notably, Prince Vorontsov objected to the church's oppressive treatment of the sectarians and intervened on their behalf in 1851, requesting that the archbishop show the Old Believers "some lenience."[85] Local diocesan authorities flouted Vorontsov's request and continued their campaign. A year later, therefore, the prince reiterated his objections much more forcefully. This time, Vorontsov emphasized that Russian statutes granted Old Believers a legal right to pursue their faith, and that in the course of twenty years he "continually heard the very best things about them." He argued that the church should not perceive the Old Believers as a threat, for they "never thought about converting Orthodox believers and they have never offered any kind of temptation." Finally, in a characteristic expression of his stance on Russia's religious pluralism, Vorontsov invoked the Catherinian legacy, and asked the archbishop to comply with "the government's eternal devotion to the system of religious toleration."[86] Vorontsov's assertions revealed an unmitigated tension over religious rights and freedoms, between his "enlightened" toleration and the church's aggressive attempts to incorporate the Old Believers. In this case, ecclesiastic authorities found enough support in other echelons of Russian bureaucracy to circumvent Vorontsov's objections.

Apart from the generally well-established settlements of Old Believers, the church attempted to attract other Russian groups, especially Molokan, Dukhobor, and Skoptsy, many of whom settled in the Tauride province in and above Crimea. In Tauride, local priests managed to convert nearly 150 Molokan to Orthodoxy in a small village located in the Melitopol district, and this inspired an enhanced effort to convert other Molokan living in nearby Berdiansk as well.[87] Neither effort generated notable reaction from state bureaucrats, partially because the campaigns were not overly successful. A local priest, Aleksandr Bershatskii, complained two years later that the mission failed because the Molokan were "surrounded on all sides by the Nogai Tatars and Mennonites." Consequently, these sectarians maintained closer, "freer" relations with "Nogai and Germans . . . than with the Orthodox."[88] This complaint reflects a common theme: church authorities frequently blamed their failure to consolidate authority on the diocese's confessional diversity.

Whereas state support splintered over converting the Old Believers and proved insignificant in converting the Molokan, nearly all state officials supported the suppression of the Skoptsy, a sect named for its ascetic denial of earthly desires through self-castration. The Russian government officially extended toleration to the Skoptsy in the early years of Alexander's reign, but reversed the decision by 1820, after officials realized that the sect's "castration of earthly desires" was a literal and not merely figurative prescription.[89] Across the empire, officials moved quickly to suppress the sect as it appeared. In 1851, priests discovered a Skoptsy settlement in Tauride's Melitopol district, relatively close to the Molokan. Diocesan authorities reacted to the spread of Skoptsy with alarm—shocked that worshippers mutilated their bodies and concerned that they might "infect" other people with their heresy. In a report to the Holy Synod, diocesan authorities noted that two women were especially dangerous, for they spread the heresy among their neighbors and even "dared to speak against the icon."[90] Because the sect was so extreme, local clergy passed the problem on to state administrators. Reports of the sect reached the highest levels, including the Tauride governor, the lieutenant governor general of New Russia, and Prince Vorontsov himself. Non-ecclesiastic authorities acted quickly to stop the spread of the sect, and established a supervisory commission to observe the villages where the sect was strongest.[91] Although the Skoptsy group was disbanded, its memory remained an important symbol of the weakness of the church in New Russia. Religious authorities feared that despite the unusual tactics of the group, the Melitopol Skoptsy would spread like a brush-fire, quickly igniting village to village.

In a letter to Prince Vorontsov, Innokentii expressed his concern for the northeastern part of the Tauride province where sects especially flourished:

> The violent spread of the *skoptsy* in the last year urgently demands my visit to Melitopol and Berdiansk districts; but with attacks on all sides from various sects—Skoptsy, Molokan, Dukhobors, I could not stay long enough for a pitched battle ... thanks to God, and due to the zealous and humble servants of mine who carried the fight forward, all victory was on our side, without any other means apart from the Gospel.[92]

As the above excerpt illustrates, the archbishop viewed the integration of schismatics as an intensely contentious affair. His battle metaphor summarized well the strategies he employed, for "re-Christianizing" Russians who had drifted away from the Russian Orthodox Church constituted the most assertive mission of his administration.

Catholics

Catholics composed another confession targeted by the Russian church. In this case, priests did not engage individuals or groups. Rather, the conflict with Catholics unfolded on an institutional level. Catholics formed a very small percentage of the non-Orthodox population in the Black Sea diocese. They mainly consisted of Armenians who predated Russian conquest, a few Polish landowners, and German, French, and Italian immigrants. Yet they had a powerful, visible presence in southern Russia after Nicholas I decided to establish a new Catholic diocese there in 1847.[93] The Catholic example particularly illustrates the association of faith with identity and suggests that church leaders could influence the state's management of other religions. In a fascinating report submitted to the Holy Synod and published posthumously, the archbishop carefully laid out his objections to the new Catholic diocese.[94] He expressed concern that the Latin diocese would not merely minister to its own flock, but would actively seek out new adherents among Orthodox populations and that it would exercise disproportionate influence in the affairs of the diocese.[95] Prior to the 1847 concordat, according to Innokentii, "there existed only one Latin priest, who unnoticed, disappeared in the crowd." From the middle of the 1840s, however, the Latin church became an obvious sight in Kherson-Tauride; it acquired more priests, an official diocese, and even a cathedral church.[96]

Innokentii argued that the government's decision to permit the diocese confused all groups in Kherson-Tauride, especially the schismatics, who interpreted the "dropping of Latinism into the middle of the Orthodox south" as the activities of the anti-Christ. He perceived the new Catholic diocese as a threat to stable Russian rule in the provinces, writing that it "impoverished not only Orthodox belief but also the Fatherland." Virtually from its existence, he maintained, the Black Sea population "uncomfortably struggled against Latin Propaganda," which followed the Poles "as a shadow follows the body."[97] Innokentii criticized the government for under-estimating the delicacy of religious identity in the Black Sea region. Instead of protecting diversity, the region needed a stronger affiliation to the Russian tsar and state, a gap that only Orthodoxy could bridge. Given the relatively small number of Catholics populating the region, he concluded that the Russian government did not create a diocese from need, but as "a thoughtless, and hasty concession to Rome." How could anyone sanction, he asked, "the government's creation of three Latin bishops from nothing, without any particular need?"[98]

Sources suggest that Innokentii was right—that the formation of a diocese was indeed a diplomatic concession. During Nicholas I's reign, Catholics in Russian borderlands suffered severely. In 1839, Nicholas I forcibly incorporated Greek Catholics into the Russian Orthodox Church and throughout his reign closed Latin monasteries and convents, which fell from 323 in 1803 to 72 in 1847, while women's convents dropped from 40 to 34. Under increasing pressures from Europe to stop anti-Catholic abuses, Nicholas I convened a special committee to discuss a concordat with Rome.[99] One result of this concordat was the formation of a new Catholic diocese, intended primarily to serve the German and Armenian populations scattered through Bessarabia, Kherson, Ekaterinoslav, Saratov, Tauride, Astrakhan, and part of Kavkaz.[100] With a seat in the city of Kherson, it covered over 700,000 square kilometers and composed one of the largest dioceses in the world.[101] Through Innokentii's intervention, however, the Catholic diocese was ultimately moved from the Odessa/Kherson vicinity to Tiraspol.[102] The archbishop could not dissolve the new diocese, but was instrumental in removing it to the periphery of his domain.

Tatars

When Russians annexed Crimea, seventy-five native inhabitants converted to Orthodoxy. Many of these were Islamicized Greeks, who retained strong ties to their Christian heritage. Other Tatars adopted Christianity to better assimilate into the new imperial state. By the late 1780s, however, this initial wave of conversion settled, and with the exception of an occasional conversion made by the Scottish Bible Society in Crimea in the 1820s, few Muslims turned toward Christianity.[103] Prince Vorontsov discouraged Orthodox proselytizing in Tauride.[104] With the exception of the temporary Feodosia-Mariupol diocese (1787–1799), established for Crimea's long-standing Greek population, the church made very little effort to expand into Crimea after annexation.[105]

The limited efforts toward Tatars that Crimean bishops did make drew criticism. In 1839, Gavriil entered a mosque and said a Christian prayer. When stories of the event reached Filaret, the metropolitan wrote: "This means, that You publicly were guilty, or implicated yourself in violating church rules. If you are not allowed to pray with heretics, how much [graver the offense must be] in the Muslim mosque. . . . Not one Muslim soul you have acquired: but the rules of the church have been broken, and Orthodoxy compromised." Filaret concluded that such methods would not bring any Muslim into Orthodoxy, but rather the "invasion of the mosque dangerously excited concerns that the Muslims will be oppressed in faith;" such a conclusion consequently raised the ire of local authorities, who "with this are preoccupied."[106] This episode effectively ended Gavriil's narrow mission to the Tatars.

Tatars presented the most numerous faith group that diocesan authorities encountered in Crimea, and for Gavriil's successor, Archbishop Innokentii, they represented the most apparent example of the contradictions inherent in the empire's approach to religion. In this case, however, Tatars typically enjoyed greater rights than their Orthodox counterparts. They could not be conscripted into the army. Although Tatars were listed as state peasants, they could not be attached to noble estates, as were Russian serfs. Nicholas I's regime reinforced the special concessions given to Tatars by his predecessors. In November of 1827, the "Conditions for Tatar population and land owners in the Tauride Province" guaranteed rights for Tatars that far outweighed those given to most Russians. This document permitted Tatars to own movable and immovable property, to sell land, and to transfer to another estate or to government lands after fulfilling agreed upon labor obligations. Tatars also could bring complaints against landlord abuses to court. As E. I. Druzhinina noted, Tatars had more rights than government peasants, demonstrating "the extent to which different religious and national groups in the Russian empire composed different estates with different juridical statuses."[107] Elsewhere in the empire, Muslim clergy enjoyed more privileges than their Orthodox counterparts, including the right to purchase land—something Orthodox clergy could not do.[108]

The legal privileges that Tatars enjoyed on paper did not always correspond to their daily experience. Most regional administrators like Prince Vorontsov did follow the policies of Catherine II, which were designed to protect Tatar autonomy. Locally, however, Russian land-grant holders exploited legal ambiguities, especially the absence of written documentation verifying Tatar land-holdings. Distance from officials in Simferopol allowed some Russians to seize land in remote areas, which they did through fencing and other illegal and immoral practices. From Catherine's reign through the 1830s, Tatars and Russian nobility constantly quarreled over land, and the government set up repeated commissions to solve the problem. Most often the committees in theory supported the Tatars; they confirmed the principles of Tatar free landholdings, yet they had little success resolving specific disputes.[109]

French eyewitnesses in Crimea during the 1830s viewed the problem as a product of local corruption:

> On his accession to the government, Count Voronzof [sic], with his natural kindness, applied himself strenuously to improve the condition of the Tatars; he took them under his special protection, and prevented the rapacity of his underlings as far as in him lay. Unfortunately, his efforts could hardly avail beyond the limits of his own estates, and all his generous intentions were baffled or worn out by the incessant pettifogging arts of the *employés*.

They noted that at the end of the decade yet another commission, this one established by Count Pavel Kiselev, head of the Ministry of State Domains, "set about the task under which Count Voronzof had failed . . . but their efforts were all ineffectual, and they soon retired in disgust from the useless struggle." In the end, these travelers concluded that they anticipated the "total extinction" of the Tatars. They elaborated that "[t]he tribes are rapidly degenerating; the moral and physical forces of the nation are daily declining; the territorial wealth of the Tatars has been destroyed, sold, or divided; the native families distinguished for their past history or for their fortunes have disappeared; the population, instead of increasing, diminishes."[110]

Despite their apparent decline, many Russian contemporaries perceived Tatars as the chief beneficiaries of Russia's religious policy. Church leaders opposed the privileges granted to Tatars, a position they could more openly take the closer the war became. In 1852, Innokentii argued that Tatar rights were incongruous with their status as a conquered group:

> Crimea was bought with the price of Russian blood, which flowed more than once from Perekop to Kerch. And obviously its defeated populations had no rights or any particular advantages [due them]; but nevertheless, Crimean Tatars received from [the Russian Empire] such distinctions and advantages, that not one Russian in our region has; they do not pay any taxes; they are not obligated to military conscription; they are not subject to landlord rights, in the same measure as our poor serfs and others.

The bestowal of an "unnatural excess of rights" to a "wild, conquered people," especially rights that exceeded those enjoyed by the Russians, created, according to Innokentii, numerous problems. Expressing the growing anxiety felt by many of his contemporaries, Innokentii claimed that excessive rights jeopardized the loyalty of Tatar populations, and that higher status actually promoted rebellious behavior rather than deterring it. Tatars, he claimed, openly paraded their "dissatisfaction with the government" in a "haughty contempt of the Russian name, disgust for Russian beliefs, and secret hopes for future political independence." The more privileges the state granted the Tatars, Innokentii asserted, the more they would demand.

More to the point, perhaps, the inequality of rights made an Orthodox mission to Tatars untenable. Because the Russian state attached privileges to confession, Orthodoxy had an identity nearly synonymous with serfdom. No Muslim would convert to Christianity and risk losing his privileges. Thus, despite his opposition to the "unnatural excess" of Tatar rights, Innokentii asserted that "[i]t would be just to demand, at the very least, that Muslims who are converting to Christianity preserve their former rights, but this is not the case. Now, he becomes Christian, and with tomorrow's day begins to submit to all obligations of our simple people." For this reason, he concluded, "many Muslims decide to remain in their faith which is joined with so many civil advantages." As the archbishop pointed out, the organization of Russian imperial subjects into categories of faith, which would seem to have certain advantages for the church elsewhere in the empire, only complicated matters in Tauride. Innokentii remained committed nonetheless to the idea of Christianizing Tatars, arguing that it was necessary to maintain stability in Crimea. The conversion of Tatars was of "first importance, not only in the relationship to the church, but also to the state, as the very government of Tauride itself recognizes."[111] Here it should be pointed out that the archbishop, like many of his contemporaries, perceived Tatar conversion as a political issue. The adoption of Christianity by Tatars, he and other authorities maintained, would facilitate their assimilation and therefore strengthen the state.

Due to the traditional restraints placed on Orthodox missions in Crimea, Innokentii, like Gavriil before him, made few overtures toward the Tatars. He did, however, take Sturdza's advice, and established Kirimtatar as a language along with New Greek in the Odessa seminary.[112] News of the course spread widely, and in 1849, Isidor, exarch of Georgia, sent a request for "two or three educators finishing the course of study at the Kherson monastery with the ability to read in Tatar." The exarch wanted these graduates to lead a mission to a group in the northern Caucasus who were on the edge of apostasy. Like in Crimea, he noted that "indifference" from state officials constituted "one of the chief reasons of the slow spread and approval of Christianity in Kavkaz." Before writing to Odessa, he admitted that he hoped the recent arrival of Greek priests who studied in Turkey might help, but "not one of them were suited for the mission."[113] When told that the course in Tatar language had only just begun and extra missionaries possessing the language would not be available for some time, Isidor empathized. "How frightening," he stated, "that in your area, they did not notice this need in Crimea for the Tatars!" Still, Isidor commented that the Odessa seminary remained at an advantage because it could draw from sons of priests living in Tatar areas who were somewhat familiar with Tatar language and culture and did not fear missionary assignments. In Georgia, he wrote, "scholars do not wish to study the Tatar language, fearing that such knowledge might determine their future post among Tatars." He concluded with a question about the position of Muslims in the empire that Innokentii had also asked: "will Muslims be truly citizens when following their own law, or will they only be decisively conquered and merged with the general fatherland, and obtain the Russian soul through Holy Christening?"[114] Isidor, like Innokentii, perceived the crux of assimilation not in terms of language or culture, but religion. From Orthodoxy, all else would follow.

In the end, the course in Tatar language did not produce any great missionaries among the Tatars, and there are no great stories of Tatar conversions to Orthodoxy on the eve of Crimea's Christianizing. Instead, the only cases of Tatar-Christian faith exchanges that appeared before diocesan authorities were those of Tatar apostates.[115] Thus, despite the evident desire to convert Tatars, church leaders in Crimea refrained from direct missionary activity. Nor did they really attempt to absorb Tatars into the body of the church at all. Rather, the church entered Crimea through the small population of native Greeks and Balkan Christian refugees. Tatars were relegated to the role of admiring bystanders to church expansion, while their claims to Crimean landscapes and history became overshadowed by Christian legends.

Colonists

Colonists composed the last group that caused diocesan authorities particular concern. Like Tatars, colonists occupied Russian lands yet failed to assimilate into the Russian population. As the table below shows, the province of Tauride had more colonies than Kherson, a total of ninety settlement groups compared with only sixty-six colonies.[116] The problems of conversion and faith-based, privileged status are well -illustrated by the unfortunate fate of a Lutheran family in Tauride's Melitopol district that converted to Russian Orthodoxy in 1849. The conversion of the members of the family met several obstacles, only one of which was being ostracized by their former fellow Lutheran colonists, who according to reports, "met the family at every appearance with various frightenings, reproaches and laughter." To escape derision, the family relocated to a new village where they could peacefully practice Orthodoxy.

If the loss of their group identity was not challenging enough, the converted German colonists also lost their special privileges. As soon as imperial authorities learned of the Germans' conversion, they began to reclassify the colonists' status. The Ministry of State Domains, which typically oversaw settlement and land distribution, transformed these free agriculturalists into government peasants.[117] To the outraged clergy, the reclassification of these German colonists symbolized the constraints that faith-based juridical status imposed upon the church's mission. Lo-

TABLE 2   **Colonies in New Russia and Bessarabia**

Ekaterinoslav	62
Tauride	90
Kherson	66
Bessarabia	108
Total	**326**

Source: Gosudarstvennyi Arkhiv Odesskogo Oblasti (GAOO), GAOO, f. 1, op. 173, d., 15 (Statisticwal Information for New Russia and Bessarabia), l. 6–7.

TABLE 3   Numbers of Colonists by Type

Type	Men	Women	Total Colonies
German	60,587	57,872	206
Bulgarian	54,877	51,588	92
Jewish	9,493	8,544	28
Total	**124,157**	**118,094**	**326**

Source: GAOO, f. 1, op. 173, d., 15, l. 6–7. Figures in this table include colonists for the provinces of Bessarabia and Ekaterinoslav, as well as Kherson-Tauride.

cal diocesan authorities petitioned imperial agents, including agents in the Ministry of the Interior, who oversaw the juridical status of foreign confessions, to reverse the decision. Innokentii himself intervened and the affair escalated to St. Petersburg. He compared the conversion from "Lutheranism to Orthodoxy in Orthodox Russia," to "a punishment usually reserved for serious criminals."[118] The diocese fought central authorities for two years over the status of the German colonists. The archival trail ends in 1851 with local authorities failing to compromise. Backed by Archbishop Innokentii, regional bureaucrats refused to comply with imperial orders and the German colonists precariously retained their privileges under the diocese's protection. The way events transpired in Tauride did not necessarily reflect events elsewhere in the empire. Paul Werth has shown, for example, that the Ministry of State Domains was particularly concerned to make the conversion to Orthodoxy easier, not more complicated, in the Volga-Kama region. The potential problem here might relate not to the colonists' adoption of faiths, but their desire to leave the German colony.[119]

In any case, the Christianizing process was bounded by Russia's confessional approach to identity. Missions to the colonists were futile until the state separated religion from juridical status. Thus, the archbishop rarely encouraged parish priests to focus their energies on the colonists. He did advocate, however, a rethinking of "the rights of the state religion relative to the confessions of the foreigners and non-Christians." The current situation in which Orthodox populations "remain at one title and rank, while foreign faiths and even non-Christians enjoy active rights," he argued to Grand Duke Konstantin Nikolaevich, only cause "the destruction and the harm of the former."[120] Rather than attempting to convert colonists then, Innokentii instead concentrated upon buttressing the visibility of the Orthodox Church in areas thick with foreign settlements.

Jews and Karaim

Russian imperial officials recognized two different Jewish groups on the peninsula, Rabbinite Jews and the Karaim. Rabbinite Jews included an unidentified number of Polish Jews who immigrated to Crimea after annexation and the pre-conquest population of Krymchaks (after the Russian term for Crimea), also called "Constantinople Jews." Numbering only a couple thousand, Krymchaks spoke a Turkic language but wrote in Hebrew characters. According to Crimean statisticians, "they speak Kirimtatar, dress and have manners like Tatars, and are hard to distinguish from Tatars."[121] Krymchaks descended from a diverse mix of immigrant Judaic peoples, including Ashkenazi, Sephardic, and Romaniote Jews, who settled in Crimea through the centuries and practiced several different rites. At the beginning of the sixteenth century, a rabbi from Kyiv settled in Kaffa (Feodosia) and organized Crimean Jews into a unique rite. With the Mongol invasion, and the subsequent immigration of Kipchaks and other Turkic tribes, Crimean Jews slowly intermingled with Turkic populations and amalgamated local practices.[122]

Like the Crimean Tatars and the Krymchaks, the Karaim are unique to Crimea. They practice a form of Judaism that can best be described as a "Jewish religious movement of a scripturalist and messianic nature."[123] Karaism rejects rabbinical authority and does not recognize the Talmud. Historically, the Karaites, who include all those who practice Karaism, have been sparsely dispersed throughout the Middle East, Eastern Europe, and the Black Sea region. Crimean Karaites, or Karaim, differ from other Karaites because they are of Turkic ethnicity and speak a Turkic tongue.

In the sixteenth, seventeenth, and eighteenth centuries, Chufut Kale, a community outside of Bakhchisarai, became the heart of Karaim culture in Crimea, and its scholars developed a wide reputation. Estimates of Karaim population in Chufut Kale vary widely depending upon the source. Official censuses typically listed fewer than one hundred households in the seventeenth century, a figure that climbed upward toward two hundred in the eighteenth.[124] With the Russo-Turkish wars and the Russian annexation, however, Chufut Kale declined along with Bakhchisarai, and the Karaim population moved westward toward Evpatoria.[125]

Over the course of the nineteenth century, the Karaim distanced themselves from the Krymchaki.[126] In 1837, the Russian government granted the Karaim recognition as an independent religious group, entirely separate from Rabbinical Jews. Subsequently, a few years later, Karaim scholars began to search for historical and archaeological evidence to provide their community with a legitimate and long-standing past. In the middle of the nineteenth century, Abraham Firkovich became the most well-known and controversial scholar of the Karaim. He traveled extensively to research the earliest traces of Karaim, and established a monumental collection of documents that suggested the Karaim arrived in Crimea in the sixth century. Such a date positioned the Karaim on the peninsula well before the Crimean Tatars arrived and even prior to the Krymchaks. However, scholars later revealed that several, but not all of Firkovich's documents were forgeries, and the origin of Karaim remains ambiguous.[127] The Firkovich episode demonstrates the political significance of religious identity in Crimea, and the complex relations between the Karaim and Krymchaks. Throughout the empire, the church expended little effort to attract Jews or Karaites, and such is the case in Crimea.

Almost immediately upon arriving at his post, Innokentii unsuccessfully attempted to separate the Kherson-Tauride diocese. In a report to the Holy Synod, he suggested that a new Orthodox bishop in Simferopol would strengthen ties to the Orthodoxy laity and ensure a population loyal to the tsar. First, Innokentii argued that a bishop could oversee the conversion of "the various numbers of schismatic sects, the most evil being Skoptsy, Molokan, Dukhobor and Nepomniak, in the Tauride districts of Melitopol, and Berdiansk." Previously, all attempts to bring these sects closer to the church were difficult, he wrote, because the sectarian settlements were located at a distance of five to seven hundred kilometers from Odessa, the diocese's current seat and only centralized vantage point over the vast territory. A bishop vested with full authority in Simferopol could work with the sectarians "much more conveniently" and "much more successfully, particularly because of the frequency that personal visits could be made."[128]

Second, a bishopric could counter the deleterious influence of foreign colonists and their faiths. As Innokentii asserted, "[t]he significant numbers of various foreign settler colonies with their confessions and forms of thought, such as the Mennonites, are all unfavorable for Orthodoxy and the Russian spirit." These faiths were particularly problematic in Tauride and demanded "brilliant pastoral vigilance" to protect productive subjects from the corrosive "infection of influence of the non-believers." Just as with the sectarians, Innokentii argued that it was impossible to counter the "decadent spirit" of the foreign faiths in the Tauride steppe and Crimea from distant Odessa. A bishop located closer "to the places of infection" would be much more effective. By the same token, Innokentii asserted that a new bishop would give the Orthodox hierarchy a clear advantage over the new Catholic diocese established in Tiraspol.

The archbishop referred pointedly to the Tatars, arguing that a bishop might inspire them to adopt Orthodoxy. Here, however, he did not talk about "converting" Tatars, but rather about "returning" them to Orthodoxy. The difference was not merely semantic. In a persistent trope, church publicists portrayed the Crimean Tatars as former Christians. This depiction served as a reoccurring legitimacy for church expansion. Rather than moving into an entirely new territory, the church intended to reclaim its authority over former adherents "violently converted to Islam." Because the Tatars, according to this line of argument, were forcibly converted to Islam, Orthodoxy was Crimea's one true religion.[129]

The recommendation to establish a separate bishop for Crimea met immediate opposition from Vorontsov, who feared inciting Tatar unrest. In a letter to the archbishop, Prince Vorontsov clarified his reluctance to allow a bishop in the province: "Almost all of the population in Crimea is Muslim and Christians are in the minority. For this reason, establishing such a powerful religious leader with a residence in Simferopol could germinate among the natives unfounded dangerous thoughts about intentions of deflecting them from Islam and converting them to Orthodoxy."[130] Vorontsov believed that a strong church might endanger the stability of Crimea; any perceived threat to Islam could potentially lead to Tatar insurgency. For him, maintaining Islam in Crimea was a practical matter of preserving social order.

Innokentii's efforts to create a separate diocese for Crimea failed in 1848, and thereafter he tried to expand church influence in more subtle ways. Instead of building churches or establishing a hierarchy, church authorities generated studies about Crimea's ancient Christians and legends of local saints. Scholars from Odessa and from across the empire rewrote Crimea's history, replacing its recent Muslim past with a Christian one. Through a complex set of ritualistic and representational practices, church leaders imposed authority over sacred landscapes, even those revered by Crimea's other faith groups. In only a couple of decades, scholars transformed Crimea's identity. Once known as the home of the Tatar Khanate, and later celebrated as the site of classical antiquity on Russian soil, Crimea became the "cradle of Russian Christianity," an eponym based on the legend of Prince Vladimir's baptism in Chersonesos. Under Innokentii, before the church even assumed a real presence there, Crimea became a holy place—a destination that attracted Orthodox Christian pilgrims from throughout the empire.

Chapter Two

FROM THE TEMPLE OF DIANA TO THE CRADLE OF CHRISTIANITY

Ivan Muravev-Apostol included the following excerpt from Lord Byron on the opening page of his Crimean travel account, published in 1820:

> —approach this consecrated land
> And pass in peace along the magic waste:
> But spare its relics;—let no busy hand
> Deface the Scenes . . . already how defaced!

With these lines, Muravev-Apostol, elite bureaucrat and father of the Decembrists having the same name, intended to draw his readers into one of the major themes of his book, the need to preserve the remnants of Crimea's ancient past that were scattered throughout the landscape. He criticized Russian colonists for their evident disregard for Crimea's historical treasure, and their use of marble from Hellenic and Byzantine ruins for the construction of Sevastopol. Muravev-Apostol had difficulty locating some of the ruins described by the eminent scholar P. S. Pallas, who "as early as 1793 contemplated the destruction of these valuable remains." "What," he asked, "remains for me to say about them in 1820?"[1] Despite the recent decades of demolition of ancient ruins, Muravev-Apostol was not disappointed. He had prepared for this journey for two years, which he admitted, was "altogether insufficient for reviewing a classic land, where diligent research served every step."[2] Linking Crimea to the writing of the ancients particularly concerned him. He speculated, for example, that the mountain Chatyrdag on the Crimean coast was depicted in the works of Strabo, and while standing on the site of ancient Panticapaeum (present day Kerch), imagined himself "in the very spot" where the blood of Mithridites flowed.[3]

In the eighteenth and nineteenth centuries, philhellenism spread through Europe as enlightened thinkers heralded ancient Greece as the apex of western civilization. Russians, like other Europeans, were fascinated by Greek antiquity and also developed a distinct phil-Orthodox movement based on a shared faith. Because Crimea was colonized by Ionians in the fifth century BCE and was later attached to the Byzantine Empire, it occupied the intersection of both Graecophilic movements. As Andrei Zorin has argued, Crimea's well-preserved collection of Greek architecture provided the Russian Empire with a western pedigree and along with it "the right to stand next to civilized European nations," while the Byzantine ruins enabled Russia to claim a direct lineage to Byzantium.[4] Reflecting the dual symbolism associated with Crimea's past, Catherine II renamed this part of New Russia "Tauride," after the Greek "Tauris," and the neighboring province Kherson, after Korsun, the ancient Russian name given to Chersonesos, the city in which the Kyivan Prince Vladimir was believed to have been baptized.[5]

Greek immigrants living in New Russia contributed to the Graecophilic discourse that surrounded Crimea; they published in Russian historical journals, taught ancient and Modern Greek in Russian schools, and searched for Hellenic and Byzantine ruins. Their support for Russian Graecophilia is not surprising. Greek nationalists hoped to translate Russian fascination with Crimea's Greek and Byzantine past into "aid to realize their political goal of a restored Byzantium to replace the Ottoman Empire,"[6] while others simply desired to strengthen the connection between their adopted nation and their homeland. Graecophilic narratives benefited Russian imperialists as well, for they created an alternative history for Crimea that demonstrated the peninsula was Greek before it was Tatar, and that it was Christian before it was Muslim.

Church historians and archaeologists also enthusiastically embraced research into Crimea's Greek past; they wrote about a variety of topics that ranged from Crimea's Grecian ruins to the Christian populations who left for the Sea of Azov. Naturally church scholars were interested in the saints' lives associated with Crimea, including a host of Byzantine-era saints and several associated with Crimea's Roman period.[7] As the nineteenth century wore on, however, official nationality encouraged Russian scholars to focus upon *Russian* subjects. Increasingly, therefore, church scholars engaged in "archaeology of the Korsun legend," or in finding evidence to substantiate the legend of Prince Vladimir's Christianizing recorded in the *Russian Primary Chronicle* associated with Nestor. Because Prince Vladimir received Christianity from the Byzantine emperor, the Korsun legend provided a convenient compromise between Russian Graecophilia and evolving Russian nationalist discourse. By the 1840s, the Greeks—who contributed fundamentally to Crimea's pre-Islamic and post-annexation Christianizing—were no longer synonymous with Crimea's Christian identity. Instead, the Korsun legend enabled Russian nationalists and church archaeologists to argue that Crimea was the center of the Russian Empire, the "cradle of Russian Christianity." When Archbishop Innokentii arrived in Odessa, Crimea's Christian pedigree had been well established by archaeology; only the program of restoration remained.

Crimea in the Shadow of Greece

The philhellenic movement in Russia can be traced to the Enlightenment and the rise of Graecophilia across Europe. Suzanne Marchand defines Graecophilia as a European obsession with classical Greece on an institutional level, a trope that echoed in university halls and "resounded through the pages of . . . prose, poetry, and scholarly literature."[8] Ancient Greece serviced European fantasies in a number of different ways, whether through democratic ideals represented by Athens or the "the pinnacle of artistic beauty and scientific genius" achieved by ancient Greeks.[9] Russians similarly evinced a fascination with ancient Greece, but due to their shared Orthodox faith with the Greeks, also expressed an affinity for Byzantium.

The history of Greeks in Crimea can be traced to the fifth century BCE, when Ionian settlers established a series of trade routes along the Crimean coast and founded Chersonesos, a thriving city that functioned primarily as a trading post.[10] Chersonesos was well known in the ancient world and appeared in the writings of Josephus Flavius, Strabo, and Pliny the Elder.[11] The city continued to be a major mercantile center for centuries and served as the eastern outpost for the Roman and Byzantine Empires. Christian missions from Jerusalem and then Constantinople targeted Chersonesos repeatedly, and the city became a gateway for missions to the steppe, from the reign of Justinian I in the sixth century CE. It was in 988 that the Kyivan prince, Vladimir, was baptized by Emperor Basil II. When Chersonesos finally fell in 1399 to the Tatars, some Greek residents followed the example of St. Constantine (also known as St. Cassius the Greek, the Wonder-worker of Uglich) and fled.[12] Remaining Greeks converted to Islam along with other Christians on the peninsula and contributed to the unique ethnic make-up of the Crimean Tatars. A few Greeks kept their Christian identity, while coastal Crimean Tatars retained certain traditions belonging to their Christian ancestors.

The story of Crimea's native Greeks—those whose connection with the peninsula stretched deeply into the Byzantine period and the Tatar Khanate—ends for the most part in 1778. Following a series of brutal conflicts between Christians and Tatars, who had previously lived together peacefully for centuries, Crimea's last Greek metropolitan, Ignatius, wrote Catherine II on behalf of his flock, requesting asylum, citizenship, and relocation within the Russian Empire. The Armenian prelate, whose seat was near Azov, encouraged Armenians to leave as well.[13] Catherine conceded, granting both Greeks and Armenians land along the Azov Sea. Thousands perished in the process of relocation; some died on the journey, while others died from starvation, cold, and the disease that spread from poor sanitary conditions during the first months of relocation. Approximately 13,500 of 18,000 Greeks survived to establish Mariupol, and 11,000 of 12,500 Armenians formed a couple of communities in Ekaterinoslav.[14] Greeks left Crimean churches in ruins, after stripping them of holy artifacts. Crimea's miraculous icon, the Bakhchisarai Mother of God, was removed from the Dormition monastery in Bakhchisarai. Not all Greeks left, and some of those who did emigrate eventually returned to Crimea. F. A. Fedorov, whose travel account was published in 1854, remarked upon the curious habits of these "native" Crimean Greeks, described as native because they used Tatar language "not only between themselves . . . but even in liturgy." Native Greek women followed "eastern customs" of wearing head coverings; men dressed in the Tatar fashion.[15] These remaining Crimean Christians made pilgrimages to the monastery in the icon's memory. Others lived in the Kerch-Enikale region and perpetuated traditions there.[16]

The continued existence of a small population of Greeks with eastern mannerisms and dress did not stop Russian and European scholars from romanticizing their memory, or distorting their historical legacy for nationalist purposes. Hellenic and Byzantine ruins captivated newcomers. Even today the Crimean peninsula resembles a living museum of ancient ruins. As one of the best preserved sites of Ionian colonists, as well as the legendary location of Prince Vladimir's baptism, Chersonesos became a favorite destination of historians, antiquarians, and archeologists. During the last years of Catherine's reign, especially following her trek to the Black Sea in 1787, amateur and professional scholars from St. Petersburg flooded Crimea with speculation about this ancient Greek city.[17] Necropolises lined the street that leads into the abandoned city, whose heart contained crumbling remains of ancient temples. Extensive urban ruins also accommodated a Hellenistic mint and an amphitheater at the city's outskirts. Eighteenth-century Russian imperialists approached the ruins with wonder and based their budding research in romanticized readings of ancient maps and manuscripts.[18] After archaeological and historical interest in antiquity waned toward the end of Alexander's reign, Chersonesos remained a chief focus of research for its legendary association with Prince Vladimir.

Apart from Chersonesos, researchers wrote about ruins of Greek, Scythian, Alan, Karaite, Tatar, Genoese, Byzantine, and other settlements that stretch from Evpatoria in the west to Kerch in the east. Scholars especially focused upon the "cave cities."[19] These are a series of hollowed dwellings carved into sedimentary cliffs that criss-crossed the internal or second row of mountains separating the steppe from the coastal tip of the peninsula. Many included traces of castles, villages, and monasteries—conglomerations that were believed to constitute ancient cities.[20] Due to their dating in the mid-late Byzantine era, these caves became popular subjects of research during Nicholas's reign.[21] Before scholars developed an interest in Crimea's Christian ruins, however, they focused on Crimea's Greco-Roman ruins, and moved the peninsula to the center of imperial discourse and representation.

The ability of Crimea to represent ties to Greece was extremely important to Catherine II. On one level, it reinforced the imperial vision of her failed "Greek project," in which she anticipated a restored Greek empire ruled by her grandson seated in Constantinople. On another, it tied into her court's neoclassical revival and celebration of Hellenic antiquity, motifs designed to affiliate the Russian court more closely to those in the west.[22] As one of the best preserved sites of Greek and Roman antiquity in Crimea, Chersonesos became the center of intellectual curiosity and the subject of imperial discourses; Catherine even created a coin with her image on one side, and ruins of Chersonesos on the other.[23] Catherine also emphasized the myth of Iphigenia, a Greek princess, who according to Euripides, traveled through the Black Sea until settling on the coast of Tauris, or Crimea. According to this legend, Iphigenia came to Crimea after being rescued from her father's plan to sacrifice her by Diana, Greek goddess of the hunt. Diana intervened at the last moment to save the princess's life and transported her safely to Tauris to serve in a temple. Court writers and lyricists revived the legend of Iphigenia during Catherine's tour through New Russia, causing scholars and travelers to speculate over the exact location of the ancient temple for decades.[24]

Reflecting imperial prerogatives as well as European antiquarian trends, the first wave of archaeological research in Crimea was organized by the

Imperial Academy of Sciences and consisted largely of identifying traces of classic architecture.[25] Apart from the representational needs of the court, practicalities of Russian rule demanded greater knowledge of the new southern territory and prompted greater study of the region. Through the Academy of Sciences in St. Petersburg, scholars organized the first stage of research on Crimea and sponsored several early expeditions dealing with immediate concerns of imperial rule. Early studies concentrated on the history of the Crimean *khanstvo*, the reforms of the last khan, Sahin Giray, and representations of Tatar customs and beliefs, especially Islam.[26] Some of this research focused on the peninsula's ruins, including a few preliminary plans of Chersonesos.[27]

One of the most important studies from this era was Peter Simon Pallas's *Travels through the Southern Provinces of the Russian Empire, performed in the years 1793 and 1794*. This work reintroduced this hitherto forgotten land to Russian and western audiences, and was published in several different languages and editions.[28] Pallas covered an array of topics pertinent to imperial governance, including climate, the flora and fauna of Crimea, and Tatar languages and customs. He also gave special attention to the peninsula's history and its impressive complex of ruins. He wrote about Crimea's major monuments, from "cliff cities" to the region's Byzantine monasteries. He especially detailed the ruins of Chersonesos, with a thoroughness that established the foundation for archaeological study for years to come. From the end of Catherine's reign through that of Alexander, travelers and scholars continued to provide accounts of Crimean ruins and antiquity for consumption by Russia and the West.

Martha Guthrie, formerly the governess of the Smolny School for girls, followed in Pallas's footsteps when she visited the ruins in Crimea and presented a synthesis of existing studies and personal impressions for a British audience.[29] A couple of prelates also participated in the early studies.[30] With few exceptions, these works, published in German, French, Russian and English at the turn of the century, focused on Greek and Roman antiquity in Crimea and reflected Catherine's project of linking Russia to the West. They also accorded Greeks a foundational role in the history of Crimea. A St. Petersburg scholar who toured Crimea at the turn of the nineteenth century, Pavel Sumarokov, credited Greeks for delivering the peninsula from barbarism. "What," he asked, "prepared Crimean peoples for enlightenment? That would be the Greeks."[31]

Crimea's popularity among scholars continued through Alexander I's reign. By the 1820s, news of Crimean ruins generated a distinctive "intellectual" pilgrimage of the Russian educated elite.[32] Foreign travelers also interiorized the Russian philhellenic obsession with Crimea, so much so that by 1825 Robert Lyall described the Black Sea region as the only valuable place to visit in the Russian Empire:

> I could have wished that our journey had been of longer duration, but at the same time, it must be remembered, that travelling Russia is not like traversing the classic ground of Greece and Italy, or even most countries of Europe, in which objects worthy of description continually present themselves. With the exception of the Krimea, and the opposite shores of the Cimmerian Bosphorus, we met with little that recalled associations with the Greeks or the Romans. Interesting objects lie widely scattered in the vast empire of Russia, and the traveller is generally contented to gallop over the ground which separates them all with possible rapidity.[33]

The obsession with Grecian antiquity had grown to such enormous proportions, that Anatolii Demidov, who visited Crimea in 1837, scoffed at the endless speculation over the Grecian past:

> Would you witness the immortal scene of the drama of the Atrides, and of the Trojan war, which the world learned as it learned to read? Advance a few steps upon this sacred promontory, and behold the scene—the imperishable scene! Far superior to that of the classical writers, it has not changed these three thousand years; since old Homer first took possession of his poetical universe. On this very spot is the Temple of Diana Tauropolitana, with its blood-stained altars: you are now upon its formidable pavement. Behold the altar of the goddess: it is that square stone—a rude and primitive altar, like those of the Druids. Why those garlands and wreaths, upon a stone ever red with blood?

He concluded his tirade, which has only been partially excerpted here, "But whither is all this poetry leading us? We are travellers, and not poets: let us return to reality."[34]

In the dawning of archaeological and historical disciplines, fascination with classic ruins eclipsed other Crimean monuments, whether the Scythian sarcophagi, ancient mosques, or Karaite scrolls. Yet, in her analysis of philhellenism in Germany, Marchand argues that "[n]o ideal is an island: each depends on a complex of other ideals, institutions, ideologies, and interest groups for its self-definitions and properties of internal cohesion."[35] In part, Marchand is saying that multiple and overlapping discourses exist within any given cultural context. Thus, in the case of Crimea, philhellenism constituted only one trope in the Russian imperial imagination.[36]

Exotic orientalism, represented by Aleksandr Pushkin's poem, "The Fountain of Bakhchisarai" (1824) was another.[37] An exotic, triangulated love story wrapped around the sixteenth-century Crimean khan Mengli Giray, the Polish and Georgian women of his harem, and the nostalgic gaze of an intrepid Russian traveler, "The Fountain of Bakhchisarai" wove legend through a clever narrative of imperial travelogue.[38] Its lyrical beauty not withstanding, "The Fountain of Bakhchisarai" mapped the provincial town into Russia's imperial geography; Bakhchisarai became an important reminder of Russia's victories to the south, the ruin of the Crimean khanate, and the decline of the Ottoman Empire. With Pushkin's help, the city became a living museum of the once great Tatar culture—Russia's exotic "other"—and a common stop of Russian tours through Crimea. While still in his post at Chigirin, Archbishop Innokentii whimsically lamented that Chigirin had no memorial as great as the "Giray fountain" of Bakhchisarai.[39]

European travelers also embraced the Tatars as a subject. Mary Holderness, a Scottish woman who lived in Crimea during the reign of Alexander I, published *Notes relating to the manners and customs of the Crim Tatars, written during a four years' residence among that people* in 1821. Her work provided a detailed description of Tatars and revealed a level of interaction with them experienced by few Russians.[40] Despite her claims of objective and impartial description, Holderness's account was anything but; it engaged many of the orientalist themes evident in the writings of others.

Tales abounded regarding the khan's harems and the beauty of the mysterious women whose veils kept the penetrative gaze of Europeans at bay. Especially adventurous travelers attempted to catch sight of the women's faces. Mme. Adele de Hell, wife of the French geologist, describes a dinner on an estate to which Tatar women were afterward invited. The men in attendance left the salon so that the Tatar women could comfortably enter. After the men exited, the women unwrapped their veils, and plied the European women with their own questions. When the male guests made noises that they were ready to return, according to Mme. de Hell's recollection, it threw the Tatar women "into the most picturesque and comical disorder" as they "ran about in all directions looking for their veils." Mme. de Hell then divulges, "In the midst of the confusion I was wicked enough to hide the veil and slippers of the young beauty, and then throw the door wide open." Thus having violated the women whom she had ostensibly befriended minutes before, Mme. de Hell continues, "It was curious to see the dismay of the poor blushing creature who knew not how to escape from the bold admiration of several men. She had never in her life been in such a situation before; so when I thought the gentlemen had sufficiently indulged their curiosity, I hastened to relieve her by returning her veil."[41] Apart from revealing a surprising lack of sympathy for Tatar women's privacy and customs, the above narrative illustrates that while many intellectuals romanticized Crimea's philhellenic heritage, as established in Catherine's court writing, Crimea was a flexible symbol and could be used in multiple ways. The one element that held early representations together was a common application of Crimea as a trope of national mythology.

In the 1820s and 1830s, the symbolic role of Crimea began to shift again, reflecting the rise of religious nationalism under Nicholas I.[42] Especially after the articulation of Sergei Uvarov's official nationality platform, "Orthodoxy, autocracy, nationality," Russian archaeologists and antiquarians looked to define Russian identity of the present through Christian artifacts of the past.[43] In place of classical or orientalist motifs, scholars pursued traces of Crimea's Christian past in the Roman, Genoese, and especially the Byzantine periods.[44]

A series of articles in *Notes of the Fatherland* during the mid-1820s reflects the growing Russian fascination with Byzantine history.[45] One anonymously published article, "About the Environs of the St. George Balaklava Monastery in Crimea," combined a discussion of ancient Grecian ruins near Balaklava with a discussion of the Korsun legend. The article's goal was to generate donations for the repair and renovation of the monastery that had been undertaken by its Greek superior, Khristos. Written in 1820, but published in 1826, the first half of the article reflected the Catherinian court's absorption in the myth of Iphigenia and argued that ruins of the temple to Iphigenia existed near Balaklava. The emphasis on antiquity, however, served to segue into the article's main thrust: the baptism of Prince Vladimir in Chersonesos. Only three kilometers from Balaklava, the article exalted, was located one of "the most unique places, a holy place." This was the city of Chersonesos, "where the Great Prince Vladimir, who enlightened all of Russia with the Faith in the Savior, was baptized." The crumbling architecture of Chersonesos bore evidence of this event: "From the [St. George] monastery, one can see the ruins of the blessed city, the walls of the city and its fortress, triumphant over time's all-encompassing destruction!"[46] Although the Korsun legend composed only a small part of this article, the article's Christian rhetoric, especially the description of Chersonesos as "holy" and "blessed" nevertheless anticipated the later mid-century project of sacralizing the ruins and reflected the transition between philhellenic and phil-Orthodox perspectives.

Crimea's Byzantine Christianity inspired interest from government agencies as well as academic circles. Shortly after the series in *Notes of the Fatherland,* the Scottish commander of the Black Sea naval forces, Admiral Aleksei Greig, sponsored the first excavation in Chersonesos with the express purpose of locating the church in which Prince Vladimir was baptized. The archaeologist in charge of the excavation, L. Kruze, produced three Byzantine churches, and determined that Prince Vladimir was baptized in the ruin with the richest findings.[47] Officials promptly decided to erect a church on the spot, a project that lay dormant until the Crimean War.[48]

Although Christian scholarship in Crimea existed prior to Nicholas's reign, it received its first major outlet with the formation of the Odessa Society for History and Antiquities. During the second half of Nicholas's reign, scholarly societies began to crop up across the empire. The Odessa Society for History and Antiquities was one of the first regional scholarly societies dedicated to the pursuit of historical and archaeological topics, and received full rights to excavate across New Russia and to publish its findings in 1839.[49] Formed by archaeologists and "lovers of antiquity" from all over the empire, the society did not recognize the disciplinary and professional boundaries that exist today, but was characterized by the same sort of "fluid intellectual milieu" that Nathaniel Knight notes in the early formation of the Imperial Geographic Society.[50] The society grouped together a hodge-podge collection of archaeologists, amateur historians, ethnographers, and philologists pulled from a variety of backgrounds and ranks, whether military officers, state officials, educators, merchants, nobility, priests, or prelates. It sponsored a wide array of archaeological studies. Researchers investigated topics ranging from numismatics to burial grounds. They gathered ancient manuscripts, and generated local histories from ancient times to the era of Russian rule.[51] The society marked a new phase in the study of Crimea, for it displaced work sponsored by the Imperial Academy of Sciences with projects having a local base.

The society's scholars did explore multiple facets of Crimean history. Many concentrated on study of Tatar history, dress, and rituals, and still others focused on the Karaim. With over one-seventh of the early members coming from ecclesiastic backgrounds, however, church archaeology and Christian topics sat at the top of the agenda.[52] Nikolai Murzakevich, the secretary and vice president of the society, professed a deep interest in the study of Crimea's Byzantine heritage, and produced a series of articles on the area's Christian past.[53] In 1836, three years before the founding of the society, Murzakevich published a comprehensive treatment of Crimea's archaeological curiosities in the pages of the Ministry of Education's journal. This article described Tatar sites in some detail, provided a discussion of Hellenic ruins, and pointed to an excavation in Simferopol that was "especially important for archaeology," with the production of Scythian monies and artifacts. Still, Murzakevich gave Christian antiquities ample attention. He highlighted the ruins of Chersonesos, which he described as "valuable to any Russian Christian, since (in 988) the Kyivan prince Vladimir Sviatoslavich took the Christian faith and from there transferred it to all his people." After discussing both ancient Hellene and Byzantine ruins in Chersonesos, Murzakevich speculated over the fundaments of a church, asking, "might this be the church in which the Saintly Prince took his baptism?" He also played the role of ethnographer, sketching habits of native Crimeans. He quoted a seventeenth-century account of Tatars fulfilling religious devotions at the Bakhchisarai monastery and concluded that the historical narrative depicting the "respect of Tatars to Christian holy places is not surprising." Even now, he wrote, Tatars make a pilgrimage "every year on the first of July on the day given to Cosmas and Damian, with other Christians," to the well that was named in memory of Cosmas and Damian. "Tatars, not minding the cold of this well, plunge themselves, and even their children up to their chests, with the intention of healing various ailments. Tatars call this water Suluk-Su, or healing waters."[54] Evidence of Christian ancestry in Tatar religious practices, like the ruins themselves, became a central theme in Crimean Christianizing narratives. Intentionally or not, scholars and the new Odessa Society for History and Antiquities slowly began to shape Crimean history in the image of its Russian conquerors. This Muslim territory increasingly acquired a Christian past.

Unsurprisingly, the impetus to research Crimea's Christian past was embraced by Russian Greeks, who encouraged Greek cultural awareness through religious education, language instruction, and literature. Alexandru Sturdza, Mikhalis Paleolog, and Zacharias Arkas are among a few of many Greeks who encouraged intellectuals to study classical languages and classical architecture. Sturdza, a diplomat in the service of Alexander I whose family had estates in the province of Kherson, promoted a shared Russian and Greek connection through Orthodoxy. Partly for this reason he encouraged Tsar Alexander I's cabinet to bring Christian principles to the forefront of imperial administration.[55] He supported the establishment of a Greek press in Odessa, instruction of the Modern Greek language in the local seminary, and the opening of a Greek gymnasium. He was a founding member of the Odessa Society for History and Antiquities.[56]

Paleolog was another founding member of the Odessa Society for History and Antiquities, and like Sturdza, he well illustrates the connection between nationalist politics and Greek antiquities. Paleolog was born in 1800 in Constantinople and immigrated with his mother to Bucharest, where he cast his support behind the Greek insurrection led by Alexandros Ypsilantis in 1821. After the insurrection failed, Paleolog, like many others, settled into a new life in Russia. He moved to Odessa, where he taught classical Greek in the Greek school until 1827. Paleolog argued that it was important for Russians to learn Modern Greek as well, and received a position in the Odessan Richelieu Lyceum in 1838 for this purpose. Finally, Paleolog also became censor of the newly founded press for which Sturdza ardently campaigned in 1846. Throughout his career, Paleolog published New Greek grammars as well as works on a number of Greek-related topics for the journal of the Odessa Society for History and Antiquities. "Until his death," one member wrote, Paleolog "never ceased being an active member of the Society, never refused to assist fellow members who needed his advice."[57] Throughout his intellectual activities, Paleolog attempted to tie the fascination with Crimea's Grecian antiquity to the more pragmatic concerns of Greeks living in the present.

Zacharias Arkas, elder brother of the more widely known admiral, Nikolaos Arkas, was another prominent member of the Odessa Society. In 1816, he entered the forty-first naval depot as a midshipman, remaining there until 1839 when he was released for health concerns. While in the navy, Arkas served under Admiral Greig during the Turkish War (1828) and distinguished himself twice for bravery. Upon his retirement, he moved to Sevastopol where he directed the naval library until his death in 1866. Once Arkas settled in Crimea, he devoted himself to scholarship and community service. He became a member of the Sevastopol Statistical Committee, a guardian of the Peter and Paul church, a patron of a local girls' school, and an inspector of the Sevastopol quarantine.[58] He also became involved with the Odessa Society and published many articles in the pages of its journal. Two major articles published there described the Black Sea fleet from its establishment through the second half of the nineteenth century.

Even though his work with the Black Sea fleet and its library may ultimately be of greater significance, Arkas is most widely known for his archaeological research.[59] He worked on one of the earliest excavations in Chersonesos and wrote up his findings in 1847 under the title, "The Ancient Heraclean Peninsula and Its Antiquities."[60] This article became more influential than earlier studies of Chersonesos and went through multiple editions and formulations, including publication in the journals of the Ministry of the Interior and the Odessa Society for History and Antiquities. It was also published in a separate edition in 1879. Arkas gave a comprehensive description of the entire peninsula with a breadth unmatched by earlier travelers and researchers. With the intention to review carefully the entire Heraclean peninsula (so called because it was settled by Heraclean Greeks), Arkas utilized information gathered by the Sevastopol Statistical Committee during a three-year period. The article carefully described the monuments and ruins in the Balaklava region, the Inkerman cliffs, the ancient city of Chersonesos, and the land in between. The article's broad agenda also speculated on the location of Iphigenia's temple and the location of Prince Vladimir's baptism. The latter subject became an object of special interest, for Arkas proposed an alternative site for the baptism of Vladimir other than that identified by Kruze. "Maybe this embankment," he wrote about the site in question, "is the same location advised by Nestor, made of the earth brought here by the residents of Chersonesos . . . during the time of the Great Prince Vladimir and the siege of the city. In this manner, there must have been located a church which was destroyed after his christening."[61] The discovery by Arkas displaced that by Kruze. Arkas thus established what is believed to be the exact spot of the Christianizing of Prince Vladimir, and therefore the exact location in which the Greeks passed Orthodoxy to the Slavs. Arkas became the new champion of the older project to build a church on the site of the ruins.[62]

GREECE IN THE SHADOW OF RUSSIA

The role of Greeks in preserving and restoring Crimean Christianity was not lost on local clergymen eager to expand Orthodoxy throughout the peninsula. Concurrent with Arkas's research, Archbishop Gavriil began to historicize Crimea's Greek community. As administrator of the Kherson-Tauride diocese from 1827, Archbishop Gavriil had regulated church affairs in Crimea for over a decade when the Odessa Society opened, and he was one of its most informed and influential members.[63] He actively patronized the society's exploration of Crimean history and archaeology and contributed several articles of his own to the society's journal, from 1844 until his death in 1859. One local scholar credited Gavriil for motivating the Odessa Society's excavations in Christian antiquity, writing: "The Society and all lovers of antiquity are largely obligated to the work of [Archbishop Gavriil]," for attracting attention to "Christian churches . . . these eloquent reminders of old."[64] Later generations of Russian scholars, including Arsenii Markevich (in 1900) and more recently O. A. Griva (in 2002), affirmed this assertion, widely attributing the foundation of directed archaeological research into Crimea's Christian antiquity to Gavriil.⁶⁵

Even though Gavriil is credited as a founding father of church archaeology, much of his work was more historical than archaeological in nature, having a phil-Orthodox emphasis on faith-based kinship ties between Greeks and Russians.⁶⁶ For instance, Archbishop Gavriil wrote a lengthy history of Christianity in New Russia, in which he reviewed the changes in diocesan structure from the era of Catherine II, and illuminated the role of non-Russian Orthodox Christians in building the church in New Russia.⁶⁷ He also contributed a couple of articles to the Odessa Society dealing with the recent exodus of Crimea's Greek Christian population before the annexation. These articles tended to portray Christianity as the "true" religion of Crimea, and typically depicted Muslims as oppressive overlords.

In an article titled "Resettlement of Greeks from the Crimea to the Azov Province," Gavriil cast Crimea's Christian exodus in the 1770s as a symbol of Muslim abuses and an example of the inherent incompatibility between Muslims and Christians. He paralleled their experience with Moses's flight from Egypt. "If it is possible to compare the small with the great," Gavriil wrote, "similar to Moses leading the Israelites from Egyptian slavery, [Metropolitan Ignatius] rescued his tribesmen from under the Tatar yoke, transferring them to Russia, their kindred by faith."⁶⁸ This article, as well as his other works on Crimea's Greeks, went far to establish a Christian history for Crimea. Unlike earlier portrayals of Russian ties to Grecian antiquity circulating during Catherine II's reign, Gavriil postulated a familial bond between Greeks and Russians in their shared faith in Orthodoxy. He also emphasized the rift between Christianity and Islam and implied that Crimean Tatars oppressed Christians. Here, Russia was depicted not only as heir to ancient Greek Christianity in Crimea, but also its savior. Gavriil's scholarship in the Odessa Society attracted attention well outside of the church, culminating in a medal conferred from Nicholas I in April 1847.⁶⁹ Coupled with the research of other society members, including the Greeks themselves, Gavriil's work slowly began to give Crimea a Christian past. Yet as a bishop of New Russia, the main goal of his research had a practical application: to build stronger connections between Greeks and Russians in his diocese.

As Gavriil and other local scholars associated with the Odessa Society for History and Antiquities studied early Christianity in Crimea, nonlocal scholars also participated in the Christianizing of Crimea's history. Makarii Bulgakov (1816–1882) wrote a work entitled *The History of Christianity in Russia before Prince Vladimir, as an Introduction to the History of the Church* (1846) which is the most influential of these works and can be seen as a mediation between local Christian scholarship and Russian imperial audiences at large. With the entire multi-volume work, Makarii established a new field, the history of the Russian Orthodox Church, and set the framework for later studies by E. E. Golubinskii and A. V. Kartashev.[70] Makarii was among the first to mine ancient sources for material on eastern Europe, and like the church archaeologists, he united Christianity with science in his work. This particular volume broke new ground as well, for it conceptualized the past of the Russian Orthodox Church in a new way. Rather than viewing Vladimir as the source of Russian Christianity, it sought to extend Russian Christianity directly to Christ. As S. A. Beliaev argues, the book redefined Vladimir's Christianizing from one great discrete event to the culmination of a thousand-year process in which Christianity had been spreading through the south of Russia (now southern Ukraine, Crimea, and the Caucasus) for years. Makarii drew upon contemporary archaeological studies to make this point: the receptors of Christianity in this region were not Greeks and Romans but the "proto-Russians," that is the Scythians and the Gett-Dacians lumped together.[71]

Crimea constituted a key area of interest throughout the book. The opening chapter, "The Proselytizing of the Holy Apostle Andrew in Our Countries," entered decisively into an ongoing debate about whether Scythia, the proto-Slavic nation, was St. Andrew's mission field.[72] The German historian, August Ludwig von Schlözer, had successfully dismissed this claim at the end of the eighteenth century.[73] After closely comparing legends with texts from the Middle Ages, Makarii challenged von Schlözer's assertion, and concluded that St. Andrew visited the southern shores of the Crimean peninsula and from there penetrated deeply into the northern Black Sea littoral and other areas of the Russian Empire in order to mission to the Scythians in AD 63.[74] In consequence of St. Andrew's visit, Makarii claimed that several early, first-century Christian communities formed, including a population of over two-thousand near Chersonesos. Effectively, Makarii's work revitalized the myth of St. Andrew, and legitimized it.

Makarii also attempted to link the Christianizing of the region to ethnic Russians, to complete the first-century pedigree. A sub-heading posed as a question illustrated the importance of this point to his overall project of Russifying Crimean Christianity: "Which peoples could have proselytized in ancient Scythia, or in the present-day New Russian Province?" He did acknowledge the overwhelming research on the Greeks, which so fascinated Russian scholars since Catherine II. "Before all, truthfully," he wrote, "there were here back then a few populations of Greeks, such as: Ol'viia, Khersones [Chersonesos], Feodosia, Pantikapeia." Yet Makarii took a novel turn, arguing: "But it is no less true, that the chief inhabitants of these countries were the barbarians, and in this number were hidden, although under alien names, a few Slavic tribes." Primarily, Makarii meant the Gett-Dacians, who he maintained, populated southern Russia and originated in Crimea.

Following his treatment of St. Andrew, Makarii mapped out a history of Christianity in Crimea through nine centuries. He drew attention to saints' lives and lay Christians, beginning with the life of St. Clement, the first-century pope exiled to Crimea by the Roman emperor Trajan. At Inkerman, according to Makarii, St. Clement found Christian communities inspired by St. Andrew, and converted more Christians himself. Subsequently, according to Makarii, early Crimea had over seventy-five churches, a number drawn from the life of St. Clement but reflected in archaeological surveys of the "cave cities."[75] Other important highlights of Crimea's Christian history included the seven martyrs of Chersonesos, who were first dispatched to Crimea in 310, when Jerusalem's patriarch sent a mission to Tauride.[76] Makarii also touched upon the life of St. Martin, who was incarcerated in Chersonesos in the mid-seventh century, and Cyril and Methodius, the famous apostles to the Slavs believed to have studied the Khazar and Jewish languages in the Crimean city. Makarii described other communities and saints among the Khazars and Scythians. Again, he admitted that Crimea's early Christians were mostly composed of Greeks yet carefully noted that "these early dioceses in Chersonesos . . . probably included a few Slavs."[77] As should be evident, Markarii's work brought competing tropes in Crimean history together in critical ways. He emphasized that Crimea was Christian before it was Muslim and that proto-Russians were present in the land along with Greeks. These early Slavs, as Makarii insinuated, were the ancient predecessors of nineteenth-century Russian imperialists. In a few deft rhetorical movements, Makarii gave Russia a first-century Christian pedigree, provided imperialists with a claim to the land, further alienated Tatars from their homeland, and eroded Crimea's Greek heritage.

St. Vladimir was by far the most important saint that Makarii dealt with. The section on St. Vladimir, which composed the last chapter of the book, provided the most significant link between Crimean and Russian Christianity and became a fundamental rationalization for the church's expansion in Crimea. Like the myth of St. Andrew, that of St. Vladimir generated intense debate. Partly this is because the conversion of Prince Vladimir occupies one of the most pivotal moments in nearly all narratives of Russia's past. In the words of Makarii himself:

> This event is without a doubt, the most important event in the history of all Russian lands. In several ways, it decided the eternal fate of all future genera-

tions of Russia, and the fate of the earthly fatherland. The Christian kingdom of Prince Vladimir began a new period of our existence in every respect: our enlightenment, customs, judiciary and building of our nation, our religious faith, and our morality.[78]

Prince Vladimir's conversion, which according to Makarii occurred in Chersonesos, defined Russia. It gave the people a Christian identity, drew them together as a nation, and created a state.[79] Later in the nineteenth century, critics challenged Makarii's version, suggesting that Kyiv was the more logical site of Vladimir's baptism.[80] Regardless of the Kyivan controversy, Makarii's work firmly established Crimea as an Orthodox symbol of Russia's self-definition.

Makarii's work attracted attention from intellectuals and officials across the empire, many of whom desired to see a stronger church presence on the Black Sea. Archbishop Innokentii was one of those most intrigued by Makarii's research. When Innokentii first learned of Makarii's publication, he immediately asked his friend and former pupil for twenty additional copies. It appears that Innokentii planned to disseminate these among the parish schools of his diocese in Kharkov, where he was then posted.[81] That Innokentii actually used the work in his later writings about Crimea is also obvious. His collected works, for example, contain one short piece, "The Propagation and Success of Christianity in Ancient Chersonesos," which carefully chronicles Crimea's communion of saints, and describes the early spread of Christianity in the region.[82] This short, abbreviated article reads like a verbatim extract from Makarii's *History of Christianity*. As soon as Innokentii arrived in Odessa, he immediately began to campaign for Crimea's recognition as a special holy place within the Russian Empire, based largely upon the peninsula's ancient Christian history and spectacular Byzantine ruins.

Due to the early activities of the Odessa Society for History and Antiquities, Crimea's Christian past became increasingly celebrated and known throughout the empire. Widespread knowledge of the *Life of St. Vladimir*, along with the discovery of Vladimir' baptistery in Chersonesos, led to a new toponym for the peninsula: this jewel in the crown of Catherine II became the "cradle of Russian Christianity."[83] Tourists expanded their itineraries to incorporate ancient Greek churches and abandoned monasteries along with traditional stops at the khan's palace in Bakhchisarai. When the imperial family visited Crimea in the second quarter of the nineteenth century, for example, the royal visits touched on Crimea's important Christian monuments. Grand Duke Konstantin Nikolaevich and other family members visited the Bakhchisarai monastery, last home to the Greek metropolitan, in the 1840s.[84] Local clergy diligently recorded these visits in the church's record book; the tsars and family signed their names on the walls, and the memory of their presence added another layer of sanctity.

Byzantine Antiquities Preserved

Archbishop Innokentii continued earlier research into Crimea's Christian history when he assumed leadership of the Kherson-Tauride diocese in 1848. Like many Russian bishops, Innokentii wore several hats. He had contacts throughout various fields of research and held memberships in multiple academic societies, including the Imperial Moscow Society of History and Antiquity, the Odessa Society for History and Antiquities, the Imperial Society of Agriculture of Southern Russia, the Imperial Russian Geographic Society, and the Imperial Archaeological Society.[85] His correspondents spread widely to include the leading intellectuals of his era, such as historian Mikhail Pogodin, the minister of enlightenment Sergei Uvarov and his son, the archaeologist Aleksei Uvarov, and the geographer Nikolai Nadezhdin. Arsenii Markevich, Crimea's famous archivist, commented that "[t]he name of Innokentii, as a leading scholar, theologian and historian . . . resounded throughout all of Russia even when he was still in Kyiv."[86]

An active participant in the scholarly debates of his day, Innokentii had a well-defined philosophy of science. He sided with a cadre of Russian nationalist intellectuals like Nadezhdin, who believed that science should be applied for the benefit of the Russian state. When invited to join the Geographic Society in 1846 by its vice president Feodor Litke, for example, he warmly replied that he met the news of the society's founding with "gratitude and surprise." The society, he said, had an important obligation to Russia; it should elevate knowledge of Russia "not only in front of the foreigners," but as he noted, "in front of our very own sons, who love to fill themselves with the burden of information about others." He told Litke that Russian fascination with abstract science, especially that oriented toward Europe, was somewhat "estranged and without use."[87] In addition to praising the society's work, Innokentii admitted that for him, the "work for the benefit of science and the fatherland will always be one of the most pleasant undertakings."[88]

Just as he believed that science should serve the interest of the state, Innokentii more importantly argued it should support the church. Science, he said, should be subjugated to faith, as a "daughter is obedient to her mother."[89] He was dedicated to intellectual pursuit and scientific inquiry, believing that scholars had a God-given responsibility to pursue truth, not only for "the benefit of the earth, but for facilitating the path to heaven."[90] His commitment to science is evident in his own theological and historical scholarship, his patronage of and community with other scholars, and especially his work in Crimea. He vowed to be active in the society's work, writing that "strengthening the fatherland history, particularly the history of the Russian Church," would "always compose favorite leisure-time activities."[91] Unlike western tendencies to portray religion and science as binary opposites, or alternative world views, Innokentii as well as many of his Russian contemporaries perceived science and religion as complementary pursuits.

Archbishop Innokentii's long-term interest in history and archaeology of the church blossomed into a full-fledged program of Christian scholarship after he assumed his post in Odessa. In a memoir published in *Strannik* in 1861, Baroness Maria Bode recalled that Crimea was at the center of Innokentii's attention: "He zealously gathered information about the various churches and scattered monasteries on the Tauride mountains, looking for indications of the saints in old monastery archives."[92] Similarly in his memoirs, Evgenii, abbot of the future monastery in Chersonesos, noted that the archbishop "paid particular attention to the Crimean peninsula" and all of its "various different faiths and elements," but foremost he was fascinated with the "Great Ancient Christian monuments."[93] Ivan Palimpsestov, secretary of the Agricultural Society of Southern Russia, described his own recollection of an expedition with the archbishop through the meandering spine of the Tauride mountains. Archbishop Innokentii, according to Palimpsestov, knew the name of each mountain, foothill, and cliff complex as well as any archeologist.[94]

According to an Odessa seminarian who later became the main priest in the St. Peter and Paul church in Sevastopol, Innokentii spent nearly three months exploring the peninsula during the first year of his appointment to the post in Odessa. Similar to many who visited Crimea, Innokentii duly appreciated the "ancient Tauride mountains with its marvelous valleys, its diverse population, and its rich gifts." Yet, unlike other travelers, Innokentii lamented the "unnatural position of the state religion in the midst of a domineering Islam," the unfulfilled "spiritual needs of the Orthodox," the "monuments of holy antiquity" that "lay in ruins," and the necessity of preserving and renewing the ruins "for historical education."[95]

Innokentii's sermons drew on the complex relationship between archaeology and faith. Throughout his proposal and his writings elsewhere, Innokentii argued that Christians had a holy duty to uncover, study, and restore Crimea's ancient churches. Nowhere was the connection between ruins and restoration more apparent than in Chersonesos. Frequently during his administration, Innokentii emphasized the necessity of restoring the Christian ruins discovered decades earlier by Kruze and Arkas. These ruins, he argued, were among the most holy in all of Russia, yet went completely ignored. In one of his sermons, he expressed shock over their condition: "The church, which according to all probability was the place that St. Vladimir was baptized, and from which began the enlightenment of the faith for all the Russian land, was not fenced in; it was left to the trampling of illiterate animals, who destroyed the last grasses that covered our cradle of Orthodoxy."[96] Literally, the ruins of Chersonesos, which bore witness to St. Vladimir's baptism, had become pasture land for farmers' herds, and according to the archbishop, the local orthodox believers betrayed their duty to protect them.

Abandonment of the ruins to the ravages of time was tantamount to sacrilege, for as Innokentii emphasized to his parishioners, the ruins themselves were holy. Russian pilgrims and travelers in the Sevastopol area were deeply disappointed not to see a monument to St. Vladimir, who turned Russians away from "idolatry and into the saving light of the Gospel." Thus, Innokentii concluded, it was important "for all of Russia . . . to build a church in memory of the Christianizing of St. Vladimir."[97] Church building and restoration in Crimea was not a matter of historic preservation, or even national representation, but of honoring and perpetuating the faith. Because the archbishop perceived the ruins as having a holy past, Christians had an obligation to rescue them from oblivion.

A revealing petition from Orthodox believers in Crimea suggests that Crimean laity received the message. Signed "Residents of the cities of Simferopol, Bakhchisarai, the village of Alushta, and other neighboring cities and villages," this petition reiterated many of the points made in the proposal and reveals local desire to see church expansion. The petition also called upon legitimizing discourses of history and archeology to advocate restoration of ruins:

> History clearly shows that the Crimean peninsula from the first centuries of Christianity was familiar with the Gospel of Christ and had abundant Christians, and martyrs for Christ. Many Christian monuments, particularly the remains of the churches in the Crimean mountains and cliffs, provide evidence of how many Christians were here. Now only one of these holy antiquities is preserved in good condition—the Balaklava Greek monastery. Others of these ancient churches, built in the mountains, disappeared into the cliffs, remaining empty and trampled underfoot.[98]

Emblematic of Christianizing discourse characteristic of New Russia's scholarly journals and newspapers, the petition emphasized that Crimea's sacred Christian history, dating to the first century, and the ruins, especially the cave churches, acted as evidence of Crimea's ancient Christian past. Rather than advocating further study and research into Crimean Christian ruins, however, the petition encouraged restoration and active use.[99]

The archbishop forwarded the petition to the Holy Synod with a much longer proposal titled "Notes about the restoration of ancient holy places in the Crimean mountains." The proposal argued that Crimea's Christian antiquities constituted an unparalleled holy place in the Russian Empire. It advocated forming a modest community of ascetic monks to oversee preservation and restoration of ruins. The monks were to live according to the Athonite rule, a rule that Innokentii often described in monolithic terms despite its variety in practices, of which he was undoubtedly aware. He argued that this monastic community could serve several purposes at once and establish a common ground between Russians and Crimea's other Orthodox populations, especially the Greeks.

Due largely to the web of Graecophilic imagery cast by Russian and European travelers, as well as the grass-roots efforts of Greek refugees, Crimea acquired a Christian identity despite the restrictions associated with the confessional empire. Although this process culminated in the opening of the Russian Athos monastic community under Archbishop Innokentii in 1850, it began with the Greek émigrés and Catherine II's philhellenic platforms decades earlier. The result was a legitimizing discourse that prepared the way for greater church authority by proving that Crimea's inhabitants were Christian before they were Muslim. And while the Greeks themselves were active participants in the Hellenizing of Crimea, they soon found their contributions to the peninsula's past and present identity trumped by the nationalizing and Christianizing drives of a conquering power.

Chapter Three

ATHOS IN CRIMEA

A Local Response to the Eastern Question

In April 1850, the Holy Synod opened a new era in Crimean history when it approved Archbishop Innokentii's proposal, "Notes about the Restoration of Ancient Holy Places in the Crimean Mountains."[1] This document proposed restoring Crimean Christian antiquities for active use. The report identified ten sites for restoration that were "most respected by the people" and that had the most profound "inner holy character."[2] Each site related to Crimea's Balkan Christians of the past and present, whether abandoned Byzantine churches, places still venerated by remaining Greek Christians, or ruins that attracted new waves of Balkan immigrants. Innokentii advocated naming the community "Russia's Athos," after Mt. Athos, the multinational holy community of monasteries in Greece.

Because the church selected communities for Russian Athos based upon previous decades of archaeological discovery, the proposal reveals the extent to which science assisted church expansion. In addition to recommending restoration of Christian antiquities, the proposal referenced archaeologists and antiquarians. Simultaneously, the plan reveals the degree to which religion and politics hybridized along the Black Sea. The choice of Athos as a model reflected Russian fascination with the variety of spiritual practices emanating from the holy mountain: desert monasticism, hesychasm, asceticism, and *starchestvo*. The significance of Mt. Athos for Crimea was not limited, however, to an expression of faith. Mt. Athos served as a complex symbol that intoned a shared past, international religious tensions, and continuous Balkan migrations. Crimea's Hellenic and Byzantine ruins created a special affinity to Mt. Athos that few places in the Russian Empire could claim. Only the Caucasus, which later in the nineteenth century developed the New Athos (Novy Afon) community, had a similar Christian pedigree. Both Crimea and Athos were borderland regions, battlegrounds of identity caught between opposing powers. Like the holy mountain, Crimea had become a gathering place for multinational Orthodox populations, and like the holy mountain, it was viewed by contemporaries as a Christian island in a sea of Islam. Crimea's location on the Black Sea made it, along with Odessa, a pilgrimage route to Athos. Athos thus offered the church more than an example of monastic practices; it provided a flexible symbol of the borderland.

The proposal to transform Crimea into Russia's Athos demonstrates the influence of immigrants on local identity, and illustrates the church's remarkable ability to adapt to an unpredictable imperial environment. Rather than imposing a monolithic identity on Crimea's multinational Orthodox population, Innokentii sought to build upon it, for he viewed the Balkan Christian immigrants as the gateway into Crimea. He stipulated that monks and hierarchs in the community should have journeyed to Mt. Athos at least once and should possess the ability to communicate in Greek. Many of the first generation of monks at Russian Athos did indeed meet these requirements, and the man chosen to lead the community, Polikarp (Radkevich, 1798–1867, later bishop of Orlov and Sevsk), had served in the consulate church in Athens.[3]

Finally, burgeoning religious tension that increasingly characterized the mood at home and abroad inspired the decision to create Athos in Crimea. Although the proposal rarely mentioned overt efforts to convert Tatars, it expressed optimism that a stronger Christian presence might attract them to the church. In its portrayal of the dangers of pilgrimage abroad, the proposal frequently referenced the uncertain political environment along the Balkan Peninsula, whether it be Ottoman persecution of Christian populations or mounting strife among Orthodox populations. Established on the eve of a war sparked by a controversy over holy lands, this small monastic community resembled a breakwater, built to fortify Crimean Christians from international pressures that pounded along the shore like the crashing waves of the Black Sea.

Religious Politics in the Borderland

Religious considerations informed Russian diplomacy from the age of Alexander I, although Alexander did not always cast his lot with Orthodox nations.[4] When confronted by the Greek revolution, the brutal hanging of Patriarch Grigorios V in Constantinople, and Turkish slaughter of the Greeks of Chios in 1821 and 1822, Alexander refused to intervene to support Russia's co-religionists, choosing instead to uphold Prussian and Austrian ties in the Holy Alliance.[5] Similarly, pragmatism guided Alexander's policy toward the Serbs, whose 1804 bid for independence he supported only after Russia declared war on the Ottoman Empire. Even then, according to David MacKenzie, Russia aided Serbs "as a tactical maneuver."[6] The course of Russian policy vis-à-vis Orthodox nations shifted with the ascension of Nicholas I, a devout Orthodox Christian who felt personally an obligation toward his co-religionists. In 1827, Russia broke with the Holy Alliance to intervene on behalf of Greece in the Russo-Turkish War.[7] Many events prompted Russia to declare war on the Ottoman Empire, not the least of which was repeated disruption of Black Sea trade. Still, the rise of public sympathy for Greek independence resonated in the private conscience of the tsar. When Russia concluded the war, the Treaty of Adrianople (1829) provided for limited Greek and Serbian independence.[8]

International religious conflict intensified toward the end of Nicholas I's reign, when the emperor's personal piety led Russia to the brink of war over access and control of holy places in the Levant.[9] Reaching a crisis in the 1850s, the controversy began with the slow filtering of Protestants and Catholics into Jerusalem. The Anglicans installed a bishop there in 1842 and the Catholics appointed a hierarch in the city in 1847.[10] Russia, whose influence had hitherto been secondary to Greeks in the Levant, established a mission of its own headed by Porfirii Uspenskii.[11] A power struggle mounted between Catholics and Orthodox, until the Catholics demanded the right to repair the cupola of the Church of the Holy Sepulchre.[12] This seemingly innocuous request upset the traditional balance of power between Orthodox and Catholics, for the religious body that oversaw the church was considered the dominant Christian faith of the region. Conflict over who repaired the cupola escalated within the administrative worlds of the Ottoman, Russian, and French governments, and became a factor in the foreground of Russia's entrance into the Crimean War.[13] This particular episode ended in a temporary peace, but only after a French warship menaced the Russian Navy in the Black Sea.

Many Russian officials took a pragmatic view of confessional politics. More Muslims than Christians from the Russian Empire visited the holy places in the Ottoman Empire, while Eastern Christians loyal to Greek, Antioch, and Jerusalem patriarchates regarded Russian overtures with suspicion. Russian consuls in the Middle East, in particular Konstantin Bazili, warned against hopes for a romantic pan-Orthodox brotherhood.[14] Other Russian diplomats felt a kinship with their co-religionists. In a position paper written for Russia's Special Committee of Eastern Affairs in the 1820s, Dmitrii V. Dashkov presented an analysis of Russia's historic protectorship over the Eastern Christians from the era of Catherine II. Each war with the Ottoman Empire and the subsequent treaties, Dashkov argued, produced a tangled web of precedents and rights of intervention that varied from one geographic location and one nation to another. He emphasized that Russia had different responsibilities for Serbia, Moldavia, Wallachia, and Greece, but noted that any provisions of protection "were a deserving award for ... sacrifices and struggles" of "our coreligionists" who assisted Russia's war effort against the Ottoman Empire.[15] Throughout, his analysis suggested that Russia's concerns for Eastern Christians extended only to those who traditionally served with Russia in the Russo-Turkish wars, who shared a common language base and a similar eastern European identity, and who were identified specifically by the series of treaties since Catherine II's reign (Kutchuk-Kainardji in 1774, Jassy in 1791, and Bucharest in 1812), that is, the Balkan Christians.

As the differing opinions of Dashkov and Bazili illustrate, Russian bureaucrats discriminated between Orthodox populations of the Ottoman Empire, and Russian opinion did not remain static, but ebbed and flowed throughout the nineteenth century. The struggle among various Greek nationalists for influence in their new state disillusioned Russians who earlier supported the independence movement. Other Russians were scandalized by the autocephaly movement of the Church of Greece (1833) and the behavior of the patriarch in Constantinople, whom critics believed was beholden to the Ottoman sultan rather than to Orthodox believers.[16] Crises in the Balkans and the Danubian principalities in the 1850s, moreover, shifted sympathy to Bulgaria and Romania, while the holy places controversy directed Russian interests to Palestine.

Through the 1830s and 1840s, Russian religious writers lamented the decline of Christianity on the Balkan Peninsula and continued to advocate Russian intervention. Russia's obligation to Constantinople occupied a central theme in many travel narratives based on the Ottoman Empire. Sergei Sviatogorets, a Russian pilgrim whose serialized accounts of his life on Mt. Athos introduced the holy place into Russian mainstream culture, also wrote passionately about the mistreatment of Balkan Christians under Ottoman rule. His description of Constantinople reflected the political nature of his religious narrative and highlighted the romantic notion that the city would once again become Christian.[17] Mainly, Sviatogorets emphasized the city's ruin under Ottoman rule: "the streets are generally narrow, crooked, slipshod, layered with wild stone and litter, and endlessly unclean ... the impression of the morals of Constantinople is pitiful. There, where in its time stood Godly churches, with a canopy of crosses, now is seen humble ruins, or churches transformed by fanaticism under the pale half Islamic crescent." He continued, "Orthodox churches in Constantinople are few, and if they do exist, they are in homes, without cupolas, and without sound."[18] He reiterated common complaints that the Catholic Church had more rights than the Greek, and that Orthodox churches were subject to Ottoman brigandage. "After reviewing Constantinople," he concluded, "the heart involuntarily makes peace with the grief over its touchingly pitiful status."[19] Even those imbued with skepticism over pilgrimage and holy places felt that Constantinople was special. Vladimir Davydov, a Russian scholar traveling through the Ottoman Empire whose account of Mt. Athos amounted to an exposé, lamented the state of Hagia Sofia. He remembered thinking to himself: "Maybe a time will come, when again they [Christians] will appear here in all their former brilliance!"[20]

First-hand narratives depicting the oppression of Balkan Christians flooded travelogues and journals. Instead of sympathizing with Greeks as was common in the first quarter of the nineteenth century, Russian travel writers during the later Nicolaevin period tended to focus upon the Bulgarians, whom they portrayed as being oppressed by Ottoman rule. To impress the plight of Balkan Christians upon his readers, the pilgrim Parfeny Ageev quotes a local priest, who attributed the poverty and misery of the country to continuous warfare and exploitation by Ottoman overlords. The priest, according to Ageev, said:

> from antiquity our country has stood on the borders, and frequently here there is war . . . when we start to recover, and flocks are reestablished, and gardens bear fruit—again begins another war; those who can, flee to Wallachia, but there they are captured by the Turks, who carry them to the middle of the country; our flocks are eaten, our homes are set on fire, gardens are emptied. In the last war, survivors again returned to their residences, again they dug themselves out of the ruins, again resumed their farming. . . . Still Turks here continue to annoy, are very evil, like their faith, always oppressing and out of control: they burn our churches, and looking for silver, they frequently kidnap icons; and there is no one to complain to: the Pasha does not accept it, Tsargrad is far away, and we are in ruins. So we patiently suffer the insults, and we wait for God's mercy, when Russia will come to us, and frees us from the heavy Turkish yoke.[21]

In this passage, attributed to a Bulgarian priest living in a village near Rustchik, Ageev summarized his view of the problem, and his favored solution—the intervention of Russia. Davydov, who traveled the region in the 1830s and who was by the eve of the Crimean War an official in the Russian Foreign Ministry, gave a similar recommendation for Mt. Athos, then under Ottoman rule: "Unfortunately, the holiness of this country falls year from year, and knowledge and manners; they need Russia to transform it and make worthy of their high appointment."²²

By the middle of the nineteenth century, pan-Orthodox sentiment and religious nationalism took shape throughout the empire and found expression in New Russia. Partly this stemmed from the many waves of Eastern Christians who had settled there from annexation forward. Ottoman law designated to Christians a lesser status than to the majority Muslim population. Eastern Orthodox Christians living in the Ottoman Empire were given the status of *Dhimmis*, People of the Book. Theoretically, *dhimmi* status granted Eastern Christians some equality under Ottoman law, but it also saddled Eastern Christians and Jews with the responsibility to pay higher taxes. This contradiction in Ottoman policy became more pronounced in the nineteenth century, and led to oppression and persecution of some Eastern Christians. Although Reshid Pasha passed a *tanzimat* pledging the equality of Christians and Muslims alike, Turkish intolerance for Orthodoxy continued.²³ The first half of the nineteenth century saw repeated upheavals in Ottoman Europe, whether the Serbian rebellions or the Greek revolution. Russian sympathy for Orthodox co-religionists gathered momentum in the Black Sea region, where powerful Greek and Bulgarian lobbies began to form.

Balkan Immigration and Crimean Christianity

The impact of refugees on the host nation, as Peter Gatrell has argued, makes for a complicated topic, one with which historians are still grappling.²⁴ Not only are refugee populations notoriously difficult to count, their influence is not always obvious to contemporaries. Immigrants from the Ottoman-held Balkan Peninsula flooded New Russia from the Russo-Turkish Wars under Catherine II through the Crimean War. Greeks composed an especially visible and numerous immigrant population. They served in the Russian foreign service, the navy, and local administration. Asylum seekers brought memories of their troubled existence under the Ottoman Empire and supported movements for national liberation. Most famously, Alexandros Ypsilantis founded the secret cell Philiki Etaireia in Odessa in 1814, a cell that plotted armed resistance against the Ottoman Empire.²⁵ The same year, Ioannis Kapodistrias helped organize a Russian branch of the Vienna-based philanthropic society Philomousos Etaireia, which actively spread Greek culture and awareness. Kapodistrias was a top foreign minister in the cabinet of Alexander I and, later, the first head of state of independent Greece.²⁶ Even after Greece won its independence, Odessan Greeks raised money for and awareness about other Greek-populated territories (Epirus, Thessaloniki and Crete) still under Ottoman suzerainty.²⁷ Russian policy from the era of Catherine II was to some degree responsible for the political consciousness of immigrants along the Black Sea coast, as elite émigrés in particular were used "to exacerbate provincial challenges to the sultan's authority."²⁸

Greeks settled throughout New Russia, but were especially visible in Odessa, where they established a mercantile base at the city's founding at the end of the eighteenth century. These Greeks typically operated as *beratlis*, or "people who . . . were entitled to diplomatic protection and immunity from Ottoman taxation and duties including the *haraç* [poll tax]."²⁹ Subjects of the Ottoman Empire became protégés of Russians and Europeans so that they could take advantage of the privileges granted by the *berat*, a title that enabled the Ottoman *millet* (non-Muslim subjects) an escape from taxes, customs, and other punitive laws. Intended for diplomats and a few extraordinary traders, *berats* became objects of corruption and were widely dispensed, especially for merchants.³⁰ Holders of the *berat* typically possessed land and had other attachments in the Ottoman Empire, but theoretically they could also have at least part-time if not permanent residence along Russia's Black Sea territory. Several Greek *beratlis* lived and worked in Odessa as either stateless traders or de facto subjects of the tsar. Given their traditional occupation as merchants in the Ottoman Empire, Greeks easily dominated trade in New Russia.³¹ In his visit to Odessa, the German geographer Johann Kohl commented that there were "from forty to fifty great commercial houses, of which the principal are Greeks."³² Further, he noted, Greek merchants were so numerous that although Russian was "the language of the common people, of servants and coachmen, of the market and the harbours, as well as the official language of the authorities," Greek was "the language of the Exchange and of commerce, and the daily Price Current."³³

In addition to commerce, Greek émigrés played an enormous role in the Black Sea fleet. Founded by Catherine II in 1783, the Black Sea fleet initially relied heavily upon non-Russians. Five of its admirals before the Crimean War were English or Scottish, with a majority of the population of sailors being Greek.³⁴ Nikolaos Arkas (younger brother of Zacharias Arkas), whose father immigrated to Nikolaev at the end of the eighteenth century from present-day Greece, was the most famous Greek in Russia's Black Sea fleet. Inspired by Greek nationalism and devotion to his adopted home, Arkas volunteered at the age of thirteen to fight, along with his two elder brothers, in the Russo-Turkish War of 1828/29. From there, he rose quickly to have a brilliant career, serving in an expedition to the Caspian Sea and in the defense of Sevastopol in the Crimean War. At the war's end, Arkas submitted a proposal to Tsar Alexander II advocating a private steamship fleet based in the Black Sea to develop trade and postal service with foreign ports. The government supported this venture, and by that summer the Steamship Society had sold over 10,000,000 stock shares to private buyers, including the Russian Orthodox Church. The new trade organization opened with five steamships able to carry 5,400 tons.[35] In the next Russo-Turkish War (1877/78), the steamships were pressed into service and Arkas became admiral of the swollen Black Sea fleet. By World War I, the Steamship Society had grown enormously, to 75 ships able to transport 200,000 tons, with destinations throughout Europe and the Near East.[36]

Greek *beratlis* and asylum seekers established a strong a presence in Crimea. One of the first waves of Greeks arrived in Crimea shortly before the Russian government ordered the relocation of Crimea's native Eastern Christians to the shores of the Azov. These Greeks comprised a special population; they were subjects of the Ottoman Empire who fought with Russia during the Russo-Turkish War of 1768–1774.[37] Misnamed by Russian authorities as the "Albanian Regiment," they were transferred to Balaklava from the east of Crimea after only a few years. The Balaklava Greeks participated in Russian conflicts from the 1780s forward and marshaled up a special unit during the Crimean War. In quiet periods, they performed a variety of tasks, as border patrol along the coast of the Black Sea from Sevastopol to Sudak and as construction brigades responsible for new roadways. They also enforced the quarantine bay when the plague hit Sevastopol in 1829.[38] In return for their service to the Russian Empire, the government awarded these Greeks plots of land. Because Balaklava is mostly mountainous, the Greeks spread their farmsteads throughout surrounding villages.

As a foreign group who fought on behalf of the Russian Empire, Balaklava Greeks achieved a near mythical status in nineteenth-century travel narratives. Ivan Muravev-Apostol, who visited the Greek community in 1820 as the guest of the Greek commander Revliottis, supplied a highly romanticized depiction of this population, comparing the Greek immigrants' history with the legend of the Sabines. Just as the Romans had to abduct the Sabines, "due to having insufficient women," he wrote, this male military colony on the Russian borderland "abducted Jews and Tatars." Whether the intermarriage between Greeks and natives took on the aggressive nature of the Sabine myth is unclear, but certainly intermarriage did occur. The Balaklava Greeks perfectly represented the exotic, chaotic composition of the peninsula in Muravev-Apostol's eyes. Several in the community, he claimed, "separately worship Mohammed, combining the descendents of Pelasgi with the heirs of Chingis Khan."[39]

The Balaklava battalion had a mixed history with the Tatars, for while battalion members interacted on a regular basis with Tatars—travelogues are rich with anecdotes of Greeks, Armenians, and Tatars working and recreating together—they also acted as informants for the Russian government and helped to subdue Tatar unrest.[40] According to Victor Amanton, Balaklava Greeks nurtured resentment against the Ottoman Empire through the 1840s, and transferred their negative feelings to local Tatars. "This transplanted Greek colony, which is in the middle of a Muslim population" Amanton wrote, "is possessed of the highest degree of hatred for the Muslims from whom they fled, and contributes to the irritation of the subject [Tatar] population, which is still an enemy of Russia today as it was from the first day of the conquest."[41] Estimates of the Greek population vary. Officially, census takers reported them around 2,500, but an Englishman who toured Crimea during the Crimean War put the Greek population of Balaklava "to the number of 8,000."[42]

Following this group, a number of other Greeks from Anatolia slowly began to filter into abandoned villages. Greeks arrived in Sevastopol and Evpatoria, and returned to Bakhchisarai. Many more Greeks settled in Perekop and filled the famous villages that Grigorii Potemkin built to give the empress the impression of progress during her tour of the Black Sea region in 1787. These villages had been rapidly erected by Russian serfs imported especially for that purpose—to create the illusion of a thriving economy so that the empress would be impressed with development in the newly conquered region. Typically, the Potemkin villages have served as a symbol of tsarist excess. With the settlement of the Greek population, however, these villages acquired a useful function.[43]

Immediately upon their arrival, Greeks began to reestablish Christianity on the peninsula and operated two active monasteries, the Dormition monastery and St. George Balaklava monastery. Before annexation, the last khan invited a Greek priest, Constantine Spiranda, to staff the Dormition monastery that Metropolitan Ignatius had evacuated.[44] Spiranda conducted services for all of the Christians in Bakhchisarai: old Greeks and Armenians who remained; new non-Russian Christians who arrived after Catherine's invitation; and Russian soldiers based there. Anecdotes describe the last Crimean khan, Sahin Giray, lighting candles in the monastery, an act that has since generated some debate over whether his actions revealed the memory of his ancestors' Christian tradition or were rather clever diplomacy. Under Spiranda, the renewal of the Dormition monastery proved to be short-lived, for turmoil caused by Russian annexation led to a wave of Christian-Muslim violence and the priest went into hiding. By 1800, authorities relegated the Dormition monastery to the status of a cemetery church, after building a new church in the name of St. Nicholas in the center of town. Decades later, however, patrons continued to visit the church in the cliffs. Archaeologists visited the monastery to study cave architecture, while pilgrims traveled there on the feast day.[45] Even the imperial family made repeated stops at the monastery between 1800 and 1850, reflecting its lasting reputation and adding to its mystique.[46]

The St. George monastery near Balaklava represents another Greek contribution to Crimean Christianity. When Crimea's original Greek settlers left for Mariupol in 1778, a few monks remained in the monastery. Whereas Spiranda had to retrieve the Dormition monastery from the utter desolation of its long closure, the St. George monastery had been continuously in operation when Russians entered the peninsula. Moreover, the Balaklava Greek battalion gave the monastery a powerful, stable base of support. Initially, the Balaklava monastery retained allegiance to the patriarch in Constantinople, whose office organized Greek Christian affairs in Crimea before the Russians arrived. Only in 1794 did Balaklava Greeks begin a relationship with the Russian Holy Synod in Moscow, although Greek abbots continued to administer the monastery until the middle of the nineteenth century.[47] For these reasons, the Greek Balaklava monastery is legendary in Crimea as a symbol of ancient Greek ties to Crimea. It also composed a central image of the Greek-Russian 'brotherhood,' when it became the base for Black Sea naval priests in 1806.[48] Greek monks at Balaklava mixed with Russian monks, and after the Crimean War, all were viewed as heroes who dedicated themselves to the defense of the fatherland.[49]

Metropolitan Agathangelos (Typaldos, 1770–1865) was the most famous abbot of the St. George monastery, which he oversaw for thirty years, from 1824 to 1854. The metropolitan's professional life followed the path of Greek national awakening. Born in Kefalonia, Agathangelos spent his early years in Constantinople and the Danubian Principalities. In 1808, Patriarch Grigorios V made him a bishop of Asia Minor, and he was later appointed the metropolitan of Kefalonia, where he served until the beginning of the Greek revolt. His career with the church had taken him from Kefalonia, which was a site of revolutionary activity, into the heart of the Ottoman Empire. Throughout this period, he was closely aligned with Patriarch Grigorios V, who was brutally murdered by Ottoman authorities during Easter services in 1821.[50] Like many of his compatriots, especially those clerics associated with the patriarch, Agathangelos fled the violence. In 1822, at the Verona Congress, Tsar Alexander I granted Agathangelos asylum and appointed him to the post at the St. George Balaklava monastery. Agathangelos led a dignified career in Crimea, and acquired such renown that he was invited to Nicholas I's coronation.[51] Several years later, in 1830, another Greek metropolitan, Iosephos, also settled on the peninsula.[52]

It is impossible to provide accurate statistics for the Greek population in Crimea, because not every city kept good records or required passports of the fluctuating refugee population. In 1846, the Imperial Academy of Sciences sent a delegation to Crimea to collect information on the non-Russian population. The academy's research, however, reveals only a partial picture, because the statisticians lumped all non-Russians together in the villages where the vast majority of Crimeans lived. In the cities, however, the researchers compiled separate statistics for the following groups in the categories of merchants and townspeople: Greeks, Armenians, Karaim, Tatars, Nogai, and "Tatar Tsegany." In Crimean cities, which were counted as Simferopol, Sevastopol, Karasubazar (Belogorsk), Bakhchisarai, Evpatoria, Feodosia, Kerch-Enikale, Staryi Krim, Perekop, and Nogaisk, the Greek population included 91 merchants and 1,432 townspeople, a similar proportion to Armenians, who numbered 93 merchants and 1,248 townspeople. Of all Crimean populations, the Karaim appear to have had the most merchants, 341 of 1,617, ten of whom even visited Britain's Great Exhibition of 1851.[53] In comparison, very few Tatars were listed as merchants, 206 out of nearly 12,000.[54] According to the data, Greeks and Armenians composed a small part of the population of the cities, with their merchants accounting for fewer than one-tenth of the total.[55] Still, more than one-third of the Greek merchants ranked in the first and second guild. Throughout the imperial period, the official estimates of the Greek population in Crimea remain quite low, rising from a few thousand at the end of the eighteenth century to 25,000 on the eve of the revolution.[56]

Because statisticians working in Crimea and along the Black Sea coast could not easily track transient populations, in reality, the actual numbers of Greeks, Armenians, and other non-Russians were probably much higher than official estimates in the first half of the nineteenth century. The government could not count *beratlis* who took residence in New Russia, and it also was surprisingly flexible in overlooking undocumented foreign workers. When passing through the Moldavian city of Akkerman, for example, Johann Kohl maintained that the population was several times greater than the Russian estimates. He writes:

> As the city enjoys a privilege of exemption from the plague of passports, its population is continually increasing, and cannot be less than 13,000, for according to the police master and the German apothecary of the place, the names of 8,000 men are inscribed in city books. It is absurdly rated in the St. Petersburg almanac as at 2,500, whilst there are at least as many houses. . . . It has like most of the cities in this part of the world, a medley population, composed of Asiatics and Byzantine Greeks, Jews, Armenians, Germans, Frenchmen, Bulgarians, and Moldavians.[57]

A couple of decades earlier, Mary Holderness described a similar problem in the population estimates for Sevastopol: "Sevastopol, or Aktiar, does not surpass" 3,000 official residents, she writes, "but as this port is the rendezvous of the Russian fleet in the Black Sea, its population, including sailors, soldiers, shipwrights and so on, is computed at from fourteen to fifteen thousand."[58]

Given the ambiguity over population statistics, the real influence of Greeks in the Black Sea region and Crimea should not be judged by numbers alone. In Crimea, the goals of Greek nationalists as well as the day-to-day activities of refugees simply trying to carve out a living space translated into a grassroots revival of Christianity.[59] Greeks did indeed arrive well in advance of the Russian civilian population, and as early as 1795, they had created Greek parishes throughout the peninsula, most notably in Kerch, Enikale, Karasubazar, Bakhchisarai, Kermenchike, Balaklava, Evpatoria, and Perekop. Their churches also functioned as the center of Greek culture in Crimea, because most contained libraries and schools with services and other affairs conducted in Greek. Festivals at the churches also remained distinctly Greek.[60]

During his trek through New Russia, Kohl stumbled across the annual celebration of the Mother of God (August 15) in Bakhchisarai, the former capital of the Crimean Tatar khanate. Christians from surrounding towns and villages streamed into the city, joining local Tatars who either recognized the feast day in their own tradition or supplied goods and services to the swollen population. Kohl described the sight as pandemonium: "Russian Troikas" and "Tatar Maydars" competed for space in the steep, narrow passages; people thronged the square, and the air filled with the din of several different languages. Most striking of all groups were Greeks, "the mountains between the towers." Their carriages "were all filled with pretty, laughing faces, and high in the midst, as on a presidential chair, sat always a remarkably beautiful woman, with a fair complexion and raven black hair, dressed in black richly decorated with gold ornaments." These Greeks, he continued "came over about twenty years ago from Asia Minor, having escaped from the outrages of the Turks at the time of the Greek insurrection, by taking refuge in Russian ships. The emperor had assigned them lands in the Crimea, where, as might be gathered from their appearance, they had prospered and grown rich."[61]

Kohl's observations reveal that despite the challenges facing church expansion in Crimea, Orthodoxy managed to flourish on the peninsula largely due to the Greek refugees who had flooded into Russia during the Greek War of Independence (1821–1829) and earlier conflicts with the Ottoman Empire. At the end of the eighteenth century, Greeks often outnumbered Russians in the Black Sea region, and as merchants, seamen, scholars, and bureaucrats they contributed significantly to the borderland's development.[62] In Crimea, they opened derelict Byzantine churches vacated during the exodus of Crimea's Christians, revived local pilgrimages, and imported new priests to serve growing parishes. In short, Greeks sustained Christianity on the peninsula when the Russian Orthodox Church could not.

New Russia and Crimea also became home to swelling populations of Armenians and Bulgarians. Armenians emigrated to Russia in great numbers after annexation; like the Greeks, their exodus in 1778 did not mean an end to the Armenian population in Crimea. New waves of Armenian settlers poured in with each major borderland conflict. As *dhimmis*, Armenians had a secondary economic and political status under the Ottoman Empire, a status that steadily worsened in the nineteenth century.[63] Armenians, like Greeks, came to Crimea in several waves: 1794, 1800, and 1832. In the 1820s, 15,000 to 25,000 Catholic Armenians appealed to the Russian government for asylum in Crimea—they claimed oppression from both Ottomans and Gregorian Armenians. Initially, the Russian government responded positively to the request, but then balked when Russian diplomats expressed concern over how accepting such refugees might affect diplomacy with the Ottoman Empire.[64] By the middle of the nineteenth century, the Tauride Statistical Committee counted 7,000 Armenians, and of those, 1,500 Catholics. The Armenian populations spread among all the cities in Crimea. Russian authorities in Crimea had come to think of the Armenians as the most desirable non-Russian populations. The Statistical Committee, for example, argued that because of their "deep tradition of faith, [being] very close to Orthodoxy, they are the easiest of all populations to get along with."[65]

Throughout the imperial period, Armenians actively contributed to Crimea's rich cultural fabric. They built many churches, created their own schools, and published books and journals in their own language. They maintained ties with Armenians living outside Crimea, especially those in Constantinople who long agitated for the formation of a cultural center in Feodosia. Finally, the Armenians produced numerous literati; the most notable is the seascape painter Ivan Aivazovskii, who himself passionately advocated for the preservation of Armenian culture in Crimea in the second half of the nineteenth century.[66]

Bulgarians were far more numerous than Armenians and were perhaps the most politically charged group on the eve of the Crimean War. They came in several waves, with the first party of Bulgarians arriving in Crimea in the early 1800s, at which time they formed small colonies in Staryi Krym and Kishlav. The title of the order that allowed Bulgarian settlement reflects the political nature of the immigration: "for the settlers in Russia of Balkan refugees, not wishing to make peace with the Ottoman powers in their homeland."[67] Bulgarian immigration continued through the Napoleonic Wars, when every month, several families entered through the ports of Kerch or Sevastopol on Greek merchant ships, waiting to be resettled in the villages vacated by the Tatars after their first exodus in 1783.

The second wave of Bulgarian settlers also consisted of refugees. These Bulgarians came along with Greeks and Armenians during the Russo-Turkish War of 1828/29. It is believed that 20,000–30,000 Bulgarians came to New Russia at that time. Many settled in Bessarabia, while approximately 2,000 arrived in Crimea. This wave of Bulgarian settlement fared far worse than its predecessors of thirty years before. These Bulgarians fled the Ottoman Empire during an outbreak of the plague, which meant that Russian authorities kept them in quarantine for an average of one month. Moreover, the imperial government did little to facilitate their transition, and instead left all preparation to the local authorities.[68] The group also suffered upon their arrival when local authorities failed to allocate them adequate resources. Still, by the mid-1850s, Bulgarians became a fixture in Crimea's diverse landscape and established their own Orthodox community.

The degree to which Crimean Bulgarian laity turned their allegiance toward Odessa rather than Constantinople is difficult to glean from the limited sources. However, an episode recalled by Aleksandr Zavadovskii suggests that the Bulgarians welcomed integration into the Russian diocese. During the archbishop's tour of Crimea in 1853, he visited the Bulgarian settlements, and it was midnight when the official deputation arrived at the first of the Bulgarian colonies, Staryi Krym. The Bulgarians were so eager to greet the prelate, according to Zavadovskii, that they refused to allow the delegation to rest outside the city. Carrying lamps on their shoulders, the Bulgarians escorted representatives from the church in Odessa into a fully illuminated city. The archbishop's party received similar treatment in Kishlav, where "hardly had the equipage been visible when all the Kishlav colony rushed to meet him. Grown Bulgarians, children, and elders crowded around the equipage, women threw flowers." The crowd was so thick "that the equipage could not move."[69]

From his arrival in Odessa, Archbishop Innokentii became actively involved in the Orthodox politics of the Ottoman Empire and pursued relationships with Porfirii Uspenskii, Archimandrite Vissarian of the mission in Bucharest, Archimandrite Sofonia of the mission in Constantinople, the general consul in Beirut, Konstantin Bazili, and many Athonite monks and pilgrims.[70] From these men Innokentii gathered information about both the Ottoman oppression of Balkan Christians and the bickering that divided Eastern Christians throughout the Ottoman Empire. Referring to quarrels between the Antioch and Jerusalem patriarchates, Bazili wrote Innokentii in 1850: "The problem now is not from the unbelievers, as it was before, nor from those of other faiths, despite their stubborn onslaught, but from the Orthodox clergy themselves." To the west, Vissarian recounted tales of Greek discrimination against Moldavian and other Balkan Christians.[71] Reports of inter-Orthodox strife from those located in the middle of controversy, however, did little to dissuade Innokentii from aiming to achieve pan-Orthodox unity in his own diocese.

In Odessa's seminary, Archbishop Innokentii required that textbooks include information about Serbs, Bulgarians, Montenegrins, Albanians, and others. The seminary also educated its students in Modern Greek following the recommendation of Alexandru Sturdza. After the Crimean War, the seminary produced fifteen students who could speak Modern Greek, more than twice the number who took courses in Kirimtatar.[72] Innokentii collected all the material he could about Balkan Christians from travelers and merchants coming through Odessa and Crimea, and his own personal library quickly became one of the largest collections pertaining to Orthodox Christians.[73] In 1851, he received the Ordination of the Savior from the king of Greece in recognition of his efforts on behalf of Greek emigrants living inside his diocese and his support for the new Greek nation abroad. The award was sponsored by Agathangelos (Typaldos), abbot of the St. George Balaklava monastery, and the abbot's brother.[74] In a letter to Karl Nesselrode, who officially informed the archbishop of the ordination, Innokentii asked, "Who of the Russians was not deeply sympathetic with and does not continue to be sympathetic with the political rebirth of this people, which formerly contributed such a rich part of the treasure of world learning and knowledge?" He portrayed Greeks as "the godfathers of the font of holy Christening" and admitted that because of his "present neighbors in the East" and "the Kherson churches, to which belong so many of all the Hellenic peoples," supporting the "various spiritual needs of the people of Greece" was a crucial part of his mission.[75] The degree to which other prelates shared Innokentii's views on the Greek question remains uncertain. It is clear, however, that the needs of the diocese and the local legacy of Greek Christianity guided Innokentii's behavior. Innokentii demonstrated an equal commitment to the Bulgarians, and especially to Odessa's Bulgarian circle.

Spiridon Palauzov and Nikolay Palauzov were the Bulgarian counterparts to the Greek lobbyists Ioannis Kapodistrias and Alexandru Sturdza. They wrote extensively about the Bulgarian issue and championed Russia's intervention on Bulgaria's behalf. They supported the flowering of Bulgarian culture in Russia, emphasizing the need for Bulgarians to have native-language publications and education. To this end, Nikolay Palauzov encouraged the continual education of Russians about Bulgaria. He worked to divert all publications about Bulgaria to the Odessa Censorship Committee rather than to the committee in St. Petersburg, for as he wrote to Archbishop Innokentii, the latter "was very difficult and slow."[76] He also formed a Bulgarian national society in Odessa.

Established officially in 1854, the Bulgarian National Society was spearheaded by N. M. Toshkov and the Palauzovs. The society was initially organized to regulate the process of donations. Previously, many Bulgarians had come to Russia seeking assistance, whether from the state or from individuals, and apparently a number of scandals had erupted over how the refugees handled their spending of the donated funds. Unfortunately, some Bulgarians, it seems, pocketed the money, or diverted the monies to other causes.[77] Therefore, the Odessa Bulgarians decided to organize the collection and distribution of funds. They vetted donations to a variety of causes, including support for Orthodox churches and religious schools in Bulgaria, and assisted the needs of Bulgarians in New Russia.[78] The Bulgarian National Society in Odessa represented one of the many important links between Russians and Bulgarians. It also demonstrated the extent to which Bulgarians maintained ties with their homeland, and the degree to which this local refugee population fostered hopes for national liberation.

The Bulgarian issue occupied many Russians, especially those associated with the Russian Orthodox Church. Andrei Murav'ev, an official affiliated with the Holy Synod, wrote about the necessity of addressing the growing breach between the Balkan Christians and the patriarch in Greece.[79] The patriarch, he charged "is not taking the development of religion in Bulgaria seriously and is not satisfactorily protecting this young church; the people of the Slavic dioceses do not understand the liturgies in Greek." Murav'ev acknowledged that the Greek patriarch attempted to address the problem by encouraging the study of Slavic language in seminary, but concluded that such efforts were insufficiently supported. The Bulgarian situation, he impressed upon his readers, was reaching crisis: "Already Bulgaria is living and thirsting for its hierarchy; already Greece feels itself alone. . . . The Affairs of the Moldavian-Wallachian church must soon be straightened out."[80]

Archbishop Innokentii shared Murav'ev's sympathies and became an outspoken advocate for the Bulgarian cause.[81] Even before the founding of the Bulgarian National Society, the archbishop took an active interest in the affairs of Bulgarian Christians, and he corresponded with members of the society in Constantinople, who advocated for an independent hierarch for the Bulgarian Church. Innokentii agreed that Bulgarian Christians needed someone who could minister to believers in their language.[82] He sent some money from Odessa to support the project and requested a copy of the journal *Tsaregradskii vestnik*, published in Bulgarian in Constantinople, in order to keep himself and other Russians informed about the Bulgarian struggle. His request required special permission from Tsar Nicholas, and it resulted in Nikolay Palauzov's appointment to the Odessa Censorship Committee to oversee the distribution of Bulgarian-language materials in southern Russia.[83]

Above all, Archbishop Innokentii promoted unity among the multinational Orthodox Christians living in the diocese. More pan-Orthodox than pan-Slav in outlook, Innokentii was optimistic that the mix of various Orthodox "tribes and nations"—the Greeks, Armenians, and Bulgarians—presented "rich material for didactic observations." With dedicated support, they could be "unite(d) with the Russian spirit."[84] Greeks and Bulgarians composed a highly visible proportion of Crimean Orthodox believers, and they had churches that conducted services in their own languages. Consistory reports following the Crimean War show seven churches "for the Greek language" and three "for the Bulgarian."[85] These figures do not account for the subsequent influx of Bulgarians through the 1860s, nor do they reveal the numerous parishes of mixed Balkan and Russian believers. Thus, one can see that Innokentii intended Russia's Athos community in Crimea as the means by which to bring together the diverse constituents of the eastern half of his diocese: Russians, Greeks, and Bulgarians.

Athos in Crimea

Considered by Orthodox populations to be a holy place as important as Jerusalem and Constantinople, Mt. Athos occupies an entire peninsula in northern Greece east of Thessaloniki. Renowned for its rugged beauty, picturesque landscapes, and wide open sea vistas, it is distinguished in both Hellenic mythology and Christian tradition and has been the site of international pilgrimage for over a millennium.[86] Whereas Jerusalem, as the birthplace of Christ, is considered holy for all Christians, Mt. Athos is considered holy among Eastern Christians for its timeless preservation of Eastern Orthodox treasures and the traditions of Orthodox monastic life. Mt. Athos has been the bastion of the Orthodox monasticism practiced by thousands of monks in living continuity with the past since the tenth century, and it contains the world's greatest collection of icons, frescos, and ancient manuscripts.[87] It has, however, one curious feature that sets it apart: the total absence of females. The prohibition against women arose during the Byzantine period and extends to all female creatures. In other words, not only does Mt. Athos not have women, it also has no female domestic pets or livestock.[88]

Through the centuries, multiple types of monasticism have been practiced on Mt. Athos in the twenty large monasteries, many skvetes, and countless hermitages.[89] Cenobitic monks live communally in monasteries. They pray, work, and eat alongside one another. Often their rule is very strict. Itinerant monks, on the opposite end of the spectrum, completely seclude themselves in a contemplative life. They live in caves or shacks and may have no relationship to monasteries. They pray when they want, eat when they are hungry, and typically forage for their own food. Finally, there are levels of monasticism in between these extremes in which monks might live independently, but share prayers or meals with others in a monastery.[90] Athos has also preserved the ancient teachings of the patristic fathers as well as a wide array of spiritual practices. In the nineteenth century, Russians became captivated with the Athonite monks who followed the "desert tradition" of Eastern fathers, characterized by isolation from the world, hesychasm or incessant prayer, and ascetic lifestyles.[91]

Some Russians were skeptical of their countrymen's interpretation of Athonite monasticism. Parish priests, for example, felt themselves superior to those in monastic orders, whom they accused of being "selfish hypocrites."[92] Critics argued that Athos attracted lazy idlers, eager to escape the hard work and tedium of everyday life. They also pointed to well-intentioned monks who slipped into madness from Athos's isolation and extreme asceticism, or were insane before they even arrived. Davydov expressed both strains of criticism and records numerous and occasionally humorous encounters with drunk, greedy and unbalanced monks on Athos. One of these was his guide, Vasilii, a character who represented what Davydov described as the "delusional" element. He writes:

> Our own Father Vasilii, who accompanied us, looked something altogether strange, although he was still a young man and generally mild, looking at him, I thought: is he not a hermit already at the end of his life? Lying close to him on the stern of the boat, I heard words coming from him, and turning to him, suggested that he talk to me, but he immediately covered his mouth with his hand, explaining that he spoke only to himself. He showed us various places, where unfortunate things happened which he assigned to evil spirits, and began to conjure them, in half a voice to himself, and then in

half a voice upbraided himself, for sinful thoughts, and for words that were barely audible and located in sin. He appeared troubled and timid in all his movements. I saw in him a sad image of a person, solely occupied with his own sins, and full of fear, without really trying anything to strengthen his soul's future beatitude.[93]

A pilgrim identified as N. A. Blagoveshchenskii, who visited Athos directly after the Crimean War and lived there more than a year, echoed Davydov's sentiments. Blagoveshchenskii took his criticism a step further to complain about the deleterious influence of Athos over Russian culture. Everyone, "even our simple people," he complains, have heard about "these notorious Athonite wanderers and collectors of good-willed legends, who ramble in every nook and cranny of our world with various soul-saving themes." These itinerants, often "under the view of religious authority, pull the wool over the eyes of simple people. . . . They talk about the exploits of the Athonite brothers, and destiny of the kingdom of heaven, about the temptations of the demons." Interspersed into these long tales of miraculous experiences, the wanderers "bitterly complain about the poverty and the godliness of the Athonite hermits. A man listens to these speeches; he glances at a dim poster of Athos" and "mistakenly believes" all the legends. Many of the so-called Athonite wanderers, Blagoveshchenskii claims, were frauds or crooks, or were otherwise selfishly motivated. Worse than the peasants, were the "baronesses" who "are continuously surrounded by sanctimonious holy fools wearing the black dress with the rosary in their hands." The wanderers "in delight give out the remains of their sincerity and wise descriptions of their former exploits," and without appearing to ask for it, "acquired money."[94]

Such criticisms of Athos and its monks cropped up throughout the nineteenth century, including in Archbishop Innokentii's own writings. Still, clergy heavily imported spiritual movements associated with Mt. Athos.[95] Metropolitan Filaret of Moscow, for example, experimented with reordering local women's idiorrythmic monasteries on the cenobitic rule associated with the Athonite revival, and established the Gethsemane skete, his interpretation of the contemplative life emanating from the Athos.[96] The Optina hermitage had acquired a reputation for the exploits of its *startsy* at the St. John the Baptist skete (founded 1821) and took the lead publishing patristic works.[97] Other monasteries in Russia followed suit and were known for their spiritual association with Athos: Valaam, the Sergei Trinity monastery in Moscow, and the Solovets monastery. Crimea, moreover, was only one place to directly recreate Athos on Russian soil. Russian monks from the Panteleimon monastery on Mt. Athos streamed into Abkhazia in the 1870s and erected a community called Novy Afon (New Athos) by 1888.[98]

In an era of religious nationalism, it makes sense that Athonite spirituality would capture the Russian religious imagination. Athos has historically been composed of all Orthodox nationalities, whether Macedonians, Vlachs, Romanians, Russians, or others.[99] Due to its multinational Orthodox composition, Mt. Athos figured prominently in pan-Orthodox movements and became a symbol of eastern European nationalist awakenings.[100] Especially following the Russo-Turkish wars, which facilitated easier movement between the Russian and Ottoman Empires, Russian pilgrims headed to Athos in greater numbers. Approximately two-hundred Russian pilgrims traveled there a year, an impressive number, but only a precursor to the flood of Russian pilgrims that would journey to Mt. Athos later in the century.[101] In the climate of religious politics following the hanging of the patriarch in Constantinople, pilgrims became emissaries, promoting Russian influence in the Ottoman Empire, and countering the missions of Catholic France and Protestant Britain.[102] With greater ease of travel following the Treaties of Adrianople (1829) and Unkiar Skelessi (1833), these pilgrims also opened a direct channel to Mt. Athos, filtering Athonite practices and pan-Orthodox sentiment back into Russia.

Russian pilgrims to Mt. Athos were not limited to monks and prelates, but included officers, bureaucrats, and scholars. Many of these pilgrims published accounts of their travels.[103] Among them, the letters of Serafim Sviatogorets about Mt. Athos were serialized in the 1840s and published in book form on the eve of the Crimean War.[104] Sviatogorets's letters are as political as they are religious, describing the treacherous path of pilgrimage through Ottoman territory, Turkish oppression of Christians, and conflicts between the Orthodox monks themselves.[105] Poised on the Black Sea between the two empires, Crimea was one of the primary gateways for pilgrims and diplomats traveling south to Mt. Athos, and like Odessa, filtered Athonite spirituality and Eastern Christian nationalism through the rest of the empire. In the 1840s and 1850s, the numbers of pilgrims grew so great that the Black Sea region was often referred to as "Russia's gateway to the Eastern faith."[106] By the end of the nineteenth century, the Athonite movement in Russia reached its highest stage; on Mt. Athos itself, Russian populations grew to outnumber the Greeks, 3,500 to 3,276. The majority of Russians were posted at the St. Panteleimon monastery and scattered among four large sketes. Although the degree to which Athonite monasticism influenced the Russian tradition can be debated, one scholar maintains that "Russian monks were influenced by Mount Athos from the very beginning."[107]

The creation of Russian Athos in Crimea was organically connected to the Athonite movement elsewhere in the empire. Perhaps more than any other of the Athonite communities, it reflected the union between religion and politics that characterized the reign of Nicholas I. When Archbishop Innokentii presented his plan to establish a holy place in Crimea to the Holy Synod, he offered a critique of the Athonite movement in Russia, one which reflected the movement's popularity and hinted at its internal tensions. Not possibly able to predict the immense proportions that Russian pilgrimage to Mt. Athos would eventually reach, Innokentii believed that in his era, the Athos movement had already overgrown its limits; he argued that neither Athos nor Russia could accommodate the spiritual needs of Russian monks. Russian monks interested in the ascetic life that was "strongly preserved in Greece on Mt. Athos," had no retreat to fulfill their spiritual practice. In "Russia," he lamented, "this occupation, the spirit of Athonite eremitic exploits, is almost impossible" due to the "physical layout of a heavily populated country."[108] He believed that Russia's industrial growth deprived the empire of virgin landscapes suitable for an isolated eremitic lifestyle. He acknowledged that a few exceptional monastic centers existed in Russia, specifically identifying the well-known communities of Solovets, Valaam, and Kanevets.[109] Yet even these were not ideally suited to Athonite asceticism, for reasons that he did not fully explain. As a result, monks with a particular interest in communal, ascetic life felt unfulfilled by "native forms of monasticism" and so had to travel to Mt. Athos.[110]

Innokentii further argued that the complex political environment related to Mt. Athos had ceased to make it a viable spiritual outlet. Rumors abounded about the numerous obstacles that pilgrims encountered simply en route to Athos, much less within the walls of its monasteries. One character in Ageev's memoirs, an archimandrite, cautioned against travel to Mt. Athos. If traveling by water, itinerants had to pay for three separate voyages, through the Black Sea, the Sea of Marmara, and the Archipelago. By land, pilgrims had to pay for hotels and food. In addition, the archimandrite warned, "you will still pay the Turks a great tax and each person pays a *haraç*. And if you go by land, through the mountains, you might find robbers—this journey is almost impassable, and if you do pass, you will meet great caravans, with weapons and guns."[111] Ageev had various unpleasant encounters throughout his journey, but none that dissuaded him from his goal. Andrei Murav'ev's narrative contains similar cautions. While he was visiting the holy mountain in August of 1849, for example, pirates stole two ships, English and French, and fell upon a caravan of Greeks and Bulgarians visiting the holy mountain for a monastery's feast day. More than one-hundred people were robbed, including his dragoman.[112]

Those pilgrims who survived the many challenges along the journey to Athos met a mixed reception. Before the Crimean War, Russians had no monastery on Athos, and struggled to maintain influence in just one skete. Russian pilgrims tended to gather around two primary locations, the St. Elijah skete and the Panteleimon monastery. In both destinations, their connection was tenuous at best, for the St. Elijah skete at that time was in the hands of Ukrainians and the Panteleimon was controlled by Greeks.[113] The relationship between Russians and other nationalities little improved, for after the war one pilgrim observed that "[w]ith each increase in Russian monasticism on the mountain, there is an ensuing debate and taking of measures; with each influential man there is the danger: is he hiding some political secret?"[114]

The plan for a Russian Athos in Crimea addressed many of these problems. Archbishop Innokentii argued that despite Ottoman promises of protection for Russian subjects, the passage through the Ottoman Empire could still be treacherous. Once Russian monks finally reached Athos, Innokentii continued, they found themselves in an increasingly crowded and hostile environment, forced into competition with Greeks for space. Alluding to the Greek-Russian struggle at the Panteleimon monastery and elsewhere, Innokentii commented that "the Greek element, as the natural leaders there, do not mix comfortably with the Russians."[115] Consequently he sympathized, "It is sad to say that the devout Russians, looking for their soul's peace in Athos . . . meet heavy constrictions." The political realities of Mt. Athos, according to Innokentii, neutralized its spiritual rewards.

Yet the problem was much greater than the disappointed souls of dissatisfied pilgrims, he warned, for these same pilgrims roamed aimlessly across Russia to "no benefit of faith or Orthodoxy, and only to the disadvantage of rumors about Athos." For these reasons, claimed Innokentii, a soul could better find its destination without "leaving the native land and subjecting itself to the arbitrariness of the Greeks and Turks." Where Mt. Athos would fail, Crimea would succeed. "How good it would be if we could build our own Russian Athos [*Russkii Afon*]!" the archbishop exclaimed. "Speaking not from the point of rivalry, in which in this holy affair could be no place," he nevertheless asserted that "Tauride far excels Athos in peace and comfort for Russian monks."[116] Rather than adopting Athonite practices as had many Russian monasteries during the period, Innokentii proposed an improvement over the original. Crimea, in other words, was not meant merely to borrow from Mt. Athos, but was intended to replace it as the holy place of the Slavs. Innokentii believed that all Slavs and Orthodox Christians were united by their shared faith, yet like many Russian nationalists, believed that Russia should take the lead.[117] Crimea's Grecian romance, it seems, was waning.

Crimea offered a local improvement over Athos, for it had everything that Athos had but was closer, safer, and cheaper. It too was mountainous woodland unspoiled by encroaching populations, roadways, industry, or agriculture. Much of Crimea even resembled Athos. It was a peninsula with steep cliffs that plummeted to the sea. It enjoyed similar temperate climates that produced abundant berries and fruit growing naturally in the wild.[118] A Russian monk seeking inner peace and an isolated ascetic lifestyle could find his soul's fulfillment in Crimea. "If the hermits on Athos are accustomed to mountains rising into the clouds, perfect silence and removal from human conflicts, proximity to the borderless sea, blessed abundance of a fruitful land: grapes, olives, figs, living and babbling springs," Innokentii enthused, "our Tauride has it all, in such perfect generosity from God."[119] Repeatedly, Innokentii emphasized that anything found in Greece, also existed in Russia.

Most crucially, Crimea was as holy as Mt. Athos. Evidence of ancient Christianity was everywhere in Crimea, from the ruins of Byzantine architecture to the cave churches of the Inkerman cliffs. Innokentii asserted that recent archaeological studies and travel narratives, especially those by Petr Keppen and S. N. Montadon, rescued "Crimea's holy memories from oblivion,"[120] and proved that Crimea had a long history of early ascetic monasticism. Like Athos, Crimea had its own communion of saints, including St. Andrew the Apostle, and the apostle to the Slavs, St. Vladimir. Many of Crimea's monasteries, including St. George at Balaklava, and the more than seventy cave churches near the Inkerman cliffs proved that Crimea had Byzantine roots as old as those on Mt. Athos.

In a typical fashion, Innokentii concluded that the history of Crimean Christianity and the remains of Byzantine architecture combined to make Crimea as holy as Mt. Athos. He wrote:

> If Mt. Athos has abundant holy monuments and memories so does Russian Athos ... here are holy traces of the visit of St. Andrew the Apostle, the blood of holy popes—Clement and Martin; here are the exploits of St. Stefan of Surozh and the first Slavic apostles Cyril and Methodius; here is the monument of St. Vladimir and his Christianizing: how many examples of faith and good deeds![121]

Crimea, it would seem, was even more holy than Mt. Athos. Not only did the ruins contain evidence of a glorious Christian past and visitation of saints, but they also continued to attract respect and admiration from local inhabitants, Orthodox and Muslim alike. Even the Tatars, who were at one time Christian according to Innokentii's frequent assertion, "express their memory of their former beliefs in their occasional pilgrimages to places sanctified by Christianity."[122]

After describing the failure of Athonite monasticism elsewhere in Russia and showing how well suited Crimea was to house the movement, Innokentii proposed the form of monasticism the monks would follow. In his proposal to the Synod, Innokentii advocated a blend of two forms of monasticism, eremitic and cenobitic. The monks would gather in small monasteries with attached cells, take a vow of poverty, occupy themselves with labor, and embrace constant, uninterrupted prayer. These monasteries would not be just "any type of monastery," Innokentii repeatedly emphasized, but would follow "the form of the ascetic life of Athos."

Apart from establishing a strict code of behavior, Innokentii created a blueprint for monastic bureaucracy. The Dormition monastery would be the chief institution and would house the archimandrite charged with supervising the entire network of monasteries. As the center of the Crimean brotherhood, Dormition monastery would have the largest appointment, including one abbot, a hieromonk, and three novices. The other "holy places," including churches named after St. Vladimir in Chersonesos, St. Clement at the Inkerman caves, and St. Anastasia near Bakhchisarai, would be under the authority of an "elder (*starets*)-hieromonk" and two or three novices. "In this manner," the archbishop tabulated, "all of Crimean Athos (*Krymskii Afon*) would have no more than nine monastic persons, and no more than twenty novices who truly follow the monastic elders."[123] The archimandrite located at the Dormition monastery would impose a rule over all the communities and would supervise the financial affairs of the various *cenoby*, including the process of restoration and construction. In addition to the officially sanctioned community, Innokentii anticipated that his Russian Athos would attract ascetic hermits who could tuck themselves into the mountainous crannies, just as they did on Mt. Athos.

In what must have been an attractive point for the church, these monks were not to be dependent upon synodal coffers, but were to be self-sustaining, reliant as much as possible upon their own labors for survival. They would gather their own food from the forests and the foothills, and would spend their spare time in scholarly and charitable pursuits. They could, as the archbishop suggested, research and record local history and folklore, paint holy icons, gather medicinal herbs, tend to shelters, guide travelers, and cultivate gardens.[124] In many ways, Russian Athos was planned as a utopian community, with every monk engaged in fruitful labor as well as spiritual pursuits. It would be, as he often stated, a local holy place—an ideal spot for Russian monks and pilgrims to commune with God.

On 15 April 1850, the Holy Synod affirmed Innokentii's proposal, finding that "Russian Athos would bring healthy religious and moral benefits for all of the country, as well as for the foreign visitors on Mt. Athos, and might also open a straight, peaceful path to Tauride's Muslim inhabitants."[125] The Synod approved five sites for renewal: the Dormition monastery, St. Anastasia, the spring at Savluk-Su, the Inkerman monastery, and the ruins at Chersonesos, each of which either existed on state lands or on Russian noble estates.[126] The sites, many of which had contested religious or ethnic symbolic importance, became new monuments that, as Innokentii argued, would serve the "glory of God, the advantage of the Church, the benefit of humanity, the honor of the Monarch and the Russian estates."[127] In addition to their layered meaning as restored sites of ancient Christianity, Innokentii endowed these restored ruins and altered landscapes with the perpetual memory of their namesake, Mt. Athos.

Archbishop Innokentii believed that the first generation of monks was crucial to the success of the new community. Primarily, he wanted Crimean monks to have experience on Mt. Athos so that they were prepared for the ascetic life and could duplicate exactly Athonite monasticism. He received a blanket of résumés, some of which fit the desired profile, and others that simply expressed an interest in the Crimean post to escape from harsh Russian winters. The archbishop ultimately selected a man by the name of Polikarp to lead the new community, a monk who had long-term experience with multinational Orthodox Christians and Mt. Athos.

Like many monks, priests, and prelates of his age, Polikarp was fascinated with the ascetic life and petitioned the Holy Synod for permission to travel to the holy places of the East. The Synod responded to his request in 1843 with an appointment to head the Russian consulate church in Athens, where Polikarp remained for seven years.[128] During his work in Greece, he traveled through Palestine, Syria, and all holy places "sanctified by the sojourn of the Lord Jesus Christ" and "all ancient ascetic communities in Arabia."[129] Living primarily in Athens, he made numerous pilgrimages to Mt. Athos.[130] Polikarp's training, love of asceticism, and dedicated pilgrimages made him an ideal candidate for Crimea's monastic community. Innokentii wrote the Holy Synod that due to Polikarp's "ecclesiastic experience and full disposition toward ascetic monasticism one might fully expect large spiritual rewards for the young Tauride monks."[131] His work in Greece also made him an effective liaison between Russian and Greek communities.

When Polikarp learned that the Synod approved the plan for Russia's Athos, he immediately assured Innokentii that he was prepared for the challenge: "You have almost resurrected my soul.... Thanks to God, thanks to God! Your Athos has already been approved.... Rocks and cliffs I am not afraid of. When I was in Jerusalem and on old Athos, I was prepared to kiss every little rock." He was, as he repeatedly emphasized, predisposed to isolated and ascetic living, and as he noted earlier, he felt ready to bring "any part of the blessings of Old Athos to the New Athos!"[132] He received his transfer the same month that the Synod approved the monastery's opening. After Innokentii secured Polikarp, he turned his attention to recruiting six additional monks, each of whom arrived prepared for an "ascetic life," and brought only the bare necessities with them.[133]

Innokentii's plan to transform Crimea into a monastic retreat entailed profound changes to the peninsula's sacred landscape. It meant an immediate increase in Christian institutions and a subsequent, subtle shift in the confessional balance. In this regard, the proposal openly celebrated Crimea's pan-Orthodox composition, and indirectly advocated conversion of the Tatars. The plans for a skete at the restored church of St. John the Baptist offer insight into the pan-Orthodox element of the proposal, for the skete was designed specifically for New Russia's Greeks. The question of converting Tatars, by contrast, appeared more subtly.

The St. John the Baptist skete was envisioned as a bridge to the Greek community. Innokentii located it near a spring close to Balaklava and Sevastopol, in the heart of Crimea's Greek settlement. Just like the Dormition monastery and the spring of Cosmas and Damian, the church of St. John the Baptist already had a popular following and was "zealously revered" by the Greeks. With the construction of only a few additional cells, Innokentii maintained, the setting would become an "excellent cenoby." He anticipated that the Balaklava Greek battalion, which controlled the territory, would readily donate land. Much as Russians populated sketes on Mt. Athos, the community at the St. John the Baptist church would form a bond between the two Orthodox nations. Innokentii succinctly summed it up, commenting that the "Greek element [would] enter into the composition of the Tauride brotherhood, in a sign of brotherly union according to the faith of both peoples." In addition to offering a spiritual accord between the Greeks and Russians, restoration of St. John the Baptist would offer "spiritual shelter for Tauride Greeks looking for the desert life."[134] The example of the Greek skete is remarkable, for it shows that Russian Athos, like the holy mountain, was to be a multi-lingual and multinational Orthodox community. For Innokentii and other church officials, it mattered little that Greeks were ethnically different, so long as they were Orthodox.

As the Christian communities prepared their openings, they indirectly tested restrictions against expanding into Muslim regions. Innokentii viewed Islam as a non-indigenous religion that had no legitimate claim to Crimea, and to some degree, placed blame upon Islam for disrupting the peninsula's natural progression to becoming a holy place. Delicately approaching the matter in his proposal, Innokentii suggested that renewal and renovation of Crimea's holy places and the benign influence of contemplative monks might "quietly and by degrees attract the Crimean

Muslims closer to Christianity."[135] The monks, meanwhile, could facilitate the process by learning Tatar languages and making connections within surrounding Tatar communities.[136] Despite Prince Vorontsov's concerns about church expansion, the archbishop envisioned the possibility of Tatar conversion through the network of Crimean monasteries.

Finally, Innokentii's attempt to create an Orthodox holy place in Russia can be seen as a local response to the religious dimension of international politics and especially the Holy Land controversy that began in the 1840s. Although the archbishop did not specifically engage these issues in his proposal, he often implied that if Russia had its own holy place on par with Athos, it would no longer need to struggle with western European countries or the Ottoman Empire over holy places in the East. Due to the safety of pilgrim passage, the glory a holy place would bring to the Russian state, and the mounting tensions between Muslim and Orthodox populations on the peninsula, renewing the sites was not only a religious issue, but also a local and national imperative. It would be, as he wrote, "an honor to the Christian faith and the Russian government in the eyes of the non-believers," while the renewal of ancient Christianity would serve as a "spiritual reward for the fatherland."[137] Here as elsewhere, Innokentii revealed his belief that a strong Orthodox presence in Crimea would strengthen both the church and the empire.

To be sure, Innokentii did not have carte blanche to build a new monastic community. In early 1849, Vorontsov ruled out one proposed site in Mangup,[138] because it occupied land located in or contingent to Tatar villages.[139] This site never made it into the proposal to the Holy Synod. Surprisingly, however, Vorontsov threw his weight behind renovation of other monastic communities, especially the Dormition monastery.[140] This unexpected turn might have been a product of Vorontsov's own interest in the renewal of ruins.[141] More than likely, however, the successful implementation of the new monastic community derived from its modest proposal. After all, the community was to be small, and its monks were to be hermits. Their existence was characterized by isolation, rather than proselytizing, and the new community would not draw upon church or state coffers, but would rely upon the donations of benefactors. As the passage of time demonstrated, however, the community exerted a symbolic influence that far exceeded its residential capacity. It also established real-life monuments to Christian faith and created a blueprint for church expansion that lasted through the revolutionary period.

Icons on the cliff at the Dormition Monastery

The Dormition Monastery

The Cave City at Chufut Kale

Historic Bakhchisarai Palace of the Crimean Khans

Mausoleum of Janike-Khanym on Chufut Kale, near Bakhchisarai and Dormition Monastery

Karaim Knessa on Chufut Kale

St. Vladimir Church at Chersonesos

The Inkerman Monastery built into the caves

Chasoven at the Cosmas
and Damian springs

Abandoned grotto
church, Balaklava

The skyline of Evpatoria with images of the dome of St. Nicholas Cathedral and minaret of the Juma-Jami Mosque

People bathing in healing waters near the St. Paraskeva Monastery

Golubinka/Fotisala, a contested sacred site

Sudak fortress, picturing a museum that has been a mosque, an Orthodox church, and a Catholic church

Anti-NATO protests in Feodosia, 2006

Chapter Four

MONASTICISM TAKES ROOT

The Russian Orthodox Church spent months preparing for the official opening of the Russian Athos community, held at the Dormition monastery on its feast day, 15 August 1850. Priests throughout the Kherson-Tauride diocese raised money to fund new building and restoration in Crimea, while monks began gardening and construction projects immediately upon arriving at their new posts. Benefactors filled the treasury of Dormition monastery, donated books, and purchased miscellaneous supplies.[1] Archbishop Innokentii required regular reports on the monastery's progress and carefully crafted an impressive public ceremony intended to convey the importance and meaning of its opening. He invited local Greek clergymen to participate in a religious procession and services, including the aging son of Constantine Spiranda, the priest appointed to Dormition monastery by the last Crimean khan, as well as the two Greek metropolitans who had settled in the region. These men were integral to the display, acting as messengers "from the Old Athos to the new one."[2]

On the feast day, carriages, wagons, and pilgrims thronged the streets; it took more than one hour to move across the small city because traffic "was stopped in every step."[3] After an elaborate religious procession wound through the center of Bakhchisarai to the distant cliffs, clergy erected a cross in front of monastery doors and blessed the founding of the new community in "the name of the Holy Mother of God, protector of Mt. Athos." In the square, Archbishop Innokentii delivered a sermon that further tied the Dormition monastery to the holy mountain:

> From now on, when you visit the monastery, it will not only have prayer and liturgies, but also the type of monasticism located on holy Mt. Athos. Who of you have not heard of this divine mountain, where thousands of good monks and humble hermits day and night warmly pray to the Lord for world peace? And here, henceforth we will have the comforting vision similar to ancient Athos in the borders of our own fatherland, in the middle of our mountains![4]

The statistician Franz Dombrovskii, who attended the procession, summarized the remainder of the archbishop's sermon in *Odesskii vestnik*, commenting that it told "how [renewal of the Dormition monastery] served as a memorial to ancient Christianity in Tauride."[5] He claimed that "one thousand people of all estates, tribes and faiths" filled the square, while the "Muslim city," was a willing and "an amazed witness to the exciting [Orthodox] Christian celebration." Not only Orthodox pilgrims attended, but also present according to Dombrovskii were "Jews, Muslims, and what is particularly wonderful, people from higher Bakhchisarai Muslim clergy." "So great was the procession," Dombrovski enthused, that even the Muslim girls and women, "forgetting the custom not to reveal their faces, which was strongly followed in Bakhchisarai—the heart of Crimean Tatars' Islam—climbed upon the fences and rooftops with open faces attracted by the desire to see the celebratory parade." The residents of Bakhchisarai, he argued, "had never before seen anything like it."[6] Another eyewitness shared Dombrovskii's view, writing that the procession in Bakhchisarai composed a stunning sight, "especially in the eyes of the *inovertsy* [non-believers]."[7] Crimean Tatars' religious practices even today contain some semblance of their Christian heritage, yet it is unlikely that they participated in the ceremony with the enthusiasm alleged by nineteenth-century Russian witnesses.

As the official opening of the Dormition monastery suggests, church authorities hoped that the Crimean Athos community would establish Christianity firmly in the peninsula. Renewing the ancient monasteries in Crimea was not simply a matter of stocking and staffing of monks. It drew deeply upon Crimea's multi-confessional past. Narratives associated with the sites integrated the established scholarship about Crimea's Greek and Byzantine history to deepen the association with Mt. Athos. They also emphasized Crimean Tatar participation in Orthodox rituals, which may or may not have reflected reality. These narratives were published in what scholars typically describe as secular mediums: scholarly journals and the *Odesskii vestnik*, the region's largest circulating newspaper.[8] An analysis of the foundation of the community's first monasteries shows that Russian Athos was the product of a complex missiology that maximized sophisticated, modern means of promotion and depended upon ceremony, text, and alteration of public space.

As the flagship community, the Dormition monastery opened first. After its success, church authorities began building monasteries at three other sites: the spring at Cosmas and Damian, the ruins of Chersonesos, and the caves of Inkerman. Next, diocesan authorities managed to bring the powerful St. George monastery into the orbit of the Russian Athos group. Each of these communities represented a unique place in Crimea's Christian memory and sacred history. The Dormition monastery occupied the most contested landscape, for it sat at the intersection of sacred Muslim and Jewish memorials. The community at Chersonesos drew upon the legacy of St. Vladimir depicted in saints' lives and elaborated in archaeological research to represent Crimea as the cradle of Russian Christianity. Similarly, Christian archaeologists contributed to the narrative of Inkerman's special holiness and investigated legends of first-century saints associated with the site. Cosmas and Damian was the only site in the first stage of Christian renewal based on natural rather than man-made phenomena and suggests how easily the church syncretized local traditions, Muslim as well as Christian. Finally, the St. George monastery provided an obvious connection to Crimea's Greek population, although its absorption into the Russian Athos community signaled the end of an era. The opening of these monasteries enabled the spread of Christianity, for they staked a Christian claim to contested or shared terrain, and increased the number of Christians residing in and visiting Crimea. In Crimea, new or renovated churches associated with Russian Athos imposed an Orthodox identity on a predominantly Muslim landscape.

Dormition Monastery

Of all the other sites that composed Russian Athos, the Dormition monastery had the greatest degree of overlapping sacred histories, for it sat at the intersection of Christian, Muslim, and Jewish monuments. The monastery is located in a dense patchwork of ruins, stretching three kilometers between Bakhchisarai—former capital of the Crimean khanate—and Chufut Kale—the ancestral home of many of Crimea's peoples, including Goth Alans, Tatars, Armenians, and Karaim.[9] These ruins contain rich material evidence of the past, which boasts of the region's ever-changing history, cultures, and faiths.

The oldest set of ruins in the region, in Chufut Kale, spreads across 113 acres on the wide plateau of the Stolovi Mountain. Ruins above ground include a Muslim mausoleum and an Orthodox baptistery. A complex cave system that contains evidence of human habitation networks the ground below. Remnants of the most elaborate of the early settlements belong to the Goth Alans, who federated with the Byzantine Empire from the sixth to the seventh centuries. In the mid-fourteenth century, the settlement, then known as Kyrk-or, or Kyrk-er (Kirimtatar for "forty fortifications"), became the first capital of the Crimean Khanate. When the Tatars moved their capital into Bakhchisarai in the sixteenth century, Karaim and Armenians took over the plateau and renamed the settlement Chufut Kale, or "Jewish fortress."[10] Karaim consider Chufut Kale their historical and religious center, and over centuries they inscribed surrounding environs with numerous sacred Jewish markers. Chufut Kale is also the place where the controversial Karaim scholar Abraham Firkovich set up his residence.[11]

Ruins from the once powerful Tatar khanate also scatter across the three-kilometer space between Chufut Kale and Bakhchisarai. Decaying buildings from Salachik, which was once a thriving village of more than 3,000 residences, can be found near Chufut Kale. The most prominent and visible ruins of Salachik are the Giray mausoleum and the Zincirli-Medresse, the earliest Muslim educational center in Europe.[12] In Bakhchisarai, the khan's palace built by Mengli Giray in the early sixteenth century occupies the memorial heart of the Tatar city. Thus, Muslim sacred sites are even more noticeable, and stretch from the boundaries of Chufut Kale to the city of Bakhchisarai.

A Greek cliff-city, Mar'iam-dere (Mariampol) sits in the middle of this diverse array of ruins; its remnants can still be seen in the vacated caves carved into the cliffs. Greeks built Dormition monastery into the cliffs, where it became the religious center of their community. Unlike the cave complexes of Mar'iam-dere, the caves of Dormition monastery remained populated and in use well into the eighteenth century. The Dormition monastery thus was only one religious marker in a diverse sacred landscape and was for many years secondary to Islamic monuments. Following Russian conquest, the monastery, like Chersonesos, became an object of imperial fascination. Today, most scholars date the monastery to the fourteenth and fifteenth centuries. At the time of Russian conquest, however, scholars dated the Dormition monastery to a period between the eighth and tenth centuries when Crimea was settled by Christian Greeks, who retreated into the Crimean mountains during a period of iconoclasm and persecution.[13]

The reopening of the monastery generated a new wave of interest in the site's Christian past that was partially satisfied by an article in the *Odesskii vestnik* recounting the legends of sacred history. Sacred histories have one main goal: to demonstrate a past distinguished by grace. Therefore, this article focused on the monastery's miracle, when an icon suddenly revealed itself in the cave city complex near Bakhchisarai. Miraculous icons constituted a common religious motif in Russian Orthodox lay and official spirituality. Vera Shevzov explains that common miracles included "self-cleaning or renewal of icons," the "unusual flickering or self-lighting" of an icon's candle, or as in this case, the spontaneous appearance, or "epiphany," of an icon. Such icons could be found in any number of places, whether a riverbank, forest, rock outcropping, or spring. The "epiphanic icon" (the spontaneous revelation of an icon) was particularly widespread and revered.[14] Crimea had multiple legends of epiphanic icons associated with the cliff faces near Bakhchisarai and the spring of Cosmas and Damian.[15] In the case of Bakhchisarai, the miraculous icon was preserved for centuries by the Greeks, who transported it out of Crimea during their exodus in 1778. Still, the icon's removal from the monastery did not deter Christian devotion, for the miracle of its appearance had already blessed the site and made it holy.

The most common version of the Bakhchisarai icon's epiphany, according to the author of the *Odesskii vestnik* article, followed a typical schema associated with miracles of self-revealing icons. A shepherd saw an icon of the Mother of God hovering seventy feet over the cliffs, while he was herding his flocks. As with most miracles, news of the shepherd's vision spread, eventually reaching the local prince, who ordered that the icon be taken down from the cliff and transferred to his palace. Despite the reverence with which the icon was taken into the prince's quarters, it disappeared, only to be found later hovering in its original spot. The same process repeated itself until the prince and his servitors finally realized that the icon wanted to remain at the cliffs. The prince built a church into the rock face for the icon, and this church eventually expanded into the Dormition monastery.

Another version that was "told jointly with the former" depicted a terrible serpent that lived in the valley at the foot of the mountain and destroyed the surrounding environs and harassed the region's inhabitants. Suddenly, the Mother of God icon miraculously appeared and hovered above the snake, which immediately shriveled and died.[16] In gratitude for the miraculous icon, the villagers built the monastery. Acknowledging that some parts of the legends were contradictory or unlikely, the author nevertheless concluded that their one common theme—the epiphany of the Mother of God icon—reflected a reality. Although the exact circumstances of the miracle could not be authenticated, the number of oral traditions surrounding the cave churches indicated a miracle.

After establishing the monastery's miraculous pedigree, the article explained that the Dormition monastery constituted the first sacred space in the region, and that Orthodoxy had sanctified the peninsula before the arrival of other faiths. More explicitly, the monastery was built when "Crimea was located still in the state close to its original wildness, and when Tatars and Bakhchisarai still did not exist." Later, the author emphasized that the monastery emerged "not fewer than six centuries ago," which occurred well "before the invasion of Mongols in Crimea, when there was a colony of Genoese and the authority was still Greek."[17] Christianity, in other words, entered Crimea well before Islam. And not only did it come to Crimea before Islam, it arrived when the peninsula was still in a primordial state of nature, and "dense forests spread across the spines of the mountains," covering all of its "ravines and cliffs." This visual panorama of a lush virginal landscape was a common representation of Crimea, dating to Catherine II's portrayal of the peninsula as a Russian Eden. In Catherine's age, the topos was meant as a "sign of autocratic intervention, the result of benevolent rule."[18] Here, the emphasis on nature styled Crimea as an unaltered space before the arrival of Christianity. Because Christians were the first to discover the territory, the passage implied, they and not the Tatars were its rightful heirs.

In an interesting inversion of confessional roles, the article appropriated the example of Tatar worshippers as further evidence of the monastery's special holiness. It repeatedly described Dormition monastery as a place of "particular respect for not only the Orthodox Christians in Crimea, but also the Tatars themselves." It referred to oral traditions that depicted the khans worshipping at the monastery's chapel. "In spite of their Muslim fanaticism," the khans "frequently sought protection in the Holy Place, and lit candles in front of the Holy Icon."[19] The high level of esteem that Tatars had for the monastery was further demonstrated following the Greek exodus. The author reasoned, "it might be expected that the Tatars would seek to erase any signs of [Greek] presence, even to destroy the church." Instead of tearing down the monastery, however, the Tatars protected it from harm, while Khan Sahin Giray invited a priest from Constantinople to serve there.[20]

Tatars may very well have been among the devotees, for their complex cultural heritage left them with the memory of Christian rituals, and some continued to recognize Christian festivals.[21] Yet, the trope of Tatar reverence for the monastery was one of the most important themes of the article, for it enabled Christians to assert Orthodox hegemony over competing claims to Bakhchisarai's sacred space. Additionally, by portraying Tatars as descendents of Orthodox Christians, this interpretation suggested that renewing Christian communities in Crimea could reunite apostatized Tatars with the church and the empire.[22] The article concluded that the Islamicization of the peninsula disrupted the monastery's predetermined destiny as a holy place.[23] "If it were not for the Tatars, and close location to the Khan's capital in Bakhchisarai, the Dormition cliffs," asserted the *Odesskii vestnik*, it "would have been raised quickly in the measure of the blessed and great monasteries."[24] As the largest, most important news source for the Black Sea region, *Odesskii vestnik*'s description reached a far larger audience than the procession had, creating a permanent and official interpretation that outlasted the fleeting impressions caused by the event itself. The narrative, it could be argued, was therefore even more important than the actual procession.

Due perhaps to the articles in *Odesskii vestnik* and the archbishop's carefully crafted promotion, Russians across the empire met the opening of the monastery with curiosity and a flurry of congratulations. Correspondence from the exarch of Georgia revealed that news of Russian Athos reached the Greek communities of his diocese as early as 1849, well before Archbishop Innokentii received formal approval from the Holy Synod.[25] Days before the procession, the architect Dmitrii Efimov congratulated the archbishop on his work establishing "New Athos,"[26] while Grand Duke Konstantin Nikolaevich "heartily" wished Russian Athos success. The first member of the imperial family to visit Mt. Athos in many years, the grand duke expressed a desire to visit Crimea, "not out of simple curiosity, but for prayer."[27] This enthusiasm reflected the breadth and success of the church publicists' active campaign to promote the new monastery and a readiness to treat Crimea as Russia's special holy place.[28]

From Mt. Athos, Serafim Sviatogorets delivered measured praise, asking a question that undoubtedly weighed heavily on others' minds as well: "Will women be allowed on Crimean Athos?"[29] In June of 1851, Sviatogorets sent Dormition monastery a small shipment of produce from Mt. Athos. The shipment included large gourds that the monks made into vessels for storing wine and transporting other liquids to "the hermit cells." Sviatogorets also included a few smaller gourds, and a box of sugar produced on the mountain.[30] In a separate correspondence, the monk promised to send saplings from Mt. Athos to be planted around Dormition monastery.[31] Sharing such goods provided another emblematic link between Crimea and the Holy Mountain.

Despite the generous outpouring of support from the Orthodox laity, the monks' first year was extremely harsh. Renovation had only just begun, so lumber and tools piled up around them. Their quarters were minimal; the seven monks shared three ancient cells carved into the cliffs, a space that was small, dark, cold, and damp. In the winter time, they crowded into two cells to preserve heat and to keep warm. Literally living in caves, these monks were true ascetics.[32] Still, the monastery grew, and by the winter of 1851, architects and builders, who carefully designed each stage of renovation to preserve the monastery's "ancient look and character," had made significant progress in the process of renewal.[33] By 1852, the Odessa news reported that the monastery had already attracted its first elder, who landed in Crimea "after various travels through the religious communities of the fatherland, Palestine, and Athos."[34]

Chersonesos

Once Dormition monastery opened, diocesan officials initiated building the St. Vladimir church in Chersonesos and the church in the names of St. Clement and St. Martin in Inkerman.[35] Authorities planned these sites together because both were located on land controlled by the Black Sea navy on the outskirts of Sevastopol. Because the *Russian Primary Chronicle* identified Chersonesos as the location of Prince Vladimir's baptism, diocesan authorities made it the next priority. Archibishop Innokentii wrote to the Holy Synod that the recently discovered churches in Chersonesos were of great symbolic value to the Orthodox laity. Both Russian and foreign pilgrims, he asserted, visited Chersonesos to "pay their holy debt" to the site of "the Christening of St. Prince Vladimir, from which the light of the Orthodox faith illuminated all of Russia."[36] Blueprints for the new monastery at Chersonesos drew substantially from archaeological research. Innokentii pointedly discussed religious artifacts stored in the Odessa Society's museum and wrote the Synod that, "Amid these ruins [in Chersonesos] lay four churches, three small, and one large."[37] Yet, for Innokentii, these remnants of Byzantium religiosity were not merely ruins, or "material evidence of the past," but the most holy of relics. In their current state, he argued to the Synod, these ruins were "a pitiful sight that [did] not serve the glory of Orthodoxy—especially in the eyes of the *inovertsy*," or those of other faiths.[38]

Consequently, the archbishop proposed building an appropriate monument for St. Vladimir. "What type of monument," he asked, should commemorate one of the holiest spots in Orthodox memory? For an answer, he turned to archaeologists who had uncovered foundations and columns of an ancient church in Chersonesos. He advocated restoring these ruins in the best possible replication of the church as it existed during the life of Prince Vladimir. He suggested that a monument be erected in honor of Prince Vladimir on the exact spot believed to be the site of his christening, literally upon the ruins themselves. The church should also replicate as much as possible the early Byzantine church in which Prince Vladimir was baptized.[39] In addition to the church, he proposed building cells for twelve monks and servitors, a hostel for pilgrims, and gardens around the monastery so the monks could be self-sufficient.[40]

After receiving official approval to begin the Russian Athos project from the Holy Synod in April of 1850, diocesan authorities mobilized local scholars and resources for Chersonesos. The consistory concluded the transfer of Chersonesos and surrounding lands from the Black Sea naval authority into the administration of the Russian Orthodox Church in March of 1852.[41] This transfer initiated a new phase of research and excavation of Chersonesos, in which the church adjudicated access to the ruins and excavations.[42] The community at Chersonesos founded and maintained a museum and digging site jointly financed by Holy Synod and the Ministry of Enlightenment.[43] In order to create an historically accurate structure, Archbishop Innokentii enlisted support from the Odessa Society for History and Antiquities. Typically ill-disposed toward the archbishop, Odessa Society secretary Nikolai Murzakevich agreed to work with an architect to create a detailed blueprint for the ancient church based on recent archaeological studies.[44] Under the guidance of Murzakevich, diocesan authorities hired an architect to build the church in the Byzantine style of the ninth and tenth centuries.[45]

Plans for the new church integrated remains of the old, so that exposed ancient walls and fundaments could be seen inside the new ones. Thus the architectural plans transformed the ancient artifacts into holy relics; the crumbling walls themselves became sacred symbols representing the baptism of Russia's great St. Vladimir. Because the church in honor of St. Vladimir would take altogether several years to build, authorities approved the construction of a small wooden church to serve the needs of the monks and pilgrims during the interim.[46]

As scholars from the Odessa Society projected blueprints, local clergymen, including Father Vasilii who was selected as head of the monastery at Chersonesos, raised money among local parishes for the new church. The church in Chersonesos quickly found support from a wealthy merchant in Sevastopol, as well as from many other philanthropists.[47] A lieutenant in the Russian navy presented a canvas of Prince Vladimir based on his research in local collections and portrayed the prince "in the same clothes he wore when he conquered Chersonesos." Still other merchant families and members of the Russian military helped to fill the church coffers.[48] On February 28, the community at Chersonesos, which included monastic cells in addition to the wooden church, was sanctified. According to Father Vasilii's report, the opening was attended by many local dignitaries, including the Greek archaeologist who conducted the most recent excavation in Chersonesos, Zacharias Arkas.[49]

After the official sanctification, local scholars continued to be involved with the church. Several months later, Arkas praised the church's work in Inkerman and Chersonesos with an expansive article in the Odessa paper that seamlessly patched together religious myths of the region, an archaeological exposition of excavations, and a contemporary review of Innokentii's plans for renewal.[50] Arkas, like Murzakevich and many other local scholars, perceived few distinctions between Christian and secular scholarship or excavation and restoration. In language redolent of the

Christian patriotism typical of his colleagues in Crimea, Arkas wrote: "In the lovely warm country of Russia, in the mountains, between fruit gardens and wild trees, four sketes [hermitages] have already been built in which Orthodox Christians can spend their days on their native land, in conversation with God."[51] Although the land transfer granted the church control over the ruins, it did not bring an end to cooperation between religious and non-religious scholars. In 1853, for example, Aleksandr Uvarov, son of Sergei Uvarov, the minister of education, conducted an excavation there under diocesan supervision. He published the results in the large volume titled *Research on the Antiquities of Southern Russia and the Shores of the Crimean Sea* (1851–1856).[52]

INKERMAN

As diocesan authorities planned for the official opening of the site in Chersonesos scheduled for February 1853, they also began work at Inkerman. Like Chersonesos, Inkerman occupied a privileged position in Crimea's sacred landscape. "Both places," the Synod reported, share a "united importance within Holy tradition." Inkerman was a common stop for religious, scholarly, and tourist groups, and attracted the "honorable attention of local inhabitants and visiting pilgrims, Russian and foreign." It was "a pitiful sight" that the Inkerman monastery was left "empty, without any supervision, serving nothing to the honor of Orthodoxy—particularly in the eyes of the non-Orthodox."[53] Inkerman, like Chersonesos, was an important zone of Orthodox memory that had to be renewed not merely for the edification of the Orthodox but for the benefit of the non-Orthodox as well.

Even though Inkerman and Chersonesos were located only two kilometers apart, Inkerman architecturally resembled the Dormition monastery; it was located in a cave-city complex, with remnants of over two-hundred structures built into the cliffs, eighty of which archaeologists determined were churches.[54] Inkerman is one of the most curious places in Crimea, and one of the most picturesque. It is an ancient city, whose origin is contested and unknown, having been inhabited by successive waves of settlers and their conquerors. Only seven kilometers from Sevastopol, ruins of the ancient city spread along the mouth of the Black River through the seaside cave city of Calamita, where remnants of a fortress and encircling wall overlook the river valley below. Inkerman-Calamita stands out as one of Crimea's most beautiful and intricate historical sites.

Archaeologists typically date the earliest fortifications at Inkerman to the second through the fifth centuries, attributing the ruins to Scythian,

Sarmation, and Alan settlers. In the sixth century, when Byzantines entered Crimea, they gravitated toward Inkerman, lured by its deep natural harbor and its gateway inland through the Black River. The Calamita fortress and its caves, according to most scholars, dated to the eighth century, when Byzantine icon-worshippers fled to Crimea during the empire's iconoclastic period.[55] Although this period saw a significant boost in Christian architecture, Inkerman's most famous churches are believed to have been built in the fourteenth and fifteenth centuries during the Genoese kingdom.[56] Given the fame of the basilica and other cave churches, Inkerman acquired the local toponym "Monastery Cliffs." In the nineteenth century, Archbishop Innokentii proposed renewing three of these churches.

Now scholars generally concur that the basilica was built by the Genoese, but in the middle of the nineteenth century speculation about its origins was rife. Some scholars even hypothesized that many of the cave churches were a first-century construction, designed by the Christian exiles or converts of Pope Clement. One of the most popular legends associated with the churches on Inkerman cliffs came from the life of the Roman pope, Clement, recorded in St. Dimitrii of Rostov's saints' lives, compiled in the sixteenth century. Pope Clement was the fourth pope of Rome, known as the first of the Apostolic Fathers, and believed to have been ordained by Peter. In 94 CE Emperor Trajan exiled Clement from Rome to Crimea. When Clement arrived there, according to St. Dimitrii's account, he found two thousand Christians living around Chersonesos in residences carved into the cliffs. These Christians were believed to have been a combination of exiled Christians and converts.[57]

Inkerman was a popular site for archaeological and scholarly research, generating far-reaching controversy among the era's most prolific academic writers. The findings of these writers provided a diverse, often contrasting, body of scholarship. An article in *Novorossiiskii kalendar'* (1855) sorted through some of the controversies, especially the debate over who founded the Inkerman fortress.[58] The author, I. Danevskii, hypothesized that Tauric Scythians founded the cliff city at Inkerman.[59]

In the mid-1850s, Archbishop Innokentii was, unsurprisingly, one of the most outspoken advocates of the St. Clement legend and asserted that in Inkerman "St. Clement, the Pope of Rome, was incarcerated, and his relics, miraculously found in the sea at Chersonesos were taken by the blessings of Prince Vladimir from Korsun [Chersonesos] to Kyiv."[60] Due to its association with St. Clement and other first-century Christians, Inkerman became one of the chief landmarks of Crimea's sacred landscapes. Because the ruins of the cliff churches bore witness to the life of Pope Clement and the history of early Christians in Crimea, church officials planned to incorporate the architecture of the original cave churches and to retouch the ancient Greek paintings on the walls.[61] Just as in Chersonesos, the restoration of the church at Inkerman was to be historically precise down to minute detail. Restoring Inkerman was essential, for as Archbishop Innokentii argued, the many travelers drawn by Christian legends and archaeological curiosity were "insulted" by the poor condition of the ruins, which had become in some cases shelters for shepherds and their flocks. Sevastopol merchants who supported construction at Chersonesos also promised to fund renewal of two churches in the Inkerman cliffs in the names of St. Martin and St. Clement, and to pay for equipment for all church services.

Plans for Inkerman included a small chapel at the bottom of the cliff, and shelter for eight brothers.[62] The church at Inkerman received land at the same time Chersonesos did; after that, restoration proceeded rather quickly. In October of 1852, Father Vasilii wrote to the consistory promising the church would be ready for sanctification by Christmas.[63] On 14 February 1853, he reported that he had worked with Archimandrite Polikarp to prepare both sites for sanctification and that the church at Inkerman was scheduled to be finished on 20 February.[64] At the end of the month, Polikarp sanctified both Inkerman and Chersonesos. In a small ceremony on 24 February, he met with the newly appointed superior of the Inkerman skete, Father Aaron, and blessed the community.[65]

Cosmas and Damian

Before receiving approval to build in Inkerman and Chersonesos, the local church began work on the site at the spring of Cosmas and Damian, a project that remained unfinished until after the Crimean War. This site was one of the few in Russian Athos inspired by nature. Known by Crimean Tatars as Savluk-Su ("healing waters"), Cosmas and Damian is a spring deep in the mountainous preserve located eighteen kilometers from Alushta and forty-five kilometers from Simferopol. The spring constituted one of many sites associated with Crimea's sacred natural landscape that Archbishop Innokentii advocated bringing into the orbit of the Russian Orthodox Church.[66] The spring originated in an *urochishche*, the Russian word given to describe natural landscape phenomena characterized by contrasts or opposites, such as a clearing in the forest or the hollow of mountains. In Russian Orthodoxy, springs, mountain peaks and valleys, grottos, even stones, trees, and unusual natural phenomena often become the location of shrines.[67] This is especially the case in Crimea, an ethnically and culturally diverse landscape that was geographically isolated from official Christendom for centuries. Thus, the sites of local miracles frequently occurred on terrain recognized by pre-Christian sacred geography, whether the epiphanic icon that appeared at the Bakhchisrai cliffs or tales of healings at the Cosmas and Damian spring. This *urochishche* in Cosmas and Damian was composed of the crossway of a mountain chain, which included the Chatyrdag foothills, the spurs of Babugana, and the slopes of the Chuchel and Chernoi mountains.[68]

Unlike several other sites, the spring had no material ties to the period of Greek Christianity. No cave cities surrounded it; no ancient ruins rose from its earth. Instead, the gossamer tissue of legend and mythology cloaked the *urochishche* in the memory of Greek Christian miracles and Tatar rituals. Christians and Tatars both had long series of oral traditions that attributed to the spring divine powers of healing and restoration. Pilgrims from both groups traveled there by the thousands on the first of July, the feast day of Saints Cosmas and Damian.

Cosmas and Damian came to the attention of diocesan authorities in the 1840s, when Archbishop Gavriil initiated an investigation after rumors reached Odessa of a popular pilgrimage to a healing spring in Crimea every year on the first of July. This annual pilgrimage to a remote mountainous spring miles from any town was supported by local parish priests, but its origins perplexed officials. When Gavriil sent inquiries to local priests near the site, he asked for a full description of where the site was situated, who visited it, and how it was that Russian priests had come to serve there on the feast day. The resulting reports give rare insight into a sacred space shared by Christians and Muslims.

According to local priests, Greek pilgrims had been visiting the site long before Russian churches in nearby villages had even begun to be constructed. Over the course of the first half of the nineteenth century, different priests vied for influence over the site. Several villages—Bakhchisarai, Mangup, Laskoi, Alushta, and Balta-Chokraskii—sent priests on the first of July. The issue was a significant one, for in addition to conducting services, village priests raised revenue by selling candles.[69] The official leading the investigation, Mikhail Radionov, personally visited the site on the feast day from his post in Simferopol. Much like a modern-day anthropologist, he was a participant observer, taking part in the ceremonies and carefully recording every detail. He arrived at the site on 29 June, where he found some people already in attendance. The spring spilled over a small waterfall at a source of the Alma river and flowed through the heart of Crimean foothills between present-day Simferopol and Alushta. Radionov reported seeing Tatars, both men and women, plunging themselves in the spring, which Tatars believed had healing powers. He counted approximately fifty people at this particular spot who, in addition to bathing, also lit candles. After camping close by, he continued further up the spring, climbing the rocks with the help of "good Christians." At the falls, he saw priests blessing the water and preparing for the services the following day. On the feast day, he counted fifty pilgrims at the top of the falls, and at least five hundred bathing in the falling waters. Radionov returned a few years later at the request of Archbishop Innokentii and found more than five hundred people.[70]

Archbishop Innokentii used the information gathered by Gavriil and Radionov to construct a sacred history for the site of Cosmas and Damian. His narrative was not written for diocesan authorities, but for a broader public. The article, "About the Crimean Spring of Saints Cosmas and Damian," published in *Odesskii vestnik* described the folklore around a spring that intersected both Christian and Tatar sacred landscapes. It explained the saints and miracles associated with the site and connected the layered history of the spring with Russian conquerors, to show that Russians, not Tatars, were the rightful authority to arbitrate access to this holy place.

According to the article, the site had been known from time immemorial as Cosmas and Damian. It was named after the second of three pairs of saints by the same name celebrated by the Orthodox Church. These saints were born in Rome during the third century. Both worked as doctors and tended to the poor, while spreading the gospel. Because they practiced medicine without material compensation, they acquired the adjective "unmercenary." The saints met their deaths in 284, when a jealous local rival had them stoned.[71] In a language that borrowed from a skepticism of science, Innokentii admitted that *Cheti minei*, the standard Russian collection of saints' lives, revealed nothing about a trip to Crimea, but reasoned that it could very well be possible because "such exiles were not unusual" for Romans persecuted in the faith.[72] "Given insufficient historical evidence," the archbishop concluded that their presence in this isolated Crimean wilderness "could only be decided with help from oral tradition." This oral tradition, not surprisingly, came from the Greeks, who, the article reminded readers, "were the first and oldest Christian residents on the Crimean peninsula, and consequently, the first sources for Christianity in Crimea."

Many of the myths associated with Cosmas and Damian include the miracle of a self-revealing icon. In one of these legends, a monk went to the spring after hearing about the vision of a local elder, who saw an icon of the saintly healers hovering in the air. Another Christian tale recounts a Greek man who visited the spring after having a vision in a dream that told him to go there. Similar to the previous tradition, he found an icon poised over the water. As he looked at the icon with bewilderment, two men walked by, shouted, "Cosmas and Damian," and hid. Archbishop Innokentii concluded that although the details of the miracle might be a little unclear, the oral traditions did provide evidence of the spring's holiness and the reality of a self-revealing icon.

The article also integrated a discussion of Tatar myths and miracles associated with the spring. One Tatar legend of Savluk-Su, for example, tells of a Tatar shepherd, who while guiding his sheep through the hills, fell and broke his leg. An inner voice commanded the shepherd to go to the spring, which he managed to do "with unusual strength." After drinking the water he immediately felt better; he then submerged his entire body and "felt healthier than before." The other Tatar miracles similarly describe shepherds or villagers, guided by an inner voice to the spring, who all experienced the water's restorative powers. Unlike Christian legends, which attributed the spring's later restorative powers to the miraculous blessings of Cosmas and Damian, Tatar tales reveal no special intervention of the saints. Rather, Tatar myths attributed the miraculous quality of the spring to the mystical powers of Tatar dervishes.

The archbishop did not dismiss the legends of Tatar miracles but instead treated them as proof of the spring's holiness. He insisted that Tatar reverence for the spring was natural, predictable, for it "follow[ed] from the older example of their Christian ancestors." That Tatars recognized the feast of Cosmas and Damian on the first of July provided further proof of their Christian ancestry. Innokentii concluded: "[H]istory indicates that the Tatar population on the Crimean mountains were not Muslim, but of Greek and Italian origin; they were enticed into Islam which led to the unhappiness of Tauride Christians during the last centuries."[73] Here, the article alleged that Crimea deviated from Christianity only after foreign, Islamic powers imposed an alien faith on the peninsula's southern population. As with Crimea's sacred histories elsewhere, the insistence upon Tatars' Christian heritage did not represent a narrative of toleration, but of Christianization.

Apart from the sacred history of miracles, the "natural" qualities of Cosmas and Damian—the spring's remote, isolated location, the extremity of the environment, and the sharp contrasts of the *urochishche*—were emphasized. Uncultivated nature compensated for the absence of ruins or other religious landmarks and constructed a different parallel with the past based in wild, remote, and pristine landscapes. In a sermon, Archbishop Innokentii described Cosmas and Damian as "one of the greatest and most deserted (*pustinnykh*) places in the middle of the Tauride mountains, which in general are so rich and picturesque."[74] He sketched a verbal portrait for his audience, asking his congregation and readers (for like many sermons, this one was published) to reflect upon the natural majesty and contrasts of the place: "Imagine in the center of this mountain gorge, a clearing surrounded by a forest of various trees and greens . . . imagine a small cliff from where a small spring stems and soon unites with a torrent flowing into the river Alma: this is the spring of Cosmas and Damian." Innokentii's depiction of the site reverberated with contrasts, from the gorge to the high mountain, from the foothills to the summit, from verdant forests to barren hollows, and from a spring to a torrent. The mystery of the earthly contrasts surrounding Cosmas and Damian revealed the wonder of God's creation. Even the temperature of the spring produced a natural phenomenon, a "cold boil," which he asserted, "overwhelms the bathers, seeming to go through the bones and brains itself."[75]

Innokentii advocated developing Cosmas and Damian, because the "*urochishche* was considered holy, and the spring healing, not only in the opinion of the Christians, but also of the Tatars."[76] Whereas renovation of the sites in Bakhchisarai, Inkerman, and Chersonesos began with churches and monks' quarters, in Cosmas and Damian, building began with hostels and bathhouses. An old, decrepit bathhouse already existed at the spring, which the archbishop attributed to the energies "of some kind of saintly hermit," but it was in poor condition and too small for the large flow of pilgrims. In its place, Innokentii advocated erecting two new and separate shelters for Christians and Muslims, both divided into male and female rooms. Most prerevolutionary accounts depicted the site of Cosmas and Damian as an example of the church's response to popular faith. Makarii, the community's first abbot, commented: "The voice of the people have long pointed to the *urochishche* where the spring was located in the name of St. Cosmas and Damian as a very convenient place for the building of a holy community."[77]

The question of popular spirituality is a complicated one, for although the bathhouses provided a more comfortable place for devotees, they also gave a structure to popular ritual on the feast day, including greater separation between the Muslims and Christians. Church officials designated separate spaces for Muslims and for Christians. In addition to the bathhouses, a small chapel for pilgrims and a set of cells were planned to accommodate overnight and extended visits.[78]

In February of 1851, local authorities informed the consistory that the application for land transfer had been elevated to the Ministry of Government Property, which officially released the land to the church in the middle of March with the tsar's approval.[79] On 1 August, the local department of forestry permitted the church to take over the land.[80] Later in August, the archbishop commemorated the land transfer around the Cosmsas and Damian skete, and the appointment of its new caretakers, with his article to the paper.[81] By 29 December, a priest blessed the water and the grounds. The brief, unattended ritual conducted in the cold, snowy silence of Crimea's winter commemorated the inclusion of the site into Russian Athos, reinforced the holiness of the spring, and ended with a prayer for the mercy of God, for holy hermits, and for the health of the tsar and all Orthodox Christians.[82] Although plans for Cosmas and Damian were set in motion before those for many of the other communities in Crimea, the war delayed completion of the work until after Innokentii's death in 1857.

St. George Monastery

The St. George monastery near Balaklava was an integral part of the Russian Athos community, and perhaps even its inspiration. The monastery's long-standing Greek identity provided the source of Archbishop Innokentii's parallel with Mt. Athos, evidenced in part by the archbishop's plan to build a church in the name of St. John the Baptist for the Greeks, to be located between Balaklava and Sevastopol. St. George monastery is located on Cape Violent, rather than in the small town its name bears. The earliest given date for the monastery is 1350, according to Metropolitan Agathangelos's report to the Kherson consistory, but its first historical record does not appear until the writings of the seventeenth-century Polish emissary M. Bronevskii.[83] A popular tradition dates the founding of the monastery to 890, when as the legend goes, Greek sailors erected the monastery in gratitude for their survival of a tempest at sea that crashed their boat onto the cliffs of Balaklava. With the blessings of a Scythian bishop, these sailors carved a church into the cliffs where the monastery still stands.[84] Although this legend remains associated with the monastery, most researchers believe now that the monastery could not have been established before the fifteenth century.[85]

Local diocesan authorities began renovating the monastery in the 1820s.[86] The site first attracted attention at the end of the eighteenth century, when archeologists and travelers began to publish broadly about antiquity in Crimea. The St. George monastery became a primary focus of regional studies especially because it was located near the ruins believed to be the ancient temple of Diana. The monastery remained under Greek supervision as Russian imperial authority began to strengthen and even after the appointment of Russian naval priests there in 1806. Despite improvements made by earlier abbots, the monastery was still in need of repair and expansion when Metropolitan Agathangelos arrived at his post. "With my appointment in 1825," Agathangelos wrote to the chief procurator of the Holy Synod, Count Nikolai Protasov, three decades later, "the monastery was in poor condition, half in ruins, and threatened with imminent collapse . . . In it," he continued, "there were no brothers, no fence, and only one small stone church with a decrepit abbot's cell."[87] The quarters outside the monastery housed no more than twelve monks. Under the administration of Agathangelos, the monastery erected a stone church at the cemetery, two two-story buildings for the brothers' cells, one building for visitors to the monastery, a dining hall, kitchen, and pantry. From 1834, the monastery housed twenty-four monks and two hierodeacons, and in 1839, it attracted a few new novices.

Due to its unique function as the residence of naval priests, as well as its continuous growth and structural improvements, St. George's exceeded its officially designated status as a third-class monastery. Before Archbishop Innokentii took over the diocese, Metropolitan Agathangelos unsuccessfully petitioned the Synod several times to elevate the monastery. In 1835, he petitioned the Synod to elevate it to stauropegion status, a change that would have entailed an increase in state support and a guarantee of Agathangelos's local authority. At that time, however, Protasov refused to circulate the request any higher.[88] Twelve years later, Agathangelos requested the monastery be raised to second degree, a request which Protasov agreed to support but never acted upon. With Archbishop Innokentii's encouragement in the late 1840s, Agathangelos re-petitioned the Synod to change the monastery's status. The Greek metropolitan argued that the monastery had grown even larger with a total of forty brothers, the majority of whom, he noted, served in the navy and local fortresses, and yet drew upon the monastery's supplies for their sustenance during the winter.[89]

In April of 1850, the synod elevated St. George monastery to the first degree, basing its decision on Archbishop Innokentii's recommendation, which contended that "the meaning of this monastery in comparison with others was unique because it must have monks appointed for serving in the entire Black Sea navy and all of the shore line along the Caucasus."[90] In order to speed the process of elevation, the archbishop proposed that the monastery obtain the first degree, but without provision of first-degree salaries, which he argued, would be unnecessary if the priests in Balaklava were fiscally attached to the accounts of the Black Sea navy. In March 1851, the Synod agreed to count the Balaklava priests as the navy's responsibility.[91] Unfortunately, the monastery's new status did very little to alleviate the financial strains on the rapidly expanding institution.

In response to the news that the monastery was elevated, Agathangelos wrote to Innokentii: "[T]he problem still exists that people in the monastery do not have enough money." He acknowledged that many of the monks did receive small stipends through the military, but explained that many of the other appointed monks received nothing at all.[92] As a potential solution to this problem, Metropolitan Agathangelos again in 1852 petitioned the Synod to elevate the St. George monastery to stauropegion status.[93] This request was also refused.

This latest attempt to elevate the monastery to stauropegion status coincided with a local controversy regarding who should exercise authority over the institution.[94] Prior to the formation of Russian Athos, Tauride had only two consistently active monasteries—St. George monastery and the Korsun monastery, located in the steppe region above the peninsula. The two monasteries were as different as they were distant, and were rarely in contact with one another. Until Innokentii's plan to restore ancient Crimean monasteries, St. George's was the only monastery on the peninsula. Coupled with its unique identity as a Greek center and residence for naval priests, St. George had a long tradition of independence from diocesan authorities, who until Innokentii's administration, remained largely in the distant post of Odessa.

With the establishment of Russian Athos and the newly created supervisory role for Polikarp, however, there arose the question of who should oversee the administration of St. George. Whereas St. George did not figure in the initial proposal, a long series of correspondence shows that its relationship to the administrative center at Dormition monastery had become unclear. Thus, the renewed petition to raise the monastery to stauropegion status can be seen as an attempt to circumnavigate the encroachment of local diocesan authorities. The Synod's refusal to grant stauropegion status added further grounds to bring St. George under the newly reopened Dormition monastery, and in the fall of 1853, Agathangelos petitioned to be released from service. In his place, Archbishop Innokentii appointed Archimandrite Gerontiia, the abbot of Bizukov monastery located in the neighboring province of Kherson, a man of "strong character," capable of maintaining a "strong monastic rule."[95] The appointment of the abbot Gerontiia, a Russian from Kharkov, brought an end to the Greek phase of the Balaklava monastery. While the transfer of the monastery was underway, Archimandrite Polikarp oversaw the monastery's affairs.[96]

Thus, while St. George in Balaklava was not officially a part of Russian Athos, it gradually assumed a role in the community. The same year St. George was elevated to a first-class monastery, priests of the Balaklava monastery sanctified a church in the name of the Holy Elevation of the

Life Creating Cross, which was designed by a local architect, V. A. Rulev. This church preceded Russian Athos, for Metropolitan Agathangelos initiated its construction in the 1830s.[97] Yet, very few local observers made this distinction. A feuilleton in *Odesskii vestnik* published in 1850 by a bureaucrat named Leontii Cherniavskii celebrated Crimea's special holiness and emphasized local lore surrounding the St. George monastery in Balaklava, including stories of Tatar reverence for Christian sites.[98] The Tatar nobility, Cherniavskii asserted, revered the St. George monastery at Balaklava, and "observed the fasts, and brought fruit and fish" to the monks. Moreover, these Tatars believed that the waters around the monastery were healing and would wash their heads and body in the water, or they would drink from the spring water "on an empty stomach for five to fifteen days."[99] Cherniavskii wrote his piece as a commentary advocating church expansion. One of the numerous supporters of Innokentii's work outside the church, Cherniavskii proposed the Balaklava monastery be considered as one of the peninsula's most holy places.

In many ways, Agathangelos's ambitious renewal of the St. George monastery set a precedent for the restoration of the other communities of Russian Athos, while the Greek heritage of St. George monastery certainly inspired the parallel with Mt. Athos. St. George's attachment to the Dormition monastery and the appointment of a Russian abbot, however, signified a new stage in the community's development and belied the pan-Orthodox principle its example inspired. In his analysis of pilgrimage to the St. Tikhon of Zadonsk shrine in the Voronezh province, Christopher Chulos has argued that "nowhere was the connection between local faith and Russian identity clearer than at religious shrines," and that "peripatetic energy was seized upon by religious and secular authorities who promoted and regulated pilgrimage sites as convenient venues for infusing old symbols of Orthodoxy and Russianness with new meaning."[100] The same is true for the St. George monastery in Balaklava and for all of Crimean Christian antiquities, which even as they represented the memory of Greeks and traditions of Tatars, acquired a new, Russian identity.

With the restored Greek monasteries, and the new community at the spring of Cosmas and Damian, Crimea slowly began to resemble Mt. Athos, although Crimea's few small sketes were a far cry from Athos's twenty large monasteries. Between yearly religious processions and through the promotion of fairly constant publications in *Odesskii vestnik*, the sites attracted even greater numbers of pilgrims. Dormition monastery achieved the success that Innokentii had hoped for, paving the way for renewal of other churches. The renewal and building of the monasteries that would compose Russian Athos before the war represents on one hand a remarkable accomplishment. Without any help from the state, Innokentii managed to open several monastic communities in only a handful of years: the Dormition monastery, the Inkerman monastery, the monastery at Chersonesos, and the skete at the Cosmas and Damian spring. By degrees, he also added another skete focused on the St. Anastasia church near Bakhchisarai, and brought the St. George monastery fully within the orbit of Russian Athos. The success of Russian Athos, however, is not due only to the energetic activity of diocesan authorities, but also to the dedication of local Russians. Scholars, clergy, officers, merchants, and other lay believers found common cause in the restoration of ancient Christian ruins.

The narratives about the miraculous histories associated with Crimea's monuments and topographies were not unusual, but part of a larger Christianizing discourse that drew in many participants. For example, Aleksander I. Budberg wrote to Innokentii about the ruins of the Greek colonies in Abkhazia, a strip of land bordering present-day Georgia across from Kerch on the Black Sea.[101] He emphasized above all that in Abkhazia, like Crimea, early Christian colonies preceded Islam and left an intact sacred landscape behind them. He wrote that although "a large part of the Abkhazia tribes now follow the study of Islam," their memory of Christianity is preserved through "observing a few fasts, [and] celebrating large Church holidays." More to the point, perhaps, Budberg argued that "the Abkhazia Muslims easily converted to Christianity around each structure of the Church."[102]

Similar narratives revolved around other areas of Crimea's landscapes, whether they were the ruins of Chersonesos, the church of St. Anastasia located deep in the forests several kilometers from Bakhchisarai, the Inkerman monastery in the cliffs near Sevastopol, the church of St. John the Baptist, or the St. George Balaklava monastery.[103] The Christian historical narratives in the Black Sea, from Abkhazia to Bakhchisarai, encoded the littoral with a profoundly holy Christian history. Some narratives dislodged Tatar and Jewish claims to Crimea's sacred spaces, but others emphasized the commonalities of faith between Islamic and Christian believers on the Crimean peninsula. The church recognized Tatar respect for the spring of Cosmas and Damian, and made plans to include the Tatar population there. The well associated with St. Anastasia also attracted both Muslims and Christians. Visitors to the well washed in the water, and left small coins and domestic treasures. When Tereshchenko visited the holy spot, he happened upon a Tatar kneeling in prayer. As he prayed, the man "drew water from the well, repeating the following blessing: 'Allah ekber' (God is Great)." To Tereshchenko, the chant sounded "touching, dear, and eloquent."[104]

The small number of monasteries had a large impact upon Crimea. These institutions increased Christian populations through pilgrims, monks, novices, and devout *startsy*. The renewed sites also went far to recreate Crimea as an Orthodox territory. Scholars uncovered Christian histories and sacred narratives for Crimea that the restored monasteries came to represent. All of this appealed to Russian state officials because the restored monasteries also legitimized the Russian presence in Crimea through Orthodox links, such as the baptism of St. Vladimir. To certain observers, the monasteries were monuments to the greatness of the Russian Empire as much as to the memory of Orthodoxy.

Archbishop Innokentii wrote to a colleague in the church:

> Our Crimea, thanks to God, is beginning to thaw the ice of Islam. The new Bakhchisarai skete apparently is attracting the friendly attention of the Tatars. A week does not go by in which some Tatar family asks to enter the cave church: upon entering, they fall on their knees in front of the icon and pray with tears. All of this encourages us in the work of our new holy place.[105]

Rather than intrusively sending out clergy among the Muslims from the central location in Dormition monastery, Innokentii remained hopeful that Muslims might join the church on their own. The relationship between the monastery and local Tatars was to be a friendly one. Despite signs of progress, he admitted however that the monastery had a significant challenge ahead "due to the variety of ethnic and national groups" in surrounding areas.[106]

Just as the project of Russian Athos began, the Crimean War brought it to an abrupt halt. The monasteries at Chersonesos and Balaklava hosted the French and English armies. Other sites suffered abandonment, neglect, and dilapidation, and many of the community's monks, priests, and abbots perished. As the next chapter will show, however, the idea of Russian Athos survived the war, and although many of the churches and new structures were utterly destroyed, the sacralization of Crimea—the idea of its holiness—took on greater strength and absorbed new sites.

Chapter Five

WAR

The Crucible of a Holy Place

On imperial order of 21 October 1853, Archbishop Innokentii read Nicholas I's declaration of war to the members of his diocese. Initially read in *Tsarskoe Selo* the day before, this manifesto expressed regret over entering war with the Ottoman Empire, and offered Russia's official justification.[1] According to the document, Ottoman abuse of the Eastern Christians necessitated Russia's intervention. The war would restore Russia's protectorship over Christians living in the Ottoman Empire that had been guaranteed through a series of treaties in the first half of the century.[2] Within a month of the declaration, the Russian navy under the command of the legendary admiral, Pavel Nakhimov, delivered a sound defeat to the Ottoman fleet near the Turkish port of Sinope. This victory turned fatal for Russia, however, for it motivated France and Britain to join forces with the Ottoman Empire.

Historians rarely accept Russia's official position for entering the Crimean War at face value.[3] Debates about the war's origins delve into the complicated politics of the nineteenth century, revealing myriad reasons why the war might have started.[4] These reasons include imperialism, domestic dilemmas over maintaining serfdom, and the existence of a "Western Question," as well as an "Eastern Question."[5] It has become a standard explanation, for example, that Tsar Nicholas I objected to Louis Napoleon's rise to power following the February Revolution of 1848, and that the French and Russian conflict in the 1850s revolved around questions of legitimacy of rule. In Queen Victoria on the other hand, Tsar Nicholas thought he had a friend, and overestimated the influence of his personal charm during his visit to London in 1844.[6] He was surprised therefore when Britain joined the allied invasion of Russia. Despite frequent protestations by Russian diplomats, the British believed that Russia had its eyes on the Ottoman Empire, and lusted after India as well.[7] Although each of these issues fed into the war, religion constituted a main ingredient.

Sympathies with the Eastern Christians remained at the forefront of the tsar's mind. He was a devout Orthodox Christian with personal connections to the holy places in the East.[8] Tsar Nicholas repeatedly stressed that religion was a chief source of conflict with the Ottomans in his personal correspondence and official pronouncements. He wrote to Frederick Wilhelm IV, for example, that he waged "war neither for worldly advantages nor for conquests, but for a solely Christian purpose." He further lamented that only Russia was willing to fight for the freedom of European Christians living under the Ottoman Empire and asked: "[M]ust I be left alone to fight under the banner of the Holy Cross and to see the others, who call themselves Christians, all unite around the Crescent to combat Christendom?"[9]

Just as Nicholas I, other Russians believed that Russia had an obligation to liberate the Eastern Christians and supported the entry into war.[10] Metropolitan Filaret, the most powerful figure in the Russian Orthodox Church in this era, remarked upon reading the declaration of war, "Really, this might be a biblical struggle, a fight of the people of God with the heathens, only if it were less infected with the usual heathens of the West."[11] The metropolitan expressed a sentiment shared by many: the war was a conflict of biblical proportions and was unnecessarily complicated by the western allies, who having placed politics over faith had abandoned Christianity. Slavophiles had long agitated for Russians to liberate the Eastern Christians and embraced the opportunity to change the face of Europe. Even if A. S. Khomiakov later interpreted the war as a sign of Russian backwardness, his poetry before 1853 cast Slavic bids for independence in providential terms, and at the opening of the struggle attached religious significance to the war.[12]

The ardently nationalist historian Mikhail Pogodin even advocated that Russia take Constantinople. In one of his many fusillades over the war, Pogodin urged his readers: "Here is our purpose—Russian, Slavic, European Christian! As Russians, we must capture Constantinople for our own security! As Slavs, we must liberate millions of our older kinsmen, brothers in faith, educators, and benefactors. As Europeans we must drive out the Turks. As Orthodox Christians, we must protect the Eastern Church and return to Saint Sophia its ecumenical cross."[13] Pogodin emphasized the religious nature of the conflict as did Filaret and Tsar Nicholas. Yet his call to capture Constantinople presented an extreme side of the spectrum. This stance may have appealed to Catherine II seventy years earlier, but not to Nicholas I, who wanted merely to secure freedom of religion for Eastern Christians, not to dissolve the Ottoman Empire. Although as David Goldfrank has suggested, Nicholas I may not have minded if the empire collapsed on its own.[14]

In Russia's Black Sea region, which became the center of fighting, Innokentii infused the moment with his own interpretation, which inveighed against religious politics. "What did we do to Turkey?" he asked the congregants gathered before him. He answered his own question:

> We demanded only what was just and necessary. We demanded that the Orthodox churches and their servitors be given their inviolable freedom, which we have given to Muslims and their mosques in our borders; we demanded that the holy places of Jerusalem, where thousands of devout Russian people flow every year, would not be transferred from hand to hand, like some place bought and sold . . . we demanded that the Orthodox faith would not be reproached for its faith in Muslim eyes; we demanded that when necessary, we could intervene upon the suffering of our brothers of faith, with the right to point out their wounds and shackles. This we demanded for the benefit and peace of the Ottoman power, in [those places] where there are three or four Muslims for tens of Orthodox.[15]

In his sermon, Innokentii reviewed the long list of Russia's complaints against the Ottoman Empire, complaints that had been building for decades and had occupied repeated Russian missions to the Porte. Mainly he emphasized Ottoman mistreatment of Eastern Christians, who as *dhimmis* had fewer rights than Muslim subjects. Interestingly, he compared Christians in the Ottoman Empire with Muslims in Russia. Only Russia, he argued, tolerated the multiple confessions of empire, a statement surely not without irony in light of his earlier critique of Russia's faith-based juridical status. He also pointed to the holy places controversy and protested Ottoman handling of Jerusalem in the wake of French and British claims. Finally, he pressed the right of Russia to intervene on behalf of Eastern Christians living within the Ottoman Empire. One of the more active lobbyists on behalf of Eastern Christians before the war started, the archbishop was one of the war's most enthusiastic supporters once war began.

He, like Filaret, perceived the war as a crusade, a holy mission ordained by God, and Russia's one destiny: "[T]his affair of Christianity is in the hands not of people, but of God. Russia accepted the challenge, made not in words, but of fire and sword. . . . Millions of our brothers in faith wait, like a holiday, for us to rescue them."[16] This pan-Orthodox perspective, characterized by a unified Orthodox world led by Russians, permeated Innokentii's sermons and writings about the war until its end. Innokentii's unswerving, confident presumption that Russia would succeed in this task was gradually replaced by foreboding pessimism as the war progressed. Yet, even at this early date, the archbishop did not anticipate an easy victory. Rather, he compared the problems in the East to a menacing storm that finally settles, "to allow nothing other than a rain of blood, with lightening and thunder of destruction."[17]

As his metaphor portended, the declaration of war opened a long struggle with tremendous loss of life on all sides. The conflict dramatically exposed the weaknesses of outmoded military traditions, while ushering in new technologies and methods of modern warfare, from the telegraph to the trench.[18] Although this war ultimately preserved the delicate balance of the Ottoman Empire, it produced major changes in Europe. It ended the Holy Alliance, catalyzed a unified Germany, and freed the serfs in Russia. The introduction of wartime correspondence and photography also forever changed the culture of war with exposés that immediately revealed to a distant yet powerful public opinion the dark underside of war.[19] Nowhere, however, was the experience of change as great as in Crimea, the primary theater of violence.

Just a few months after Russian troops crossed the Danube in fall of 1853, fighting moved into the Black Sea and transformed Crimean culture and life in immediate, tangible ways. From the first bombardment of Odessa in April of 1854 until the last stage of the siege of Sevastopol in September 1855, the Black Sea region and the peninsula in particular were almost unrecognizable.[20] Enemy troops covered the full shoreline of Crimea, from the western gate of Evpatoria through the Kerch straits in the East. Russia lost tens of thousands of soldiers to fighting and disease, with figures as high as one thousand per day in the summer of 1856. Vast series of barracks dotted the once bucolic countryside; public buildings became hospitals, private homes became officers' quarters, and roads became trenches. Crimea became the focus of the empire and Sevastopol emerged as the mythical "city of Russian glory."[21]

In Crimea, war was accompanied by religious fervor; wartime propaganda portrayed the conflict as one between Orthodoxy and Islam. British, French, and Ottoman troops, in this representation, struck at the heart of Russian Orthodoxy. At stake was not merely the integrity of the Russian state, but the glory of God. On the peninsula itself, Orthodoxy began to replace Islam, and Crimea's special Christian holiness was transmitted across the empire. State officials and military governors viewed Orthodoxy as an essential component of Russia's mission in the Black Sea region, as well as a moral grounding for the troops fighting the war and the citizens under attack. Local priests and prelates became heroes, and like soldiers, they received numerous imperial commendations for their activities, while the new Russian Athos community became the scene of battle. Enemy troops took over and settled themselves in monasteries; other sites became way stations for refugees. While all this transpired, sermons from Crimea were read in various corners of the empire—transmitting both news and religious interpretations of battle.

As Christianity ascended, Islam fell under suspicion. Because Tatars constituted over half of Crimea's population, officials feared that they would side with their Turkish co-religionists and use the war as an opportunity to throw off Russian imperial rule. When the Ottomans settled into Evpatoria in September of 1854, Russian anxieties intensified. Local officials bombarded St. Petersburg with reports about "the mood" of the Tatars, which became more ominous as the Allies progressed through the peninsula. Skirmishes between Tatars and Russians, especially in Evpatoria, Perekop, and Yalta, seemed to legitimize official anxieties.[22] Although these Tatar uprisings were isolated occurrences that rarely spread, Russian officials had already grown impatient with Catherine II's legacy of religious toleration. The Russian military police set up an investigation of Tatars suspected of illegal activities and even infiltrated Tatar villages with spies. Police targeted suspects of all ages, from fifteen-year-old boys to seventy-year-old men. The majority were convicted of treason without trial or evidence. Rarely did the police inform family members of the prisoners' whereabouts, and many of the prisoners died in custody. Furthermore, Tatar villages were exploited by allied and Russian troops; both sides robbed Tatars of livestock, food, and monies.

Before the war, the pace of Christianizing was subtle—unfolding through the artful processes of ritual and memory. During the war, Christianizing became overt and unfurled with the assistance of Russia's military elite. It is in this context, the pain and bloodshed of war, that Crimea's special Christian holiness became fixed in people's minds. The sites selected for the Russian Athos monastic community were made all the more holy by the sacrifice and suffering of Russian troops fighting for Orthodoxy. In Crimea, war created the holy place; it decimated Crimea's Muslim identity and, with it, traditional obstacles to church expansion. After the war, the Russian Orthodox Church became a chief architect of the peninsula's reconstruction.

ODESSA AND THE PRECEDENT OF CLERICAL ACTIVITY DURING THE WAR

The violence of the Crimean War first entered the diocese through Odessa, when French and English troops anchored off the shore and bombarded the city on 10 April 1854, the Saturday before Pascha. Such timing reinforced claims that the Crimean War was a religious war. M.

V. Iuzefovich wrote Pogodin shortly after: "It seems that we stand upon a threshold of a new period in Christianity," a time in which European powers have no respect for the Christian calendar.[23] As Innokentii wrote Count Protasov: "Such rude scorn and neglect for holy days produced distress in all, even the foreigners wonder at this recklessness of Admirals Dundas and Hamelin."[24] For many Russians, the bombardment carried an indisputable religious symbolism, a point that church publicists repeatedly emphasized. At this moment, however, the bombardment was not serious, and the Pascha spray of cannon was most likely intended as a warning. Nonetheless, when Crimean authorities spotted enemy ships on the horizon in the summer of 1854, they took few chances. They encouraged all non-military populations to leave.[25] Only the soldiers, clergy, and the poor Tatar peasants who could not afford to flee remained. By September, the commander of the forces in the Black Sea, Prince Menshikov, had 38,000 troops and 18,000 sailors distributed along the shores of southwestern Crimea, and 12,000 troops in the east around Kerch and Feodosia.[26]

The bombardment of Odessa, in addition to prompting authorities to fortify the Crimean peninsula, established the stage for the church's highly visible role in nationalist myth-making and patriotic discourse. Through a series of sermons that was widely distributed across the empire, Archbishop Innokentii constructed a religious narrative of events that imperial authorities adopted. The sermons portrayed the war as a holy crusade against Islam—the fulfillment of Russia's destiny. They also dramatized the city's heroism, much as later sermons would encode Sevastopol. These sermons depicted Odessans (as well as the soldiers encamped there) as sacrificial victims, called upon to offer their lives to the empire and Christian faith. Through sermons, church publicists generated official and unofficial representations of the war; their efforts were encouraged and rewarded by the highest authorities.

The archbishop and his priests remained in the city to perform their religious obligations, an act that in itself appeared courageous to contemporaries, none of whom could have predicted the relative harmlessness of the bombardment. The archbishop received recognition for his sermons, which not only set out a religious interpretation of the war but also framed official representations of the struggle until its end. Russia entered the war, the archbishop told his congregants, because it "wants freedom of faith and conscience for our brothers in the faith, living under the Muslim yoke, and to save the Cross of Christ and the Gospel from perfect destruction by the Koran." He portrayed Russia as the last Christian nation in Europe to carry the banner of faith and the battle against Islam. In their unholy alliance with the Ottoman Empire, Innokentii argued, France and England shamefully betrayed their Christian duties.[27] Through the rest of the war, the archbishop reinforced the distinctions between Orthodoxy, Catholicism, and Protestantism. Europe's failure to support Russia and the Eastern Christians in the struggle against the Ottoman Empire, he maintained in his sermon, resembled Pontius Pilate's politically motivated refusal to "see the truth" of Christ's holiness.[28]

As Archbishop Innokentii sympathized with the plight of the Eastern Christians, he reinscribed the conflict in deeper religious symbolism associated with the passion of Jesus Christ.[29] All Orthodox Christians, he impressed upon his congregation, would be wiser to develop their inward spiritual strength than to be concerned with the "external," worldly spectacle of the enemy ships anchored in Odessa's harbors. With clean consciences and fortified souls, he promised his anxious diocese, "your fear and your confusion will be removed."[30] He paralleled the plight of the Odessans, who were being bombarded during Easter, to the suffering of Jesus. It was a privilege, he endeavored to convince them, to "suffer for the Orthodox faith." Whether he convinced his congregation to embrace the role of self-sacrifice, he did impress this image upon the empire. His sermons reached an audience far wider than those in his church, for they were printed in *Odesskii vestnik* and released independently in small pamphlets.[31] Periodicals in Russia's largest cities, including the *vedomosti* of Moscow and St. Petersburg, quickly picked them up as well. The sermons' reach extended beyond Russia's reading public, as the words were often read aloud in churches. Their influence, therefore, might better be compared to the wartime *lubki*, or broadsides, which were accessible to a wide stratum of Russian society and not merely to the literary elite.[32]

In addition to interpreting the war through sermons, the church inscribed the war in public religious rituals, a process of representation encouraged by local military elites. On 11 April, 1854 for example, after French and English ships pulled away from Odessa, General Osten-Saken, who commanded Russian forces on the right side of the Bug, invited the archbishop to perform a liturgy at the women's monastery in Odessa jointly with a short military ceremony in the square. Innokentii blessed the soldiers with holy water and performed a service in the name of the tsar and all of Russia's military. In a letter to Baron Korff, he echoed the patriotic sentiments he delivered in Odessa: "There is nothing better than the Orthodox military of ours" that "now burns with the impatience to spill all its blood for the grave of the Lord and for the Orthodox faith."[33] Repeatedly, church publicists portrayed Russian soldiers as Christian crusaders fighting for Orthodoxy. Whether or not military generals like Osten-Saken or Menshikov perceived their obligations in such a messianic light, they encouraged religious mythology presumably because it presented the war in terms most meaningful to the general public. The crisis of war, as the Odessa example shows, quickly bridged the distance between church and state that Prince Voronstov—who retired from his post at the beginning of the war—so long attempted to preserve in New Russia.[34]

The state expressed its approval of Archbishop Innokentii's activities and representation of the conflict by awarding him one of the first commendations issued in the Black Sea theater of war. Immediately after the bombardment, local and regional authorities generated a flurry of reports to the Holy Synod about what they described as the archbishop's courageous, steadfast performance of all liturgies during Holy Week. Documents praised Odessa's local clergy, who did not "swerve from the fulfillment of their callings." Reports seamlessly combined the spectacle of religious ritual with the spectacle of war, writing that "the liturgies were accomplished in all churches of the city on Holy Friday when the enemy navy arrived in Odessa; on Holy Saturday, on the very day of the bombardment when he continued twelve hours in a row; on the Great night of Holy Sunday, and on the following morning, equally as on the previous days."[35]

With dramatic, patriotic rhetoric, imperial accounts praised Innokentii for bravely conducting the liturgies against the threat of menacing warships, falling bombs, grenades, and the spray of bullets. Throughout this dangerous time, reports asserted that Innokentii's sermons "served to raise spirits and to comfort the residents and to support the city with peace and order during an extremely grave time."[36] General Osten-Saken corroborated these reports, writing that the prelate "tirelessly carried out his duties" and insured a general "peacefulness" among the population during the English and French invasion.[37] In consequence, the tsar and the Holy Synod passed an ukase formally recognizing Archbishop Innokentii for "pastoral zealousness" during the bombarding of Odessa.[38] Tsar Nicholas commended Innokentii for bravely appearing in the "theater of war" and concluded that he "had an advantageous influence on the residents and on the military."[39] In the margins of the report, Tsar Nicholas jotted the note, "Praiseworthy."[40] In most historical accounts, the liturgical celebration of Pascha constituted an inseparable part of the day's patriotic memory. In fact, the bombardment of Odessa, despite its minimal consequences, composed a central event in the city's biography, a myth no doubt perpetuated by annual religious processions that commemorated the event until the Russian Revolution.[41]

The bombardment of Odessa proved to be only a minor event of the Crimean War. Yet, it set an important precedent for the diocese and presaged active church participation in the affairs of the military. The church also served as an interface between local Russian subjects and the military. At services, church officials disseminated official news, such as the very declaration of war, and regular church rituals helped preserve order. As the war spread through Crimea, the Russian Orthodox Church assumed greater authority in the lives of its adherents and participated more directly in the war effort. Local priests and newly placed monks became heroes for marching with soldiers and dying in the crossfires. The newly built monasteries and more notably the long-standing St. George monastery at Balaklava fell to enemy troops and housed local and foreign military. The monks and priests who escaped these fallen monasteries fanned out across the peninsula, ministering to soldiers and civilians. Many joined the nurses and the doctors to serve in impromptu hospitals and *lazarety*, or camps. By the end of the war, Russian prelates and clergy in Crimea, who were virtually unnoticed prior to Innokentii's proposal for Russian Athos, had acquired an empire-wide reputation for bravery. They linked Orthodoxy to the peninsula in ways that intensified connections to the sacred previously established mainly by Christian scholarship.

ORTHODOX SERMONS AND THE INVASION OF CRIMEA

The allied invasion of Crimea in September of 1854 amplified holy war propaganda. In a series of sermons that were immediately published in several formats and distributed across the empire, Innokentii placed Orthodoxy at the center of Russian patriotism, and Crimea at the center of Russian national identity. The first series of sermons began when the archbishop rushed to the eastern half of his diocese after allied troops landed in early September. He informed the Synod of his decision, writing that Crimea was in a state of "confusion" due to the "extreme conditions of the war" and the "mutinous uprising of the Tatars."[42] Carrying a locally revered icon from Odessa, Innokentii arrived in Crimea's provincial capital, Simferopol, to embark on his tour. With the icon and an entourage, Innokentii traveled to Feodosia, Bakhchisarai, Karasubazar, and Genichesk to ritually bless the cities most in danger. Due to the impassable conditions of the roads, the group could not reach Sevastopol. Nevertheless, the archbishop aimed his sermons toward the city under siege and publicized its sufferings to distant corners of the empire.

As with the series of sermons in Odessa, those in Crimea cast the struggle with the Ottoman Empire and western allies as a religious conflict. Literally, Innokentii described the war as "a holy war (*bran' sviashchennaia*)—fought not for worldly advantages, but for the holiness and the honor of the cross of Christ."[43] Much as before, he portrayed the Crimean

War as a culmination of Russia's destiny and the fulfilling of a Christian obligation. Russia had a "great and holy calling to be the protector of the Orthodox faith," to "free its brothers in faith and in ethnicity from the Muslim yoke."[44] The tropes of Ottoman despotism, messianic Russia, and the centrality of Orthodoxy to Russian identity paralleled themes in the sermons first delivered in Odessa. An increasing emphasis on martyrdom and heroic sacrifice, however, distinguished the sermons in Crimea from earlier ones. In the early stages of the war in Crimea, Archbishop Innokentii portrayed the peninsula and its inhabitants as willing, selfless victims, prepared to sacrifice their lives for the war. Their hardships, he insisted, would not be in vain, but would serve "all of orthodox Christianity" and "great, all-powerful Russia."[45] Here as elsewhere, Innokentii established a trope that invoked sympathy for Crimea from all imperial observers.

These sermons also contained more pronounced elements of coercion and persuasion, to motivate soldiers and remaining civilians to flee in order to commit selfless acts of heroism. Innokentii asked them: "[W]ouldn't it be better, if in the various places of the empire people were to say that you exceeded expectations, in your bravery and in your firm spirit?" He emphasized that all eyes in Russia were upon Crimea and that "all true sons of the fatherland, and even the blessed Monarch" expected only the most courageous and daring of feats, and not "weak spirits or short-sightedness." He asked his audience whether they preferred "eternal glory, or eternal shame—blessings or indelible reproach."[46] He argued that the war was quickly passing, and those who waited to express their heroism and generosity of spirit would lose their chance.[47] Through sermons, therefore, Innokentii urged soldiers to fight fearlessly for Russia, and implored civilians to meet the soldiers' needs, to provide food, shelter, and anything necessary. Throughout, he emphasized civic duty, clarifying that Russia would not attain victory without the support of its subjects.[48]

Just as the sermons portrayed Crimeans as martyrs for the faith, they also depicted the peninsula as a special holy land, a representation that imperial officials readily adapted. Sermons extended the prewar Christianizing discourse into a basis for religious patriotism. Archbishop Innokentii emphasized that because Crimea was the site of ancient encounters between Islam and Orthodoxy, it was uniquely destined to host the current fray. Prince Vladimir, as Innokentii later reminded his congregation, was baptized in nearby Chersonesos, which brought a "special grace" to the peninsula, and likewise obligated all of its inhabitants to fight the "union of unbelievers arriving from the west."[49] He urged his congregation forward to show that it was not for nothing they "lived in the very cradle of [Russian] Christianity and the land of the martyrs and saints."⁵⁰ He reinforced the idea of Crimea's holiness by invoking its history of saints: "Isn't it from here that the light of the Orthodox faith shone on all of Russia? Did not the saints of Chersonesos lay down their lives for our souls?" All of the efforts of the saints, he argued, "might remain in vain," and the "cross of the Christianity" would not be able to overcome the "Crescent of the Muslim," if Crimean residents neglected their patriotic duty.⁵¹

As one of the church's most prominent prelates and passionate preachers, who was himself living through the most extreme theater of battle, Archbishop Innokentii presented an authoritative, powerful, and influential narrative of the war. His sermons influenced popular interpretations of the war and were sanctioned and encouraged by the government. He received official recognition for the second time since the beginning of the war when an imperial ukase commended him for the "pastoral zeal" he displayed during his visit to Crimea in the middle of "war circumstances and the mutinous uprising of the Tatars, which produced confusion in the local orthodox population."⁵² In the ukase, officials in St. Petersburg praised Innokentii for voluntarily exposing himself to the hardships of war. The ukase also expressed a reoccurring belief that the words of the archbishop provided an element of comfort and order to a distressed population.

The reoccurring themes of holy war and courageous sacrifice quickly found a reflection in newspapers and other literary mediums across the empire. After the storm of 2/14 November 1854, which damaged the allied fleet and gave Russia a temporary advantage, a feuilleton in *Odesskii vestnik* concluded that the storm was evidence of divine intervention.⁵³ "Isn't it obvious," the writer asked, "that the hand of God raised the elements against our arrogant enemies?" Now the allies could plainly see that God sided with Tauride and its "indestructible courageous defense of the Monarch, the Orthodox faith and the fatherland."⁵⁴ This particular feuilleton was composed by F. M. Dombrovskii, the scholar who had earlier described the religious procession in Bakhchisarai for *Odesskii vestnik*. As the example above demonstrates, Dombrovskii continued to participate in Crimea's Christianizing discourse. In this case, Dombrovskii's views were picked up by newspapers across the empire, including *Moskovskie vedomosti*. In concert with religious authorities, Russian scholars in the Black Sea region continued to cast their environment in Orthodox terms, a process that gained increasing attention as the war took over the peninsula.

In addition to infusing patriotic discourse with Orthodox themes and rhetorically constructing Crimea as holy, the sermons also inspired residents to build new monasteries and churches. Even during the most extreme moments of war, the archbishop did not forget his Russian Athos project. In Feodosia, he motivated parishioners to build a church in the name of St. Stefan of Surozh, who he argued, protected them from the devastating attacks occurring in the western side of the peninsula. St. Stefan was a local saint known for opposing the iconoclastic rule of the eighth-century emperor Leo III the Isaurian (717–714).[55] As a seasoned fighter for the faith, St. Stefan stood "at the throne of God as a continuous petitioner and strong protector."[56] He urged congregants to embrace their local saint, to petition that saint to faithfully celebrate his holiday, and to teach his memory to their children. If the residents wanted to preserve peace, they should encourage the "wealthy" to build a small church for the saint.[57]

Similarly, a year later, Innokentii encouraged the people of Crimea to support building at the spring of Cosmas and Damian. This time, he employed much stronger rhetoric to construct a parallel between Russia's losses in the war and the neglect of the churches in Crimea: "Maybe this fiery battle has risen as a response to our former coldness to our ancient holy sites *(sviatyn)*." Innokentii proposed to his congregation: "If God were to see that we have changed and have sufficient feelings of zealous faith, and all that that entails . . . an end to the destruction will come and we will return to the peace and blessings that God wishes for you and for our country."[58] Renewing ancient churches and building the bathhouse at the spring of Cosmas and Damian, the archbishop argued, would restore Crimea to grace. Delivered in July 1855, these words can also be seen as an attempt to rationalize Russia's apparent losses. Whatever their rationale, Innokentii's sermons had their desired effect, because after the war, Feodosia's congregation established another skete in the "Russian Athos" complex under the name of St. Stefan, and laity across the peninsula contributed for a monastery at the spring of Cosmas and Damian.

Archbishop Innokentii and the Last Siege of Sevastopol

The sermons that became most central to religious patriotism and Crimea's Christian identity were delivered in Sevastopol at the beginning of the third stage of the siege. With the Crimean War, Sevastopol acquired another layer of nationalist meaning—Russia's "city of glory." Similar to the myths following the battle of Borodino, which prefaced Russia's strategic withdrawal from Moscow in 1812, the extraordinary losses Russia suffered in Sevastopol became the basis of the city's heroism.[59]

The circumstances of the siege of Sevastopol are well known. For over a year, allied ships laid siege to the city. Sevastopol's success in withstanding the attack has been attributed to the autocracy's ability to rapidly mobilize resources and to the brilliance of the chief engineer Eduard Totleben, whose memoir reconstructed the scene for posterity.[60] More popular accounts credit the city's long-standing survival to sailors' and soldiers' selfless bravery. Most of the heroes were cast as martyrs for the faith, men willing to sacrifice their lives for Orthodoxy and for Russia. Orthodoxy occupied the center of these popular and official representations of Sevastopol, while martyrdom and religious imagery permeated patriotic discourse on multiple levels. Here as elsewhere in this chapter, one can argue that Innokentii's sermons provided the primary religious framework for interpreting the siege for the rest of the empire. Innokentii himself became a hero of the siege and entered into representations, memoirs, and other nationalist writings as a key subject, much like other heroes in the military.

Archbishop Innokentii visited Sevastopol from 24 to 27 June 1855. He conducted liturgies in the camp parish at the upper fortifications and in the middle of the city at the Nikolaev church. (At this point in the war, Russia's troops were losing about 300 to 400 men a day, a number that would climb to 1,000 with the bombardment of August.)[61] Innokentii's sermons had become among the most legendary of the war and reiterated familiar themes of religious patriotism. He began with words of sympathy, recognizing that there was no place of battle that had suffered like Sevastopol, "nowhere has the grief been greater, nowhere have the wounded been more ill." He emphasized that all of Russia knew of Sevastopol's suffering, and that throughout the empire, "there is not one son in the fatherland whose thoughts are not continuously occupied with the brave defenders" of the city.[62] He told the soldiers going into battle to firmly remember: "Russia is behind you and God is above you."[63] The sermon openly addressed the imminence of death with the words: "there is a time to act, a time to pray, and if necessary, a time to die as Christians and sons" of Russia.[64] This sermon was delivered at the behest of General Mikhail Gorchakov, the supreme commander of the military in Sevastopol who had replaced Prince Menshikov, at the most extreme point of battle. It became the most famous of Innokentii's wartime writings, and constituted a legendary moment in the war. It also elevated Innokentii to the status of a venerated war hero. A spectacular broadside from the Crimean War, in fact, centers on the sermon of 26 June.

The *lubok*, or broadside, pictured below depicts the scene of the sermon, widely attended by all estates in Crimea, with allied ships in the background. The archbishop and local priests from Sevastopol occupy

Sevastopol: the troops receive a blessing. Courtesy of State Historical Museum, Moscow, Russia (lubok, inv. GIM 46639 I III chrom. 8121)

the focal point of the picture, and images of local orthodox churches are clearly evident in the upper right-hand corner. Each clergy member holds a religious object to be used in the blessing of the city. Russian troops, military elite, and townspeople surround the priests. The caption lists the most illustrious attendees by name, including Gorchakov and Admiral Nakhimov. It also excerpts pieces of the sermon, ending with a note that "the scene was very moving."[65]

The print seen here in Figure 16 supplies only one popular representation of the sermon. Many others appeared in local newspapers and, after the war, in memoirs. An interesting example connects the sermon of 26 June with one of Sevastopol's military heroes, Admiral Nakhimov. Although Nakhimov was a secondary figure in the defense of Sevastopol, popular accounts identified him as the inspiration for the city's defense.[66] His death provided further material for his lionization. He was struck by a bullet while inspecting the city's third and fourth bastions on 28 June/ 10 July and died during the night three days later.[67] The account below romanticizes his death and includes a story about Nakhimov spending his last days praying with the archbishop:

On June 26, as if to say goodbye to this world, the admiral attended the celebratory service and religious procession on the square, arranged by the famous spiritual orator Archbishop Innokentii, whose strong able speeches expressed the meaning of Sevastopol for all of Russia—speeches having particular strength delivered against the loud thunder of artillery and bombs. At the completion of the ceremony, each of the bastions received a blessing of the icon.[68]

Above, the memoir not only links Nakhimov's valor to the archbishop, but casts Innokentii in heroic terms as well. It emphasizes that the archbishop placed himself in danger, in the midst of the "thunder of artillery and bombs," to piously bless the soldiers. The memoir also iterates the theme of this chapter, that Innokentii "express[ed] the meaning of Sevastopol for all of Russia." In addition to achieving recognition for his heroism in the press, Innokentii received another commendation from the tsar for his performance. The archbishop was extolled for "his blessings to the military, which he sent from the garrisons to the battery" and for the "eloquent sermons, that wished new success for the defeat of the enemy."[69] From the beginning of the war in Odessa to the siege of Sevastopol, these sermons shaped a religious patriotic discourse that permeated official and popular treatments of the war. They found a permanent echo in Leo Tolstoy's *Sebastopol Sketches*, which frequently alluded to the importance of Orthodoxy in soldiers' views of the war.[70]

Innokentii's sermons and their popular representation forged a lasting identity for the peninsula. Throughout each of his sermons, the archbishop maintained that the peninsula would become more important in the empire, more Christian, more Russian. The sacrifice of the Tauridians would attract "special attention and the heart of the Monarch . . . the sincere respect of all Russia . . . new blessings from the heavenly kingdom," and the gratitude of all of Russia. The accomplishments of the war would not only put Tauride on the map, but would also literally transform it. The Crimean War, he often asserted, marked the final stage of Crimea's reunion with Russia, and returned the territory to its former sacred status:

> I see already Tauride finally rising from the dust of a half-existing society—from the unhappy remains of the barbaric leadership of the Tatar khan. I see how all parts of this peninsula entered into the lively and powerful status of Russia, taking from it a new life and fortification; how Khersones-Tauride returns fully to its ancient Christianity, and eternal holiness revealed by the ruins.[71]

Similar to the view found in his prewar Christian scholarship, Innokentii portrayed Tatar rule in Crimea as an ill-fated anomaly, an interruption of the peninsula's destiny as a Christian holy place of great renown. He also perpetuated themes of Crimea's Christian history and sacred ruins. The war did not displace earlier Christianizing discourses with new ideas, but extended and intensified pre-existing ones.

PRIESTS IN THE FIELDS AND IN THEIR CHURCHES

The metaphoric ascendancy of Orthodoxy on the peninsula had a dramatic reflection in the enhanced role of the Orthodox clergy. With the tremendous loss of life following the battle of Alma (20 September 1854), through the last siege of Sevastopol in September of 1855, the Orthodox clergy of Crimea found themselves in an increased level of mobilization and in a more direct participation in the war effort. As Menshikov transformed Crimea into a state of war-readiness, local diocesan authorities in Crimea moved quickly to prepare its priests and parishes for war. Innokentii believed that the churches and monasteries were uniquely situated to assist the military.[72] In the middle of November 1854, Innokentii reported to Count Protasov that "various places in Crimea," even "the roads that lead into the villages," reported an insufficiency of field priests and an "extreme need" for clergy to tend and to confess the wounded. The chain of communication, originating with local priests through Innokentii to the Holy Synod, demonstrated a surprising efficiency and flexibility to respond to the immediacy of crisis and the needs of its own. One innovation included a supplementary cadre of diocesan priests to minister to the thousands of sailors and soldiers who composed Russia's army and navy. These priests were assigned to the authority of Dormition monastery, and were stationed in the military camps and in the "very fields of battle."[73] They also became the subjects of patriotic representations, a theme the archbishop actively promoted.[74]

Russian Orthodox priests in Crimea did contribute significantly to the war effort and received recognition for their work. Many attained visibility by working with the Russian Sisters of Mercy founded by Grand Duchess Elena Pavlovna.[75] In October 1854, the grand duchess received permission to establish another society, the Order of the Exaltation of the Cross (*Krestnovozdvizhenskaya*). Supervised by the grand duchess, the society was composed of nurses, who with "warm love and personal selflessness," would care for the wounded and the ill and "relieve suffering through Christian comfort," work to be done in close cooperation with medical authorities in the war hospitals.[76] The nurses were placed in Crimea's war hospitals under the authority of the leading medical professor Nikolai Pirogov.[77] Given the perceived spiritual nature of their duties, however, Elena Pavlovna requested Protasov to enlist additional support from Crimean priests.[78] Diocesan authorities quickly concurred with the wishes of the grand duchess and appointed twelve monks and priests to work with the sisters in several different camps: Sevastopol, Bakhchisarai, Kherson, Simferopol, Karasubazar, Feodosia, and Perekop.[79]

In addition to working with the sisters, many priests were appointed to Russian camps to perform liturgies and give final rites. With the onset of the winter in 1854, the allied and Russian armies remained moored in gridlock. The long, difficult winter depleted both sides, and the hospitals filled up with men stricken by scurvy, cholera, and typhus.[80] As the war intensified, so did the demand for priests, who were needed to tend to the ever-increasing numbers of wounded and dying. Priests suffered along with Russian soldiers, especially those stationed on the front. In January 1855, a monk appointed to Inkerman monastery, but restationed to a camp in Sevastopol at the northern flank of the army, reported that many of the priests on the southern shores were deeply unhappy, impoverished with the upheavals of the war, and starving.[81]

In the middle of their difficulties, priests acquired reputations for bravery and courage. Many were praised for voluntarily participating in the war, while others gained recognition for heroic deeds. Stories of Father Ioann Savinov, a naval priest who fought in the Kamchatka line during the siege of Sevastopol, inundated broadsides, newspapers, military memoirs, and patriotic poetry.[82] According to most accounts, Savinov did not fight, but rushed into battle with his regiment to inspire and bless the troops with holy religious objects. A story in a St. Petersburg newspaper describes Father Savinov marching "with our columns, holding a cross in his hands, inspiring the military and calming the wounded during all times of the war."[83] *Russkii invalid*, a chief publication of the Ministry of War, counted Father Savinov among the pantheon of Crimean heroes from the siege of Sevastopol, along with Gorchakov, General Lieutenant Khrulev, and others. Like Innokentii, Savinov was the subject of *lubki*. In the picture here, captioned "Hieromonk Savinov's exploit," Father Ioann appears as a central figure—clearly distinguished in the right foreground—outstretched arms, raising a cross over troops in battle. Innokentii actively promoted the myth of Savinov's heroism, emphasizing that the cleric selflessly volunteered to be with the troops "despite the spray of bullets and the possibility of being taken captive."[84] The tsar awarded the monk, who ultimately died from a contusion suffered during the siege, the St. Gregory Medal of the fourth degree.[85]

In addition to Father Savinov, Archbishop Innokentii actively promoted all priests as heroes and argued that servitors "who remained in their places despite extreme danger" should be counted as "senior or junior

Hieromonk Savinov's exploit. Courtesy of State Historical Museum, Moscow, Russia (lubok, inv. GIM 46639 I III chrom. 21768)

warriors." The archbishop often invoked the story of Father Briukhovskii, a priest who refused to evacuate Yalta when it was taken by the Allies in September 1854. For days, according to this legend, Briukhovskii barricaded the church against British soldiers, who "swearing, drinking and breaking things," pounded on locked doors.[86] When these soldiers finally forced their way into the church, they stole money the parishioners had placed in front of icons, and they dismantled the windows.[87] Once Yalta fell to British occupation, Briukhovskii was transferred to Berdiansk, a city hundreds of kilometers away, which at that time had seen no military activity. In the summer of 1855, however, troops entered Berdiansk at least two times. Due to Briukhovskii's "energetic and courageous supervision," neither of the churches in Berdiansk lost valuables. Instead, according to Briukhovskii, French troops came to pray:

The Vice Admiral appeared at the door of the church around nine o'clock in the morning. He took off his hat, and entered the church. He looked into the interior and around at the iconostasis. He then kneeled at the altar, and left, saying that he would not bother the church. A half an hour later, a French officer with a few soldiers came to the church, and through a translator, asked if they could look around. After the respect shown by the Vice Admiral, I nodded, taking the key. I opened the door, and they, taking off their hats, entered behind me, and asked about the local icons. Then they asked if they might look at the altar. I, through a translator, said that the officer might enter, but that the soldiers were forbidden. After looking at the altar, the officer thanked us for complying with their request, and together with the soldiers, left the church. At one o'clock in the afternoon, the enemy left the city for their ships, and a couple of hours later, left the city altogether.[88]

The preceding account, which circulated to the Holy Synod, portrayed the French as showing deep reverence for Orthodoxy, a theme starkly in contrast to Briukhovskii's earlier experience with the British. Whereas Briukhovskii had been praised for attempting to protect the church from British troops, here he was commended for revealing to the enemy the glory of the Orthodox faith. The archbishop praised him again for his "selfless priesthood" and for "conducting services even to the respect of the enemy itself."[89] For his efforts protecting the churches, Innokentii elaborated by saying, "despite the removal of all residents from the city, Briukhovskii did not once abandon his post, even during the time of bombardment."[90] Priests like Briukhovskii and Savinov were meant to represent the heroic actions of all of Crimea's Orthodox clergy who were assigned to troops or hospitals, or to tend refugees. The images of these clergy reinforced the role of Orthodoxy during the war, and more locally, the new vital role of the clergy in Crimea. After the war, it was impossible to separate the peninsula from either the heroic priests or its martyrdom.

The Monasteries

In addition to the work of the archbishop and the priests, the monasteries assumed a heroic role of highly visible proportions. Monks at the monasteries, especially Dormition monastery in Bakhchisarai, played vital parts and contributed to the war as much as parish clergy. Three of the monasteries associated with the new Russian Athos community were at scenes of battle: St. George at Balaklava and the monasteries under renovation at Inkerman and Chersonesos. Monks of the new Crimean skites, the archbishop argued later to the Holy Synod, "showed untiring energy in the spiritual supervision of the war wounded" and sacrificed their own lives to the fever and disease that quickly overtook the camps.[91]

Due to its distance from the theater of battle, the Dormition monastery in Bakhchisarai organized communication between the prelates and the parish priests.[92] After the devastating battle of Inkerman, and the perplexing battle of Balaklava, better known for the Charge of the Light Brigade, the monastery assumed new responsibilities for refugees. Following the Charge of the Light Brigade, in which priests reported that the foolhardy British cavalry "fought like lions," because "up to the last of them were drinking,"[93] the monastery absorbed scores of refugees who "flowed like lava" on the road between Bakhchisarai and Balaklava.[94]

By the fall of 1854, the centrally located Dormition monastery became a waypoint for many of the refugees evacuating Sevastopol, Evpatoria, Balaklava, and surrounding villages. The abbot expressed the seriousness of the situation to diocesan authorities, remarking that "the enemies, like locusts, are surrounding Crimea, and are squeezing the cities, causing people to flee. Not wishing to judge the runners, I nevertheless have to ask, to where will they run?" He noted that the monastery had already absorbed the priests and servitors from the community at Chersonesos, and anticipated the arrival of those from Inkerman. The numbers of monks flowing into Bakhchisarai from the new monasteries were overwhelming, and he asked the archbishop to accommodate new arrivals in monasteries further north.[95]

While Dormition monastery caught overflow from the towns lining the coasts, other monasteries struggled to survive. The Inkerman skete, which was located close to the enemy's camp, survived the battle of Inkerman with minimal damage. All of its movable property was transferred to Dormition monastery, where its brothers were also staying.[96] By virtue of its proximity to Sevastopol, however, Chersonesos fared much worse. It became a target from the first bombardment in October 1854.[97] All of the new structures in Chersonesos were occupied by the French battalion that used the monks' quarters to store munitions.[98] The new church had been burned to the ground, and the roads to Chersonesos, including that which lined the territory surveyed by Aleksandr Uvarov, had been transformed into trenches.[99]

While all three monasteries and their servitors received recognition for their suffering during the war, the one that attracted most attention by far was the St. George monastery at Balaklava. Allied forces took over the monastery on 14 September 1854 and quickly transformed it into a base of operations. The fate of the monks concerned diocesan authorities and captured imaginations across the empire. For months, diocesan authorities pressed civil and military officials for information about the monks. In early February, Innokentii finally received correspondence from Archimandrite Gerontiia, the abbot of the monastery. He obtained this letter through the express permission of General François Canrobert, the French chief of command.[100] The archimandrite reassured diocesan authorities that all of the community, "thanks to God, are living and are healthy." French officials allowed the monks to perform Orthodox rituals and left them to their own devices.[101] A year later, during the siege of Sevastopol, Innokentii received a second correspondence from the monastery through the cooperation of the French commander and the Russian general, Osten-Saken. As before, the archimandrite wrote that all monks were healthy and that they performed religious services everyday.[102] After the war, the naval monks and all other brothers associated with St. George monastery received medals: "For Defending Sevastopol" and "In Memory of the War of 1853–1856."[103] The monks of Balaklava became heroes, just as the priests who walked with soldiers in battle and the archbishop who delivered sermons on the bastions of Sevastopol.

For the diocese, the war in the Black Sea ended the same way it began, with the enemy flotilla anchored in Odessa's harbors.[104] On 26 September at nine o'clock in the morning, allied boats appeared in the harbors and remained there for several days. Especially after the devastating bombardment of Sevastopol, the sight of the flotilla sent some residents of the city into total panic; many fled, anticipating that Odessa would bear similar losses. Businesses and government offices closed, and the city prepared for evacuation. During the allied occupation of Odessa's harbors, however, the archbishop and the entire clergy of the city remained calm. They performed a continuous liturgy in the cathedral church, focusing all prayers on the Mother of God icon there.[105] The church services, according to the archbishop, "comforted the population who could see the enemy's navy."[106] Altogether, the allied navy stayed for six days, but did not fire on the city. On Sunday, 2 October, the enemy lifted anchor and sailed to sea. Later, Innokentii would credit the city's preservation to the protection of the miraculous icon.

Due to his energetic participation in the war in both halves of his diocese, Archbishop Innokentii acquired the epithet, "great patriot of the fatherland," a descriptor first coined by Pogodin. On the occasion of the archbishop's death in 1857, Pogodin waxed eloquent:

> This was not only a prelate, theologian, and orator, but a great citizen of Russia, whose soul felt all pressing questions of the fatherland, whose heart broke with all its wounds, whose mind was continuously occupied with thoughts of its healing, who was always prepared to sacrifice his life. . . .

> During the first news of the enemy invasion of Crimea, he flew there, placing himself in the middle of danger to bless the Russian military for their holy feats and to animate their faith . . . In Odessa, in the middle of falling bombs and cannons, Innokentii accomplished liturgies on Great Saturday, without trembling underneath the fire of bullets from the enemy flotilla and supported the entire people with sacred guardians.
>
> Innokentii appeared in all bastions, in all camps, in all hospitals, and did not miss one occasion during the continuation of three fatal years, in order to bring everywhere words of life, hope, and faith.[107]

Pogodin's assessment covered the primary feats attributed to Innokentii, namely, his patriotic sermons in Odessa and Sevastopol. In addition to the three commendations of bravery Innokentii received with the support of General Osten-Saken, Prince Menshikov, General Gorchakov, and both of the tsars, Nicholas and Alexander, he was also awarded the St. Gregory Medal in 1856. He received the medal in "recognition of [his] military participation from 13 September 1854 to 27 August 1855 in defense of Sevastopol." The order announcing the medal praised the archbishop for "visiting the city, and under heavy enemy fire, bringing to the church of God warm prayers to the Highest Creator, sprinkling holy water on the brave defenders of Sevastopol and blessing them with the Holy icons, and for unprecedented exploits, evidently sharing the general danger of the military there."[108] The awards given to Innokentii paralleled those distributed to the monks and priests, many of whom received special commendations for their bravery.

THE TATARS

As the Russian prelate emphasized the religious character of the Crimean War, the majority of Tatars in Tauride went to great lengths to distance themselves from the mutinies that occurred in Evpatoria, Perekop, and later in Feodosia. On 6 October 1854, for example, the Tauride Muslim Spiritual Assembly passed a resolution stating their rejection of the mutineers. They began by referencing the event: "Information has revealed that a number of Muslims in the Tauride province, taking an oath to the Tsar of Imperial Russia to be faithful subjects, violated the oath, and many have already passed over to the enemy that has appeared in the borders of Russia in the city of Evpatoria." The resolution continued in no uncertain terms: "Breaking the oath is strongly forbidden, by Russian, and equally by Islamic law." They concluded their statement with a long discussion of the severe punishments for disloyalty according to Islamic law, which included amputating the hand and foot, and even the death sentence.[109] Here, the Tatar Muslim Spiritual Assembly unequivocally cast their support behind the tsar and military, and clarified that they would prosecute any Tatars proven to be traitors.

The Nogai Tatars, who occupied the northern parts of the Tauride province in the Dnepr, Melitopol', and Berdiansk districts, also expressed their disproval of the Tatar actions in Evpatoria. Their petition, dated 12 October 1854, clarified their loyalty to the tsar: "Located more than 70 years under the scepter of the Great Tsar of Russia, the Nogai feel themselves to be fully happy in their status and wish to show their gratitude and recognition, for the generous care of the government, and together with this to show how separate they are from those ill-intentioned and ungrateful Crimean Tatars who demonstrate friendly disposition to the enemies of Russia."[110] To prove their loyalty to the war effort, each district donated food, clothing, and money to the imperial Russian army. They concluded their petition by emphasizing that the "Nogai do not have any kind of relationship with the ill-willed Crimean Tatars," and reiterated their oath "to the throne and the fatherland."[111]

At first, the imperial government accepted these two petitions at face value. The Tauride governor Vladimir Pestel' received these petitions in good faith, and forwarded them to Prince Menshikov, who in turn forwarded them to the tsar. "After listening to excerpts of the resolution and petition" from Tauride Tatars, Tsar Nicholas announced "to the Tauride Muslim Assembly and the Nogai tribes" his gratitude "for their expression of their loyalty."[112] Convinced that the mutiny of a few did not characterize the attitude of the entire population, Tsar Nicholas agreed that the Muslim Spiritual Administration should carry on as it always had, including trying Tatars accused of crimes. Despite official support from Tsar Nicholas, however, many local administrators remained suspicious of all Tatars.

After investigating the Tatar mutinies in Evpatoria up to the end of the war, authorities in Crimea generated report after report of Tatars who had been collaborating with the enemy, revealing the whereabouts of Russian forces, and providing the enemy with stores of food. None of these reports was based on hard evidence. Rather, the reports were a loose collection of rumors and denunciations, which appear to have begun as early as April of 1854 with speculations about the "mood of the Tatars" published in a German newspaper. Although some sources credit Prince Menshikov with designs to relocate the Tatars after the allied landing on Evpatoria, Count Adlerberg, the military governor general of Simferopol and Tauride, was the chief driving force behind surveillance of Tatars.[113] Before arriving in Crimea in 1854, Adlerberg had a long career in Russian service. He fought in campaigns in the Caucasus and led Russian troops into Hungary in 1849. A devout Orthodox Christian, he also recorded a memoir of his travel through holy places, published in 1853 under the title *Iz Rima v Ierusalim*.[114] Throughout the war, Adlerberg organized the intelligence around the Crimean Tatars. He collected reports on their activities and was responsible for having several arrested and exiled to Kursk.

None of the allegations against the Tatars are likely. The majority of Tatars in Crimea were illiterate and impoverished; it is hard to imagine their organizing a spy ring, much less voluntarily relinquishing food and animals that they themselves desperately needed. According to some sources, Tatars applied repeatedly to the Russian government for protection from the invading allied forces that terrorized the countryside. Yet the government did not, or could not, come to their aid. Making matters worse, Don and Ural Cossacks entered Crimea from the north, through Simferopol, and subjected the Tatars to another wave of terror. The Cossacks, self-organized in unofficial and unsupervised units, were drawn into Crimea in the fall of 1854 by Menshikov, ostensibly to give local Crimeans support against the Allies. The results were predictably disastrous; the Cossacks failed to protect the Tatars and instead reenacted centuries' old hostilities.[115]

With continued devastation of war, Tatars found themselves caught between Russian surveillance, marauding Cossacks, and hungry Allies. They began to leave Crimea in a slow trickle from the fall of 1854 through the spring of 1855. Among the first people to detect their absence were the land commissioners. On 30 June 1855, the Simferopol land adjustor reported to Adlerberg that a local aristocrat by the name of Abdulla Murza Dzhaniiskii together with thirteen members of his family gathered their property and "went to the enemy [Ottoman Empire]."[116] According to the adjustor, Dzhaniiskii invited other members of the village to join him, but no one else at that time wanted to go. Later, in December of 1855, forty-six men and fifty women abandoned their homes in the village of Kuchuk-koi.[117] Only one elderly man and four women remained. When questioned by Yalta authorities, they explained that "they did not know what happened, for the residents left in the middle of the night." These early departures caused some concern among local officials, but they did not prepare the officials for the masses of people who left after the war was over.

On 22 April 1856, 4,500 Tatars left Balaklava for Constantinople, because as the governor-general's office of New Russia reported: "The Turkish government secretly invited Crimean Tatars to relocate in Turkey." This mass exodus of Tatars so alarmed local officials that they brought the matter to the tsar himself, asking if they should throw up barriers to prevent the future departure of Tatars. Alexander II, who assumed the throne after Nicholas I passed away in March 1855, responded that there was no reason to prevent relocation of Tatars and, in fact, wrote that "it would be advantageous to rid the peninsula of this harmful population."[118] Subsequently, the tsar's statement was forwarded to all of Crimea's districts, including those most affected by the war: Perekop, Yalta, Theodosia, and Evpatoria.[119] In this area of the empire, the tsar-liberator Alexander II, who was credited with the Great Reforms, is known as the tsar-oppressor, responsible for the massive relocations along the Pontic rim.[120]

The new Russian general-governor, Count Aleksandr Stroganov, the callous bureaucrat who replaced the enlightened administrator of New Russia, Prince Vorontsov, interpreted the tsar's words strictly and communicated to regional officials in Crimea that "His Imperial Greatness ordered that it was *necessary* [my emphasis] to free the region of this harmful population."[121] Thus, with the change of regime at the end of the Crimean War, the Russian government officially approved and encouraged the departure of Crimea's native population, and Stroganov even changed the idea of Crimean Tatars leaving from being "advantageous" or desirable, to "necessary." Here under Stroganov and Tsar Alexander II, the state came to its closest articulation of policy: official encouragement of Tatar emigration.

The Crimean War re-created, at home, the international conflict between Eastern Christians and Muslims. Churches were robbed, monasteries were occupied by enemy troops, and many church structures were razed to the ground. At the same time, however, the crisis of war provided an opportunity for the church to take a leading role in the peninsula. It brought an end to religious toleration and cleared the way for overt Christianizing. The physical destruction of Crimea was accompanied by an ideological reconstruction. Legends of the Tatar khanate were dismantled to make way for tales of Russian suffering, and a new pious Christian history was erected in its place.

At the same time, the war accelerated the Tatar's decline, as nearly 200,000 Tatars emigrated to the Ottoman Empire in the following decade. Before the war, Christianity spread subtly through the peninsula in sacred discourses and architectural renewal. The church strove to create a foundation of special holiness for the peninsula based in Christian antiquity, Byzantine ruins, and parallels with Mt. Athos. Now, however, following the intensive experience of war, religion acquired a new meaning on the peninsula. After the uprisings of the Tatars, Catherine's program of religious toleration seemed no longer applicable, while the Tatar departure left a void that was easy for the church to fill. Russian Orthodoxy became synonymous with Russian patriotism and Crimea became a sacred outpost of holy Russia.

Chapter Six

THE LEGACY OF WAR FOR CRIMEAN CHRISTIANITY

In 1869, a man who identified himself only as D. Sokolov asserted that "Crimea is known more or less in all places of Russia," a fact that he attributed to the Crimean War. During the last war, he argued, "all branches of literature published the activities of western enemies and familiarized Russia with the localities of Crimea." The sacrifices of the heroes who fought and fell in Sevastopol "flowed for the glory of the faith, the Tsar and the fatherland, uniting Crimea with Russia in one family." Throughout the empire, "*Crimea* was repeated in the speech of merchant estates and in the stories of simple people, its name began to be more well known, not only as before when only people of the higher ranks knew about it, or those close to it in neighboring territories."[1] The war, Sokolov contended, put Crimea at the center of the empire.

As the war familiarized Russians with Crimea, it changed the peninsula forever. Islam declined and Christianity moved into its place. Population exchanges between the Russian and Ottoman Empires altered demographic composition and hence the confessional balance. Remarks by Bishop Germogen (Dobronravov, 1882–1885) summarize the role of the war in the peninsula's Christianizing: "In general before the Crimean War the Christian population grew slowly and from year to year, new churches increased by one, by two, and sometimes by three . . . but after the Crimean War, when 85,000 [sic] Tatars left Crimea for Turkey and especially after the foundation of an independent Tauride diocese, the number of churches and parishes significantly increased."[2]

Prior to the war, the governor-general of New Russia and viceroy of the Caucasus, Prince Vorontsov, actively opposed the spread of Christian institutions in Crimea. He repeatedly blocked efforts to establish an Orthodox hierarchy there, fearing it would "germinate among the natives unfounded dangerous thoughts about intentions of deflecting them from Islam and converting them to Orthodoxy."[3] Wartime religious rhetoric and exaggerations of Tatar mutinies added new fuel to the prewar Christianizing drive. Count Stroganov did not share his successor's concerns about the Tatars, and instead advocated strengthening Russian institutions in Crimea. Postwar shifting demographics further altered the balance between Christians and Muslims. When Crimean Tatars emigrated, Christians moved in to take their place. Initially, however, these Christians were not Russians, but Bulgarians—refugees from the Ottoman Empire similarly displaced by the war. Still, growth of parishes matched that of the population.[4] In another watershed event, Crimea received a permanent Orthodox bishop.

The monasteries of Russian Athos also rapidly expanded. In addition to the new parishes created in the aftermath of war, the church quickly erected and rebuilt the monasteries and churches associated with the plan for Russian Athos. In 1848, the province of Tauride only had two monasteries, St. George monastery in Balaklava and Korsun monastery in the northern steppe.[5] By the time of the revolution, Crimea had nine active monasteries. The others, built immediately before and after the Crimean War, included St. Vladimir monastery in Chersonesos, Dormition monastery, the skete at St. Anastasia, St. Clement Inkerman monastery, St. George in Katerles, St. Cosmas and Damian monastery, the St. Stefan of Surozh community at Kiziltash, and St. Paraskeva monastery near Topla.[6] Between them, these monasteries housed several hundred people, many times more than the figure of thirty initially projected in the proposal for Russia's Athos.[7] In other ways, the monastic community became unrecognizable from the original plan for its development. The monasteries gradually lost their pan-Orthodox identity, as the Russian population grew and the waves of Balkan immigration subsided, while the challenges of real-world administration tested the utopian framework that characterized the community's founding.

In tandem with the prewar sacred narratives and Christian scholarship, wartime religious patriotism changed the way Russians looked at Crimea. Crimea became an important site of military memory and locus of Russia's religious national identity. On a more tangible level, the war accelerated the Christianzing process. The anti-Islamic sentiment that framed Russia's outlook in Crimea during the war brought an end to Catherine II's all but forgotten policy of religious toleration. Simultaneously, the synod invested heavily in church expansion and gave the Russian Athos project official support for the first time since its inception.

The Crimean War officially came to a close with the Treaty of Paris on 30 March 1856, a month after hostilities had formally come to an end. Negotiations for peace revolved around the Five Points and resulted in Russia's ceding parts of Bessarabia and relinquishing influence over the Danubian Principalities of Wallachia and Moldavia; treaty signatories agreed to the demilitarization of the Black Sea, and created an international waterway on the Danube. Although the war ended badly for the Russian Empire, it did secure greater rights for the Eastern Christians living under Ottoman rule. In an effort to forestall western interference in Ottoman affairs, the sultan passed an edict before European negotiations began on 18 February 1856, in which he declared the equality of all faiths and races, and asserted policies of religious toleration.[8]

The Crimean War preserved the integrity of the Ottoman Empire for a few more decades. It brought an end to the Concert of Europe, ushering in the age of realpolitik in which European powers emphasized unilateral polices over cooperative platforms in the preservation of order on the continent. In Russia, the results of the Crimean War produced the most apparent changes. They temporarily terminated Russia's involvement in European diplomatic affairs, and inspired the decade of Great Reforms that resulted in the freeing of the serfs.[9] The Crimean War also spanned a change of regime when Alexander II succeeded Nicholas I in February of 1855.

As much as the Crimean War changed the face of European imperial affairs, it more dramatically altered the Crimean peninsula. A majority of the war's causalities, which included an estimated 95,000 French troops, 22,000 British troops, and 475,000 Russian troops, occupied the peninsula.[10] Some sources ascribe 100,000 men lost in Sevastopol alone. The population of Crimea dropped precipitously.[11] In addition to the horrendous loss of life to battle, disease, and migration, many of the peninsula's cities suffered utter devastation. Sevastopol especially had been bombarded until nothing remained. Other cities and towns, such as Yalta, Evpatoria, and Balaklava, were looted or laid to waste by ever-consuming encampments of both sides. Many places, especially along the coast, had been abandoned by their populations; apart from its large military hospital, Feodosia "resembled more of a desert than a city."[12]

The peninsula by degrees recovered through the end of the 1850s.[13] With the transfer of occupied territories back to Russian control in the summer of 1856, Russian authorities began the arduous and overwhelming task of cleansing and restoring the peninsula to its prewar status. In Evpatoria authorities struggled with the removal of two years of human waste and manure deposited by more than 100,000 people and 2,000 horses.[14] Cities slowly reestablished themselves; residents returned to their homes. The majority of these faced certain and terrible poverty. Not only had many lost their homes to enemy fire and depredation, they had also lost their livelihoods. Crops were devastated, livestock were slaughtered, factories were stripped, and merchant vessels commissioned, looted, and ruined.

The principal consequence of the Crimean War, however, was a population exchange between the Ottoman and the Russian Empires. Throughout the war, the Tatars' precarious position was evident to contemporaries, and many viewed it as a catalyst for a decline already begun. One English observer stationed in Crimea in 1855 commented:

> The Tatars are a rapidly diminishing race; and failing numbers is accompanied with declining moral energy. This melancholy fact is referable to their position as a conquered people, spoiled of territorial wealth, social and political importance and exposed to the harassing peculation of subaltern agents of government. It is painful to reflect, that the present war must be an additional disaster to them, arresting industrial employment, taking away their master, and conferring upon them no boon, however successfully closed by the allied armies.[15]

Here, this eyewitness describes Tatars as victims of imperial conquest.[16] Blame for their decline is laid not so much upon the malicious premeditation of government, but upon the consequences of imperial expansion that might occur in any dominion: loss of lands, decreased political autonomy, and greed of local agents.[17]

As the war drew to a close, the Russian government gave extremely meager reparations to Tatars for devastated houses, flocks, and crops. Such compensation did not replace Tatar losses, and fell well short of providing Tatars with means of supporting themselves in the immediacy of peace.[18] The migrations that began in 1855 steadily continued. By 1860, the number of Tatar emigrants had reached well over 100,000. In 1867, when Russian authorities, who compiled statistics based on police reports, were sure that the emigration had stopped and had the time to calculate how many Tatars actually left, they determined that, altogether, 104,211 men and 88,149 women had abandoned Crimea for good.[19] Behind them, these Crimean Tatars left 784 villages completely empty, and they abandoned 457 mosques.[20]

New Christian populations flooded into Crimea as Tatars left. What had once been Tatar villages suddenly became populated by other people. And not just Russians settled in former Tatar residences, but also Greeks, Bulgarians,

TABLE 4 Population Shift in Tatar Villages after the Crimean War

District	Number of villages abandoned by Crimean and Nogai Tatars	New Settlements	
Berdiansk	68	3	Russian refugees from Bessarabia
		38	Bulgarians
		17	state peasants
		1	state peasants: Molokan
		8	In Ruins
Melitopol	9	7	Russians and Ukrainians [*Malorussians*]
		2	Bulgarians
Perekop	278 villages (47,331 Tatars emigrated)	1	Bulgarian
		4	Czechs from Bohemia
		3	Nogai Types [sic]
		4	Estonians
		6	German colonists
		4	Ukrainians [*Malorussians*]
		256	In Ruins
Simferopol	24 villages (7,459 Tatars left a total of 146 villages, but 128 villages retained some Tatar population)	1	Estonian
		1	Settlers from Voronezh
		1	Settlers from Kursk
		23	In Ruins
Feodosia	67 villages	3	Bulgarians from Kishlav and Staryi Krym
		1	Russians from Berdiansk
		2	Russians from Voronezh
		13	Russian
		1	Russians from Kursk (state peasants)
		4	German colonists
		2	German Mennonites
		1	Turkish citizens (Greeks)
		18	Bulgarian colonists/mixed
		16	In Ruins

TABLE 4   **Population Shift in Tatar Villages after the Crimean War** *(continued)*

Evpatoria	196 villages	11	Russian
		3	German
		79	Tatars
		15	mixed (incl. Tatars, Greeks, Armenians and Moldavians)
		39	Empty

Source: Taken from *Pamiatnaia Kniga 1867* (416–36). The number of new settlements does not necessarily correspond to the number of abandoned villages, nor do the numbers of immigrants equal that of emigrants.

Germans, Czechs, Estonians, and others. In 330 villages, the Russian government resettled refugee populations from the territory it lost in Bessarabia during the Crimean War. Bulgarians, fleeing from persecution in the Ottoman Empire, took residence in the homes vacated by the Tatars. They established several colonies and completely occupied many former Tatar villages.[21] The Tatars in turn settled in the lands vacated by the Bulgarians.[22]

The church contended with this rapidly growing lay population by turning to the land vacated by Tatars. In 1861, the new archbishop, Aleksei (Rzhanitsyn, 1860–1867), wrote to Stroganov, asking to transfer the abandoned mosques that had been absorbed by the Ministry of State Domains: "The Tatar population is decreasing and decreasing. In their place, appear settlers from Orthodox Russia, who need Christian churches." Aleksei asked if the abandoned buildings, land, and sums set aside to support the mosques in the Muslim Spiritual Assembly could be transferred to the new consistory in Simferopol. The governor general of Tauride refused Aleksei's request, on the grounds that Tatars who did not emigrate would object, while many Tatars had decided to return.[23]

CREATION OF A NEW DIOCESE

The war deeply impressed upon Crimean laity the need to strengthen the official church, so they prepared a petition requesting an Orthodox bishop, even as ink dried on the Treaty of Paris. The petition reveals the degree to which Crimean Christians interiorized the voluminous prewar writings about the holiness of Crimea's Christian antiquities, and new concerns over the visibility of Islam on the peninsula. "The Tauride Peninsula, since the Christianizing of our great Prince Vladimir," began the petition, "has served as the cradle of Orthodox faith for all of Russia, from the first centuries of Christianity." The petition provided a list of Crimean saints who were located in Crimea "from the first centuries," briefly summarized the Greek contribution to local Christianity, and the shameful "persecution [of Crimean Christians] under the cruel rule of the Mongols, Tatars and Turks."[24] Without an active bishop, believers maintained, "Islam remained the governing faith in Crimea." The theory of toleration applied to Crimea had failed. Instead of incorporating the Muslim population, the Russian government "rewarded Muslims for their former political independence." Vorontsov's policies of religious and cultural autonomy served only to give "Muslim fanatics" the impression of living still in the "dominion of the Tatar Khans," and while the church remained weak, Islam grew. "Crimean Islam, in the person of its Mufti, has its own highly-ranked spiritual authority," petitioners pointed out, "but the Orthodox church appears in front of the Tatars only in the persons of its lowly ranked servitors." Petitioners circled back to Crimea's historic legacy for the Russian Empire, emphasizing the "unnatural position of Orthodoxy, in this country for which all of Russia is the cradle of Christianity." The laity lectured the Holy Synod on Crimea's "extreme importance to the empire for its closeness to the Islamic East."

For this reason, petitioners argued that it would be "advantageous for the Orthodox Church and the Fatherland" to establish an Orthodox hierarchy in Crimea. Clearly smarting from memory of the war, believers argued that a bishop would provide "a bastion against the dominance of Islam" and would "enable Christians to heal from the ulcer of the harmful invasion and mutinous uprisings of the native Tatars."[25] The military and civilian governors of Tauride signed the document, as did the mayor and regional officials from all of Crimea's principal towns and cities. To be sure, elite Christians in Crimea, rather than the peasants, composed and signed the petition. Still, the petition demonstrates a prevailing desire for a stronger Orthodox presence and a heightened sensitivity to religious tension along imperial borders.

Archbishop Innokentii forwarded the petition to the Holy Synod in 1857, attesting that "during frequent trips to Crimea, I always found such a desire," which increased with intensity in the summer of 1856. The request originated, he said, with "the Crimean citizenry, which knows the detailed status of the Orthodox Christians in the middle of prevailing Islam, on one side, and on the other, many sects of foreign colonists and our own sects."[26] In February, Count Stroganov responded that he "fully shared the opinion that a bishopric is necessary, especially in relation to the other faiths who populate Tauride and who remain fully represented with greater means for religious and political activity."²⁷ The Orthodox churches in Crimea, Stroganov asserted, should be no less influential than the mosques of the Tatars or the synagogues of the Karaim.

Archbishop Innokentii passed away before the Synod resolved to create a separate diocese in Crimea. On 22 June, nearly three weeks after Innokentii's death, the Synod passed an ukase that requested more information from the consistory in Kherson about the particulars of establishing a new diocese in Crimea, and in 1859 it issued official approval. The next year, the two provinces, Kherson and Tauride, officially separated their diocesan hierarchies, marking a watershed event in the history of Christianity in Crimea.²⁸ Crimean clergy were granted independence from Kherson and the Russian Orthodox Church expanded into the Muslim territory with official sanction from the state. Catalyzed by the religious fervor during the Crimean War, this diocese heralded a new era in the political dynamic of Crimea's religious life. In fewer than fifteen years, the diocese established the first seminary for Tauride, and within twenty years, it had more than doubled the number of Crimean churches.²⁹

RECOVERY FROM THE WAR

As the diocese underwent the process of separation, Crimea's new monasteries and older churches struggled to recover from the war. Sevastopol suffered the most. Only one church that was still under construction before the war survived the enemy invasion, while the most prominent church in the city, according to consistory reports in 1857, "was devastated by bombs and missiles until it did not resemble a church but a hideous skeleton, incapable of renovation." Similarly, bombardment destroyed the church of Genichesk, located on the riverbanks of the Azov Sea; "[it] burned completely to ash." Most of the Greek churches located in the villages surrounding Balaklava suffered severely, after troops transformed them into stores and arsenals. Many churches were robbed of their icons and utensils by allied troops; at least one French officer several years after the war returned an icon he had taken. The officer presented the icon to an Orthodox nun who in turn presented it to the tsar. Eventually, the piece made its way back to the city of Sevastopol, where religious authorities determined it was an icon of St. Mitrofan.³⁰ Several local merchants from Simferopol came forward to fund the restoration of Sevastopol churches, while the Greek community, "as soon as they came back," made restoring churches the first order of business. Other churches, such as the Peter-Paul church, the consistory in Odessa wrote to the Synod, "cannot find the means [for restoration] among the destroyed and impoverished inhabitants."³¹

Crimean monasteries suffered a fate similar, if not worse, to that of the churches during the war years, the consistory pointed out, because violence devastated the buildings "in their youngest age." Most of the new sketes were completely destroyed. Of the St. Vladimir skete in Chersonesos, "not a rock or splinter remained" after the Allies used the grounds for the chief battery of their left wing. A close witness to battles of the war, neighboring Inkerman fared much better because ancient Christians built their churches deep into the hollowed out cliffs. Still, British troops established a battery there and violence caused destruction of all external structures. The Katerles skete named for St. George near Kerch, built in 1853 on the eve of war, suffered bombardment with the city. It lost the roof, the floor, the windows, and three of its four walls. Dormition monastery and Balaklava monastery survived the war mostly intact. Located in Bakhchisarai, Dormition monastery did not directly experience battle, while the Balaklava monastery owed its survival to the protection of allied officers who used it as headquarters. Still, both suffered the "disadvantages of wartime, particularly high prices and insufficient workers."[32]

Postwar restoration of Crimean antiquities presented no easy task. In 1856, Father Vasilii left his post in Chersonesos to collect funds to rebuild the church and monastery, but tragically drowned in the Don that summer.[33] His successor, monk Evgenii, managed to convince a wealthy merchant in Sevastopol, P. A. Telatnikov, to underwrite the bulk of the work. By early spring of 1857, cells had already been built, and the church was under construction. Workers erected a fence that encircled nearly fifty acres of land, while monks began to cultivate gardens.[34]

By March of 1857, the abbot resumed services and readied the cells for the return of the monks and novices. Workers continued to labor over repairs, while Russian officials sanitized the space. In a report to the Holy Synod, the archbishop predicted that by the end of the spring, the sixty-five acres surrounding Inkerman monastery would be completely combed over for mines, and the monastery would return to its prewar status, with fully renovated cells and a revived garden and vineyard on top of the cliffs.[35] General Lieutenant Vesslitskii assisted restoration of Inkerman by ordering that all churches in territories still under his command provide a "notebook for entering donations for the renewal of churches."[36]

On the eastern side of the peninsula, authorities initiated work on the Katerles community in the name of St. George.[37] By the end of 1856 and the beginning of 1857, the local clergy found sponsors: a local merchant who funded decoration of the inside of the church and a city official who committed to building a residence for the brothers. After the conclusion of the war, the city head approved the transfer of over fifty acres of land, a step the diocese had struggled to accomplish years before.[38] Although construction was still in progress, the clergy arranged to consecrate the small monastery on 23 April, the day devoted to St. George. In this manner, as Innokentii wrote the Synod, "all of Kerch is very happy due to their love and respect for ancient holy places."[39] The community had fewer than twenty brothers at the end of the nineteenth century, and only the small wooden church sanctified in April of 1857.[40]

In addition to beginning work on St. George, diocesan authorities founded the St. Stefan of Surozh community in Kiziltash, a mountain located between Theodosia and Sudak. This site, which had acquired a reputation as being particularly holy before the war, became a substitute for the renovation of the St. Matthew church in the Sudak fortress, which was considered too inaccessible.[41] Father Arsenii from Balaklava monastery transferred to the new site to oversee construction, as Father Radionov negotiated with General Zhukov over the transfer of land to the new community.[42] Priests sanctified the monastery at Kiziltash in 1857. The quarters housed twenty monks, who tended to two small chapels, one named for the Dormition of the Mother of God, and the other for St. Stefan of Surozh.[43]

Until his death, Archbishop Innokentii remained the most active supporter of the monasteries. An astute investor as well as a devout subject of God, the archbishop tracked Odessa's burgeoning growth and invested his own capital in the Black Sea Society of Steamships and Trade, founded by Nikolaos Arkas. Innokentii bequeathed all certificates, worth 150 rubles each, for a total of 24,350 rubles, to the monasteries of Russian Athos. He encouraged the monasteries to use only the interest and to leave the capital in the certificates.[44] He also petitioned the Holy Synod to publish an account of the "suffering of the skates in newspapers throughout all of Russia." The synod approved Innokentii's request several months after his death.[45] It fell to the new archbishop of Kherson-Tauride, Dimitrii (Muretov), to prepare an article for the empire's newspapers.[46]

By the time Tauride received its own diocese in 1860, most of the monasteries had been restored. As if to emphasize the point, the imperial family visited Crimea the next year to survey the recovery. In August 1861, Alexander II, his wife Maria Alexandrovna, and their children inspected the reconstruction of Sevastopol and lingered at Crimea's top tourist destinations, including Chufut Kale in Bakhchisarai. Local officials took great pains to provide the imperial family with a carefully organized itinerary. Diocesan authorities actively participated, escorting the family through the new communities of Russian Athos. The imperial family visited the Dormition monastery in Bakhchisarai and the St. George monastery in

Balaklava, a location not particularly easy to reach today, that must have seemed quite remote one hundred and fifty years ago in the absence of automobiles. They also stopped at Chersonesos, where they admired the ancient Grecian ruins and played starring roles in sanctifying the holy place. The visitation of the imperial family is legendary in Crimea. It received attention in contemporary imperial religious periodicals and has become part of the history of each church where the family prayed.

The imperial family's first stop was in Chersonesos, where the church hierarchy involved them in the sanctification process of the church in honor of St. Vladimir, under reconstruction after it was destroyed in the war. The sanctification tied together the history of the ruins, the autocracy, and Russian Orthodoxy. The ceremony featured Christian artifacts found in Chersonesos, including a cross with a Greek inscription believed to be a thousand years old, and relics of St. Vladimir that the monastery acquired from Kyiv especially for the opening. After a procession, the bishop blessed the ground of the new church. Each member of the imperial family laid one of the first stones of the church's foundation. Elite officials, including Governor General Stroganov and Crimean War dignitaries Count Adlerberg and engineer Eduard Totleben, followed suit. The ceremony concluded with the imperial family kneeling in front of the ruins believed to be the place where Prince Vladimir was baptized. They family left the area of Sevastopol at 12:00 p.m. and continued on the rest of their tour of Crimea, which took them next to Dormition monastery.[47]

According to an unsigned article in *Tserkovnaia letopis'*, Aleksei, the new Tauride bishop, greeted Tsar Alexander, his spouse Tsarina Maria, and their daughter at the steps of the Dormition monastery on 24 August at 10:00 a.m. The tsar and his family kissed the cross and received a blessing with holy water. As they followed Aleksei up the stairs into the cliff's caves and through the catacombs, they listened to the bishop's history of the monastery. Aleksei related the legends associated with the church's holy icon, and told how local populations continued to hold the monastery in great esteem even after the Greeks abandoned the church in the 1770s. Aleksei told the tsar about the monastery's restoration in 1850, and the difficult first years of the founding monastic community. He concluded with reference to the Tatars, who "show not insignificant attention to our holy cliff."[48] The next day, the family visited the St. George monastery in Balaklava, where they attended a prayer service. Their visit became legendary in the history of Crimea's holy places, because tsarist approval, much less participation in the process of sanctification, secured the importance of place.

The monastic community in Crimea evolved into a large, thriving network in the years following the Crimean War. In the 1890s, three decades after the imperial family laid the first stones in the foundation, twenty-five brothers lived in the St. Vladimir monastery in Chersonesos. The monastery had accommodations for ordinary pilgrims and dignitaries in addition to the rooms for the monks, the abbot, and for dining. It had two churches, including the large one built in memory of St. Vladimir over the ruins. Nearby Inkerman monastery also grew and attracted illustrious visitors. It had twenty brothers during the 1890s and distinct churches.[49]

Three new women's monasteries formed in Crimea by the end of the nineteenth century. The St. Paraskeva monastery opened in Topla after a Bulgarian hermittess, Konstantina, founded a community there. Konstantina grew up in the Bulgarian colony of Kishlav in Crimea. The ascetic life attracted her from an early age. She first settled into a site on the Kiziltash mountain where she spent seven to eight years living as a hermit in the caves. After two other monks arrived to establish a hermitage in the name of St. Stefan of Surozh, Konstantina found a new place for peace and reflection at a healing spring known in Kirimtatar as Chokrak Savluk, and among Christians as the spring of St. Paraskeva.[50]

Like the site at Cosmas and Damian, the spring in Topla reportedly attracted Muslims, Karaim, and Christians from "time immemorial." After Russians annexed the territory, the land eventually fell into the hands of the secretary general of Tauride, whose wife donated a large parcel to religious authorities upon her death. Konstantina lived there until 1874, acquiring a reputation as a great Bulgarian hermit and elder. One by one, other female hermits took her example, and in the space of only a few years, the spring had become a women's spiritual community. Eventually, these women attracted the attention of the diocesan authorities, who granted them a monastery charter in 1864. The monastery quickly became the largest in the region, with six churches. In addition to the abbess, the monastery had 30 nuns, nearly 60 novices, and approximately 125 individuals living "on monastery food." On the eve of the Russian Revolution, the monastery had nearly 250 sisters.[51] It founded a school for girls in Feodosia that had 58 students at the turn of the century.[52] Expanding beyond capacity, Paraskeva nuns eventually colonized the Cosmas and Damian men's monastery.

In 1899, the Holy Synod agreed to transform Cosmas and Damian monastery into a women's monastery. At that time, Cosmas and Damian was one of the smaller communities of Russian Athos, with 35 brothers. It had several buildings, including a summer and winter church, bathing houses, and a stone chapel over the spring. The brothers of Cosmas and Damian had their choice of which men's monastery in Crimea they would relocate to. In their place, Varsofonia, a highly ranked nun from the monastery at Topla, established 25 of her sisters there.[53] The Katerles community transitioned to a women's monastery in 1900, and by 1912, records indicate that over 90 women lived on monastery resources.[54] The women's communities in Crimea reflect the growth of women's monasticism elsewhere through the empire, as well as the reinterpretation of the Athonite male-centric model for changing conditions in Crimea.[55]

Crimean Christianity in the Russian Imagination

The Great Reforms opened possibilities of travel for non-elite Russians, a transition facilitated by developments in railroad and steamship lines. The Odessa Steamship Society established a regular schedule between Odessa and Sevastopol in the decades after the Crimean War. In response to the expanding tourist trade on the peninsula, the Crimean Mountain Club formed in 1890. With an office located in Odessa, and intentions to spread knowledge of Crimean flora, fauna, and ruins, the pages of its journal also mapped out Crimean terrain for the casual hiker.[56] Travelers reveled in Crimea's climate, seashores, mountains, and exotic populations. War monuments attracted new devotees and blended with Crimea's historical markers: the Hellenic ruins in Chersonesos, the khan's palace in Bakhchisarai, the Karaim settlement in Chufut Kale, and the Genoese forts in Sudak and Balaklava. Visits to Crimean Christian antiquities became a part of the tourist itinerary, drawing devout Russian Christians and curiosity seekers alike.

Mikhail Bernov, a traveler who regaled Russians with serialized publications of his many journeys on foot, from St. Petersburg to Paris, and from Paris to Africa, trekked through the New Russian provinces in 1894.[57] This experienced world traveler compared the town of Simferopol, with its "population of all possible peoples: Russians, Jews, Tatars, Turkmen, gypsies, Karaim, Greeks," to Constantinople and the Casbah in Algiers.[58] He walked through Crimea's most famous archaeological monuments and duly appreciated Tatar architecture. Christian monuments did not occupy the center of his narrative, but did appear as the backdrop for other excursions. Of his visit to Balaklava, for example, Bernov wrote more about swimming in the Black Sea, in waters "clean, like crystal, and fresh," at the base of the cliffs on which the monastery was located, than the monastery itself.[59] He sandwiched a description of the Dormition monastery in a longer, more elaborate exposition of the khan's palace and Chufut Kale, and praised the milk, fresh eggs, and home-cooked meal that he received from the monks at Inkerman, rather than commenting on the way in which the liturgy touched his soul. Christian sentimentality rarely entered his narrative, although it did infuse his visits to memorials of the Crimean War: "I go into the Vladimir church and kneel at the remains of the four teachers and heroes of the Black Sea navy: Lazarev, Kornilov, Nakhimov, and Istomin."[60] Chersonesos, the "Russian Pompei," also elicited religious sentiment: "Chersonesos (ancient Korsyn)," he wrote, "is our Russian holy place [*sviatyna*], because as is well known, Korsun is the city of the Christianizing of Prince Vladimir in 988."[61]

Decades earlier, a lesser known author identified only as K. Zhukov traveled to Crimea in 1864 after his St. Petersburg doctor prescribed a warmer climate for the cure of various ailments. His account, therefore, tended to focus on the salubrious effects of Crimea's climate and outdoor activities. He too visited Crimea's many historical monuments, including Chersonesos, "an excellent place for bathing." After briefly sketching the St. Vladimir church, its proximity to the ruins and the kindness of the monks, he described the beach surrounded by small stone cliffs, the rise and fall of gentle waves "that fortify the body." He concluded: "I am not surprised that in the church you see fifteen, healthy, strong and boistrous brothers."[62] Still, the holiness of Crimea's antiquities was not lost on pragmatic Zhukov, who in contrast to Bernov was most struck by the St. George Balaklava monastery, "one of the communities of God, where one can be in ecstatic praise of His great name." Zhukov recounted the history of the monastery, including its discovery by the Greeks, its visits from the imperial family, and its survival during the war, expressing relief that "the enemy spared this holy place."[63] In most travel accounts, the meanings of the Christian places morphed into the changing landscape of Crimea. Depending upon the traveler, Christian antiquities became a tourist destination, no more or less significant than other sites in Crimea. In other cases, the memory of the war clung to Crimea's churches and monasteries, and even the most experienced and skeptical of Russian travelers expressed some recognition of their importance to Russian identity.

Other sources more pointedly addressed Crimea's Christian holiness. F. V. Livanov published one of the most commonly used guides to Crimea in Moscow in 1875. His lengthy narrative comprised more than fifty chapters often reprinted as separate pamphlets. It elaborated the history and contemporary status of Crimean monasteries and holy sites in great detail. His depiction of Chersonesos reflects the degree to which associations with the holy persisted through the pre-revolutionary period:

> What fortune for Russia, that she possesses the first baptistery of its Christianity, there on the same corner of earth where Vladimir converted from paganism to Christianity, and where receiving higher inspiration, burning

with zealotry, enlightened all of pagan Russia with Christianity . . .! This place, like Palestine and Jerusalem, is truly holy for Russian Christians.[64]

In the excerpt above, Livanov expresses what had become a much repeated theme: that Crimea was particularly holy because it was the source of Christianity for all of Russia. Most striking perhaps was his parallel between Crimea and Jerusalem. Others noted that the communities of Russian Athos attained the highly ascetic, romanticized life envisioned by the community's founders. Evgenii Markov wrote: "Monks, who chose Inkerman as their community, are truly poetic. Such pure thoughts and such fresh feeling for these silent and happy honorable men!"[65]

Similar travel accounts resonated through pilgrim literature. Separate pamphlets or articles in journals such as *Strannik* and *Russkii palomnik* published narratives devoted to the Dormition monastery, Chersonesos, and other sites.[66] Andrei Murav'ev, the religious writer who spent part of his career in the office of the Holy Synod, compiled one of the most famous pilgrimage accounts to Crimea as a postwar revision to his 1830s series *Journey to Holy Places in Russia (Puteshestvie po Sviatym Mestam Russkim)*. Since the first edition of his description of Russian holy places (which did not reference Crimea), Murav'ev wrote, "many changes have occurred, people have passed, and a few noteworthy communities have been established." He counted the ruins of Chersonesos (along with the Gethsemane skete) as one of the newest and most inspiring pilgrimage attractions. He even claimed to have had the inspiration to "preserve the unrivaled place, and to raise a monument to the Equal to the Apostle St. Vladimir" in 1847, two years before Innokentii submitted his proposal to the Synod.[67] In addition to his focus on Chersonesos, Murav'ev described the Inkerman and Dormition monasteries. He also gave particular attention to Sevastopol war monuments. Sevatopol offers "no peace to the Russian heart," he wrote, which "delights in the all the beauties of the southern shore, but knowing its past is left with a sad impression."[68]

Crimean monasteries and churches relied on donations to grow, and in 1888, the anniversary of Prince Vladimir's baptism in Chersonesos, Muscovite pilgrims along with the nuns from a women's monastery in Moscow raised money to restore a remote chapel located near the St. Anastasia skete.[69] A few years later, Moscow millionaire A. G. Kuznetsov funded the construction of one of the most famous churches in Crimea, the Christ Resurrection church high on the cliffs along the Sevastopol-Yalta road. Visiting this spot in 1895, church historian A. P. Lopukhin was struck by the beauty of the church built on the "natural throne of God" that "attracts attention from all travelers wandering through the exotic southern Crimean coast."[70]

A. A. Pavlovsky's 1907 guide for pilgrims included Crimea among Russia's holy places. It described the St. George monastery at Balaklava as having many "natural wonders," and portrayed the monastery in Bakhchisarai as "picturesque" and "wild," still visited by the miraculous icon. Reflecting earlier discourses associated with the spring of Cosmas and Damian, Pavlovsky's guide also noted that the St. Stefan of Surozh community in Kiziltash was built on a spring considered holy by all of Crimea's faiths.[71]

Crimean antiquities continued to fascinate scholars outside of the church throughout the end of the revolutionary period as well. Decades after the founding of the Odessa Society for History and Antiquities, the Imperial Archaeological Society formed in 1869. It too made Crimea the center of its research.[72] When it met in 1884 in Odessa, the society's ninety members sailed to Crimea for an excursion of the ruins. A local priest guided them around Chersonesos and Inkerman.[73] Shortly thereafer, scholars created the Tauride Archival Commission, which evolved into the Tauride Society for History, Archaeology, and Ethnography. Christian archaeology in Crimea remained a chief focus of the organization as was evident in its meeting agendas and publications. The commission dedicated one of the earliest journal issues (volume 5, 1888) entirely to the Korsun legend, describing each of the excavations that searched for the baptismal site of Prince Vladimir in detail. The issue also elaborated the process of restoring the St. Vladimir church in Chersonesos, and published Archbishop Innokentii's notes on Russian Athos. Aleksandr Kristianovich, one of the founding members of the Tauride Archival Commission, advocated producing this 1888 volume in honor of the anniversary of Prince Vladimir's Christianizing of Rus.[74]

Through the revolution, the church arbitrated access to the ruins of Chersonesos and other locations with Christian antiquities. The first conflict between the state, the church, and the archaeologists unfolded before the Crimean War in Chersonesos. In 1853, excavations of Aleksei Uvarov, son of the minister of education, produced an impressive number of artifacts, including the first Byzantine mosaic floor discovered in the Russian Empire. Before Uvarov could ship his findings to the Hermitage, however, Archbishop Innokentii intervened to protest the removal of local artifacts to the distant capital. Ensuing debate was resolved by a compromise: church artifacts remained with the church in Crimea and the rest could be sent to St. Petersburg.[75]

After the war, the church gradually assumed more control over the excavations, so that archaeologists associated with the Odessa Society for History and Antiquities had to obtain permission from the monastery's abbot before conducting their research. In 1861, the society wrote to Archbishop Aleksei, to request his patronage of archaeological excavation in the lands under diocesan auspices: "In the borders of the Tauride diocese, where there was once an ancient Hellenic population, now exist new cities and villages, where buried in the ground are ancient money and marble items of various forms [that] might include historical information." The society requested that the archbishop "encourage your spiritual flock, on the occasion that they find money, or marble items with inscriptions, that they fill out a form" and inform society members. For his participation, the society granted Archbishop Aleksei full membership.[76]

Annual reports of the Chersonesos monastery—in addition to listing the number of monastic servitors, their salaries, the buildings and resources of the monastery—also included regular archaeology reports. Year to year, monastery files thus included descriptions of excavated architecture, recovered crosses, mosaics, monies, vessels, and various artifacts of interest.[77] The Holy Synod contributed one thousand rubles a year from 1877 on for the maintenance of excavations and an archaeological museum on the site.[78] Archaeologists conducted excavations around Inkerman as well, and monks themselves occasionally stumbled across artifacts. In 1876, a monk found a metal cross while working on the monastery's walls and clearing the area. After the brothers cleaned it, they realized they had discovered an ancient treasure. Made of either gold or bronze (the brothers did not know which), the cross had the word "Panagea" inscribed on it, with an image in each of its corners.[79]

The monastery at Balaklava, which had a burst of growth in the 1890s, attempted to capitalize on the fascination with archaeology.[80] In *Toward the History of Christianity in Crimea, a Passage of One-Thousand Years. Considerations and Activities of the St. George Balaklava Monastery,* A. L. Berte-Delegarde used archaeological and historical evidence to establish 891 as the date of the monastery's founding.[81] This publication prompted the monastery's new abbot to advocate for a one-thousand-year anniversary commemoration, an act that would have raised the monastery in Balaklava on par with that in Chersonesos. Quite often, Crimean prelates found themselves in the position of negotiating these historical controversies. In this case, the archbishop questioned the accuracy of Berte-Delegarde's claims and resisted the abbot's efforts. In the end, the abbot and the archbishop reached a compromise. They did not craft a millennial celebration, but did use the study to raise money to restore an ancient church.[82]

LOCAL CONTROVERSIES

Despite the spread of Crimea's reputation as a center of monasticism, these "godly Eremites" who "lingered on that hallowed spot" (adapting

Lord Byron's description), were not without their controversies. In Bishop Germogen's lengthy analysis of the Tauride diocese published in 1886, he remarked that the dream of Archbishop Innokentii to build Athos in Russia had come true, "although maybe, not quite as he would have wished."[83] Probably Germogen intended the comment as a reference to the monasteries' financial struggles. The majority remained independent of the Holy Synod and therefore dependent upon benefactors. Such a status did not have the security that the community's creator desired.[84] Germogen might also have been referring to the proliferation of women's monasteries. With three active women's monasteries, Crimea had departed from the all-male monastic community of the Athonite model. Contemporary readers, however, might have read Germogen's oblique statement as an allusion to the intrigues and controversies that surrounded many of the monasteries.

Christian ruins discovered at Inkerman and Chersonesos contributed to the atmosphere of holiness that surrounded Crimean sites, but not all such discoveries were authentic. In 1886, a Moscow newspaper ran an article about an archaeologist who discovered the bones of early Christian martyrs in the caves of Inkerman. The Kyivan church that sponsored the excavation submitted the story and claimed rights to the relics. Unhappy diocesan authorities in Crimea read the article with surprise, since archaeological research at the monasteries fell under their jurisdiction, but until this point they had heard nothing of this archeologist's work. They contacted the archimandrite of Russian Athos to explain the situation, who in turn contacted the hieromonk at Inkerman. The distressed monk, Methodius, responded that an archaeologist arrived in the middle of October, desiring to make a plan of the cave city's layout, with a special focus on the churches. The archaeologist found a small collection of bones, which he claimed were the bones of first-century Christians. Methodius pointed out in his letter to the synod that these bones were not necessarily human, and certainly gave no evidence of dating to the first century. He protested their use as relics, writing: "do not put these bones, which are of unknown origin, on the same level as the bones of relics of the Saintly Martyrs esteemed by the Orthodox Church."[85] Here, it is the clergy who urged caution in the celebration of Crimea's sacred space. Nevertheless, the archaeologist cemented his career with this huge "discovery," and before the revolution, devout Christians in Kyiv may have unwittingly directed their respect to the bones of sheep rather than first-century martyrs.

Apart from the exploitation of ambitious archaeologists, the monasteries also fell victim to corruption. In the mid-1890s, an exposé publicized poverty and mismanagement at the Cosmas and Damian monastery. In the 1880s, the men's monastery reached 50 monks, at least 30 men beyond ideal occupancy; the community's small income could not sustain such a large population. Brothers went hungry and the monastery was unsanitary. Visitors to the community increasingly reported high incidences of alcohol abuse and disrespect to holy vessels. A series of changes in the monastery's abbots in the late 1880s and 1890s made a deteriorating situation worse. After visiting the monastery in 1896, one man wrote: "It's dirty there, like a pigsty . . . outside the monastery, nothing grows . . . there is gossip here, quarrels, and jealousy . . . the abbot is an idiot," and all, he assured his readers, behaved like thieves. The writer even complained about the spring itself, which at the low temperature of six degrees made it "strange that the ill bathe here." He noted a rumor that that several young and elderly monks actually died after catching cold from bathing in the spring.[86] For these reasons, religious authorities in Crimea decided to scatter the monks, and transferred the monastery to the women of Topla.

In addition to the Cosmas and Damian monastery, which acquired a very poor reputation before it was transformed into a women's monastery, the Dormition monastery in Bakhchisarai reached a point of internal crisis. By the turn of the century, this monastery had more than 40 monks and novices, some of whom lived in the caves while others were in a comfortable complex removed from the cliffs. Over the years the monks built a general dining hall, a bath house, stables, and five separate small churches. The monastery had the makings of a small village, for it contained a hospital, a building for crafts, and quarters for pilgrims.[87]

In 1905, the Tauride consistory sent auditors to the monastery to investigate rumors of disarray. The resulting report gives much detail about the challenges of administering remote holy places in Crimea. The auditors found the monastery in crisis on all levels. Zosima, the abbot, often left the monastery without supervision and was not even present for the audit. Monastery accounts were in shambles, and the auditors discovered evidence that Zosima falsified reports to the consistory. The brothers often quarreled, and no one liked Zosima. In the absence of any real authority, the rule of the monastery collapsed. Young servitors failed to perform the most rudimentary tasks, few brothers attended main meals in the dining halls, and many frequented the city of Bakhchisarai without permission and for questionable purposes. Only the elders kept the monastery functioning, yet this meant that men who were old and infirm performed the hardest labor—they trudged with pails of water up and down the mountain, moved heavy bricks, and tilled the soil. Most dire, the auditors wrote, "the internal life of the brothers is weak, and insufficiently spiritual."

The auditors found several instances of monks having abandoned their own spiritual development. Not everyone attended liturgies, which were performed poorly. Servitors read passages hastily, without proper grammar, and some brothers walked out in the middle of services. Worse still, the auditors witnessed the monks who lived in the caves "wallowing in their beds," one wearing only his undergarments. When auditors approached, these men carried on their conversation as if no one else were present. "This is even more unbecoming," they reported, "when the skete in the summer is visited by significant numbers of tourists and pilgrims, including women." The monks, like others encountered at the Dormition monastery, were "dirty and unpleasant." The auditors prompted the authorities in Simferopol to remove Zosima and to assist the new abbot to draft a path of recovery.[88]

Some communities at Russian Athos clashed with local residents. In the mid-nineteenth century, as the Orthodox Church asserted a Christian sacred narrative of Crimea, Karaim self-awareness also began to bear fruit. Before the war broke out, Karaim had begun to write about their history and identity. After the war, this process intensified, and they laid claim to the mountain plateau Chufut Kale as their homeland. The two groups, Karaim, and Orthodox, intersected in the two-kilometer territory joining the Dormition monastery and Chufut Kale. Although the competition for land neighboring the Dormition monastery has erupted more seriously in the post-Soviet period, the memoirs of a Russian priest hint at early conflict between the struggle of the Karaim for self-definition and the will of the Dormition monastery to expand. In particular, memoirs allude to a controversy surrounding the research of a Karaitem rabbi of Chufut Kale, Solomon Beim, one of the most important figures in the early movement to study Karaim culture and history.[89] He, like Abraham Firkovich, moved his residence to Chufut Kale and emphasized that the plateau was an historic settlement of great symbolic importance to his people. Beim's research proved enormously influential among certain regional scholars, yet met opposition from the church. Diocesan authorities dismissed the rabbi as a "good for nothing man," who "compos[ed] a fable, filling it with ridiculous and unbelievable facts," and they maintained that before Jews ever settled in Chufut Kale the fortress belonged to the Christian Genoese kingdom. They interpreted Beim's act as a direct threat to the monastery and accused the rabbi of "forcibly dragging Jews" to Chufut Kale and "confusing everything in order to hamper the completion of the monastery." The monastery escalated the complaint to the Tauride governor, who refused to intervene.[90] This episode suggests the increasing relevance of ethnic histories to contemporaries, and it presaged future controversies associated with Crimea's overlapping sacred sites.

Church expansion met some resistance from the Crimean Tatars—

whose population went into serious decline after the war and experienced yet another wave of migration on the cusp of the Russo-Turkish War of 1878/79—when a law was passed that intended to conscript Tatars into service.[91] In the last quarter of the nineteenth century, Tatar migration slowed due in large part to Ismail Gaspirali, the outspoken Tatar activist who passionately campaigned for his people to remain in their homelands and to restore their cultural institutions.[92]

Tensions between Tatars and Christians came to a climax in the 1860s, following the mysterious disappearance of an abbot at Kiziltash monastery, the abbot Parfeny, in a shocking episode that later became the subject of a socialist-realist novel by A. B. Derman.[93] In August of 1858, Parfeny was appointed abbot of the Kiziltash monastery, after distinguishing himself in the Crimean War. He was regarded as a capable man, someone who could transform a remote monastery with few resources into a thriving community. From the beginning, his appointment was fraught with challenges. Initially, the problems paralleled those of other monasteries on Crimea—few resources. In Kiziltash, the lack of land compounded the shortage of resources, so that the monks were entirely dependent upon donations from infrequent pilgrims or proceeds from surrounding forest lands. Even worse, the Tauride diocese used the Kiziltash monastery for *epitimia*, or the paying of penance for transgressions. Thus, Parfeny's brotherhood contained an inordinate number of alcoholics and men with murky backgrounds. Few of these monks engaged in self-reflection; most persisted in the same questionable behaviors that caused expulsion from their home parishes and monasteries.

As the abbot Parfeny mediated the conflicts within his monastery, he also clashed with local Tatars who denied or simply ignored the transfer of their ancestral lands to the monastery a few years earlier. The abbot appealed in vain to authorities in Feodosia to prevent the Tatars "from robbing the forest." When the government refused help in 1863, he asked Archbishop Aleksei for defense "from the arbitrary robbers and plunderers, protected by the powers of the Tauride government: otherwise there is no possibility of preserving the monastery's interests from criminals and robbers."[94] Parfeny alleged that the Tatars escaped penalty because they bribed the court with wine. Affairs were so poor in Kiziltash that Father Parfeny repeatedly requested to be transferred. When he was presumed dead after failing to return from an official visit to Sudak, local police opened an inquiry yielding results that remain controversial even now.

The police captain assigned to the case concluded that the abbot was murdered by three Tatars from the village of Taraktash, who carefully planned the event and then burned the body afterward. On the heels of the Great Reforms, this case was tried publicly. To deliver their defense, Tatars hired Aleksei Petrovich Baranovskii, who argued that police arrested the Tatars on false denunciations and that they were victims of racial policies. Despite a passionate defense, the court found the three guilty of murdering Father Parfeny and sentenced them to death. An executioner hanged the Tatars in the last public execution before the revolution. Today, both Russians and Tatars have memorials at both sites of violence. The abbot's memorial, built shortly after the affair, consists of a cross with an epigraph reading: "Father Parfeny, abbot of the Kiziltash Kinovii, murdered and burned by Taraktash Tatars, 22 August 1866, 51 years old." Tatars have added their own symbol for the martyrdom of the three Muslim men believed to be wrongfully convicted and executed.[95] Parfeny was not the only abbot at Kiziltash to suffer a tragic fate. In 1907, Father Erasm was found with his head brutally chopped from his body.[96]

Despite apparent tensions between Russians and Tatars, authorities in Crimea maintained the collective fiction of a benign imperial rule. In 1883, the city of Simferopol held a three-day celebration of the "reunion of Crimea with Russia." It was an elaborate affair that commenced with the blessing of holy water for the sanctification of a statue of Catherine II. Military and civil dignitaries joined Russian clergy in the ceremony. Through the next few days, Russian priests and prelates led the celebration with services and religious processions. The holiday concluded with church bells ringing across the city and the reading of a telegram from Alexander III. The tsar's telegram announced his commitment to the policies of his predecessors, referring to Catherine II, and his concerns for the "success and well-being of Crimea and the various tribes of her population."[97]

Even within this climate of official toleration, some Russians openly expressed antipathy for Tatars and for Islam. Several observers represented Dormition monastery as a site of perennial conflict between Islam and Christianity in Crimea. One pamphlet, for example, alleged that the "chief purpose" of the monastery was to "support the spirit and energies of Christian struggles against Islam."[98] Another argued that the "monastery unified all Christians and protected the faith against the wild onslaught of Islam."[99]

Reaching perhaps an even broader audience than the travelogues, one adventurous traveler published the following observation about Dormition monastery in *Niva*, a St. Petersburg literary journal, after picking his path through Crimea in the 1870s:

> The Bakhchisarai Dormition skete occupies one of the most prominent places of Crimea's many wonders. It represents the deep holiness and uniqueness of this spectacular corner [of the empire]. As a sacred, holy place, Dormition monastery is a memorial to Christianity in Crimea—erected in terrible years of persecution in the very center of Muslim settlement, it defended orthodox affairs through the nearly five centuries of struggle with Islam.[100]

The above passage emphasizes the monastery's holiness—a uniquely sacred spot in a very unique corner of Russia. Yet the "five centuries of struggle with Islam" imbued the commentary with an ominous tone. By the 1870s, on the eve of another Russo-Turkish war, Russia's Athos became a symbol of the troubled Muslim-Christian relations in and surrounding Crimea.

Another case of Muslim-Christian tension involves the monastery at Inkerman, which had expanded into space that Tatars also considered holy. In 1890, the abbot of Inkerman monastery ignited a controversy when he requested permission to build a fence to keep out Tatars who gathered at the Inkerman monastery every year in May to pay homage to an ancestral burial ground. Monks of Inkerman protested the waste that the gathering of two thousand people and horses left behind. They took their complaints to the police, whose cooperation they sought before the next Tatar holiday. The police in turn escalated the issue to the regional government authorities. In the end, the monks' request was refused, for the Crimean government argued that the Tatars had the right to conduct their religious practices freely.[101]

Whereas the Inkerman case reveals aggression from the monastery toward the Tatars, another case involving the Cosmas and Damian monastery shows the reverse, a Tatar seizure of land. Between the Crimean War and the Revolution of 1917, Tatars in the Alushta district were slowly disenfranchised, displaced by ever-growing waves of Russian settlers. This was especially the case with the land surrounding the Cosmas and Damian monastery. The Alushta district had long been one of the most desirable locations on the peninsula for elite Russians. Before the revolution, it was the location of the tsar's hunting lodge in the south. Over the years, the Crimean Tatar Society of Alushta found their landholdings whittled away, and in 1904 and 1905, they forcibly reclaimed some of this land, which had been assigned to the monastery in 1901.[102]

In contrast to the site of the Dormition monastery and the conflicts with the Tatars in Inkerman and Cosmas and Damian, the St. Anastasia community appears to present a model of cooperation. Expecting the worst after reviewing the Dormition monastery in 1905, auditors were pleasantly surprised with St. Anastasia, which had only ten brothers and two small churches. Hard-working brothers kept the churches neat and in good repair. In contrast to lazy, indolent Zosima, the auditors described the monk in charge of Anastasia as "a man of strong character, energy, enterprising, very intelligent." Under his care, the auditors believed that the community of St. Anastasia could thrive. The only problem the auditors identified could also be interpreted as an asset—boxes of regular candles were mixed in with the beeswax candles used for liturgies. The monk explained that local Tatars donated the regular candles, which monks used in their homes, but not in services. Unfortunately, the trail of cooperation with Tatars ends with this small anecdotal evidence. However, the Tatar donation of candles suggests that Christian-Muslim relations were not always poor, and that at least the community of Anastasia had the ability to construct positive dialogue with area inhabitants.[103]

Even though the Russian Athos community was developed before the revolution, it never achieved the Christianizing of the Tatars. Edward Lazzerini quotes Germogen's sermon from the 1880s: "O Crimea, Crimea, our beloved Crimea! How much of you still is not Russian, how much is still not Orthodox!"[104] Lazzerini interprets the bishop's comments as an indication of a general Russian frustration with the failure of Tatars to adopt Christianity and assimilate into Russian culture. Yet, as Lazzerini himself goes on to elaborate for a different purpose, such an interpretation only tells part of the story. In the context of this book, the excerpt succinctly sums up the foundation of the church's aims; the lament "O Crimea" revolved around the land and not its inhabitants. This point is far more than semantic, for the church was not so much interested in altering the consciousness of native inhabitants as it was concerned with consolidating its position among Orthodox inhabitants and creating a homogeneous identity for the peninsula. Tatars, in this perspective, were either off-handedly pushed aside or treated as admiring foils of Orthodox rituals. The church maintained its monopoly over Crimean identity until the revolution, a revolution that not only overturned political powers, but destroyed Crimea's sacred landscapes.

To commemorate the 153rd anniversary of the fall of Sevastopol in September 2008, Crimeans held a ceremony attended by representatives from the Crimean Parliament, the Council of Crimean Ministers, the Russian commander of the Black Sea naval feet, and the Simferopol city council. Russian activists turned out in force from all regions of Crimea, flying the tri-colored Russian flag and flags from the party called Russian Bloc.

Crimean officials spoke at the cemetery of the St. Mary Magdalene church. Sergei Tsekov, member of the Crimean Parliament, invoked rhetoric surrounding the sanctity of war memorials when he remarked: "[T]hirty-five thousand of the fallen soldiers are buried here in this holy place."[105] The Metropolitan of Simferopol and Crimea, Lazar (Shvets), delivered a prayer service that commemorated the soldiers who lost their lives in the Crimean War. Once the ceremony had finished at Mary Magdalene, the group boarded buses to travel to another monument of the Crimean War, the St. Nicholas church, where a similar service was performed.[106]

The assembly of local officials, clergymen, and Russian patriots who marked the anniversary of the Crimean War was similar in form and tenor to such events in pre-revolutionary times. For the participants, the anniversary of the Crimean War symbolized the bravery and sacrifice of Russian soldiers who had given their lives in Sevastopol not once, but three times: during the Crimean War, the revolutionary era, and World War II. The Soviet and post-Soviet era have inscribed these memorials with alternative meanings.

When Crimea was part of *Novorossiia*, the commemoration did not incorporate the diversity of peoples who could have turned out for public events. Later, Soviet deportations removed tens of thousands of Greeks, Germans, Armenians, Bulgarians, Czechs, and others who gave New Russia its unique identity, groups (except for Armenians fleeing the Armenian-Azerbaijan conflict) that never returned.[107] Tatars, whose devastation during the Soviet period is more widely understood, have slowly repopulated Crimea in recent decades.[108] They too did not attend what might have been a more inclusive public commemoration of an event that so affected their history. On another level, the government officials in attendance represented the influential Russian state to be sure, but not the state in power; neither the Ukrainian commander of the Black Sea fleet, nor the Kyiv-leaning mayor of Sevastopol attended. Metropolitan Lazar, moreover, is connected to the Ukrainian Orthodox Church of the Moscow Patriarchate, not the Ukrainian Orthodox Church of the Kyivan Patriarchate or the Ukrainian Autocephalous Orthodox Church. Mired in nostalgia for an earlier age, this event commemorates both Russian rule and the Crimean War, as the Russian Orthodox Church reprises its former leading role.

Epilogue

After seventy years of official atheism in the Soviet Union, Orthodox Christians are reestablishing Crimea as a holy place of the Slavs. *Welcome to Ukraine's* 1998 magazine reflects this development with a fascinating article that reads as much like a travel brochure as a pilgrim's narrative.[1] The author, Father Andriy Vlasenko, laments the perennial challenge that every pilgrim faces—the distant destination. "All the places particularly holy for Christians seem to be situated far beyond the borders of Ukraine. For people with limited funds and for those who wish to go on foot but do not have enough time for long journeys," he writes, "such places are hardly accessible." Having, as he admitted, "neither enough money nor enough time" to travel to distant places, Vlasenko realized that he did not have to go to Jerusalem, Constantinople, or Mt. Athos, because there are "enough holy places in Ukraine." "In fact," Vlasenko asserted, "Ukraine is not at all inferior in this respect, say, to Greece." He concludes that the Crimean mountains, full of holy monuments, saints' relics, ancient churches, and tales of Christian heroism, enabled him to "know the true God."[2]

The current treatment of Crimea as a special Orthodox holy place has an historical antecedent in the Orthodox refashioning of Crimea in the nineteenth century. Today, the church reasserts its claims to sacred sites that have been considered especially holy by Christians for hundreds of years. Currently, the Simferopol and Tauride diocese associated with the Moscow patriarchate offers more than fifty different pilgrim itineraries.[3] The chief sites that occupy the center of Crimea's Christian revival include the ruins of Chersonesos, featured in *Archaeology* magazine in 2002, the Inkerman monastery, and the Dormition monastery in Bakhchisarai, which now prints its own journal, *Krymskii Afon (Crimean Athos)*.[4] But this renewal is not without challenge. Orthodoxy seeks its footing in a very troubled Crimea, a region haunted by painful traumas of the Stalinist era and the conflicted memories of the pre-revolutionary past. Dormition monastery has drawn some criticism for its expansion into lands also claimed by Tatars, while the Chersonesos community and others have struggled to reestablish themselves in state parks created during the Soviet period. Restitution of religious property in the wake of the Soviet collapse throughout Ukraine raises uncertainty over which church—the one associated with Ukraine or the one associated with the patriarch in Moscow—is the rightful heir. In Crimea, this process is even more complicated, as returning Tatars stake their own claims to overlapping sacred sites.

As the church negotiates these choppy waters, it draws upon tools from the pre-revolutionary past. In light of Soviet atheism, nineteenth-century publications on Crimea's sacred history naturally have formed the basis for current thinking about Crimean Christianity. Orthodox Christians have revived Archbishop Innokentii's blueprint for Russian Athos, and have restored the network of Crimean monasteries. Crimea has once again become a destination for Orthodox Christians, and it is promoted by Christian tourist agencies throughout Ukraine and Russia. In many ways, the restoration of Crimea resembles the Christianizing process of the past, and it proceeds as rapidly. Post-Soviet developments, of course, imbue the process with new meanings. In recognition of the changed political environment, Russian Athos has been named *Crimean* Athos (not *Ukrainian* Athos). While Crimean Athos invokes Crimea's Grecian heritage, the traditional Balkan Christian population that played an active role in the creation of Russian Athos suffered deportation during World War II and no longer exists. Expansion of the church occupies the center of debates about identity, as Crimeans ask: Is Crimea Russian or Ukrainian? A center of Christianity or Islam? Or can Crimea become again a home for all three Abrahamic religions?

Religion reemerged quickly through the 1990s in the wake of seventy years of official atheism. New and restored churches, mosques, and synagogues cropped up everywhere across the territory of the former U.S.S.R. People embraced the chance to worship freely.[5] Official religion proved to be as resilient as popular faith, and the Orthodox Church arose as one of the most potent political voices in Russia and Ukraine.[6] Religion offered post-Soviet states a tool to rally populations "when the older twentieth-century political identities rooted in the October Revolution [were] no longer viable."[7] As a result, registered religious organizations in Russia and Ukraine have multiplied. The Russian Federation has listed more than 21,000 organizations in a recent report. By contrast, the smaller state of Ukraine has 30,000 registered religious organizations, or "1 religious community per 1,000 adult citizens of the country."[8] These numbers reveal the proliferation of denominations inspired by western missionaries whose success also prompted concerns about western cultural and religious hijacking.[9] Russian officials subsequently ejected Jehovah's Witnesses, the Salvation Army, and other "foreign denominations" from Moscow.[10]

Cults also account for the high percentage of registered religious organizations. To be sure, cults such as Hare Krishna existed in the former Soviet Union long before its collapse.[11] With the freedom of religion in the post-Soviet era, these cults have spread exponentially. The Great White Brotherhood, a cult that followed Marina Tsvigun as the Maria Devi-Kristos (Maria-Jesus), offers one of the most salient examples. The cult anticipated the end of the world following the self-sacrifice of Maria Devi-Kristos in the center of Kyiv in November 1993. Media frenzy surrounded the anticipated event, but instead of the mass suicide of 150,000 followers, Kyivans witnessed her arrest.[12] Other cults in Ukraine draw upon the region's pre-Christian pagan beliefs. Some cults, as Russian archaeologist Victor Shnirelman has pointed out, make dangerous connections to an Aryan-pagan ancestry.[13] Years ago Soviet scholars concluded that youth fascination with cults derived from official atheism's "negation of religion," a reason that still may explain the wider phenomenon of post-Soviet religious revival.[14]

While the spread of western denominations and cults has created some concern among Ukrainian officials and citizens, they do not pose a threat to Ukrainian stability. Yet the conflicts between Ukraine's traditional religions do. For nearly two decades, Ukraine has been divided between branches of the Orthodox Church that are vying for influence, property, government favor, and land. Moreover, these splinter churches have also clashed with Ukraine's other faiths, Islam and the Ukrainian Greek Catholic Church.[15] Since independence, the government and the churches have actively interfered with one another's affairs, despite claims to the contrary from both sides. Battles rage over religious land and property restitution. Crimea has among the most intense religious rivalries. And again, just as in the nineteenth century, the holy places there convey political as well as spiritual meanings.

When Ukraine separated from the Soviet Union, its Orthodox hierarchs made a bid for independence from the Russian Orthodox Church. Thus in 1991, several Ukrainian prelates separated from the Russian Orthodox Church (known in Ukraine as the Ukrainian Orthodox Church of the Moscow Patriarchate—UOC-MP) and formed the Ukrainian Autocephalous Orthodox Church (UAOC). At the same time, the Ukrainian Greek Catholic Church (UGCC) went into ascendancy in the western regions of the nation, particularly in Galicia.[16] Due to internal church politics, some members of the UAOC split off and formed the Ukrainian Orthodox Church of the Kyivan Patriarchate (UOC-KP), which quickly became the stronger of the two, and emerged as the chief rival of the Russian-based Ukrainian Orthodox Church of the Moscow Patriarchate. Despite attempts at autocephaly, the Russian Orthodox Church remains dominant in Ukraine, and presides over a network of 10,384 parishes in Ukraine, compared with 11,525 parishes in Russia.[17]

Ukraine is one of the most religiously diverse post-Soviet states, home to the various Orthodox branches and to Greek Catholics, Islam, and a variety of protestant denominations, as well as the cults described above. Quite often, Ukraine's religions are geographically demarcated, so that the majority of Catholics live in the west, the Muslims in Crimea, and the Russian Orthodox in the east.[18] The autocephaly movement, meanwhile, is concentrated in the center. Not surprisingly, these regions also have different cultural and historical identities. Western Ukraine retains evidence of its former ties to Poland; the Black Sea region still contains evidence of its past in the Ottoman world; Eastern Ukraine is predominantly Russian speaking, and Russian leaning.[19] Irina Borowik has described post-Soviet religious revival as "above all a return to tradition . . . a test of the reconstruction of memory, the search for a way to reconnect the severed links of the past."[20] In this climate, "religion is fundamentally linked to politics, to national identity, and to the transformation process in Ukraine."[21] She suggests that cooperation between religious identities is critical to the success of the new Ukrainian state. Repeatedly, however, religious identities have been divisive rather than constructive.

The first post-Soviet presidency of Leonid Kravchuk demonstrates these challenges. Under his administration, the Kyivan Church (UOC-KP) received government sanction. Although Kravchuk advocated a policy of separation of church and state on paper, he believed that Ukraine needed to establish itself as a distinct entity from Russia, which included diminishing Russian influence over language, culture, and religion. Government support for the UOC-KP did not last long, however, for Kravchuk's successor and challenger, Leonid Kuchma won the presidential bid by appealing to pro-Russian voters. He drew his support from Ukraine's ethnic Russian population (20 percent of the total), as well as from the culturally Russian Ukrainians in the south and the east. One of his first actions in office, therefore, involved bolstering government favor of the UOC-MP, an issue that had taken on crucial significance to many voters.[22] The government has since learned painful lessons about interfering in religious affairs, and now it attempts to promote unity between the splinter branches rather than supporting one branch over the over.[23]

In addition to the splintering of Orthodox churches, one of the more difficult challenges to religion in Ukraine involves restitution of religious property and jurisdiction over holy places. Questions of property restitution result from the need to restore property confiscated according to Lenin's nationalization policies. Such confiscations during the Soviet period have resulted in today's conflicts among the splinter branches of the Orthodox churches and other denominations.[24] In Kyiv, for example, the splinter churches jockey for control over two particular holy sites in the city. The fiercest battles have been waged over the Kyiv-Pecherskaya Lavra and the St. Sophia Cathedral, which number among the most sacred sites in Ukraine. From 1992, the UOC-MP managed to exert control over at least the Lower Caves of the famous Kyiv Lavra, which upset its rival greatly. Neither the UOC-MP nor the UOC-KP has been able to establish itself over the St. Sophia Cathedral. Recognizing the enormous consequences of allowing the cathedral to fall to one church or the other, the Ukrainian government has chosen to administer it directly. The apparent delicacy of guardianship over this holy site was publicized as early as 1990 when Aleksii (Ridiger), patriarch of Russia, attempted to visit the cathedral but was met at the front doors by advocates of the autocephalous movement. Ultimately, the patriarch did manage to enter the side door, but the tricky circumstances of his visit served as a dark forewarning of troubles to come. Three years later, the White Brotherhood, the sect that believes in Maria Devi-Kristos, unsuccessfully attempted to take over the church.[25] Most memorable was the standoff between the Orthodox churches and the Ukrainian government in 1995 when the patriarch of the UOC-KP, Volodymyr (Romaniuk), stipulated his wishes to be buried on the grounds of the St. Sophia Cathedral. The Ukrainian government refused the request. On 18 July, a funeral procession transported the body of the deceased patriarch to the grounds of St. Sophia, blatantly disregarding the government's decision. UOC-KP members then proceeded to dig a grave on the cathedral grounds. Ukrainian police, who had no luck dissuading the crowd, resorted to violence. Several people were injured in this fight over a holy place, causing the episode to be remembered as "Black Tuesday."[26]

Religion twisted and turned throughout the 1990s as the new Ukrainian state attempted to define its identity. Succeeding presidents Leonid Kuchma and Viktor Yushchenko have made little progress.[27] Certainly part of the problem stems from the churches themselves, which despite claims to uphold separation of church and state, actively interfere in political matters.[28] Ten years later, these churches still wage battles against one another. They also draw the government into their contests for recognition and restitution of religious property throughout Ukraine. In November 2006, members of the UOC-KP and the UOC-MP clashed in front of the St. Nicholas church in Poltava. When one group organized to hold a *panikhida* (memorial service) for those who suffered from Soviet terror, the other blocked the front door to the church. The solemn occasion was interrupted by brusque pushing, shoving, and swear words.[29] Similar conflicts ensued at St. Catherine's in Chernihiv, the Church of the Holy

Spirit in Vytylivka, and countless others. Repeatedly the churches have called in Ukrainian police and Ukrainian courts to resolve disputes. There seems to be no end in sight to this ongoing conflict.[30] Crimea offers little exception to the pattern of religious revival and rivalry. In fact, the process is perhaps more complicated in light of the particular challenges facing Crimea in the post-Soviet era.[31]

Scholars have described Crimea as the "dog that did not bark." Unlike other places with deep ethnic and confessional cleavages—Chechnya, Bosnia, Georgia, Armenia, and Azerbaijan—Crimea managed to resolve its problems peacefully after the collapse of the Soviet Union.[32] These problems have been significant. The majority Russian population and Russian-speaking Ukrainian population initially resisted unification with Ukraine after its independence, protesting that Crimea's attachment to Ukraine in 1954 violated its constitution. When it became apparent that the Soviet Union was fracturing, members of the Crimean Parliament pushed for independence, which it passed in September 1991. Independence was later peacefully commuted to an autonomous status within Ukraine, not in recognition of Crimean Tatar claims to the peninsula as homeland (as in the creation of the autonomous republic), but because Russians did not want to be subsumed under Ukraine.[33] Three years later Crimea again survived a potentially cataclysmic situation when Crimean president, Iurii Meshkov, made another bid for independence. This lasted a month before infighting broke the movement.[34] Ultimately, Ukraine suppressed the Crimean independence movement; rather than breaking out in violent opposition, the Crimean population accepted their new parent state.

As Crimeans wavered between Russian and Ukrainian identities and stark political realities in the 1990s, the division of the Black Sea fleet presented another problem. Some scholars alleged that Russia initially fanned Crimean movements for independence as a bargaining chip with Ukraine for the fleet. Between 1992 and 1995, however, Russian policy toward Ukraine shifted as politicians in Moscow realized that stable border states were critical to its own success. Especially during the crisis of Chechen secession, Moscow strategists took the perspective that "Ukraine is more important than Crimea." For such reasons, Andrei Malgin maintains that Russia retreated from interfering in Crimean independence, which in turn prompted Ukrainian cooperation on the division of the Black Sea fleet. By 1997, the two states had reached an agreement. Russia was to rent the naval base from Ukraine for a twenty-year period with the possibility of renewal every five years. Some 525 vessels were divided between Russia and Ukraine; three of the five bays went to Russia, one went to Ukraine, and the last one remained de-militarized. Finally, Russia's rental cost for the naval base, $97 million, was to be applied toward Ukrainian gas.[35]

A decade after the failed bids for Crimean independence and the peaceful division of the Black Sea fleet, post-Soviet compromises appear to be wearing thin. Recently, Russia and Ukraine have renewed talks about the base and the division of the fleet. Tensions mounted in 2006, when Ukraine insisted on increasing Russian payments from $97 million to $2 billion in response to Russia's raising of gas prices. Absent that, Ukraine has undertaken other efforts to chip away at Russian holdings in Crimea, including direct occupation of lighthouses and navigation stations.[36] Russia's use of its Black Sea fleet in 2008 to intimidate Georgia further strained relations with Ukraine, prompting another set of rash statements and negotiations over the fleet.[37]

Russians in Crimea remain skeptical of Ukrainian policies, while cleavages have deepened between Crimea's Russian-speaking population and the Crimean Tatars. Recent investigations of Crimean identity politics have shown that Russians, at least to some degree, are adjusting to Ukrainian statehood. Russians accepted Ukrainian as the state language without major resistance, and are making efforts to learn it. More significantly, Russian calls for autonomy have subsided.[38] To claim, however, that the Russian nationalist movement is weak, or "mild," is an overstatement. Discontent over Ukraine's NATO aspirations have been raging in Crimea for years. In the summer of 2006, protestors from all over Ukraine and Russia poured into the peninsula to protest the landing of a U.S. ship for the Sea-Breeze exercises.

In the fall of the same year, Leonid Grach, head of Crimea's communist party, conducted a popular referendum over Ukraine's potential NATO membership. Polls in Crimea demonstrated a 98 percent opposition to NATO based on a 60 percent voter turn out. While this figure may well be the product of vote tampering, it nonetheless demonstrates Crimean ambivalence over Ukraine's western leanings. Russian politicians still view Crimea as a Russian territory, evidenced by their Moscow mayor Lushkov's million dollar investments in the peninsula, their continued support for the Black Sea fleet, and their insistence that Sevastopol, in fact, belongs to Russia.[39] An unknown number of Crimeans hold Russian passports, a number that appears to be growing, and these Crimeans actively support Russian news media.[40]

Crimea has a diverse media, with Ukrainian, Russian, and Crimean newspapers and television stations. Crimean Tatars themselves have a few publications and an evening news-segment in Kirimtatar on a Black Sea television network. Most dominant in Crimea are the Russian-language sources, many of them originating inside of Russia. While Moscow officially declares a non-intervention policy in Crimean affairs, unofficially, Russian opinion influences Crimean politics on numerous levels. In November of 2006, Rossiya-TV, the state-operated channel, produced a four-part segment on Crimea. The program criticized Ukraine's poor management of the region, arguing that "New Ukrainians" descended from Kyiv to build in Crimean nature reserves, while neglecting museums and public buildings.[41] The program also portrayed Russians and the Russian language in Crimea as subjects of state oppression. The most dangerous element of the broadcast was its focus on Crimean Tatars, whose struggle for land and resettlement was conflated with Islamic extremism. The announcer linked Crimean Tatar protests with the radical Islamist group Hezb-e Tahrir, which according to the program, planned to seize "the peninsula's main roads and bays," an action that "would be an excellent platform for an amphibious assault."[42] As Russian media sources emphasize the threat of Hezb-e Tahrir and other extremist groups, few sources acknowledge the vast majority of Crimean Tatars, represented by the Mejlis, repeatedly distance themselves from it.

Similarly, *Izvestiia* ran a series about Crimea that began after Ukrainian ministers championed the peninsula in Moscow to encourage Russian tourism. This series quickly turned negative with the media storm over the NATO protests in June 2006. While the articles focused on many of the issues raised in the television program, they consistently highlighted the case of the Crimean Tatars from an unsympathetic perspective. In May, for example, a reporter described Ukraine's attempts at attracting Russian tourists as feeble in light of Crimean Tatar demonstrations. "It is no secret," wrote the reporter, "that income in Crimea to a large part depends upon Russian tourists. Recently, however, this has become a big question, over all the affairs of the Crimean Tatars." The reporter portrayed Crimea as embroiled in "many protest acts" by Tatars who demand an "autonomous Crimea."[43] The most extreme article in the *Izvestiia* series invoked panic and anti-western sentiments. The article, "Crimea Might Become the Ukrainian Kosovo," complained bitterly about the return of Crimean Tatars to Crimea, and advocated the position of the leader of Proryv (Breakthrough), Aleksei Dobychin.[44] Dobychin, described as the "protector of the Russian-speaking population" on the peninsula, is one of the chief anti-Tatar propagandists and was banned from Crimea by the Ukrainian government. In short, the author claimed that the discontent of Crimean Tatars would "soon turn Ukraine into a new Kosovo."

Crimeans are quick to point out that the Russian media exaggerates the level of crisis on the peninsula. Ukrainian media, while on the whole more sensitive to Crimean Tatar issues of return, has also conflated Islamic extremism with peaceful Muslim organizations. In April 2006, the organization ARRAID (the Ukrainian Muslim Interregional Association of Civic Organizations) protested Kyiv's Special Correspondent program for claiming that Islamic fundamentalists were funded by ARRAID.[45] The media hype is very important for a couple of reasons. First, Russians and Russian-speaking Crimeans tend to read and are influenced by Russian television and Russian publications. As such, media hype fuels expectation of a crisis. Second, even if blown out of proportion, the media does reveal a critical problem in Crimea today: the Crimean Tatars' struggle for rights. Whereas Crimean Tatars may have been hopeful about prospects when they arrived in Ukraine in the early 1990s, fifteen years later, they are frustrated with lack of progress.[46] Because the Ukrainian government feared that Russian media heightened separatist tendencies, it imposed a ban on Russian television in Ukraine in 2008. This ban has lifted after an outpouring of criticism from the Russian-speaking population.[47]

Deep religious fractures compound escalating political and ethnic divisions and divide the peninsula more sharply than ever before. Just as elsewhere in Ukraine, when the Soviet Union collapsed, religion rushed into Crimea to fill the void left by Marxist ideology. With a population numbering about two million people, Crimea has 1,180 registered religious organizations, 60 percent of which are Christian.[48] Of the Orthodox organizations, the vast majority belong to the UOC-MP, 512 of 563. The others are divided between the UOC-KP (25), the UAOC (12), Old Believers (3), and Greek and Armenian churches. There are approximately 300 registered Protestant organizations, 7 Catholic, and 14 Roman Catholic. The rest are composed primarily of Muslim organizations, which number about 350, and a handful of Jewish groups including Krymchaks and Karaim.[49] As the numbers indicate, the most active group on the peninsula is the UOC-MP.

Immediately after Ukrainian independence, UOC-MP officials in collaboration with the church hierarchy in Moscow began planning the revitalization of houses of worship. Crimea's identity as a holy place, which was consciously constructed in the nineteenth century, had not been forgotten in the long years of Soviet rule. The church republished nineteenth-century religious pamphlets that espoused Crimea's Christian heritage while scholars reexamined old and new evidence of the peninsula's Christian past. Nadezhda Proskurina published one of the first comprehensive new studies on Crimea's Christian past in 1997, and others have followed suit.[50] Crimean newspapers, including the communist organ *Krymskaia pravda*, run series after series of articles about Christian holy sites.[51] The Orthodox Church (primarily the UOC-MP) reclaimed old houses of worship from local authorities that the Soviets had turned into movie theatres, laundry halls, and other buildings of public use. Just as elsewhere in Ukraine, the reclamation of religious property is an ongoing and expensive process.

In addition to renovating churches, Orthodox believers in Crimea reclaimed and restored the old monasteries. In under a decade, monasteries that had been closed for sixty and seventy years were operating again. Among the first to open were the Dormition monastery in Bakhchisarai and the Inkerman monastery outside of Sevastopol. Because both of these had been built into the cliffs, the integrity of the original structures remained intact. Of course the monastic complexes—the cells, the dining hall, the hostels—had suffered significantly at the hands of the Soviets, yet the main churches still existed. Monks quickly manufactured at least rudimentary shelters to cover their heads while they erected more permanent structures, and by 1993 Inkerman and Dormition monasteries had made remarkable progress.[52] Some sites had to be completely rebuilt from the ground up, such as the monastery at Cosmas and Damian and the church in Chersonesos, whose buildings had been destroyed during World War II.[53] Diocesan authorities campaigned for their restoration from the 1990s. Priests now hold services in both places, and monks have rebuilt the monastery at the site of Cosmas and Damian. In addition to renewal of the monasteries, sketes have also developed, such as the Spaso-Preobrazhenskii community near Ternovka. The Spaso-Preobrazhenskii skete represents the degree to which Orthodoxy in Crimea has rebounded, and to which the monastic complex still retains its nineteenth-century association with Mt. Athos.

The Spaso-Preobrazhenskii skete has historically been an extension of the Inkerman monastery; before the Russian Revolution, it became a "small monastery within a monastery." Local Christians believe that monks lived in the region since the era of Theodore Studite and St. Stefan of Surozh, the eighth-century Crimean icon-protector whose miracle of prayer produced a spring at the site. Byzantines named the spring after Theodore Studite, and Tatars retained this connection, renaming the spring Ai Todor. Russians claimed this land from the Tatars in the second half of the nineteenth century, and established a small monastery on the site of the spring, right on the foundation of the original church erected by Byzantine monks. This community, which gained official recognition in 1896, lasted until 1922. Like many of the other churches and monasteries of Crimea, local residents tore down the structures of the skete after the Russian Revolution and used the bricks to build small homes. In 1996, one hundred years after its founding, Slavic monks returned to the site, to reconstruct it for a third time. Two years later, the skete became a thriving community with eight monks who profess to live by the rule of Mt. Athos.[54]

As the building continued on the Spaso-Preobrazhenskii skete and other sites throughout the 1990s, the Orthodox Church created a new pilgrimage department advocated by Proskurina among others. The diocese officially opened the department in 1997 and had approximately ten different routes fully functioning by the year 2000.[55] A popular newspaper columnist described the opening of the department as "one more tradition that has been renewed on Crimean land—the tradition of pilgrimage to holy places."[56] Metropolitan of Crimea and Simferopol Lazar explained that "Orthodox holy places are valuable memorials to history and culture from apostolic times to our day. It is important to know our roots, and that [Crimeans] lived in an unusual land." He emphasized that conducting pilgrimage was as important to following the Orthodox faith as was fasting and other spiritual feats. Crimea itself, he pointed out, was influenced by the pilgrims. "Pilgrimage," he argued, "sanctified the land, which means that it itself changes, . . . and becomes blessed." The new pilgrimage department, then, not only introduced Crimea's holiness to visitors and natives, but also covered the peninsula with renewed blessings.[57] He refers to the cycle of holy places: faithful hearts and faithful prayers uttered in a holy place make a place that much more holy. In turn, the enhancement of holiness draws more believers.

Today, pilgrims from Russia can travel to Crimea through a variety of commercial tourist organizations that organize twelve-day tours of "Crimean Athos," as well as the pilgrimage department attached to the Simferopol and Crimea diocese. Tours combine excursions to historical sites on the peninsula with Christian sites. Thus for example, participants can visit the twelfth-century church of the Twelve Apostles and ruins from the Genoese fortress in Balaklava. The stop in Sevastopol includes the St. Vladimir church in the city (initially planned by the naval admiral Lazarev in the 1840s), a tour of battleships, and all the sights of Chersonsesos. The package provides comfortable quarters in a guest house that has an Orthodox library and a priest available for conversation.[58]

In another cycle typical of religion and politics, the activities of the UOC-MP in Crimea has tightened the link to the center. The center in this case is not Kyiv, but Moscow. Patriarch Aleksi of Russia has given his full support to the re-creation of Crimea as a holy place. In a speech reminiscent of earlier Christianizing discourses, he elaborated why Crimea's sites were of special importance to Russians. "Almost one thousand years," the patriarch began, "from the preaching of Apostle Andrew the First Called in Chersonesos, stands the great event of the Christianizing of Russia. Namely, Tauride became for many people from all of Eastern Europe the source of life-giving water, quenching the spiritual thirst of each person striving to find the way to the Holy Land." Just as they had more than a century before, Russian prelates claimed that Crimea was central to Russian Christianity and Russian identity. Aleksi continued in his speech to identify all those saints who occupied Christian scholars in the nineteenth century: Popes Clement and Martin, the seven martyrs, Stefan of Surozh, Cyril and Methodius and Vladimir.[59] He confirmed that the formation of the pilgrimage department was a big step in the construction of Crimea as a holy place, a step that enjoyed wide support throughout the Orthodox community.

In many ways, the re-creation of Crimea as an Orthodox holy place bears a striking resemblance to the past. Today as in the nineteenth century, clergy and scholars draw upon Crimea's deep Christian history to make an argument of holiness. In fact, today many people interested in establishing Crimea's Christian holiness rely upon the precedents set more than one hundred years ago. Moreover, the pace of Christian building and renewal of Crimean Athos is similar to what took place during the creation of the area's nineteenth-century predecessor, Russian Athos. Both incarnations of this Christian holy place have been built following a crisis of international proportions. In the nineteenth century, it was the Crimean War and today, the collapse of the Soviet Union. And just like before the revolution, the monastic community still follows the example of Mt. Athos. The Dormition monastery in Bakhchisarai even produces its own journal titled *Krymskii Afon*.[60]

Yet, the present community is beset by new challenges following the seventy years of communist rule in Crimea, especially the complicated questions of land restitution. When Leonid Kravchuk passed the law, "Measures for Returning Property to Religious Organizations," in 1992, Ukrainian officials contended with the sensitive problems of taking property from one group and giving it to the other, amid the logistical nightmare of transferring government property used by myriad bureaucracies, organizations, and institutions.[61] The law contained a section especially devoted to Crimea, requiring the Crimean Council of Ministers to work with officials in Kyiv and Sevastopol to transfer "buildings that were initially a means for religious worship, and that are being used for other purposes, to religious communities' ownership or use without charge." The law also called for an inventory of moveable religious property in archives and museums and subsequent transfer to the religious communities to which the property originally belonged. Finally, the law encouraged officials to "assist religious organizations in constructing buildings meant for religious worship," to facilitate charitable foundations, and to aid support centers for Crimean Tatar returnees.[62]

The 1992 law was a tall order.[63] Central and local governments had to fund their own relocation, no small feat for a territory in severe economic depression and simultaneously dealing with a powerful secessionist movement. Some sites could not be easily turned from their new uses. Following the Russian Revolution, for example, Soviet officials confiscated monastic territory located in the ancient city of Chersonesos and transformed it into an archaeological preserve. This is no great surprise; the area is known as "Slavic Pompeii" for its vast array of ruins dating back to the fifth century BCE.[64] In accordance with the law on religious property, however, the Orthodox Church wished to reclaim its former leading role in the preserve. Archaeologists had long ago transformed any remaining buildings once associated with the monastery into offices, museum space, or libraries, and were continuing to excavate the ruins.[65] Thus, when the Orthodox Church attempted to reclaim that space after the collapse, it met serious opposition; officials in the archaeological preserve feared that church plans might encroach upon previous and ongoing archaeological research.

The ensuing controversy began quietly, when a monk known as Father Paissy arrived asking to establish a hermitage on the site of the ruins. Sympathetic preserve officials designated a space for his hut in the location of the former church of St. Vladimir. Gradually, the monk's living quarters spread, first with a small garden plot, then with a small shed, then with new monks. Suddenly, or so it seemed, the preserve realized that a community of monks squatted on a space significantly larger than that allotted them. Moreover, these monks had begun plans for building in earnest and had initiated a correspondence campaign to put pressure on the government to approve further building. It was later revealed that the ascetic monk Father Paissy was an active agent of UOC-MP who had led other land reclamation initiatives elsewhere, using similar, indirect methods.[66]

Conflict between the church and the preserve escalated as the millennial celebration of Crimean Christianity approached, for President Kuchma approved the reconstruction of the St. Vladimir church on the spot of the original structure. UOC-MP expansion in Chersonesos continued in an assertive manner until 1997 when the church hired a helicopter to airlift a gazebo to mark the baptismal font of St. Vladimir in the ruins. This act was accomplished against the express wishes of the Ministry of Culture. Once church officials installed the gazebo, however, it proved impossible to remove for it had the devotion of Orthodox believers who delivered it to the site during their pilgrimages. Matters grew worse in the summer of 2000 when Father Paissy, with several other monks, took over the museum's property at gun point.[67]

The relationship between the archaeological preserve and the Russian Orthodox Church reached peaceful resolution, and one of the directors describes the relationship as quite cordial.[68] Reasons for the warmer relationship are varied and can be partially attributed to the departure of Father Paissy and the decision of Patriarch Aleksi of Moscow to retreat from claims on Chersonesos. Nonetheless, the church on the ruins retains its old attraction to state powers; both President Vladimir Putin of Russia and President Kuchma attended the elevation of the church's cross on 28 July 2001.[69]

A similar controversy has unfolded between the Cosmas and Damian monastery and the nature preserve outside of Alushta. Before the revolution, the monastery occupied a vast tract of land used as imperial hunting grounds. The Soviets turned this space into a nature preserve. For decades environmental officials governed this piece of land under strict ecological regulations, and in the hustle and bustle of Crimean tourism, the preserve remains a pristine natural environment where only backpackers and trekkers can move freely. When the Council for Religious Affairs in Ukraine recognized the Cosmas and Damian monastery in 1992, the church immediately attempted to renew the monastery, and a few monks established a hermitage there.[70] From the perspective of the preserve's officials, an expanding monastery had the potential to offset the delicate ecosystem. The influx of pilgrimage traffic into the preserve, which brought smog from vehicles, human waste, and garbage, most concerned environmentalists.

Currently the Cosmas and Damian monastery has a chapel over the spring and a small chapel closer to the monastery, where an attractive two-story building houses the brothers. Several monks live at the monastery, all of whom had very different backgrounds before dedicating themselves to a life in the service of prayer. The abbot of the monastery, Father Nikanor, has said in an interview that all monks were educated professionals: "one was a director of an orchestra, a musician, the other was a diplomat, the third a microbiologist, another managed an agro-industrial complex."[71] With the collapse of the Soviet Union and the freedom of religion that has emerged in the aftermath, these professionals are now able to pursue their true calling. At Cosmas and Damian, they lead rich lives of prayer and maintain the grounds of the spring in anticipation of pilgrims. The monastery even has one of its original icons. A local village woman hid the monastery's icon during the Soviet period, and passed it back to the complex upon her death.[72]

Despite a significant outpouring of support from the Orthodox community, Father Nikanor described each phase of monastery growth as a point of delicate negotiation with preserve officials. For example, when the monastery erected cells for the brothers containing showers, heat, and toilets, which he said, "one can not go without," the administration of the preserve initiated a suit, calling the development "illegal construction." Another point of concern involves the fees that pilgrims must pay in order to reach the monastery. Like many nature preserves, the park near Alushta requires a special pass and an entrance fee in order to enter park grounds. Father Nikanor has protested placing what he describes as a price on religious rituals. He further complains that while the preserve earns revenue from pilgrims, it does not share anything with the monastery, which leaves the latter dependent upon believers who have already paid once for the trip. The biggest obstacle to the preserve-monastery relationship is land. Before the revolution, the monastery administered more than one hundred acres, and now has only a small plot. The monastery claims that according to Ukrainian law, the preserve must hand over all the land. This still has not happened, and probably will not happen.[73]

There are many other controversies surrounding the renovation and reclamation of religious sites, and the two described above are meant only as examples of a wider phenomenon that is occurring not just in Crimea, but across all of the former territory of the Soviet Union. For the most part, government officials in Crimea have been quite supportive of Orthodox restoration and the expansion of Christianity. Critics allege, however, that support of the Orthodox occurs at the expense of other faith groups, especially the Crimean Tatars, who are attempting to restore their own monuments. A researcher with the Religious Information Service of Ukraine has adroitly summed up the problem: "property was returned to churches mostly on the basis of only one criterion, namely, denominational affiliation and the religious inclinations of the officials who made decisions about the return of the property." Thus, according to this researcher, the process of religious property restitution was not handled fairly by courts of law. Rather, decisions were made according to the denomination of the court. The researcher further points out that in Lviv "the Ukrainian Orthodox Church (Moscow Patriarchate) was given back not a single of dozens or even hundreds of church buildings, and in the eastern regions of Ukraine not a single building was given back to the Kyivan Patriarchate or the Ukrainian Autocephalous Orthodox Church."[74] In Crimea, the issue of religious property restitution was even more pronounced, for in most cases involving Tatars, decisions were made by administrators who profess Orthodoxy.

Crimean Tatars lost control over their religious monuments well before the revolution. Russian rule had gradually encroached upon their property since the era of Catherine II,[75] and it accelerated during the Crimean War, about the same time the Orthodox began the first transformation of Crimea into a holy place. Soviet hostility toward ethnic as well as religious groups ushered forward the dismantling of Tatar mosques and holy places. Today, as Crimean Tatars return, they are working to restore the monuments of their ancestors. In some cases, such as the khan's palace in Bakhchisarai, they have been successful. The khan's palace has been beautifully restored with an internal museum and a walking tour that informs visitors of the palace's history. Other places in Bakhchisarai have not been so fortunate. The Zincirli Medresse, for example, sits in a state of ruins. It is not abandoned; local Tatars carefully supervise it. However, they do not have the money to fund its restoration. A much worse case has been that of an old cemetery in the center of Bakhchisarai, Azizler (Saints), which had been torn down by the Soviets and later transformed into a market.[76]

From the beginning of their return in the 1990s, the Crimean Tatars attempted to reclaim the cemetery, and applied to local authorities to remove the market.[77] The government of Bakhchisarai under the laws of Ukraine agreed to assign the cemetery the status of an historic landmark and to order the relocation of the market. Years later, nothing had changed, and the market had even expanded. Throughout the summer of 2006, Tatars met the opening of the market in Bakhchisarai every morning with a peaceful demonstration. Each day, merchants pushed past praying Tatars to conduct their business. Tensions were high between the two groups, but they managed to avoid violent confrontation. On this particular day, however, Cossacks, organized into paramilitary groups with racial agendas, descended into Bakhchisarai to block Tatar protests.[78] The Cossacks and their supporters closed roads leading into and out of the city, and they sent several Tatars to the hospital. Rumors of this attack reached Kyiv and a public response motivated the newly elected prime minister, Viktor Yanukovich, to visit Crimea and meet with the leader of the Mejlis, Mustafa Jemilev. Yanukovich and Jemilev agreed upon a series of measures to address Tatar grievances, including the prosecution of the attackers, the provision of Ukrainian funds to build a Tatar memorial in the market, and measures to relocate the market. After local Crimean officials refused to approve the agreement in August, another violent outburst occurred when an angry crowd stoned Tatar protestors. This compelled local officials to sign the document. At the time of writing, the territory of the cemetery has passed into the hands of the historical preserve, and the market is in the process of relocating.[79]

The situation with the market in Bakhchisarai illustrates the severity of conflict over restoration of holy sites. On one hand, the struggle ensues over a particular piece of land. On the other, it is a battle for Crimea itself. In the nineteenth century, the expansion of the Orthodox Church occurred following the exodus of the Crimean Tatars. Now, in the post-Soviet period, the Crimean Tatars are returning, and they too wish to restore important places in their pre-revolutionary history, including their own holy places. As one prolific journalist has written, "Many memorials have been ruined in the period of the deportation of Crimean Tatars, and their preservation is now being encroached upon."[80] In the middle of the nineteenth century, the majority of Tatars were without the cultural and economic tools necessary for protest. Today, Tatars are equipping themselves with knowledge about their past and about the present laws. Therefore, each new phase of church expansion meets a public debate over how such expansion will affect Tatars.

Two outstanding cases demonstrate the conflict between Tatars and Christians. The Dormition monastery shares a boundary with the Gaspirali complex, a Tatar site that contains the ruins of the Zincirli Medresse, Ismail Gaspirali's home and grave, and an historic mausoleum of the Giray clan. After World War II, the Soviets confiscated all land between the Medresse and the monastery, and transformed both historic monuments into a neurology-psychology care center. When the Soviet Union collapsed, conflict emerged between returning Tatars and the reemerging Orthodox Church over land restitution; among the issues at stake was the exact boundary between the Dormition monastery and the Gaspirali complex. In 2001, Tatars gathered in the square of the Dormition monastery to protest what they described as an illegal transfer of public land to the monastery.[81]

Controversy continued and in an article published four years later, Oleg Markelov commented that the Dormition monastery, a place that was "one of the most ancient Orthodox holy places on the peninsula," a place that helped make Crimea a holy place of "the first level apart from Palestine," stuck "like a bone in people's throats."[82] Nor did Markelov see the problem resolving any time soon. A year later another conflict broke out between the Tatars in Bakhchisarai and the monks of the monastery, when according to the Tatars, the monastery encroached illegally upon a shared border. In this case, Ukrainian special forces joined with Cossacks to block a Tatar protest that opposed monastery construction on the border between the Medresse and the monastery.[83]

In the same province of Bakhchisarai, another controversy involves the village of Golubinka/Fotisala, a small agricultural community that has become the center of a Crimean media storm. Both Christian and Muslim communities in Crimea claim one mound at this site as having particular holy significance. Conflict between local Tatars and the Christians desiring to build a church first arose in 2001 after local Tatars, who long considered the mound a sacred place, were surprised to witness the first stages of new construction—an archaeological survey. They were alarmed at this sign, for according to local Tatars, no one had been given advance warning.

Construction on the site came to a halt not with Tatar protests, but with discoveries of the surveyors. Archaeologists found human bones in the mound. Tatar representatives contacted the director of the Bakhchisarai State Historical and Cultural Preserve (BGIZ), who informed them that the local Orthodox Church in the village of Golubinka had long ago entered into an arrangement with BGIZ to receive a small allotment of land on the mound to build a church. The Tatars immediately protested this distribution of land as unfair and requested an impartial archaeological excavation to analyze the site. According to Ukrainian law, any land of potential historical and archaeological value must be researched and properly preserved before its fate is decided. Tatars contended that neither happened in this case.[84] When archaeologists produced their reports, they concluded that the bodies were buried with Christian, not Muslim, rituals. Still, the Tatars refused to budge.

The situation in Golubinka came to a head in the summer of 2006 when an article appeared in the newspaper *Krymskaia vremia*. The article title expresses the seriousness of the allegations: "Weakness of the Authorities and the Lawless Rise of Tatar Terrorism." Expectations to the contrary, the article did not analyze terrorism. Rather, it criticized the non-violent Tatar protest in Golubinka. Author Natalia Kiseleva argued that continued Tatar protests against Christian building on the site was a product of "Tatar chauvinism," and a "dog's nonsense."[85] She pointed out that archaeologists had produced evidence of twenty graves with burials reflecting Christian rites. Kiseleva maintained that Tatars were objecting to construction of a Christian church because they objected to church expansion in general. She concluded the article with a description of the architectural plans for the new church. The local priest designed the church to have a glass floor, so that worshippers could maintain a clear connection with their Christian ancestors and the sacred space of the past by seeing through the glass to the excavation below.

Kiseleva's article prompted an outcry from the Tatar community, which currently is struggling to define itself against a wave of anti-Islam that has swept down from Moscow. Since the war in Chechnya began, Russian and Ukrainian news media frequently conflate Islam with terrorism, and have recently begun to label Crimean Tatars in a like manner.[86] Kiseleva's vitriolic title reflects this larger phenomenon, and it produced an immediate response from Crimean Tatars. The historian journalist Ibraim Abdullaev, author of numerous articles on Crimea's past in local newspapers, was prompted by Kiseleva's piece to explain Tatar interest in the site. He countered Orthodox claims on the mound with his own historical revision, which he grounded in archival research and archaeological reports. In short, Abdullaev agreed the site had a Christian past. Yet, he was careful to note that given both the location and the dates associated with the burials, the mound was not an Orthodox site, but a Catholic one, belonging to medieval Genoese conquerors and their descendents. As such, Abdullaev argued that the site represented Tatar heritage, for Crimean Tatars are descendents of these Islamicized Crimean Christians, whether Catholic, Greek Orthodox, or Armenian. Moreover, Abdullaev found evidence in the form of records of epigraphs taken by pre-revolutionary archaeologists that indicated a mixture of Tatar and Christian names on the burial markers. Thus, Abdullaev concluded, the site represented the heritage of Crimean Tatars, which was confessionally mixed, and it extended back through Crimea's history for centuries. It did not, he pointedly stated, belong to the Russian population, which settled in the region "in the last sixty years, but which [was] surrounded by archaeological and architectural evidence of more than 1,000 years."[87]

Throughout Muslim and Christian dialogues in Crimea, interpretation of the relationship between religion and landscape is consistently evident. In the year 2000, the Russian Orthodox Church prepared for the two-thousand year celebration of Christianity in Crimea. To commemorate this momentous date, diocesan authorities readied all local churches and monasteries. Those structures that were under renovation, like the St. Vladimir Cathedral in Chersonesos, were rushed toward completion. This rush in itself did not cause alarm. However, the UOC-MP also decided to erect crosses throughout the peninsula on "population points," that is, entrances to and exits from Crimean cities and heavily populated villages.

Plans for the celebration of the two-thousandth anniversary of Christianity had begun as early as 1997, which coincided with the formation of the pilgrimage department in Crimea, and initially UNESCO became involved in these church plans. In some cases, Orthodox authorities presented their plans to raise a cross at population points to a village council, which later led Christian authorities to claim that the plan to establish crosses had received Tatar approval. These authorities also argued that the practice of standing crosses at city outskirts was not a novel idea, but represented pre-revolutionary, and in some cases ancient Slavic Orthodox, traditions. To support this claim, authorities drew upon scholarly studies, a process that reflects the Orthodox Church's old nineteenth-century facility with rational knowledge and social sciences.[88]

Tatars believed that the religious symbols were being used as propaganda, and in the middle of the night, protesters pulled down the crosses. Abdullaev linked the raising of the crosses directly to politics and the bid of the Russian population to reunite Crimea with Russia. "The activities of the Crimean diocese," he argued, were aimed at "destabilizing the political situation on the peninsula." Here, Abdullaev reflects a concern shared by many Tatars, that when Iurii Meshkov's attempt to separate Crimea from Ukraine failed in 1994, pro-Russian factions in Crimea tried religion.[89] To be more explicit, Abdullaev and others point out that for the most part, the Orthodox Church that has been taking control of the restoration of Christian holy places has not represented any of the splinter Ukrainian Orthodox branches, but rather the Ukrainian Orthodox Church of the Moscow Patriarchate.

The way out of this conflict between Muslims and Christians in Crimea seems as difficult as a union between Ukraine's divided Orthodox churches. At one time, Crimea did have an interconfessional council called "Peace: God's Gift," which promoted healthy dialogue between Jews, Christians, and Muslims on the peninsula. After the incidents of putting up crosses in the summer of 2000, however, the Crimean Tatars pulled out in protest. They have yet to rejoin.[90] And noticeably absent, apart from the Tatars, is Bishop Klyment, the prelate in Crimea from UOC-KP. He would like to participate but has been barred from doing so.

The future of Crimea is uncertain. Article after article in the Crimean and Russian media predict an ethnic and religious conflict on the level of that seen years ago in Yugoslavia, or more recently in Chechnya. On the most extreme sides, Tatars who see parallels between crimes of the past in the discriminations of today accuse Russians in Crimea of enacting an "eternal dream" of ethnically cleansing the native inhabitants. The emergence of Cossack paramilitary groups who have brought weapons into peaceful protests and employ terror tactics to silence Tatars demanding equal rights certainly give them grounds for concern.[91] So does the Russian media, which exacerbates local tensions with predictions of a rise of Islamic fundamentalism in Crimea on the level seen in Chechnya or Uzbekistan. Tatars themselves admit that radical Islamic activists have turned their attention to Crimea. Yet, the vast majority of Crimean Tatars are quite clear that they reject violence as a bargaining tool and have no desire "to burn down the house in which they live."[92]

Today, as in the nineteenth century, religion occupies the center of Crimea's transformation. Gwendolyn Strasse argues that in Crimea, "symbols and myths from the imperial Russian period, kept alive during the Soviet era, dominate Russian public imagination."[93] Religious monuments in Crimea remain among the most important symbols of the pre-revolutionary period and often become the battleground for identity. For all religions that attach significance to place, moreover, it is natural that believers wish to protect landscapes considered holy. Jews, Muslims, and Christians, one scholar writes, are concerned that a holy place might be "in danger of contamination" by those who are spiritually "unclean," or who do not know how to worship correctly. Therefore, "to guarantee the spiritual cleanliness of the holy places," it is imperative that they are in the hands of the rightful guardians.[94]

Most agree that the first step toward resolving religious tension in Crimea is dialogue, and despite Tatar reluctance to rejoin the interconfessional council, both Christians and Muslims in Crimea have made efforts to keep channels of communication open.[95] For example, in 2004, Metropolitan Lazar and Mufti Emirali Ablaiev issued a joint declaration against the manipulation of religious belief in political platforms. In it, they express the spirit of religious restoration, as well as the stark controversies that have emerged: "Our current era on the peninsula is a process of active rebirth and renewal of Orthodoxy and Islam as the two founding confessions in the autonomous republic." They acknowledge that this renewal was fraught with challenges, for as they warned in their statement, "certain politicians and the mass media give one-sided coverage of interethnic and inter-religious relations in Crimea to gain political advantages." The two religious leaders are appealing "to the representatives of all confessions, representatives of government powers, and members of the press to understand that . . . playing with the interconfessional relations might have tragic results for future populations."[96] One hopes the interfaith dialogue expressed in this statement will continue to guide Crimeans as they negotiate sacred landscapes and adapt the legacy of nineteenth-century Christianizing to the needs of the present.

Notes

Introduction

1. Anatoly Demidov, *Travels in the Crimea; through Hungary, Wallachia, and Moldavia, during the Year 1837* (London, 1853), 342.

2. Artemii Tereshchenko, "Ocherki Novorossiiskago Kraia. Nekotoriia mestnosti iuzhnago Kryma," *Zhurnal ministerstva narodnago prosvieshcheniia* 84, no. 2 (1854): 40.

3. Crimea's early Christianity has attracted archaeological and historical research from the nineteenth century to the present. A representative, but by no means an exhaustive, bibliography includes the following works: D. Strukov, *Drevnie pamiatniki khristianstva v Tavride* (Moscow, 1876); D. V. Ainalov, *Pamiatniki khristianskogo Khersonesa*, vyp.1, *Razvaliny khramov* (Moscow, 1905); A. G. Gertsen, O. A. Makhneva, *Peshchernye goroda Kryma* (Simferopol, 1989); T. Iu. Iashaeva, *Peshchernyi kompleks v okruge Khersona. Problemy istorii i arkheologii Kryma* (Simferopol, 1994); Iu. M. Mogarichev, *Peshchernye tserkvi Tavriki* (Simferopol, 1997); V. M. Zubar and S. B. Sorochan, *U istokov khristianstva v iugo-zapadnoi tavrike. Epokha i vera* (Kyiv, 2005).

4. Alan Fisher, *The Crimean Tatars* (Stanford, 1978), 3.

5. Ibraim Abdullaev, "Mechet Kryma," *Golos Kryma* 30, no. 193 (1 August 1997): 5.

6. Apollon Skal'kovskii, *Opyt' statisticheskogo opisaniia novorossiiskogo kraia*, chast' 1, *Geografiia, etnografiia, i narodochislenie novorossiiskogo kraia* (Odessa, 1850), 272–73.

7. Boris Zasypkin, *Pamiatniki arkhitektury Krymskikh Tatar* (Crimea, 1927), excerpted in *Krymskie Tatary. Khrestomatiia po etnicheskoi istorii i traditsionnoi kul'ture*, ed. M. A. Aradzhioni, A. G. Gertsen, et al. (Simferopol, 2005), 211.

8. A. I. Markevich, "Pereseleniia Krymskikh Tatar v Turtsiu v sviazi s dvizheniem naseleniia v Krymu," *Izvestiia Akademii nauk SSSR*, Seriia 7, otd. Gumanitarnykh nauk, 4–7 (1928): 375–89. Kemal Karpat, who has studied Tatar migration from the Ottoman perspective, argues that altogether approximately 1,800,000 Tatars left Crimea between 1783 and 1922. Kemal H. Karpat, *Ottoman Population, 1830–1914: Demographic and Social Characteristics* (Madison, 1985), 66. See also the discussion of Russian annexation in the classic account by Alan Fisher, *The Russian Annexation of Crimea, 1772–1783* (Cambridge, 1970).

9. For a good treatment of Crimean Greeks and Armenians during the reign of Catherine II, see Gregory L. Bruess, *Religion, Identity, and Empire: A Greek Archbishop in the Russia of Catherine the Great* (New York, 1997); M. A. Aradzhioni, "Vozvrashchenie v Krym starozhitel'cheskogo khristianskogo naseleniia posle emigratsii 1778," *Materialy po arkheologii, istorii, i etnografii Tavrii* 8 (2001): 485–501.

10. Several works have provided insights into the European immigration to New Russia: Skal'kovskii, *Opyt' statisticheskogo opisaniia novorossiiskogo kraia*; K. V. Khanatskii, *Pamiatnaia kniga Tavricheskoi gubernii* (Simferopol, 1867); E. I. Druzhinina, *Iuzhnaia Ukraina v 1800–1825* (Moscow, 1970); and Willard Sunderland, *Taming the Wildfield* (Ithaca, 2004).

11. Traveling through Crimea in 1843, Iurii Bartenev noted, for example, that the Tatars and gypsies of Evpatoria were "very poor," but "they loved" the city authorities "for their fairness and goodwill." Iurii Nikitich Bartenev, "Zhizn' v Evpatorii," *Russkii arkhiv* 9 (1899): 120.

12. Victor Amanton, *Notices sur les diverses populations du Gouvernement de la Tauride et spécialement de la Crimée. Moeurs et usages des Tatars de la Crimée* (Besançon, 1854), 3–4.

13. Amanton, *Notices sur les diverses populations*, 3–4.

14. Robert Crews reminds us that "toleration" had a "much different meaning in eighteenth- and nineteenth-century Europe" than it does today. Robert D. Crews, *For Prophet and Tsar: Islam and Empire in Russia and Central Asia* (Cambridge, 2006), 9.

15. Russian and Ukrainian scholars have explored the spread of Christianity in Crimea. See Iu. A. Katunin, *Iz istorii khristianstva v Krymu. Tavricheskaia eparkhiia, vtoraia polovina XIX-nachalo XX veka* (Simferopol, 1995); Katunin, *Monastyri Kryma v XIX–XX vekakh: po materialam krymskikh arkhivov* (Simferopol, 2000); Katunin, *Simferopol'skaia krymskaia eparkhiia v 1950–1964 godakh* (Simferopol, 2004); and V. G. Tur, *Pravoslavnye monastyri Kryma v XIX-nachale XX veka*, 2nd ed. (Kyiv, 2006).

16. My understanding of the distinction between Christianization and conversion in an imperial context is drawn from a variety sources, including David Snow and Richard Machalek, "The Sociology of Conversion," *Annual Review of Sociology* 10 (1984): 167–90; Lewis R. Rambo, *Understanding Religious Conversion* (New Haven, 1993); V. Bailey Gillespie, *The Dynamics of Religious Conversion* (Birmingham, 1991); Jean Comaroff and John Comaroff, *Of Revelation and Revolution: Christianity, Colonialism, and Consciousness in South Africa* (Chicago, 1991). In the context of the Russian Empire, the works of Nicholas Breyfogle and Paul Werth have most influenced my thinking. See Nicholas Breyfogle, *Heretics and Colonizers: Forging Russian Ties in the South Caucasus* (Ithaca, 2005); and Paul W. Werth, *At the Margins of Orthodoxy: Mission, Governance, and Confessional Politics in Russia's Volga-Kama Region, 1827–1905* (Ithaca, 2002).

17. Nicholas V. Riasanovsky, *Nicholas I and Official Nationality in Russia, 1825–1855* (Berkeley, 1959), 16.

18. Cynthia H. Whittaker, "The Ideology of Sergei Uvarov: An Interpretive Essay," *Russian Review* 37, no. 2 (1978): 158–76; here, 161; see also Whittaker, *The Origins of Modern Russian Education: An Intellectual Biography of Count Sergei Uvarov, 1786–1855* (DeKalb, 1984); Andrei Zorin, *Kormia Dvuglavogo Orla . . . Literatura i gosudarstvennaia ideologiia v rossii v poslednei treti XVIII-pervoi treti XIX veka* (Moscow, 2001), 337–74.

19. Riasanovsky, *Nicholas I*, 84.

20. For an account of Crimean *kraevedenie*, see A. A. Nepomniashchi, *Ocherki razvitiia istoricheskogo kraevedeniia Kryma v XIX–nachale XX veka* (Simferopol, 1998); *Zapiski puteshestvennikov i putevoditeli v razvitii istoricheskogo kraevedeniia Kryma (posledniaia tret' XVIII–nachalo XX veka* (Kyiv, 1999); and *Muzeinoe delo v Krymu i ego staratelі (XIX–nachalo XX veka). Biobibliograficheskoe issledovanie* (Simferopol, 2000).

21. "God na iuzhnom beregu kryma (1852–1853)," *Russkaia beseda*, 3, no. 5 (1856): 47.

22. Aleksandr Ivanov, "Vospominaniia o Vysokopreosviashchennom Innokentii, arkhiepiskopie khersonskii i tavricheskii," published from no. 23 *TEV* (1900), 15–16.

23. Prot. Arsenii Lebedintsev, "Stoletie tserkovnoi zhizni Kryma, 1783–1883," *ZOOID* 13 (1883): 214.

24. Innokentii inspired mixed reactions among his contemporaries, who both praised and condemned his contribution to theology. For the latter, see the characterization based on Filaret's thought in Georges Florovsky, *Ways of Russian Theology*, ed. Richard S. Haugh and trans. Robert L. Nichols (Belmont, 1979); for praise, see T. Butkevich, *Innokentii Borisov, byvshii arkhiepiskop khersonskii* (St. Petersburg, 1887); Nikolai Barsov, ed., *Materialy dlia biografii Innokentiia Borisova, arkhiepiskopa khersonskogo i tavricheskogo* (St. Petersburg, 1884); Nikandr Levitskii, *Vysokopreosviashchennyi Innokentii, arkhiepiskop khersonskii i tavricheskii* (Moscow, 1904).

25. On the problematic definition of "Church/church," see Vera Shevzov, "Letting the People into Church: Reflections on Orthodoxy and Community in Late Imperial Russia," in *Orthodox Russia: Belief and Practice under the Tsars*, ed. Valerie A. Kivelson and Robert H. Greene (University Park, 2003), 60. See also Mark D. Steinberg and Heather J. Coleman, *Sacred Stories: Religion and Spirituality in Modern Russia*, (Bloomington, 2007), 16.

26. Robert P. Geraci and Michael Khodarkovsky, eds., *Of Religion and Empire: Mis-*

sions, Conversion, and Tolerance in Tsarist Russia (Ithaca, 2002), 335.

27. For an excellent discussion of the literature, see Robert Crews, "Empire and the Confessional State: Islam and Religious Politics in Nineteenth-Century Russia," *American Historical Review* 108 (2003): 50–83. Other studies that look at the imperial process more broadly and deserve special note, include: Robert Geraci, *Window on the East: National and Imperial Identities in Late Tsarist Russia* (Ithaca, 2001); Daniel R. Brower and Edward J. Lazzerini, eds. *Russia's Orient: Imperial Borderlands and Peoples, 1700–1917* (Bloomington, 1997); and Charles Robert Steinwedel, "Invisible Threads of Empire: State, Religion, and Ethnicity in Tsarist Bashkiria, 1773–1917," (Ph.D. diss., Columbia University, 1999).

28. Notable analyses of Orthodox missions include: Paul D. Garrett, *St. Innocent, Apostle to America* (Crestwood, 1979); Gregory Freeze, "The Rechristianization of Russia: The Church and Popular Religion, 1750–1850," *Studia Slavica Finlandensia* 7 (1990): 101–36; Werth, *At the Margins of Orthodoxy;* and Geraci and Khodarkovsky, *Of Religion and Empire*.

29. See Agnes Kefeli, "Constructing an Islamic Identity: The Case of Elyshevo Village in the Nineteenth Century," in *Russia's Orient*, ed. Brower and Lazzerini, 271–91.

30. Randon Jerris has examined the Catholic Christianizing of landscapes: Randon Jerris, "Cult Lines and Hellish Mountains: The Development of Sacred Landscape in the Early Medieval Alps," *Journal of Medieval and Early Modern Studies* 32, no.1 (Winter 2002): 85–108.

31. Scholars have emphasized that the church professionalized missions only after the Great Reforms. See J. Eugene Clay, "Orthodox Missionaries and 'Orthodox Heretics' in Russia, 1886–1917," in *Of Religion and Empire*, ed. Geraci and Khodarkovsky, 38–69; John D. Strickland, "Remembering Rus in Modern Russia: The Orthodox Church and its Cultural Mission before the Revolutions," in *Modern Greek Studies Yearbook* 14/15 (1998/1999): 151.

32. See the classic studies: Ernest Gellner, *Nations and Nationalism* (Ithaca, 1983); Eric Hobsbawm, *Nations and Nationalism since 1780: Programme, Myth, Reality* (Cambridge, 1990); Benedict Anderson, *Imagined Communities: Reflections on the Origin and Spread of Nationalism* (London, 1991); and Liah Greenfeld, *Nationalism: Five Roads to Modernity* (Cambridge, 1992).

33. For traditional treatments of both movements, see the classic work by Hans Kohn, *Pan-Slavism: Its History and Ideology* (Notre Dame, 1953); Andrzej Walicki, *A History of Russian Thought from the Enlightenment to Marxism* (Stanford, 1979), 111–15 and 300–8; and more recent articles by Andreas Renner, "Defining a Russian Nation: Mikhail Katkov and the 'Invention ' of National Politics," *Slavonic and East European Review* 81, no. 4 (2003): 659–82; and Olga Maiorova, "War as Peace: The Trope of War in Russian Nationalist Discourse during the Polish Uprising of 1863," *Kritika: Explorations in Russian and Eurasian History* 6, no. 3 (Summer 2005): 501–34.

34. Laurie Manchester shows that the sons of priests continued to shape public discourse well after the Great Reforms technically disbanded the clerical estate. Laurie Manchester, *Holy Fathers, Secular Sons: Clergy, Intelligentsia, and the Modern Self in Revolutionary Russia* (DeKalb, 2008).

35. Representative works include: Theofanis George Stavrou, *Russian Interests in Palestine, 1882–1914: A Study of Religious and Educational Enterprise* (Thessaloniki, 1963); Stephen K. Batalden, *Catherine II's Greek Prelate: Eugenios Voulgaris in Russia, 1771–1806* (New York, 1982); Theofanis George Stavrou and Peter R. Weisenel, *Travelers to the Christian East from the Twelfth to the Twentieth Century* (Columbus, 1986); Theophilus Prousis, "Russian Philorthodox Relief during the Greek War of Independence," *Modern Greek Studies Yearbook* 1 (1985): 31–60 and *Russian Society and the Greek Revolution* (Dekalb, 1994); Bruess, *Religion, Identity, and Empire*; Lucien Frary, "Russia and Independent Greece: Politics, Religion, and Print Culture (1833–1844)," (Ph.D. diss., University of Minnesota, 2003).

36. A few scholars have examined these questions during the period covered in this book: Alan W. Fisher, "Emigration of Muslims from the Russian Empire in the Years after the Crimean War," *Jahrbücher für Geschichte Osteuropas* 35, no. 3 (1987): 356–71; Willis Brooks, "Russia's Conquest and Pacification of the Caucasus: Relocation Becomes a Pogrom in the Post-Crimean War Period," *Nationalities Papers* 23, no. 4 (1995): 675–86; Brian Williams, "The Hijra and Forced Migration from Nineteenth-Century Russia to the Ottoman Empire: A Critical Analysis of the Great Crimean Tatar Emigration, 1860–1861," *Cahiers du Monde russe*, 41, no. 1 (2000): 79–108; Mark Pinson, "Russian Policy and the Emigration of the Crimean Tatars to the Ottoman Empire, 1854–1862" (2 parts), *Güney-Dou Avrupa Ara tırmaları Dergisi* (1972): 37–55 and (1973/74): 101–14.

37. Steinberg and Coleman, *Sacred Stories*, 2.

38. I have elaborated this theme elsewhere: "Ruins into Relics: The Monument to St. Vladimir on the Excavations of Chersonesos, 1827–1857," *Russian Review* (October 2004): 655–72; and in the introduction and the chapter entitled "Challenges of Church Archaeology in Post-Soviet Crimea," in *Selective Remembrances: the Construction, Commemoration, and Consecration of the Past*, ed. Philip Kohl, Mara Kozelsky, and Nachman Ben-Yehuda (Chicago, 2008), 71–98.

39. See, for example, Rossiiskii Gosudarstvennyi Istoricheskii Arkhiv (RGIA), f. 796, op. 129, d. 1815 (About the conditions of the dioceses for 1847); RGIA, f. 796, op. 130, d. 983 and d. 1636 (About the conditions of the dioceses for 1848); RGIA, f. 796, op. 131, d. 67 (About the status of the dioceses for 1849); RGIA, 796, op. 139, d. 2484 (About the status of the dioceses for 1857), and so on.

40. The Holy Synod approved of the creation of a new diocese in 1859, but the new bishop did not arrive in his seat until 1860. For a standard complaint about the burdens upon the consistory, see RGIA, f. 796, op. 133, d. 81 (About moving the Kherson consistory into a new status).

41. In addition to various works previously cited, see Edward Lazzerini, "Local Accommodation and Resistance to Colonialism in Nineteenth-Century Crimea," in *Russia's Orient*, 169–87; Edward A. Allworth, ed., *The Tatars of Crimea: Return to the Homeland. Studies and Documents*, 2nd ed. (Durham, 1998); Brian Glyn Williams, *The Crimean Tatars: The Diaspora Experience and the Forging of a Nation* (Boston, 2001) and a series of articles by the same author, including "The Deportation and Ethnic Cleansing of the Crimean Tatars," in *Ethnic Cleansing in Twentieth-Century Europe*, ed. Steven Vardy and Hunt Tooley (New York, 2003); Greta Lynn Uehling, *Beyond Memory: The Crimean Tatars' Deportation and Return* (New York, 2004); Kelly Ann O'Neill, "Between Subversion and Submission: The Integration of the Crimean Khanate in the Russian Empire, 1783–1853," (Ph.D. diss., Harvard University, 2006); Gul'nara Bekirova, *Krym i krymskie tatary, XI–XX veka* (Moscow, 2005); and the many interesting articles by Ibraim Abdullaev in *Golos Kryma*.

42. See O'Neill, "Between Subversion and Submission."

43. M. A. Aradzhioni, *Greki Kryma i priazov'ia istoriia izucheniia i istoriografiia etnicheskoi istorii i kul'tury* (88e gg. XVIII v.–90e gg. XX v.) (Simferopol, 1999) and *Hreky Krymu. Istoriia i suchasne stanovyshche. Etnokul'turna sytuatsiia ta problemy etnopolitychnoho rozvytku* (Simferopol, 2005).

1: THE LIMITS OF TOLERATION AND THE CHALLENGES OF CONVERSION

1. *Pis'ma Filareta, Mitropolita moskovskogo i kolomenskago k vysochaishim osobam i raznym drugim litsam* (Tver, 1888), 73.

2. *Pis'ma Filareta*, 79–80.

3. Serafim Serafimov, *Vospominaniia o Preosviashchennom Gavriilie* (Odessa, 1859), 28.

4. *Novorossiiskii kalendar' na 1847* (Odessa, 1846), 71.

5. A. S. Sturdza to Innokentii, Odessa, April 5, 1848, Rossiiskii Natsional'naia Biblioteka (RNB), f. 313, d. 42, l. 31 (Documents from the correspondence of Archbishop Innokentii of Kherson, 1841, 1847–1850); reprinted in *Pis'ma A. S. Sturdza k Innokentiiu, arkhiepiskopu khersonskomu i tavricheskomu* (Odessa, 1894), 20.

6. Werth, *At the Margins of Orthodoxy*, 74–79.

7. James P. Niessen, ed. *Religious Compromise, Political Salvation: The Greek Catholic Church and Nation-building in Eastern Europe* (Pittsburgh, 1992); Barbara Skinner, "The Irreparable Church Schism: Russian Orthodox Identity and Its Historical Encounter with Catholicism," in *Polish Encounters, Russian Identity*, ed. David L. Ransel and Bozena Shallcross, 20–36 (Bloomington, 2005); Theodore R. Weeks, "Between Rome and Tsargrad: The Uniate Church in Imperial Russia," in *Of Religion and Empire*, ed. Geraci and Khodarkovsky, 70–91; Robert O. Crummey, *The Old Believers and the World of Antichrist: The Vyg Community and the Russian State, 1694–1855* (Milwaukee, 1970); Roy R. Robson, *Old Believers in Modern Russia* (DeKalb, 1995).

8. Werth, *At the Margins of Orthodoxy*, 86–95.

9. Clay, "Orthodox Missionaries and 'Orthodox Heretics' in Russia, 1886–1917," in *Of Religion and Empire*, ed. Geraci and Khodarkovsky, 38–69; John D. Strickland, "Remembering Rus in Modern Russia: The Orthodox Church and its Cultural Mission before the Revolutions," *Modern Greek Studies Yearbook* 14/15 (1998/1999): 149–67; Geraci, *Window on the East*.

10. Freeze, "The Rechristianization of Russia," 108.

11. Firouzeh Mostashari, "Colonial Dilemmas: Russian Policies in the Muslim Caucasus," in *Of Religion and Empire*, ed. Geraci and Khodarkovsky, 229–49.

12. *Izvlechenie iz otcheta po vedomstvu dukhovnykh del pravoslavnago ispovedaniia za 1857 god* (St. Petersburg, 1859), 69–70.

13. Werth, *At the Margins of Orthodoxy*, 86–95.

14. See for example, *Izvlechenie iz otcheta po vedomstvu dukhovnykh del pravoslavnago ispovedaniia za 1836* (St. Petersburg, 1837) [listed under "Ekaterinoslavskoi,"]: 124–25. Corresponding excerpts were published in St. Petersburg for 1841 (1842): 38–41, for 1848 (1849): 44–47, and for 1857 (1859): 44–47.

15. Mustafa Özgür Tuna, "Gaspirali v. Il'minskii: Two Identity Projects for the Russian Empire," *Nationalities Papers*, 30, no. 2 (2002): 265–89; Steinwedel, "Invisible Threads of Empire," 155–84.

16. Innokentii, Archbishop of Kherson-Tauride, *Poslednie dni zemnoi zhizni Iisusa Khrista* (Moscow, 2007). For more information on the Pavskii inquiry, see P. Kazanskii, "Mysli i chuvstvovaniia mitropolita Filareta po delu otobraniia litografirovannago perevoda knig vetkhago zaveta," *Pravoslavnoe obozrenie* (1878): 106–18. For more on Pavskii, see N. I. Barsov, "Protoierei Gerasim Petrovich Pavskii. Biograficheskii ocherk po novym materialam," *Russkaia starina* 7, nos. 1–4 (1880), discontinuous pagination. Barsov, ed., *Materialy dlia biografii Innokentiia Borisova*, 32–35; A. Dobroklonskii, *Rukovodstvo po istorii russkoi tserkvi. Sinodal'nyi period, 1700–1890* (Moscow, 1893), 268–71.

17. The Russian National Library holds, for example, twenty editions published in the pre-revolutionary period and five editions published between 2000 and 2008.

18. Lev Matseevich, *Vysokopreosviashchennyi Innokentii Borisov, arkhiepiskop khersonskii i tavricheskii. Materialy i zametki* (Minneapolis, 1983), A–E .

19. Barsov, "Protoierei Gerasim Petrovich Pavskii," 32–35. The majority of his writings and sermons advocated a "moral theology," similar to the system developed by Marianus Dobmayer in Austria, which aimed to give believers a full codex of rules for daily behavior. Innokentii argued that fulfilling the obligations and rituals of faith were not enough. Instead, believers should follow in the footsteps of Jesus through a path based in sincerity, humility, and selflessness. Moral theology, according to Innokentii, would enable the Holy Spirit to transform humanity's "naturally evil heart," into an

image of God. For a longer discussion, see N. Arkhangel'skii, *Innokentii, arkhiepiskop khersonskii, kak uchitel' khristianskoi nrabnosti (po povodu 40 letiia so dnia ego konchiny – 27 maia 1857 g.)* (Kazan, 1899), 8–10.

20. Mikhail Maksimovich, *Vospominanie o Tavride. Pis'mo k kniaziu Petru Andreevichu Viazemskomu* (St. Petersburg, 1871), 44; Florovsky, *Ways of Russian Theology*, 196–200; Vasilii Vasil'evich Zenkovskii, *A History of Russian Philosophy*, trans. George L. Kline (London, 1953), 298.

21. For a record of Innokentii's service, see *Venok na mogilu Vysokopreosviashchennago Innokentiia, arkhiepiskopa tavricheskago* (Moscow, 1864), 1–8.

22. Barsov, "Protoierei Gerasim Petrovich Pavskii," 31–33; V. P. Zubov, *Russkie propovedniki. Ocherki po istorii russkoi propovedi* (Moscow, 2001).

23. This book draws upon multiple editions of Innokentii's collected works: *Sochineniia Innokentiia arkhiepiskopa khersonskago i tavricheskago*, 11 vols. (St. Petersburg, 1872–1877); *Sochineniia Innokentiia*, 12 vols. (St. Petersburg, 1901); *Sochineniia Innokentiia*, 11 vols. (St. Petersburg, 1908–1911).

24. Matseevich, E.

25. J. M. Neale, *Voices from the East: Documents on the Present State and Working of the Oriental Church*, ed. Rev. J. M. Neale (London, 1859), vii.

26. Barsov, ed., *Materialy dlia biografii Innokentiia Borisova*, 4. In addition to Materialy, a brief bibliography of Barsov's work includes: *Istoriia pervobytnoi khristianskoi propovedi* (St. Petersburg, 1885); *Istoricheskie, kriticheskie, i polemicheskie opyty* (St. Petersburg, 1879); *Predstaviteli dogmatiko-polemicheskogo vida propovedi v IV veka na Vostoke* (Kharkov, 1886); *Materialy dlia biografii Moskovskogo Metropolita Filareta* (St. Petersburg, 1882).

27. Nikandr Levitskii, *Vysokopreosviashchennyi Innokentii, arkhiepiskop khersonskii i tavricheskii* (Moscow, 1904), 23–27.

28. See *O nachale Khristiansvta v Pol'she* (St. Petersburg, 1842; repr. Kyiv, 1886).

29. Andrei Zorin, "Star of the East": The Holy Alliance and European Mysticism," *Kritika: Explorations in Russian and Eurasian History* 4, no. 2 (2003): 314.

30. A. Sturdza to Archbishop Innokentii, Odessa, September 1846, *Pis'ma A. S. Sturdza k Innokentiiu, arkhiepiskopu khersonskomu i tavricheskomu* (Odessa, 1894), 12 .

31. Makarii, Bishop of Tambov, "Biograficheskaia zapiska o preosviashchennom Innokentie, arkhiepiskope khersonskom i tavricheskom," *Venok na mogilu vysokopreosviashchennago Innokentiia, arkhiepiskopa tavricheskago* (Moscow, 1864), 19.

32. I. U. Palimpsestov, *Moi vospominaniia ob Innokentii, arkhiepiskopa. khersonskom i tavricheskom* (St. Petersburg, 1888), 1–2; for a brief biographical sketch, see the obituary "Izvestie konchine I. U. Palimpsestova," *TEV* 7 (April 1, 1901): 416–17.

33. *Zhitie sviatitelia Innokentiia khersonskogo* (Odessa, 1997). Innokentii is also recognized in Ukrainian Orthodox branches.

34. The statistics on the diocese's churches can be found in the *Novorossiiskii kalendar' na 1848* (Odessa, 1847), 77; and *Novorossiiskii kalendar' na 1855* (Odessa, 1854), 104. These figures do not reflect the number of churches damaged during the war. For his orders to the churches, see Gosudarstvennyi arkhiv odesskoi oblasti (GAOO), f. 167, op. 1, d. 4, ll. 9–10ob (Service-related correspondence of Archbishop Innokentii).

35. See Archbishop Innokentii's petition to raise the status of the Kherson Consistory in line with the western dioceses, Rossiiskii gosudarstvennyi istoricheskii arkhiv (RGIA), f. 796, op. 133, d. 81, ll. 1–10 (Petitioning for elevating the status of the Kherson consistory).

36. Alexander Langueron, quoted in D. Atlas, *Staraia Odessa, ee druz'ia i nedrugi* (Odessa, 1911), 13.

37. Patricia Herlihy, *Odessa: A History, 1794–1914* (Cambridge, 1986), 126.

38. Local histories for Kherson and Nikolaev are unfortunately scarce. Some gen-

eral works include: *Khersonu dvesti let, 1778–1978. Sbornik dokumentov i materialov* (Kyiv, 1978); P. M. Vybornyi, *Nikolaev* (Odessa, 1973); Viktor Lifanov, *Nikolaev, 1789–1989. Stranitsy istorii, spravochnik* (Odessa, 1989).

39. As a result of the constant flow of Russian troops, population statistics are especially difficult to calculate, for as E. I. Druzhinina pointed out, officials did not always include the ever-swelling body of military servitors in provincial censuses. In the middle of the nineteenth century, for example, the city of Kherson had a population of approximately 40,000 people, but it is not known how many of that number were soldiers. By contrast, however, it is known that 25,000 of Nikolaev's 38,000 people were involved in the Russian military. E. I. Druzhinina, *Iuzhnaia Ukraina v period Krizisa Feodalizma, 1825–1860* (Moscow, 1981), 7–8.

40. Apollon Skal'kovskii, "Prostranstvo i narodonaselenie novorossiiskago Kraia, v 1845 godu," *Novorossiiskii kalendar' za 1849* (Odessa, 1850), 354.

41. *Novorossiiskii kalendar' na 1848* (Odessa, 1847), 73–74.

42. Anthony L. H. Rhinelander, *Prince Michael S. Vorontsov: Viceroy to the Tsar* (Montreal, 1990), 107–20.

43. RGIA, f. 797, op. 19, d. 42668, l. 3 (About founding a religious procession in Odessa).

44. Metropolitan Filaret, "Zamechanie Preosviashchennago Filareta na donesenie Tavricheskoi Palaty i Gosudarstvennykh imushchestv o prichenakh slabago vlianiia dukhovenstva Tavricheskoi eparkhii," *Mneniia otzyvi i pis'ma Filareta, mitropolita moskovskogo i kolomenskago, po raznym voprosam za 1821–1867* (Moscow, 1905), 7 March 1840. The petitioner complained that the problem in Crimea existed partly because most villages were located 15 or 20 kilometers from the churches but also from the "manner of life and behavior of the clergy" themselves, who taught the villagers dissolute habits of laziness and drunkenness.

45. Archbishop Innokentii to Grand Duke Konstantin Nikolaevich, Odessa, 27 February 1852, *Russkaia starina* 25 (1879), 192–93. For more on the grand duke, see Jacob W. Kipp, *The Grand Duke Konstantin Nikolaevich and the Epoch of the Great Reforms, 1855–1866* (Ph.D. diss., Pennsylvania State University), 1970.

46. Skal'kovskii, "Prostranstvo i narodonaselenie," 358.

47. GAOO, f. 1, op. 173, d., 15, ll. 6–22 (Statistical Information for New Russia and Bessarabia), 22.

48. GAOO, f. 37, op. 1, d. 1790 (Statistical Table for the Tauride Government), l. 12.

49. GAARK, f. 37, op. 1, d. 1782 (Table of churches and clergy from the Kherson diocese in 1856), l. 113

50. Bartenev, "Zhizn' v Evpatorii," 120.

51. Tereshchenko, "Ocherki Novorossiiskago Kraia," 64.

52. "God na iuzhniu beregu kryma (1852–1853)," 66.

53. Rhinelander, *Prince Michael S.Vorontsov*, 84–85.

54. "God na iuzhniu beregu kryma (1852–1853)," 60.

55. Stepan Semenovich Kutorga, "Otryvkii iz puteshestviia v Kryme, 1833 godu," *Zhurnal ministerstva narodnago prosvieshcheniia* 1 (1834): 84.

56. Tereshchenko, "Ocherki Novorossiiskago Kraia," 51.

57. RGIA, f. 796, op. 18, d. 41463 (About building the St. Vladimir Church), ll. 10–11.

58. RGIA 796, op. 130, d. 1607 (About building a church in the village Ivanovka), l. 136.

59. RGIA, f. 796, op. 135, d. 101, (Recognizing a Lieutenant for building a church), ll. 1–2.

60. RGIA, f. 796, op. 130, d. 2399/110 (About building in the port city of Kerch a

stone church in the name of the Holy Mother of God), ll. 1–17.

61. See for example, his letter to Maksim Perepelchitsyn, "Pis'ma Preosviashchennago Innokentiia k protoiereiu Maksimu Perepelchitsynu," in *KhEV*, supplement (1878): 100–104.

62. RNB, f. 313, d. 37, l. 273, 26 November 1853, Sv. Daniel Diakovskii to Archbishop Innokentii.

63. RNB, f. 313, no. 41, l. 24–32, 19 December 1851, Feodosia, Aleksandr Zavadovskii to Archbishop Innokentii.

64. RNB, f. 313, no. 41, l. 1, 22 November 1851, Simferopol, V. I. Pestel.

65. Steinwedel, "Invisible Threads of Empire," 155–85.

66. See for example, the petition to establish a religious procession in Nikolaev: RGIA, f. 796, op. 134, d. 226 (About establishing a yearly religious procession in Nikolaev with the icon Kasperovka Mother of God), ll. 8–10; in Odessa, RGIA, f. 796, op. 130, d. 429, (About founding a religious procession in Odessa); and RGIA, f. 796, op. 132, d. 1117 (About founding in the city of Kherson a yearly religious procession), l. 3.

67. Aleksandr Zavadovskii, "Iz vospominanii o preosviashchennom Innokentie, arkhiepiskopie khersonskom i tavricheskom," *TEV* 2 (1880), 72.

68. For a few general comments pertaining to the state's treatment of Orthodox sectarians, see Breyfogle, *Heretics and Colonizers*, 19–38.

69. Crummey, *The Old Believers*, 207–8.

70. Robson, *Old Believers*, 17.

71. For more on the Odessa's women's monastery, see: *Istoricheskaia zapiska o zhenskom Odesskom s devichymi monastyri* (Odessa, 1844).

72. For a more detailed description of the *edinoverie*, see Robson, *Old Believers*, 29–30.

73. Serafimov, *Vospominaniia o Preosviashchennom Gavriilie*, 52–53.

74. Serge A. Zenkovsky, "The Russian Church Schism: Its Background and Repercussion," *Russian Review* 16, no. 4 (1957): 51–52.

75. Skal'kovskii, "Prostranstvo i narodonaselenie," 358.

76. Breyfogle, *Heretics and Colonizers*, 149–58.

77. RGIA, f. 796, op. 133, d. 2069 (About closing schismatic churches).

78. RGIA, f. 797, opis 23, otd. 2, d. 41 (About the schismatics); also GAOO, f. 167, op. 1, d. 4, l. 31 (Service-related correspondence of Archbishop Innokentii).

79. Willard Sunderland, "Peasants on the Move: State Peasant Settlement in Imperial Russia, 1805–1830s," *Russian Review* 52, no. 4 (1993): 473.

80. See for example, Frederick Kagan's recent study of the military reforms from 1832–1836. Frederick W. Kagan, *The Military Reforms of Nicholas I: The Origins of the Modern Russian Army* (Bloomsburg, 1999).

81. RGIA, f. 797, op. 18, d. 41207 (Turning the war population in the village of Nikol and Kherson from schism to edinoverie).

82. RNB, f. 313, d. 42, l. 189, Count Aleksei Nikitin to Innokentii: Kremenchug, 5 April 1849.

83. RGIA, f. 797, op. 22, otd. 2, st. 1, ll. 1–2ob (About the destruction of Old Believer chapels and prayer houses in Odessa, Tiraspol, and Maiak).

84. Crummey, *The Old Believers*, 209.

85. RNB, f. 313, d. 37, l. 8 (Documents from the correspondence of Archbishop Innokentii of Kherson, 1851–1854), Prince Vorontsov to Innokentii, 17 February 1851, Tiflis.

86. RNB, f. 313, d. 37, l. 120, Prince Vorontsov to Innokentii, 10 August 1852.

87. GAOO, f. 1, op. 173, d. 33 (About building a church near Novosil'evk for turning Molokan to Orthodoxy).

88. For additional news about the Molokan in New Russia, see the report stored

in Archbishop Innokentii's personal files: RNB, f. 313, d. 37, l. 241, Protierei Aleksandr Bershatskii to Innokentii, 9 April 1853.

89. For more on the *skoptsy*, see Laura Engelstein, *Castration and the Heavenly Kingdom: A Russian Folktale* (Ithaca, 1999).

90. RGIA, f. 797, op. 21, d. 46129, ll. 1–3 (About a Skoptsy Sect in the Melitopol District).

91. RGIA, f. 796, op. 132, d. 1171 (About the appearance of Skoptsy in the Melitopol district).

92. GAOO, f. 167, op. 1, d. 4, ll. 21–21ob.

93. Catholics had only 10 churches in Kherson-Tauride compared with nearly 600 Orthodox churches in 1848. "Statisticheskiia Tablitsy novorossiiskago Kraia i Bessarabii," *Novorossiiskii kalendar' na 1849* (Odesssa, 1848), 79.

94. "Zapiski Innokentiia, arkhiepiskopa khersonskago i tavricheskago, o novouchrezhdennoi eparkhii rimsko-katolicheskoi v Khersone," *Russkii arkhiv za 1868* (1869), 416–35.

95. For more on the Catholic Church in Russia, see D. A. Tolstoi, *Rimskii katolizm v Rossii. Istoricheskoe izsledovanie* (St. Petersburg, 1876); James J. Zatko, *Descent into the Darkness: The Destruction of the Roman Catholic Church in Russia, 1917–1923* (Notre Dame, 1965).

96. "Zapiski Innokentiia, arkhiepiskopa khersonskago i tavricheskago, o novouchrezhdennoi eparkhii Rimsko-Katolicheskoi v Khersone," 419.

97. "Zapiski Innokentiia, arkhiepiskopa khersonskago i tavricheskago, o novouchrezhdennoi eparkhii Rimsko-Katolicheskoi v Khersone," 423–24.

98. "Zapiski Innokentiia, arkhiepiskopa khersonskago i tavricheskago, o novouchrezhdennoi eparkhii Rimsko-Katolicheskoi v Khersone," 417–18.

99. Sophie Olszamowska-Skowronska, "La Correspondance des Papes et des Empereurs de Russie (1814–1878)" in *Miscellanea Historiae Pontificiae* 29 (Rome, 1970), 65–76.

100. "Articles convenus entre les Plenipotentiaires de S. M. L' Empereur et celui de S. S. le Pape à Rome le 22 iuillet/2 août 1847 // Usloviia, podpisannya Upolnomochennymi Ego Imperatorskago E. Sv. Papy v Rime 22 iiulia//3 avgusta 1847," in *Akty i Gramoty o ustroistve i upravlenii Rimsko-Katolicheskoi tserkvi v imperii rossiiskoi* (St. Petersburg, 1849), 193–212.

101. Richard J. Bollig, "The German Catholic Schools in Southern Russia," Catholic University of America Educational Research Monographs, vol. 6, no. 2 (Washington, D.C., February 1931): 20.

102. Zatko, *Descent into the Darkness*, 18–21.

103. For information about Tatar converts to Orthodoxy at the time of annexation, see O'Neill, "Between Subversion and Submission," 378–79. For the failure of the Bible Society, see Hakan Kirimli, "Crimean Tatars, Nogays, and Scottish Missionaries: The Story of Katti Giray and other Baptized Descendents of the Crimean Khans," *Cahiers du Monde russe* 45 (2004): 61–108.

104. Rhinelander, *Prince Michael S. Vorontsov*, 12–26.

105. Lebedintsev, "Stoletie tserkovnoi zhizni Kryma," 208–9.

106. *Pis'ma Filareta*, 82–83.

107. Druzhinina, *Iuzhnaia Ukraina v period Krizisa Feodalizma, 1825–1860*, 17.

108. Steinwedel, "Invisible Threads of Empire," 75.

109. O'Neill, "Between Subersion and Submission," 274–315.

110. Xavier Hommaire de Hell, *Travels in the Steppes of the Caspian Sea, the Crimea, and the Caucasus* (London, 1847), 423.

111. "Archbishop Innokentii to Grand Duke Konstantin Nikolaevich, Odessa, June 20, 1852," *Russkaia starina* 25 (1879): 368–69.

112. Ivanov, 8.

113. RNB, f. 313, d. 42, l. 160, Exarch Isidor (Nikolaevskii) of Georgia to Archbishop Innokentii, 24 December 1849.

114. RNB, f. 313, d. 42, l. 370, Exarch Isidor (Nikolaevskii) to Archbishop Innokentii, 23 January 1850.

115. RGIA, f. 796, op. 130, d. 1530 (Nikit Lukianovich); and RGIA, f. 796, op. 130, d. 927 (Tatar Seledin).

116. Kherson's total population of foreign colonists (at 50,000) numbered significantly more than Tauride's, whose population came to only 35,000 or so. The difference might be located in the largest Jewish colonies in and around Odessa. These numbers give only the broadest picture of foreign and Jewish populations, however, for they do not include the many smaller categories that Russian state officials and statistical committees used to categorize its peoples. GAOO, f. 1, op. 173, d., 15, ll. 6–22 (Statistical Information for New Russia and Bessarabia).

117. RGIA, f. 797, op. 19, d. 42693, ll. 1–14 (About the colonists taking Orthodoxy).

118. "Archbishop Innokentii to Grand Duke Konstantin Nikolaevich," 369.

119. Another study has shown that Russian authorities in Crimea fought disincentives against Tatar conversions to Orthodoxy in the 1820s. Whether efforts to combat disincentives were unsuccessful or if something changed between then and the 1840s is unclear. Werth, *At the Margins of Orthodoxy*, 87–93. O'Neill, "Between Subversion and Submission," 379.

120. "Archbishop Innokentii to Grand Duke Konstantin Nikolaevich," 369–70.

121. See for example, the description of Krymchaks in Khanatskii, *Pamiatnaia kniga Tavricheskoi gubernii*, 201–2.

122. I. V. Achkinazi, *Krymchaki. Istoriko-etnograficheskii ocherk* (Simferopol, 2000) and "Krymchaki," in *Tiurskie narody Krima. Karaimy, krymskie tatary, krymchaki*, ed. S. Ia. Kozlov and L. V. Chizhova (Moscow, 2003), 358–93; Ken Blady, *Jewish Communities in Exotic Places* (Northvale, 2000), 116–18.

123. Meira Polliack, preface to *Karaite Judaism: A Guide to Its History and Literary Sources*, ed. Meira Polliack (Leiden, 2003), xvii.

124. Golda Akhiezer, "The History of the Crimean Karaites," *Karaite Judaism: A Guide to Its History and Literary Sources*, ed. Meira Polliack, (Leiden, 2003), 732–33.

125. Philip Miller, "The Karaites of Czarist Russia, 1780–1918," in *Karaite Judaism: A Guide to Its History and Literary Sources*, ed. Meira Polliack (Leiden, 2003), 821.

126. See for example, Khanatskii, *Pamiatnaia kniga Tavricheskoi gubernii*, 202.

127. Miller, "The Karaites of Czarist Russia," 823–25.

128. RGIA, f. 796, op. 133, d. 798, ll. 3, 8–10 (Establishing a Diocese).

129. RGIA, f. 796, op. 133, d. 798, ll. 3, 8–10.

130. RNB, f. 313, d. 42, l. 129, Prince Vorontsov to Archbishop Innokentii, 12 July 1848.

2: From the Temple of Diana to the Cradle of Christianity

1. Ivan Mateevich Muravev-Apostol, *Puteshestvie po Tavride v 1820 god* (St. Petersburg, 1823), vii.

2. Muravev-Apostol, *Puteshestvie po Tavride*, 73. Russian destruction of ruins and the subsequent efforts to preserve them are explored in greater detail in Kelly O'Neill, "Constructing Imperial Identity in the Borderland: Architecture, Islam, and the Renovation of the Crimean Landscape," *Ab Imperio* 2 (2006): 178–79.

3. Muravev-Apostol, *Puteshestvie po Tavride*, 49 and 295.

4. Zorin, *Kormia dvuglavogo orla*, 100.

5. Ibid.

6. Theophilus Prousis, "Aleksandr S. Sturdza: A Russian Conservative Response to the Greek Revolution," *East European Quarterly* 26, no. 3 (1992): 310.

7. Manchester, *Holy Fathers, Secular Sons*, 127–29.

8. Suzanne L. Marchand, *Down from Mount Olympus: Archaeology and Philhellenism in Germany, 1750–1970* (Princeton, 1996), xvii-xviii.

9. Ibid., 6.

10. The archaeological and historical literature on Greek antiquity covering the northern Black Sea littoral is vast. For a comprehensive survey of the literature on Tauric Chersonesus, see Sergei J. Saprykin, *Heracleia Pontica and Tauric Chersonesus before Roman Domination, VI–I Centuries B.C.* (Amsterdam, 1997). For a bibliographic discussion of early Christian communities in Crimea, see Mogarichev, *Peshchernyie tserkvi Tavriki*. For earlier studies, see Ainalov, *Pamiatniki Khristianskago Khersonesa*.

11. National Preserve of Tauric Chersonesos, "The Ancient Period," <www.chersonesos.org/?p=history_ant&l=eng> (accessed 25 May 2005). This excellent website is compiled by an international team of archaeologists, who not only have synthesized existing studies, but are also updating the site as excavations progress. See also Joseph Coleman Carter and Glen Randall Mack, *Crimean Chersonesos: City, Chora, Museum, and Environs* (Austin, 2003).

12. Constantine fled to the Despotate of Morea to the protection of Thomas Paleolog and from there to Rome. In 1472, he joined a small number of Greek émigrés in Muscovy when he accompanied the niece of the last Byzantine emperor, Constantine XI to the northern Russian capital. There Sophia married Ivan III. See D. Strukov, *Drevnie pamiatniki khristianstva v Tavride*, 49.

13. For information about the Armenian exodus, see V. A. Mikaelian, *Na krymskoi zemle. Istoriia armianskikh poselenii v Krymu* (Erevan, 1974), 150–55.

14. Aradzhioni, "Vozvrashchenie v Krym starozhitel'cheskogo khristianskogo naseleniia," 485–501.

15. F. A. Fedorov, *Krym s Sevastopolom, Balaklavaiu, i drugimi ego gorodami s opisaniem rek, ozer, gor, i dolin; s ego istroieiu, zhiteliami, ikh pravami, obychaiami, i obrazom zhizni; s trema vidami i planom*, 2nd ed. (St. Petersburg, 1854), 66–67; Kutorga, "Otryvkii iz puteshestvie v Kryme," 84.

16. Lebedintsev, "Stoletie tserkovnoi zhizni Kryma," 205.

17. For an excellent summary of these early studies produced by the St. Petersburg Academy of Sciences, see A. A. Nepomniashchii, *Zapiski puteshestvennikov i putevoditeli v razvitii istoricheskogo kraevedeniia Kryma (posledniaia tret' XVIII–nachalo XX veka* (Kyiv, 1999), 9–38.

18. For a good historiographic essay on early representations of Chersonesos, see G. D. Belov, *Khersones tavricheskii. Istoriko-arkheologicheskii ocherk* (Leningrad, 1948): 5–13. A partial translation of Belov's work into English can be found on the website of the National Preserve of Tauric Chersonesos, see "A Review of the Historiography of Chersonesos according to G. D. Belov," National Preserve of Tauric Chersonesos <www.chersonesos.org/eng/History/history.sour.htm> (accessed 15 December 2002).

19. Gertsen and Makhneva, *Peshchernye goroda Kryma*. In *Peshchernye goroda Kryma*, Gertsen and Makhneva note that these settlements have been the subject of scientific interest for decades and appeared in documented sources over one thousand years ago.

20. Gertsen and Makhneva, *Peshchernye goroda Kryma*, 6. Many scholars now believe that the caves were formed out of the Byzantine Empire's desire to fortify its borders. Based upon literary and epigraphic sources, this interpretation dated the caves to the early middle ages, at the turn of the fifth and sixth centuries. Another school of thought dates the formation of the caves a few centuries later, from the tenth to the eleventh centuries.

21. Gertsen and Makhneva, *Peshchernye goroda Kryma*, 8.
22. Richard Wortman, *Scenarios of Power: Myth and Ceremony in the Russian Monarchy* (Princeton, 1995–2000), 137–39.
23. Belov, *Khersones tavricheskii*, 7–8.
24. Sara Dickinson provides an interesting discussion of an early Russian resuscitation of the myths surrounding the Temple of Diana by Catherine II's retinue. Sarah Dickinson, "Russia's First 'Orient': Characterizing the Crimea in 1787," *Kritika: Explorations in Russian and Eurasian History* 3, no. 1 (2002): 9–13.
25. G. S. Lebedev, *Istoriia otechestvennoi arkheologii, 1700–1971* (St. Petersburg, 1992), 73–78.
26. See, for example, *Vypiska iz puteshestvennikh zapisok Vasil'ia Fedorovicha Zueva, kasaushchikhsia do poluostrova Kryma, 1782 goda* (St. Petersburg, 1790).
27. For a good discussion of the development of archaeology in Khersones, see S. F. Strzheletskii, *Kleryi Khersonesa tavricheskogo. K istorii drevnego zemledeliia v Krymu* (Simferopol, 1961), 7–29; and Nepomniashchii, *Zapiski puteshchestvennikov i putevoditeli*, 22–25.
28. See for example: Peter Simon Pallas, *Travels through the Southern Provinces of the Russian Empire performed in the years 1793 and 1794 by P. S. Pallas, Councillor of State to the Emperor*, trans. from German by Francis Blagdon (London, 1803).
29. Pallas widely influenced official studies and more casual travelogues. For an early account based on Pallas, see Martha Guthrie, *A tour, performed in the years 1795–6, through the Taurida, or Crimea, the ancient kingdom of Bosphorus, the once-powerful republic of Tauric Kherson, and all the other countries on the north shore of the Euxine ceded to Russia by the Peace of Kainardji and Jassy*, ed. Matthew Guthrie (London, 1802).
30. Strzheletskii, *Kleryi Khersonesa tavricheskogo*, 9; Metropolitan Evgenii [presumed to be Bolkhovitinov, of Kyiv] "O sledakh drevnego grecheskogo goroda Khersona," *Obshchestvo istorii i drevnosti rossiiskikh*, 4, no. 1 (1820), 102–115.
31. Pavel Sumarokov, *Dosugi krymskago sud'i, ili vtoroe puteshestvie v Tavridu* (St. Petersburg, 1803), 91.
32. Lebedev, *Istoriia otechestvennoi arkheologii*, 76.
33. Robert Lyall, *Travels in Russia, the Krimea, the Caucasus, and Georgia* (Edinburgh, 1825; reprint, NY, 1970), xi.
34. Demidov, *Travels in the Crimea*, 2:63–64.
35. Marchand, *Down from Mount Olympus*, xxii.
36. The multiple uses of Crimea as a symbol of empire have received attention from many scholars. See, for example: Kerstin S. Jobst, "The Crimea as a Russian Mythical Landscape (18th–20th Century)," in *Mythical Landscapes Then and Now. The Mythification of Landscapes in Search for National Identity*, ed. Judith Peltz and Ruth Büttner (Yerevan, 2006), 78–91; Andreas Schönle, "Garden of the Empire: Catherine's Appropriation of the Crimea," *Slavic Review* 60 (2001): 1–23; and Dickinson, "Russia's First 'Orient,'" 9–10.
37. The first edition of the poem appeared in 1824, with a critical essay discussing the poem's historical accuracy. The poem was subsequently published in many different editions and excerpts, including the version in *Otechestvennyia zapiski*. See, A. Pushkin, "The Bakhchisarai Palace," *Otechestvennyia zapiski* 29 (1827): 3–4. For a discussion of the poem's first edition, see Katya Hokanson, "Pushkin's Captive Crimea: Imperialism in the Fountain of Bakhchisarai," in *Russian Subjects: Empire, Nation, and the Culture of the Golden Age*, ed. Monika Greenleaf and Stephen Moeller-Sally (Evanston, 1998), 123–50.
38. There have been numerous English-language interpretations of the poem, from its gendered narrative to its imperial discourse. See, for example: Stephanie Sandler, *Distant Pleasures: Alexander Pushkin and the Writing of Exile* (Stanford, 1989); and Susan Layton, *Russian Literature and Empire: Conquest of the Caucasus from Pushkin to Tolstoy* (Cambridge, 1994), 196–200.

39. Archbishop Innokentii to Prince M. S. Vorontsov, 16 October 1837, *Arkhiv Kniazia Vorontsova. Bumagi fel'dmarshala Kniazia Mikhaila Semenovicha Vorontsova* (Moscow, 1891), 490.

40. Mary Holderness, *Notes relating to the manners and customs of the Crim Tatars; written during a four years' residence among that people* (London, 1821).

41. Hommaire de Hell, *Travels in the Steppes of the Caspian Sea*, 390.

42. This use of archaeology to support the nationalist agenda of the state was not unique to Russia, but dove-tailed with general currents in Europe. Lebedev, *Istoriia otechestvennoi arkheologii*, 68–70.

43. This is not to say, however, that scholars were not interested in other cultures or completely abandoned antiquity. In 1830, for example, P. A. Dubruks uncovered a Scythian burial ground of the Kul'-oba near Kerch, while A. B. Ashik and D. V. Koreish initiated a wave of interest in Scythian culture. Scythian burial grounds remained one of the most important categories in Black Sea archaeology, and received their first full-length published summary in P. I. Keppen, *Spisok izvestneishikh Kurganov v Rossii* (St. Petersburg, 1837). See Lebedev, *Istoriia otechestvennoi arkheologii*, 75–76.

44. Skal'kovskii, "Prostranstvo i narodonaselenie," 208–10; 270–72. For an early study of the Genoese in New Russia, see N. N. Murzakevich, *Istoriia Genuzaskikh poselenii v Krymu* (Odessa, 1837).

45. See for example, "O mestopolozhenii Balaklavskago Georgievskago monastyria v Krymu," *Otechestvennyia zapiski* (1825): 97–104; "Obozrenie puteshestviia izdatelia otechestvennykh zapiskok po Rossii v 1825 godu," *Otechestvennyia zapiski* (1826): 91–117 and 440–67; and I. A. Stempkovskii, "Mysli otnositel'no izyskaniia drevnostei v Novorossiiskom Krae," *Otechestvennye zapiski* (1827): 41–72. Crimea already had a couple of small museums devoted to archaeology and antiquity prior to this series. In 1811, S. M. Bronevskii opened a museum in Feodosia, which was later transferred to the jurisdiction of the Odessa Society. Another museum was opened in Kerch in 1826, but was organized as a branch of Odessa's museum. For more on early museums in Southern Ukraine, see A. A. Nepomniashchii, *Razvitie istoricheskogo kraevedeniia v Krymu XIX nachale XX veka* (Simferopol, 1995), 47.

46. "O mestopolozhenii Balaklavskago Georgievskago monastyria v Krymu," 97–102.

47. E. G. Surov, *Khersones tavricheskii. Lektsii po spetsial'nomu kursu i materialy k seminaru dlia zaochnogo otdeleniia* (Sverdlovsk, 1961), 20; A. S. Glushak, I. A. Antonova, V. F. Filipenko, N. V. Naumova, and S. M. Cherviakov, *Krym khristianskii* (Simferopol, 1996), 98–99. RGIA, f. 797, op. 18, d. 41463, l. 2.

48. For more on the church of St. Vladimir initiated by Admiral Greig, see "Istoricheskaia zapiska o sooruzhenii v Khersonis khrama Sv. Ravnoapostl'nago kniazia Vladimira," *Izvestiia Tavricheskoi uchenoi arkhivnoi komissii* 5 (1888): 5–18.

49. Surov, *Khersones tavricheskii*, 20.

50. Nathaniel Knight, "Constructing the Science of Nationality: Ethnography in Mid-nineteenth century Russia" (Ph.D. diss., Columbia University, 1994), 10.

51. The provincial paper of the Kherson government published regular updates on the society's activities. See, for example, "Otchet obshchestva istorii i drevnostei s 14 noiabria 1847 po 14 noiabria 1848 goda," *Khersonskie gubernskie vedomosti* 20 (19 May 1849), 179.

52. "Letopis' Obshchestva," *ZOOID* 1 (1844): 565–80. For a discussion of *tserkovnaia arkheologiia*, see Mara Kozelsky, "The Challenges of Church Archaeology in Post-Soviet Crimea," in *Selective Remembrances*, ed. Kohl, Kozelsky, and Ben-Yehuda, 71–98.

53. See, for example, N. N. Murzakevich, "Nekotoriia podrobnosti o tserkvi sv. Ionna Predtechi v Kerchi," *ZOOID* 1 (1844): 625–27 and "Svedeniia o nekotorykh pravoslavnykh

monastyriakh eparkhii khersonskoi i kishnevskoi," *ZOOID* 2 (1848): 302–29.

54. Nikolai Murzakevich, "Poezdka v Krym 1836," *Zhurnal ministerstva narodnago prosvieshcheniia* 13 (1837): 625–91.

55. Prousis, "Aleksandr S. Sturdza," 318.

56. Irina V. Tunkina, "The Formation of a Russian Science of Classical Antiquities of Southern Russia in the Eighteenth and Early Nineteenth Centuries" <www.pontos.dk/publications/books/bss-1-files/BSS1_24_Tunkina.pdf> (accessed 24 May 2009).

57. F. Brun (Braun), "Nekrolog. Mikhail Grigor'evich Paleolog," *ZOOID* 5 (1863), 953–956, 955.

58. N. N. Murzakevich, [Nekrolog] "Zakharii Andreevich Arkas," *ZOOID* 6, no. 3 (1867): 492–94.

59. Z. A. Arkas, "Opisanie Irakliiskogo poluostrova i drevnostei ego," *ZOOID* 2 (1848): 245–71.

60. Z. A. Arkas, "Drevnosti Irakliiskago Poluostrov," *Zhurnal ministerstva vnutrennikh del* 19 (1847): 91–116.

61. Arkas, "Drevnosti Irakliiskago Poluostrov," 95.

62. Murzakevich, "(Nekrolog) Zakharii Andreevich Arkas," 492.

63. Sv. Feodor Milianovskii, *Pamiatnaia Knizhka dlia dukhovenstva khersonskoi eparkhii* (Odessa, 1902), VII–LII [7–52].

64. The scholar here, Franz Martinovich Dombrovskii, was the secretary of the Tauride Statistical Committee, and editor of *Tavricheskii gubernskii vedomosti*. F. M. Dombrovskii, " Feleton. Otkrytie skitskago pustynnozhitel'stva v uspenskoi skala bliz g. Bakhchisaraia," *Odesskii vestnik*, 74 (13 September 1850); for more information on Dombrovskii, see A. A. Nepomniashchii, *Ocherki razvitiia istoricheskogo Kraevedeniia Kryma v XIX–nachale XX veka* (Simferopol, 1998): 15–19.

65. O. A. Griva, "*Tserkovnaia arkheologiia. Uchenaia distsiplina i uchebnyi predmet*," in *Pravoslavnyie drevnosti tavriki. Sbornik materialov po tserkovnoi arkheologii*, ed. V. Iu. Iurochkin (Kyiv, 2002), 10–14; Arsenii Markevich, "*Neskol'ko slov o deiatel'nosti v Tavride Innokentiia, arkhiepiskopa khersonskago i tavricheskago*," *TEV* 1 (1900): 30–31.

66. Prousis parallels Russia's "phil-orthodox" movement to similar philhellenic currents in the West, arguing that it primarily emerged after the hanging of Patriarch Grigorius V in Constantinople and the ensuing war for Greek independence. For discussions of Russian philhellenism and phil-orthodoxy, see, Prousis, "Russian Philorthodox Relief," 31–60.

67. Archbishop Gavriil (Rozanov), "Ostatki khristianskikh drevnostei v krymu," *ZOOID* 1 (1844): 320–28.

68. Gavriil, Archbishop of Kherson and Tauride, "Pereselenie grekov iz kryma v Azovskuiu guberniiu i osnovanie gotfiiskoi i kafiiskoi eparkhii," *ZOOID* 1 (1844): 196–204.

69. Serafimov, *Vospominaniia o preosviashchennom Gavriile*, 60–61.

70. Evgenii Golubinskii, *Istoriia russkoi tserkvi* (Moscow, 1880); A. V. Kartashev, *Sv. velikii kniaz Vladimir, otets russkoi kultury* (Paris, 1938).

71. S. A. Beliaev, "Istoriia khristianstva na Rusi do ravnoapostol'nogo kniazia vladimira i sovremennaia istoricheskaia nauka," in *Istoriia russkoi tserkvi*, kniga pervaia [book 1], *Istoriia khristianstva v rossii do ravnoapostol'nogo kniazia Vladimira kak vvedenie v istoriiu russkoi tserkvi*, by Metropolitan Makarii [Bulgakov] (Moscow, 1994), 33–35.

72. The debate is summarized in "St. Andrew," *Catholic Encyclopedia* <www.newadvent.org/cathen/01471.htm> (25 March 2003).

73. Beliaev, "Istoriia khristianstva na Rusi," 37.

74. Metropolitan Makarii [Bulgakov], *Istoriia russkoi tserkvi*, kniga pervaia [book 1], *Istoriia khristianstva v rossii do ravnoapostol'nogo kniazia Vladimira kak vvedenie v istoriiu russkoi tserkvi* (Moscow, 1994), 105–6.

75. Ibid. 107–10.

76. These saints are known as the Holy Priest Martyrs. They are Basil, Ephraim, Eugene, Elpidias, Agathodoros, Etherias, and Kapiton, and are celebrated on 7 March/20 March. For a comprehensive list of Crimean saints, see "Kratkii krymskii paterik," in V. Iu. Iurochkin, *Pravoslavnyie drevnosti tavriki: sbornik materialov po tserkovnoi arkheologii* (Kyiv, 2002), 175–78.

77. Metropolitan Makarii, *Istoriia russkoi tserkvi*, 114.

78. Ibid., 226.

79. For a brief review of the interpretations, see Dimitri Obolensky, "Cherson and the Conversion of Rus': An Anti-revisionist View," *Byzantine and Modern Greek Studies* 13 (1989): 244–56.

80. N. M. Karamzin, *Istoriia gosudarstva rossiiskogo* (Moscow, 1989), 145–60.

81. "Pis'ma Makarii Bulgakova k Arkhiepiskopu Innokentiiu," in *Materialy dlia biografii Innokentiia Borisova*, ed. Barsov, 69–71.

82. Archbishop Innokentii, "Nasazhdenie i uspekhi khristianstva v drevnem Khersone," *Sochineniia Innokentiia* 11 (St. Petersburg, 1877), 383–86.

83. Archbishop Evgenii of Yaroslavl to Archbishop Innokentii, 3 April 1848, RNB, f. 313, d. 42, l. 91. This is also a phrase that Innokentii himself frequently used. See for example, Archbishop Innokentii, "Slovo v den' pamiati sv. Bezsrebrinnikov Kozmy i Damiana," read in the Simferopol Aleksander-Nevsky church, 1 July 1855, *Sochineniia Innokentiia* (St. Petersburg, 1901) vol. 5: 307–8.

84. A. Umanets, *Istoricheskie rasskazy o Kryme* (1888); reprint, *Brega Tavridy* 1 (1992): 253.

85. (GAOO), f. 167, op. 1, d. 3, ll. 2, 14–34 (Correspondence about the scholarly activities of Archbishop Innokentii). RNB, f. 313, d. 42, l. 228 (Documents from the correspondence of Archbishop Innokentii of Kherson, 1841, 1847–1850).

86. Arsenii Markevich, "Neskol'ko slov o deiatel'nosti v Tavride Innokentiia arkhiepiskopa khersonskago i tavricheskago," *TEV* 1 (1901): 31.

87. For Russian nationalism in the Geographic Society, see Nathaniel Knight, "Science, Empire, and Nationality: Ethnography in the Russian Geographical Society, 1845–1855," in *Imperial Russia: New Histories for the Empire*, ed. Jane Burbank and David L. Ransel (Bloomington, 1998), 108–41.

88. Archbishop Innokentii to F. P. Litke, *Pis'ma Innokentiia, arkhiepiskopa khersonskago i tavricheskago, k raznym litsam* (St. Petersburg, 1885), 15.

89. Arkhangel'skii, *Innokentii, arkhiepiskop khersonskii*, 27.

90. Quoted in Arkhangel'skii, *Innokentii, arkhiepiskop khersonskii*, 8–10.

91. Archbishop Innokentii to F. P. Litke, *Pis'ma Innokentiia*, 12–13.

92. Maria Bode, "Vospominaniia o Preosviashchennom Innokentie arkhiepiskopie khersonskom i tavricheskom," *Strannik* 2 (1861): 5.

93. Evgenii, Igumen (St. Vladimir monastery, Chersonesos), RNB, f. 313, ed. khr. 47 (Life after death: article about Archbishop Innokentii).

94. Palimpsestov, *Moi vospominaniia ob Innokentie*, 86n.

95. Sv. Arsenii, "Vospominaniia o preosviashchennom Innokentie, arkhiepiskopie khersonskom i tavricheskom," *KhEV* (1862) 5: 30–62.

96. Archbishop Innokentii, "Slovo v den' pamiati sv. Bezsrebrennikov Kozmy i Damiana" (Simferopol, St. Alexander Nevsky Cathedral, 1 July 1855), *Sochineniia Innokentiia* (St. Petersburg, 1901), vol. 5: 309–10.

97. Archbishop Innokentii, "Zapiski o vostanovlenii drevnikh sviatykh mest' po goram krymskim," in "Arkhivnye dokumenty, otnosiashchiesia k istoriiu khersonesskago monastyria," *ITUAK* 5 (1888): 181.

98. "Arkhivnye dokumenty, otnosiashchiesia k istoriiu Khersonesskago Monastyria," *Izvestiia Tavricheskoi uchenoi arkhivnoi komissii* 5 (1888): 81–83; 81.

99. Mogarichev, *Peshchernye tserkvi Tavriki*, 97.

3: Athos in Crimea

1. "Zapiski o vostanovlenii drevnikh sviatykh mest' po goram krymskim," in the series Arkhivnye dokumenty, otnosiashchiesia k istoriiu Khersonesskago Monasteryia, *Izvestiia Tavricheskoi uchenoi arkhivnoi komissii (ITUAK)* 5 (1888): 87–97. The "Zapiski" are published from the holdings collected in GAARK, f. 118, op. 1, d. 5780.

2. Archbishop Innokentii, "Zapiski o vostanovlenii drevnikh sviatykh mest' po goram krymskim," 89.

3. Prot. Petr Polidorov, "Preosviashchennyi Polikarp, episkop orlovskii i sievskii (ocherk ego zhizni)," *Strannik* (1870): 239–63.

4. Zorin, "Star of the East," 313–14. Zorin points out that even though two Greek advisors helped edit the treaty that would form the Holy Alliance, Alexander I also submitted drafts for review to the mystical group associated with Baroness Juliana von Krüdener.

5. Zorin, "Star of the East," esp. 336–41; see also Theophilus Prousis, whose work demonstrates that Alexander I was more concerned with maintaining diplomatic and trade connections with the Ottoman Empire and that phil-Orthodoxy subsided in public opinion in the mid-1820s: Theophilus C. Prousis, *Russian-Ottoman Relations in the Levant: The Dashkov Archive* (Minneapolis, 2002) and *Russian Society and the Greek Revolution* (DeKalb, 1994).

6. David MacKenzie, "Serbia and Russia to 1918," *Modern Greek Studies Yearbook* 16/17 (2000/2001): 133.

7. John Shelton Curtiss, *Russia's Crimean War* (Durham, 1979) 12, 18–19.

8. David Goldfrank has argued that the Crimean War developed from the "power, policies, and personality" of Nicholas I. Theophilus Prousis has opened our understanding of Russian policies in the Levant by examining trade and phil-Orthodox movements. David M. Goldfrank, *The Origins of the Crimean War* (London, 1994), 271–84. See Prousis, "Russian Philorthodox Relief," 31–60 and other works cited above.

9. David Goldfrank, "The Holy Sepulcher and the Origin of the Crimean War," in *The Military and Society in Russia: 1450–1917*, ed. Eric Lohr and Marshall Poe (Leiden, 2002), 491–506.

10. Goldfrank, *Origins of the Crimean War*, 78–79.

11. For more on Porfirii Uspenskii, see Theofanis George Stavrou, *Russian Interests in Palestine, 1882–1914* (Thessalonki, 1963), 34–39.

12. Curtiss, *Russia's Crimean War*, 41.

13. Ibid., 107–66.

14. Eileen M. Kane, "Pilgrims, Holy Places, and the Multi-Confessional Empire: Russian Policy toward the Ottoman Empire under Tsar Nicholas, 1825–1855" (Ph.D. diss., Princeton University, 2005). For another perspective on Bazili, see James Tabor, "Konstantin Bazili and Russia on the Orthodox East on the Eve of the Crimean War," *Modern Greek Studies Yearbook* 20/21 (2004–2005): 43–61.

15. Dashkov was a diplomatic advisor who served in the Russian embassy in Istanbul during the Greek Revolution. See Dmitrii V. Dashkov, "Obozrenie glavneishikh snoshenii Rossii s Turtsieiu i nachal, na koikh dolzhenstvuiut onye byt ustanovelny na budushchee vremia," Prousis in *Russian-Ottoman Relations in the Levant: The Dashkov Archive*, 125–29.

16. The Church of Greece broke with the patriarch of Constantinople in 1833. See Charles A. Frazee, *The Orthodox Church and Independent Greece, 1821–1852* (Cambridge, 1969); for Russian reaction, see the multiple works by Prousis cited above, and Frary, "Russia and Independent Greece."

17. This is not to say that Russians were not aware of other travel accounts to Athos. Rather, it was Serafim Sviatogorets who popularized travel to Athos. For an ar-

gument about the importance of Sviatogorets's account, see N. A. Blagoveshchenskii, *Afon'. Putevyia vpechatleniia* (St. Petersburg, 1864), 1–2.

18. Serafim Sviatogorets, *Pis'ma sviatogortsa k druz'iam svoim o sviatoi gor Afonskoi* (Moscow, 1895), 9.

19. Sviatogorets, *Pis'ma sviatogortsa*, 9–14.

20. Vladimir Davydov, *Putevyia zapiski. Vedenniia vo vremia prebyvaniia na Ionicheskikh ostrovakh, v Gretsi, Maloi Azii, i Turtsii v 1835 godu* (St. Petersburg, 1839), 35.

21. Parfeny Ageev, *Skazanie o stranstvii i puteshestvii rossii, moldavii, turtsii i sviatoi zemlie postrizhenika sviatyia goryi afonskiia inoka parfeniia* 4 vols., 2nd ed. (Moscow, 1856), 2: 46–47.

22. Davydov, *Putevyia zapiski*, 2: 182. Here Davydov refers to salvation from Greek intrigues as well as Ottoman exploitation.

23. Curtiss, *Russia's Crimean War*, 29. Roderic H. Davison, "Turkish Attitudes Concerning Christian Muslim Equality in the Nineteenth Century," *Essays in Ottoman and Turkish History, 1774–1923, The Impact of the West* (Austin, 1990), 112–32.

24. See Peter Gatrell, *A Whole Empire Walking: Refugees in Russia during World War One* (Bloomington, 1999).

25. Prousis, "Aleksandr S. Sturdza," 318–20.

26. Prousis, *Russian Society and the Greek Revolution*, 14–19.

27. Grigorii M. Piatigorskii, "The Cretan Uprising of 1866–1869 and the Greeks of Odessa," *MGSY* 14/15 (1998/1999): 129–48.

28. Batalden, *Catherine II's Greek Prelate*, 96.

29. Prousis, *Russian-Ottoman Relations in the Levant*, 4.

30. Prousis, *Russian-Ottoman Relations in the Levant*, 4–7. It is important to note that all *reaya* (Ottoman subjects protected by and responsible to the government) could benefit from the *berat*.

31. Herlihy, *Odessa: A History*, 92.

32. Johann Georg Kohl, *St. Petersburg, Moscow, Kharkoff, Riga, Odessa, the German Provinces on the Baltic, the steppes, the Crimea and the Interior of the Empire* (London, 1842), 418.

33. Kohl, *St. Petersburg, Moscow, Kharkoff, Riga, Odessa*, 420.

34. C. E. B. Brett, *Towers of Crim Tartary: English and Scottish Architects and Craftsmen in the Crimea, 1762–1853* (Donnington, 2005), 2–3.

35. Russkoe Obshchestvo parakhodstva i torgovli, *Putevoditel' Russkago Obshchestva parakhodstva i torgovli na 1912* (Odessa, 1912), 3–4.

36. Russkoe Obshchestvo parakhodstva i torgovli, *Putevoditel'*, 17, 4–5, 21.

37. The policy of settling refugees from the Ottoman Empire in Russia did not begin with Catherine. Rather, Empress Elizabeth had established Serbian communities in southern Russia in the 1750s. See A. P. Bazhova, "Iz Iugoslavianskikh zemel'—v Rossiiu—" *Voprosy istorii* 2 (1977): 124–37. For literature on Bulgarians living in New Russia territory, see Druzhinina, *Iuzhnaia Ukraina v 1800–1825*, 110–17; V. M. Kabuzan, *Zaselenie Novorossii (Ekaterinoslavskoi i Khersonskoi Gubernii) v XVIII - pervoi polovine XIX veka (1719–1858)* (Moscow, 1976), 83–85. For the status of the church during this time, see M. G. [presumed to be Paleolog], "Perechen' sobytii, otnosiashchikhsia k istorii khersonskoi eparkhii," pribavlenie k [supplement to] *KhEV* 5 (1862), 266–67. Also see Bruess, who connects Catherine's foreign policy initiatives with the era of Ivan IV: *Religion, Identity, and Empire*, 48–54.

38. "Balaklava," *Novorossiiskii kalendar' na 1846*, (Odessa, 1845), 338–42.

39. Muravev-Apostol, *Puteshestvie po Tavride* 101–2.

40. For examples of the Greek battalion subduing or spying on Tatars, see O'Neill, "Between Subversion and Submission," 59; Mara Kozelsky, "Casualties of Conflict: Crimean Tatars during the Crimean War," *Slavic Review* 67, no. 4 (2008): 862–91.

41. Amanton, *Notices sur les diverses populations du Gouvernement de la Tauride et spécialement de la Crimée*, 22.

42. Rev. Thos. Milner, *The Crimea, Its Ancient and Modern History: The Khans, the Sultans, and the Czars. With notices of its scenery and population* (London, 1855), 303–4.

43. S. Moiseenkova, "Staroobriadtsy v tavricheskoi gubernii v kontse XVIII–nachale XX v.," *Materialy po arkheologii, istorii, i etnografii Tavrii* (Simferopol, 1996), 5:201; Skal'kovskii, *Opyt' statisticheskago opisaniia novorossiiskago kraiia*, 215.

44. "Panagiia, ili Uspenskii Bakhchisaraiskii v krymu skit," in *Krymskii Afon (Bakhchisaraiskii Uspenskii monastyr' istoricheskikh opisaniiakh* (Simferopol, 1995), 11–14; M. Protopopov, "Uspenskii skit v Krymu bliz Bakhchisaraia," in *Krymskii Afon (Bakhchisaraiskii Uspenskii monastyr' istoricheskikh opisaniiakh* (Simferopol, 1995), 38.

45. "Panagiia, ili Uspenskii Bakhchisaraiskii v krymu skit," in *Krymskii Afon*, 14; Innokentii, "Zapiski o vostanovlenii drevnikh sviatykh mest' po goram krymskim," 89.

46. They visited on the following dates: Catherine II (21 May 1787); Tsar Alexander I (1818 and 1825); Tsar Nicholas I (26 June 1817 and September 1837); Tsaritsa Alexandra Fedorovna (13 September 1837); Tsarevich Alexander Nikolaevich (14 September 1837); Grand Princess Maria Nikolaevna (13 September 1837); Grand Princess Maria Pavlovna (30 May 1838); Grand Princess Elena Pavlovna (1 September 1838); Grand Prince Constantine Nikolaevich (2 September 1845 and 19 May 1850); Grand Princes Nikolai and Mikhail Pavlovich (1 October 1854); Duke George Maklenburg (1 November 1855); Tsar Alexander II and Tsaritsa Maria Alexandra with their children (1 November 1861); Tsarevich Alexander Alexandrovich (13 September 1863); Tsar Alexander III and Tsaritsa Maria Fedorovna with their children (4 May 1886). Nicholas II and his family visited several times (last visit being on 30 August 1913). For more on visits by the imperial family, see A. Umanets, *Istoricheskie rasskazy o Kryme* (1888), 253.

47. V. G. Shavshin, *Balaklavskii Georgievskii monastyr'* (Simferopol, 1997), 150.

48. GAARK, f. 118, op. 1, d. 6065 (Information about the Balaklava St. George first-class monastery in Tauride for 1873), l. 670–71; Dariia Petrovna Sheviakova, "Rol' Grecheskogo naseleniia Sevastopolia v vozrozhdenii pravoslaviia v Krymu (kontsa XVIII–nachala XX vv)," in *Russkie v istorii Tavridy. Materialy nauchno-prakticheskoi konferentsii*, ed. V.B. Gaidamaka (Simferopol, 2003), 138.

49. Shavshin, *Balaklavskii Georgievskii monastyr'*, 32.

50. See Prousis, *Russian Society and the Greek Revolution*, 55–83, for a general discussion of the Greek revolt, as well as the numbers of Greek refugees who made their way into Russia after this event. The burial of the patriarch in Odessa ignited a local religious riot between Greeks and Jews, resulting in 17 deaths. For more discussion of the hanging of the patriarch and a bibliography of the literature, see Prousis, "Russian Philorthodox Relief," 34–35; 57 n. 8 and *Russian Society and the Greek Revolution*, 55–56. For a detailed account of the patriarch's return to Greece in 1871 see, *Torzhestvo Pravoslavnykh v Odesse po sluchaiu pereneseniia tela vselenskago i konstantinopol'skago patriarkha Grigoriia iz Odessy v Gretsiu* (Odessa, 1871).

51. A. Leonid, "Metropolitan Agafangel," *KhEV* 15 (1865): 299–301.

52. For more on the Greek prelate, see RGIA, f. 797, op. 18, d. 41676 (about providing support for Metropolitan Joseph); GAOO, f. 167, op. 1, d. 4, ll. 11–12, 13 (service-related correspondence of Archbishop Innokentii).

53. Milner, *The Crimea*, 355.

54. GAARK, f. 26, op. 1, d. 15142, ll., 25–27ob (information about the numbers of non-Russian residents located in the Tauride Province).

55. Sheviakova, "Rol' Grecheskogo naseleniia Sevastopolia v vozrozhdenii pravoslaviia v Krymu," 134–35, 136. The number of Balaklava Greeks Sheviakova gives is at odds with the archival data. However, this number pertains only to those in Balaklava affiliated with the battalion. See GAARK, f. 26, op. 1, d. 14800 (Information about the population of the city of Balaklava).

56. O. A. Gabrielian, S. A. Efimov, V. G. Garubin, et al., *Krymskie repatriany. Deportatsia, vozvrashchenie, i obustroistvo* (Simferopol, 1998), 26; M. A. Abdullaeva, "Svyaschenyky Parafii grekiv krymu naprikintsi XVIII–na pochatku XX st.," in *Podvyzhnyky i Metsenaty: Hretski Pidpryiemtsi Ta Hromadski Diiachi V Ukraini XVII - XIX*, ed. Valerii Smolii (Kyiv, 2001), 71–75.

57. Kohl, *St. Petersburg, Moscow, Kharkoff, Riga, Odessa*, 443.

58. Holderness, *Notes relating to the manners and customs of the Crim Tatars*, 2.

59. Abdullaeva, "Svyaschenyky Parafii grekiv krymu," 68–80; Bruess's work provides further evidence of this point.

60. Abdullaeva, "Svyaschenyky Parafii grekiv krymu," 71.

61. Johann Georg Kohl, *St. Petersburg, Moscow, Kharkoff, Riga, Odessa*, 458.

62. For more about Greeks in Crimea, see Aradzhioni, *Greki Kryma* and *Hreky Krymu*.

63. Mikaelian, *Na krymskoi zemle*, 157.

64. Ibid., 160.

65. Khanatskii, *Pamiatnaia kniga Tavricheskoi gubernii*, 200.

66. Mikaelian, *Na krymskoi zemle*, 189–99.

67. Quoted in Nina Noskova, *Krymskie bolgary v XIV—nachale XX v. Istoriia i kul'tura* (Simferopol, 2002), 23.

68. Ibid., 32–35.

69. Zavadovskii, "Iz vospominanii o preosviashchennom Innokentie," 77.

70. Some of these letters are printed in Barsov, ed., *Materialy dlia biografii Innokentiia Borisova*.

71. Barsov, "Pis'ma s vostoka k Preosviashchennomu Innokentiu," here Archimandrite Vissarion to Innokentii, 15 January 1851, and K. Bazili to Innokentii, undated, (1–3).

72. *Izvlechenie iz otcheta po vedomstvu dukhovnykh del pravoslavnago ispovedaniia za 1857 god* (St. Petersburg, 1859), 69–70.

73. Ivanov, "Vospominaniia o Vysokopreosviashchennom Innokentii," 9.

74. Barsov, "Pis'ma s Vostoka k Preosviashchennomu Innokentiu," 8.

75. Archbishop Innokentii to K. V. Nesselrode, May 1851, in Sv. S. Petrovskii, ed., *Innokentii, arkhiepiskop Khersono-Tavricheskii k stoletiiu dnia ego rozhdeniia* (Odessa, 1901), 20.

76. RNB, f. 313, d. 42, l. 423, N. Kh. Palauzov, 23 January 1850, Odessa.

77. Apparently, the problem of fraudulent priests and collections for Orthodox Christians was nothing new. See Bruess, *Religion, Identity, and Empire*, 99–100.

78. "Ot Odesskago Bolgarskago Nastoiatel'stva," *Novorossiiskii kalendar' na 1864* (Odessa, 1863), 60–62.

79. For a recent biography, see N. N. Lisovoi, "A. N. Murav'ev i ego kniga *Puteshestvie ko sviatym mestam v 1830 godu*," preface to Andrei Nikiloevich Murav'ev's *Puteshestvie ko sviatym mestam v 1830 godu* (Moscow, 2007).

80. A. N. Murav'ev, *Pis'ma s vostoka v 1849–1850 godakh*, 2 vols. (St. Petersburg, 1851), 405–6.

81. "Rech v den' pominoveniia pochivashago Sviatiteliia Innokentiia arkhiepiskopa khersonskago i tavricheskago, Trudy arkhiepiskopa Innokentiia na pol'zu pravoslavnoi Bolgariia," in *Innokentii Arkhiepiskopa Khersono-Tavricheskii k stoletiu so dnia ego rozhdeniia*, ed. Sviashchennik S. Petrovskii (Odessa, 1901), 39–46; "Prilozhenie k Broshui Tridstatiletie deiatel'nosti Odesskago Bolgarskago Nastoiatel'stva (1854–1884)," in *K materialam dlia istorii osvozhdeniia Bolgarie* (Odessa, 1895).

82. RNB, f. 313, d. 41, l. 220–221 (Documents from the correspondence of Archbishop Innokentii of Kherson, 1830, 1851–1855).

83. RNB, f. 313, d. 41, l. 60, 11 September 1851, Ministry of Internal Affairs to Archbishop Innokentii.

84. Archbishop Innokentii to Grand Duke Konstantin Nikolaevich, Odessa, 27 February 1852, *RS* 25 (1879), 192–93.

85. GAOO, f. 37, op. 1, d. 1790 (Statistical table of the Tauride Province), l.12.

86. Philip Sherrard, *Athos: The Holy Mountain* (London, 1982), 12–13.

87. The association of Mt. Athos with the task of preservation has been so repeatedly emphasized that Mateja Matejic felt compelled to clarify: "Mount Athos is NOT a museum—it is a LIVING COMMUNITY." Mateja Matejic, *The Holy Mount and the Hilandar Monastery* (Columbus, 1983), 3.

88. The British tourist Cecil Stewart watched as a monk brought a male cat into Athos to combat the rats, and sympathized "Poor, tragic creature, so naturally amorous, doomed to celibacy." Cecil Stewart, *Byzantine Legacy* (London, 1947), 55.

89. There is substantial English-language literature on the practices of Mount Athos. For recent works, see Graham Speake, *Mount Athos: Renewal in Paradise* (New Haven, CN: Yale University Press, 2002); Archimandrite Vasileios of Stavronikita, *Beauty and Hesychia in Athonite Life*, trans. from the Greek by Constantine Kokenes (Montréal, 1996).

90. For the variety of traditions on Mount Athos, see Matejic, *The Holy Mount,* 4–14. The remaining idiorrythmic monasteries on Mount Athos shifted to cenobitic monasticism in the nineteenth century, Speake, *Mount Athos,* 144.

91. In addition to centuries of preserving Orthodox tradition, Mount Athos draws a Christian mystique from myriad legends. The most important of these legends is based on an apocryphal account in which the Theotokos was believed to have visited the mountain in 49 A.D., when her ship, bound to meet Lazarus in Cyprus, was blown off course. She landed on Athos, and pooceeded to convert and baptize all local inhabitants. This story, according to Philip Sherrard, is also connected with the twelfth chapter of Revelation, which depicts a mother fleeing into the desert after her son ascends to heaven. "This desert," Sherrard notes, "is understood as Athos," and has become a metaphor for the simple, austere lifestyle for which monks on Athos are typically known. Another legend describes Athos as the heir to the monasticism of the early desert fathers, who were believed to have relocated to Athos after Arab powers conquered Egypt and Syria. Since then, numerous other accounts of saints, miracles, and miraculous icons have been associated with Mount Athos including apparitions of Mary and icons that speak or come to life. Sherrard, *Athos,* 12–29, 5.

92. Manchester, *Holy Fathers, Secular Sons*, 87.

93. Davydov, *Putevyia zapiski,* 2:163.

94. Blagoveshchenskii, *Afon',* 3. This could be the popovich ethnographer identified in Laurie Manchester's *Holy Fathers, Secular Sons*, 222.

95. For a detailed account of this movement, see especially I. K. Smolich, *Russkoe monashestvo, 988–1917, zhizn' i uchenie startsev* (Moscow, 1997), 280–366.

96. Robert Nichols, "The Orthodox Elders (Startsy) of Imperial Russia," *Modern Greek Studies Yearbook* 1 (1985): 17; Brenda Meehan-Waters, "Metropolitan Filaret (Drozdov) and the Reform of Russian Women's Monastic Communities," *Russian Review* 50 (1991), 310–23.

97. See Nichols, "The Orthodox Elders," 12–13, and Fr. Sergii Chetverikov, *Optina Pustyn'. Istoricheskii ocherk i lichnie vospominania* (Paris, 1926), 44–54. Optina Hermitage's publishing activity began during the nineteen-year administration of Father Makarii (Ivanov), 1841–1860.

98. G. A. Amichba, *Novyii Afon i ego Krestnosti (istoricheskii ocherk)* (Sukhumi, 1988), 72–75.

99. Mount Athos also had a population of Orthodox believers from North Africa and the Middle East, including Syrians and Egyptians. Given its complex history and unusual ethnic make-up, Athos, Fennell argues, had a "vital role in Near Eastern his-

tory," and he contends that "knowledge of Athonite history provides a useful insight into the complexities of the Eastern Question and the situation in the Balkans today." Nicholas Fennell, *The Russians on Athos* (Bern, 2001), 20, 23.

100. Alexander Schmemann, *The Historical Road of Eastern Orthodoxy*, trans. Lydia Kesich (New York, 1977), 276–90.

101. Nichols, "The Orthodox Elders," 17.

102. Stavrou, *Russian Interests in Palestine*, 31–40.

103. For a list of published pilgrimage literature, see the compilation: Theofanis G. Stavrou and Peter R. Weisensel, *Russian Travelers to the Christian East from the Twelfth to the Twentieth Century* (Columbus, 1985). Famous visitors to Mount Athos in the prerevolutionary period include Porfirii Uspenskii, the prelate who headed the first Russian Jerusalem Ecclesiastical Mission in 1847; Grand Duke Konstantin Nikolaevich, who visited Mt. Athos in 1845; P. A. Viazemskii, the poet and literary critic; A. N. Murav'ev who was an official of the Holy Synod; and the Slavicist V. I. Grigorievich. Many of these pilgrims, including V. P. Orlov-Davydov, V. I. Grigorievich, A. N. Murav'ev, Grigorii I. Shiriaev, and Parfeny (Petr Ageev) published accounts of their travels on Mt. Athos.

104. Sviatogorets, *Pis'ma sviatogortsa* and "Pis'ma s Afonskoi gory," *Maiak* 19, 21, 22, 23, 24 (1845). The letters of Sviatogorets have been republished in a number of different editions and serialized versions. See Stavrou and Weisensel, *Russian Travelers to the Christian East*, 253–55. For a list of Russian monasteries and religious settlements that existed on Athos by the turn of the twentieth century, see A. A. Pavlovskii, *Vseobshchii illustrirovannyi putevoditel' po monastyriam i sviatym mestam Rossiiskoi Imperii i Afonu* (St. Petersburg, 1907).

105. K. B., "Pis'ma Sviatogortsa k druz'iam svoim o sv. gor' Afonskoi," *St. Peterburgskaia vedomosti* 63 (1850), and "*III. Severnaia pchela*, 1850 g., no. 156," reprinted in Serafim Vesnin, *Sochineniia i pis'ma Sviatogorets, sobranie posle ego smerti* (St. Petersburg, 1858) viii–x.

106. See for example: Archbishop Innokentii, "O novouchrezhdennom krestnom khod, v pamat' osnovaniia goroda Odessy," *OV* 66 (17 August 1849).

107. Sergei Bolshakoff, *Russian Mystics* (London, 1977), 237–39; 272–73.

108. Archbishop Innokentii, "Zapiski o vostanovlenii drevnikh sviatykh mest' po goram krymskim," 94.

109. For more on these communities, see Chetverikov, *Optina Pustyn'*, 289–90. Valentine Zander, *St. Seraphim of Sarov*, trans. Sister Gabriel Anne s.s.c. (New York, 1975), 15—16; Leonard J. Stanton, "Zedergol'm's Life of Elder Leonid of Optina as a Source of Dostoevsky's *The Brothers Karamazov*," *The Russian Review* 49 (1990): 443–46.

110. Archbishop Innokentii, "Zapiski o vostanovlenii drevnikh sviatykh mest' po goram krymskim," 94.

111. Ageev, *Skazanie*, 2:10.

112. Murav'ev, *Pis'ma s vostoka*, 2:170.

113. See, for example, Ageev's comments about the Ukrainians, in *Skazanie*, 2: 110–19; and Sviatogorets's description of Russian-Greek relations, *Pis'ma sviatogortsa*, 45–49. The clashes between the Orthodox populations on Mount Athos is the focus of Fennell's *Russians on Athos*.

114. Blagoveshchenskii, *Afon'*, 168.

115. Archbishop Innokentii, "Zapiski o vostanovlenii drevnikh sviatykh mest' po goram krymskim," 94.

116. Archbishop Innokentii, "Zapiski o vostanovlenii drevnikh sviatykh mest' po goram krymskim,"95.

117. Innokentii's thought as characterized in the proposal sounds similar to the pan-Slavic and pan-Orthodox movements that historians typically associate with the period following the Crimean War. For traditional treatments of both movements,

see Andrzej Walicki, *A History of Russian Thought from the Enlightenment to Marxism* (Stanford, 1979), 111–15 and 300–8. See also the classic work by Kohn, *Pan-Slavism*; and finally, *Against the Current: Selections from the Novels, Essays, Notes, and Letters of Konstantin Leontiev*, ed. and with an introduction and notes by George Ivask, trans. George Reavey (NY, 1969).

118. Archbishop Innokentii frequently stressed this point. See for example, Archbishop Innokentii, "Slovo pri pogrebnii general-fel′dmarshala, svetleishago kniazia Mikhaila Semenovicha Vorontsova," *Sochineniia* 3 (St. Petersburg, 1908): 194–209.

119. Archbishop Innokentii, "Zapiski o vostanovlenii drevnikh sviatykh mest′ po goram krymskim," 94.

120. Archbishop Innokentii, "Zapiski o vostanovlenii drevnikh sviatykh mest′ po goram krymskim," 95. P. I. Keppen was one of the more prolific writers on Crimean antiquity and published several archaeological studies and travelogues during the 1820s and 1830s on the cave cities. See P. I. Keppen, "Opisanie Turkskoi peshchery v Krymu," *Trudy vysochaishie utverzhdennogo Vol′nogo obshchestva liubitelei rossiiskoi slovesnosti* 14 (1821): 220–49 and Keppen, "O krymskikh peshcherakh," *Russkii zritel′* 5–6 (1828): 132–36.

121. Archbishop Innokentii, "Zapiski o vostanovlenii drevnikh sviatykh mest′ po goram krymskim," 94.

122. Archbishop Innokentii, "Zapiski o vostanovlenii drevnikh sviatykh mest′ po goram krymskim," 88.

123. Archbishop Innokentii, "Zapiski o vostanovlenii drevnikh sviatykh mest′ po goram krymskim," 95.

124. Archbishop Innokentii, "Zapiski o vostanovlenii drevnikh sviatykh mest′ po goram krymskim," 96.

125. RGIA, f. 797, op. 20, d. 44614, l. 3 (About building Uspenskii Skete on the cliffs near Bakhchisarai by degrees and founding other desert residences on the Tauride peninsula).

126. RGIA, f. 797, op. 20, d. 44614, ll. 1–3ob.

127. Archbishop Innokentii, "Zapiski o vostanovlenii drevnikh sviatykh mest′ po goram krymskim," 90.

128. The Russian consulate church is covered in the dissertation of Lucien Frary, who gives some detail on Polikarp's position there. Frary, "Russia and Independent Greece," 161.

129. Umanets, *Istoricheskie rasskazy o Kryme* (1888), 254–57.

130. Umanets, *Istoricheskie rasskazy o Kryme* (1888), 257.

131. RGIA, f. 796, op. 131, d. 1276, ll. 1–2 (Report about Polikarp's transfer to Uspenskii).

132. RNB, f. 313, d. 42, l. 413, Polikarp to Archbishop Innokentii, 21 April 1850.

133. M. G. "Otkrytie glavnago skita Uspenskago, v Krymu bliz Bakhchisaraia," *OV* 70 (2 September 1850); RGIA, f. 796, op. 134, d. 925, l. 4 (About the elevation of the igumen of the Bakhchisarai Skete in recognition of excellent service to the rank of archimandrite).

134. Archbishop Innokentii, "Zapiski o vostanovlenii drevnikh sviatykh mest′ po goram krymskim," 92.

135. Archbishop Innokentii, "Zapiski o vostanovlenii drevnikh sviatykh mest′ po goram krymskim," 88.

136. Archbishop Innokentii, "Zapiski o vostanovlenii drevnikh sviatykh mest′ po goram krymskim," 96.

137. Archbishop Innokentii, "Zapiski o vostanovlenii drevnikh sviatykh mest′ po goram krymskim," 88.

138. This complex received attention in the first half of the nineteenth century

in the works of Dubois de Montpereaux, who offered some illustrations and described a monastery complex near Teshkli-burun. The complex at Mangup is believed to date to the fourteenth and fifteenth centuries during the kingdom of Feodoro. Mogarichev, *Peshchernye tserkvi Tavriki*, 54; Frédéric Dubois de Montpereaux, *Voyage autour du Caucase, chez les Tscherkesses et les Abkhases, en Colchida, en Georgie, en Arménie, et en Crimée* (Paris, 1843), 16, 280.

139. RNB, f. 313, d. 42, l. 212, Prince Vorontsov to Archbishop Innokentii, 21 April 1849.

140. RNB, f. 313, d. 42, l. 268, Prince Vorontsov to Archbishop Innokentii, 12 August 1849, St. Petersburg.

141. For more on Vorontsov's interest in regional studies and involvement with local scholarly societies, see: N. N. Murzakevich, "Ocherk zaslug sdelannykh naukam svetleishim kniazem Mikhailom Semenovichem Voronstovym" *ZOOID* 4 (1858): 395–413.

4: Monasticism Takes Root

1. Rossiiskaia Natsional'naia Biblioteka (RNB), f. 313, d. 42, l. 491 (Documents from the correspondence of Archbishop Innokentii of Kherson, 1841, 1847–1850), Igumen Mitrofan to Archbishop Innokentii, 17 July 1850.

2. M. G., "Otkrytie glavnogo skita Uspenskogo, v Krymu bliz Bakhchisaraia."

3. M. G., "Otkrytie glavnogo skita Uspenskogo, v Krymu bliz Bakhchisaraia."

4. RNB, f. 313, d. 27, l. 1–7. "Slovo, skazannoe pri otkrytii v Bakhchisaraiskoi skale novouchrezhdennogo skita Uspenskogo." This sermon has been published as "Slovo skazannoe Innokentiem, arkhiepiskopom khersonskim i tavricheskim, pri otkrytii skita v Bakhchisaraiskoi pustyn', 15 avgusta 1850 goda," *TEV* 16 (1900): 1135–38.

5. Dombrovskii, "Feleton."

6. Dombrovskii, "Feleton."

7. M. G. "Otkrytie glavnogo skita Uspenskogo, v Krymu bliz Bakhchisaraia."

8. A great discussion of the terms "modern" and "secular" in application to Russian Orthodoxy can be found in the introduction of Steinberg and Coleman, *Sacred Stories*, 1–21.

9. A. G. Gertsen and Iu. M. Mogarichev, "Salachik—Uspenskii Monastyr'—Chufut-Kale," in *Bakhchisaraiskii istoriko-kul'turnyi zapovednik* (Simferopol, 1995), 35–50.

10. Gertsen and Mogarichev, "Salachik," 41–42.

11. For more about Firkovich, see V. L. Viknovich, *Karaim Avraam Firkovich. Evreiskie rukopisi, istoriia, puteshestviia* (St. Petersburg, 1997).

12. Gertsen and Mogarichev, "Salachik," 36.

13. For varying expositions of the site's history, see: V. G. Tur, *Krymskie pravoslavnye monastyri XIX–nachala XX veka. Istoriia. Pravovoe polozhenie* (Simferopol, 1998), 74; S. L. Belov, *Zhemchuzhina pravoslaviia Kryma. Novyi grad* (Simferopol, 1997); Gertsen and Makhneva, *Peshchernye goroda Kryma*; Iashaeva, *Peshchernyi kompleks v okruge Khersona*.

14. Vera Shevzov, "Miracle-Working Icons, Laity, and Authority in the Russian Church, 1861–1917, *Russian Review* 58, no. 1 (January 1999): 26–28.

15. While Innokentii is often credited with compiling these legends from local histories, several also appeared in G. I. Spasskii, *Kniga Bol'shomu chertezhu* (Moscow, 1846).

16. Anonymous publication [presumed to be authored by Archbishop Innokentii], "Novootkrytyi Uspenskii Bakhchisaraiskii skit" *OV*, nos. 15, 16, 17, and 18 (20, 23, 27 February, and 1 March 1852), here no. 15.

17. [Innokentii] "Novootkrytyi Uspenskii Bakhchisaraiskii skit," no. 15.

18. Andreas Schönle, "Garden of the Empire: Catherine's Appropriation of the Crimea," *Slavic Review* 60, no. 1 (Spring 2001): 1–23; here, 4.

19. [Innokentii] "Novootkrytyi Uspenskii Bakhchisaraiskii skit," no. 15.

20. [Innokentii] "Novootkrytyi Uspenskii Bakhchisaraiskii skit," no. 16.

21. Kozlov and Chizhova, eds., *Tiurskie narody Krima*, 307–12.

22. For more on the church's approach to apostatized Tatars, see Kefeli, "Constructing an Islamic Identity," in Brower and Lazzerini, eds.,, *Russia's Orient*, 271–91.

23. M. G. "Otkrytie glavnogo skita Uspenskogo, v Krymu bliz Bakchisarai."

24. Innokentii, "Novootkrytyi Uspenskii Bakhchisaraiskii skit," 15.

25. RNB, f. 313, d. 42, l. 159, 485, Isidor, Exarch of Georgia to Innokentii, 20 December 1849 and 26 July 1850 (Documents from the correspondence of Archbishop Innokentii of Kherson, 1841, 1847–1850).

26. RNB, f. 313, d. 42, l. 367, Dmitrii I. Efimov to Archbishop Innokentii, 12 August 1850.

27. RNB, f. 313, d. 37, l. 63, Grand Duke Konstantin to Archbishop Innokentii, 19 March 1852 (Documents from the correspondence of Archbishop Innokentii of Kherson, 1851–1854).

28. In 1849, Archbishop Innokentii's ally and friend in the chancellery of the Holy Synod, Konstantin Serbinovich, noted, "I attentively read your notes about Crimean Athos." Somewhat later, F. P. Opochinin wrote to Innokentii from St. Petersburg revealing that he "followed after the progress of our fatherland's Athos—and shared Your joy to build this great affair, which will bring, with Blessed God, advantages not only in relations to religion, and but also in relationship to politics." RNB, f. 313, d. 42, l. 270, Konstantin Serbinovich to Archbishop Innokentii, 18 October 1849; RNB, f. 313, d. 42, l. 535, F. P. Opochinin to Innokentii, 31 August 1850.

29. Serafim Sviatogorets to Innokentii, 10 April 1852, in *Pis'ma s vostoka k Preosviashchennomu Innokentiiu arkhiepiskopu khersonskomu* (St. Petersburg, 1887), 13–14.

30. Serafim Sviatogorets to Archbishop Innokentii, 21 June 1851, RNB, f. 313, d. 41, l. 84–85 (Documents from the correspondence of Archbishop Innokentii of Kherson, 1830, 1851–1855).

31. Serafim Sviatogorets to Archbishop Innokentii, 10 April 1852, in *Pis'ma s vostoka k Preosviashchennomu Innokentiiu*, 13–14.

32. [Innokentii] " Novootkrytyi Uspenskii Bakhchisaraiskii skit ," no. 17.

33. Securing the land allotted to the monastery proved one of the most significant challenges. It involved the surveyor in Simferopol, the regional council in Simferopol, and the Muslim Spiritual Assembly. RNB, f. 313, d. 41, Ivan Gorgoli to Archbishop Innokentii, 9 February 1851.

34. [Innokentii] " Novootkrytyi Uspenskii Bakhchisaraiskii skit," no. 17.

35. Rossiiskii gosudarstvennyi istoricheskii arkhiv, (RGIA), f. 797, op. 20, d. 44614, l. 10 (About building Uspenskii Skete on the cliffs near Bakhchisarai by degrees and founding other desert residences on the Tauride peninsula).

36. RGIA, f. 797, op. 20, d. 44614, ll. 13–13ob.

37. Archbishop Innokentii, "Zapiski o vozstanovlenii drevnikh sviatykh mest' po goram Krymskim," *ITUAK* 5 (1888): 90.

38. RGIA, f. 797, op. 20, d. 44614, ll. 13–13ob.

39. Archbishop Innokentii, "Zapiski o vozstanovlenii drevnikh sviatykh mest' po goram Krymskim," 90–91.

40. RGIA, f. 797, op. 20, d. 44614, ll. 13–13ob.

41. RGIA, f. 797, op. 20, d. 44614, ll. 12–13ob.

42. Nepomniashchii, *Muzeinoe delo v Krymu i ego starateli*, 205.

43. RNB, f. 313, d. 37, l. 67. For the building process, see Ieromonk Vasilii to

Archbishop Innokentii (undated); and RNB, f. 313, d. 37, l. 127, Vasilii to Archbishop Innokentii, Oct. 31, 1852.

44. N. Murzakevich to Archbishop Innokentii, November 1852, "Materialy dlia russkoi istorii pervoi poloviny XIX stoletiia. Pis'ma raznykh lits Arkhiepiskopu Innokentiiu Borisovu," *Chteniia v imperatorskom obshchestve istorii i drevnostei Rossiiskikh pri Moskovskom Universitete* 4 (October/December 1884): 53–54; for Murzakevich's negative assessment of Archbishop Innokentii, see "Zapiski N. N. Murzakevicha, 1806–1883," *Russkaia starina* (1889): 237–38. For a refutation, see I. U. Palimpsestov, "Oproverzhenie klevety—otvet na stat'iu ob Innokentie khersonskom v *Russkoi starine*," *Strannik* (1861): 1–27.

45. N. Murzakevich, "Khersonisskaia tserkov sv. Vasiliia (Vladimira)" *ZOOID* 5 (1863): 996–97.

46. N. Murzakevich to Archbishop Innokentii, 24 November 1852, *Pis'ma raznykh lits znamenitomu Arkhiepiskopu Innokentiiu Borisovu*, 54–55.

47. RGIA, f. 797, op. 20, d. 44614, l. 13ob.

48. RNB, f. 313, d. 37, l. 265. Ieromonk Vasilii to Archbishop Innokentii, Spring 1853 (date unclear).

49. Ieromonk Vasilii to Archbishop Innokentii, l. 265.

50. Z. A. (Arkas), "Osnovanie skitov okrestnostiakh goroda Sevastopolia vo imia Sv. Ravnoapostol'nogo kniazia Vladimira i Sv. Klimenta, papy Rimskogo, i osviashchenie ikh," *OV*, 2 May 1853.

51. Z. A. (Arkas), "Osnovanie skitov okrestnostiakh goroda Sevastopolia."

52. Lebedev, *Istoriia otechestvennoi arkheologii*, 94–101.

53. RGIA, f. 797, op. 20, d. 44614, l. 10.

54. M. Obolenskii, "Skazanie sviashchennika Iakova," *ZOOID* 2 (1850): 687–92. The first description of Inkerman, as this article reveals, appeared in the writings of the priest, Iakov; See also, V. F. Filippenko, "K istorii Inkermanskogo peshchernogo monastyria (pervyi etap sushchestvovaniia)," in *Istoriia i arkheologiia Iugo-Zapadnogo Kryma* ed. Iu. M. Mogarichev (Simferopol, 1993).

55. Iashaeva, *Peshchernyi kompleks v okruge Khersona*, 93–94.

56. Mogarichev, *Peshchernye tserkvi Tavriki*, 9–10. Mogarichev hypothesizes that the St. Gregory Basilica was built in the fourteenth and fifteenth centuries because the volume of the church required materials and expenditures of a large, organized government that existed only in the Feodoro (Genoese) kingdom, and that the dramatic architecture of the large cave monastery was elevated as a symbol of the power of the new kingdom.

57. "Zhitie i stradanie sviatogo sviashchennomuchenika Klimenta, papy rimskago," in *Zhitiia Sviatykh na russkom iazyke izlozhennyiia po rukovodstvu Chetikh-minei sv. Dimitriia Rostovskogo, s dopolneniiami, ob'iasnitel'nymi primechaniiami, i izobrazheniiami sviatykh* 3 (25 November) (Moscow, 1992): 701–15.

58. I. Danevskii, "Ocherk Istorii Inkermana" *Novorossiiskii kalendar' na 1855* (Odessa, 1854), 398–413.

59. Ibid., 400–401.

60. Archbishop Innokentii, "Zapiski o vozstanovlenii drevnikh sviatykh mest' po goram Krymskim," 91–92; RGIA f. 797, op. 20, d. 44614, ll. 13–13ob.

61. Archbishop Innokentii, "Zapiski o vozstanovlenii drevnikh sviatykh mest' po goram Krymskim," 92.

62. RGIA, f. 797, op. 20, d. 44614, ll. 13–13ob.

63. RNB, f. 313, d. 37, ll. 127, Ieromonk Vasilii to Archbishop Innokentii, 31 October 1852.

64. RNB, f. 313, d. 37, l. 226, Ieromonk Vasilii to Archbishop Innokentii, 14 February 1853.

65. RNB, f. 313, d. 37, l. 265, Ieromonk Vasilii to Archbishop Innokentii, spring 1853 (date unclear).

66. The intersection between Christianity and pre-Christian sacred landscapes has been the ongoing subject of Ivan Kovalenko's research. See: Ivan Mikhailovich Kovalenko, *Pravoslaviia i priroda Kryma* (Simferopol, 2006); *Dostoprimechatel'nye derev'iia Krima* (Simferopol, 2004); and *Sviashchennaia priroda Kryma. Ocherki kul'tovoprirodookhrannykh traditsii narodov Kryma* (Kyiv, 2001).

67. This is the case for Christianity generally. See Christopher Parks, *Sacred Worlds: An Introduction to Geography and Religion* (London, 1994), 247.

68. Liudmila Iasel'skaia, "Kosmodamianovskii monastyr'," Simferopol'skaia i Krymskaia eparkhiia [Diocese of Simferopol and Crimea (official site)] <orthodox.sf.ukrtel.net/MONASTYR/kosdam.htm> (accessed 10 June 2003).

69. Gosudarstvennyi arkhiv avtonomoi respublika kryma (GAARK), f. 118, op. 1, d. 4, ll.3–6 (About the spring called Savluk-Su by the Tatars).

70. GAARK, f. 118, op. 1, d. 4, ll. 8, 25.

71. The Orthodox calendar includes three pairs of the Saints Cosmas and Damian (1 July, 17 October, and 1 November), whose lives all bear strong resemblance. Cosmas and Damian are regarded as the patrons of physicians. "Den' pervyi. Stradanie sviatykh muchenikov Kosmy i Damiana," *Zhitiia Sviatikh*, vol. 11 (Moscow, 1968–1969): 5–10.

72. [Anonymous], "O krymskom istochnike sv. Kosmy i Damian," *OV* 66 (1851).

73. "O krymskom istochnike sv. Kosmy i Damian."

74. Archbishop Innokentii, "Slovo v den' pamiati sv. Bezsrebrennikov Kozmy i Damiana," *Sochineniia Innokentiia* (1901), 5:305.

75. Ibid., 305–6.

76. Archbishop Innokentii, "Zapiski o vozstanovlenii drevnikh sviatykh mest' po goram Krymskim," 90.

77. "Kosmodamianovskaia kinoviia, v Krymu, i vospominaniia o pervom nastoiateli onoi, igumen Makarii," *TEV* 3 (1882): 133.

78. Archbishop Innokentii, "Zapiski o vozstanovlenii drevnikh sviatykh mest' po goram Krymskim," 90.

79. RNB, f. 313, d. 37, l. 41, Ivan to Archbishop Innokentii, 10 February 1851.

80. "Kosmodamianovskaia kinoviia, v Krymu, i vospominaniia o pervom nastoiateli onoi, igumen Makarii," 138; "O krymskom istochnike sv. Kosmy i Damian," 66. The article gives 16 March as the official date for the transfer of property into church authority, although other sources give the date as 19 March.

81. "O krymskom istochnike sv. Kosmy i Damian," 66.

82. "Kosmodamianovskaia kinoviia, v Krymu, i vospominaniia o pervom nastoiateli onoi, igumen Makarii," 133.

83. Shavshin, *Balaklavskii Georgievskii monastyr'*, 24.

84. Ibid., 24–25; A. L. Bert'e-Delagard, *K istorii khristianstva v Krymu. Mnimoe tysiachletie. Vymysel i deistvitel'nost' v istorii Georgievskogo Balaklavskogo monastyria* (Odessa, 1910), 56. According to Bert'e-Delegarde, however, an abbot of the monastery, Nikon, created this legend in 1862. The legend does not appear among the materials associated with Archbishop Innokentii's period, including the *OV* article by Leontii Cherniavskii, "Feleton: Balaklavskii Georgievskii monastyr'," *OV* 75 (20 September 1850).

85. Shavshin, *Balaklavskii Georgievskii monastyr'*, 25–26.

86. See an account of this restoration in Cherniavskii, "Feleton," 75.

87. RGIA, f. 797, op. 20, d. 44602, l. 2.

88. RGIA, f. 797, op. 20, d. 44602, l. 19.

89. RGIA, f. 797, op. 20, d. 44602, l. 2.

90. RGIA, f. 797, op. 20, d. 44602, ll. 2, 5.

91. RGIA, f. 797, op. 20, d. 44641, ll. 1–3.

92. Agathangelos to Archbishop Innokentii, 21 July 1850, RNB, f. 313, d. 42, l. 405.
93. RGIA, f. 797, op. 20, d. 44602, l. 16 (About raising the Balaklava St. George monastery to first class).
94. RGIA, f. 797, op. 20, d. 44602, ll. 14, 14 ob.
95. RGIA, f. 796, op. 134, d. 1377, ll. 1–4, 21 (Transferring Archimandrite Gerontiia from Bizukov monastery to St. George monastery in Balaklava). The Synod formally approved the transfer on 21 December 1853.
96. See the correspondence between Polikarp and Agathangelos in RGIA, f. 797, op. 20, d. 44602, ll. 15 to 18 ob.
97. Shavshin, *Balaklavskii Georgievskii monastyr'*, 50.
98. Cherniavskii, "Feleton," 75. Cherniavskii noted further, that "The Tatars in general had respect for the water of these places which were sanctified by the Orthodox faith and frequently visited it as if coming closer to Christianity." Later, he argued that the Tatar reverence for the Christian sites protected the monastery from certain destruction after the Christian exodus: "This starets convinced me that the respect of the Tatars to the water was the reason that the monastery was not destroyed like the other similar holy places in Crimea, and particularly in the time directly preceding Tauride's unification with Russia."
99. Cherniavskii, "Feleton." 75.
100. Christopher Chulos, *Converting Worlds: Religion and Community in Peasant Russia, 1861–1917* (DeKalb, 2003), 5.
101. RNB, f. 313, d. 42, l. 229, Aleksander Ivanovich Budberg to Archbishop Innokentii, 11 February 1849. These letters can be found in "Materialy dlia biografii Innokentiia, arkhiepiskopa khersonskago. Pis'ma raznykh lits k preosviashchennomu Innokentiiu," *Khristianskoe chtenie* 1–2 (1888): 46–49.
102. RNB, f. 313, d. 42, l. 229, Aleksander Budberg to Archbishop Innokentii, 11 February 1849.
103. All of these sites were discussed in both articles about Dormition Monastery and Cosmos and Damian.
104. Tereshchenko, "Ocherki Novorossiiskago Kraia," 76.
105. Archbishop Innokentii to Archbishop Gavriil, 19 December 1850, "Pis'ma arkhiepiskopa khersonskago i tavricheskago Innokentiia k Gavriilu, arkhiepiskopu Riazanskomu, 1829–1857," *ZOOID* 14 (1886): 764.
106. Archbishop Innokentii to Archbishop Gavriil, 19 December 1850, "Pis'ma arkhiepiskopa khersonskago i tavricheskago Innokentiia k Gavriilu, arkhiepiskopu Riazanskomu, 1829–1857," 764.

5: War

1. "Vysochaishii manifest ot 20 oktiabria 1853 ob ob'iavlenii voiny Porte," in *Materialy dlia istorii krymskoi voiny i Oborony Sevastopolia. Sbornik izdavaemyi komitetom po ustroistvu sevastopol'skago muzeia*, ed. N. Dubrovin, 5 vols. (St. Petersburg, 1871–74), 1:129–31.
2. "Vysochaishii manifest ot 20 oktiabria 1853 ob ob'iavlenii voiny Porte," 129.
3. For a fairly recent expression of the debate, see David Goldfrank, "Policy Traditions and the Menshikov Mission of 1853," and V. N. Vinogradov, "The Personal Responsibility of Emperor Nicholas I for the Coming of the Crimean War: An Episode in the Diplomatic Struggle in the Eastern Question," in *Imperial Russian Foreign Policy*, ed. Hugh Ragsdale (Cambridge, 1993), 119–58 and 159–70.
4. There is a vast body of literature on the Crimean War, which it is not my intention to review in this chapter. Excellent bibliographies can be found in David Goldfrank's article listed above and in his book *The Origins of the Crimean War* (New York,

1994), as well as in Winifred Baumgart, *The Crimean War, 1853–1856* (London, 1999).

5. See Goldfrank, *The Origins of the Crimean War.*

6. W. Bruce Lincoln, *Nicholas I: Emperor and Autocrat of All the Russias* (Bloomington, 1978), 331–40. For an account of the tsar's blunderings with Prussia and Austria, see pages 326–30.

7. Curtiss, *Russia's Crimean War*, 12–34.

8. For more on the influence of Nicholas I's personal religiosity and the origins of the Crimean War, see David Goldfrank, "The Holy Sepulcher and the Origin of the Crimean War," in *The Military and Society in Russia, 1450–1917*, ed. Eric Lohr and Marshall Poe (London, 2002), 491–505.

9. Quoted in Nicholas V. Riasanovsky, *Nicholas I and Official Nationality in Russia, 1825–1855* (Berkeley, 1959), 265.

10. For an interesting insight into the church's interpretation of the Eastern Question, see Filaret, Metropolitan of Moscow, *Sobraniia mnenii i otzyvov Filareta mitropolita moskovskago i kolomenskago. Delam pravoslavnoi tserkvi na vostok* (St. Petersburg, 1886).

11. Filaret, after reading the Manifest (on 20 October 1853), in *Zhizn' i trudy M. P. Pogodina*, ed. Nikolai Barsukov, vol. 3 (St. Petersburg, 1899), 9.

12. A. S. Khomiakov, *Stikhotvoreniia i dramy* (Leningrad, 1969), 124–43. For more on Slavophiles and the Crimean War, see Nicholas Riasanovsky, *Russia and the West and the Teachings of the Slavophiles* (Cambridge, 1952), 180–82; and Peter J. S. Duncan, *Russian Messianism: Third Rome, Revolution, Communism, and After* (New York, 2000), 28–32.

13. Pogodin expressed his feelings about the Crimean War in a series of letters that were later collected in vol. 4 of *Sochineniia M. P. Pogodina*, titled *Istoriko-politicheskiia pis'ma i zapiski v prodolzhenii k krymskoi voiny, 1853–1856*, ed. N. Barsukov (St. Petersburg, 1899). This series of letters has received significant analysis by Curtis Hunter Porter, *Mikhail Petrovich Pogodin and the Development of Russian Nationalism, 1800–1856* (Ph.D. diss., Vanderbilt University, 1973), 308–65. This quote was taken from Porter, 333.

14. Goldfrank, "Policy Traditions and the Menshikov Mission of 1853," 156.

15. Innokentii, Archbishop of Kherson and Tauride, "Rech' po prochtenii vysochaishago manifesta o voine s turtsieiu," *Sochineniia* 8 (St. Petersburg, 1874), 9.

16. Innokentii, "Rech' po prochtenii vysochaishago manifesta o voine s turtsieiu," 10.

17. Innokentii, "Rech' po prochtenii vysochaishago manifesta o voine s turtsieiu," 8.

18. Initially, the war was known in the West as the Russian War. Crimea was centrally positioned with the early classic account by Alexander Kinglake, *The Invasion of Crimea: Its origin and an account of its progress down to the death of Lord Raglan*, 8 vols. (Edinburgh, 1863); for the classic Russian perspective, see E. V. Tarle, *Krymskaia voina*, 2 vols. (Moscow, 1944; reprint Moscow, 2003).

19. Kingsley Martin, *The Triumph of Lord Palmerston: A Study of Public Opinion in England before the Crimean War* (1923; reprint, London, 1963).

20. The best treatment of life in Crimea during the war remains Arsenii Markevich, *Tavricheskaia guberniia vo vremia krymskoi voiny po arkhivnym materialam* (1905; reprint, Simferopol, 1994). All citations are to the reprint.

21. Serhii Plokhy, "The City of Glory: Sevastopol in Russian Historical Mythology," *Journal of Contemporary History*, 35, no. 3 (July 2000): 369–83.

22. Markevich, *Tavricheskaia guberniia*, 15–22. It's important to note that these reports characterize the activities of only a few Tatars. The majority remained loyal to the Russian state, and many received medals for their valor. Several formed into volunteer regiments that were transferred to the north. For Crimean Tatars who received medals, see Markevich, *Tavricheskaia guberniia*, 32–33; for Crimean Tatar regiments during the

war, see M. M. Muftiizade, *Ocherk stoletnei voennoi sluzhby Krymskikh tatar, 1784–1904* (Simferopol, 1905).

23. M. V. Iuzefovich to M. P. Pogodin, 22 May 1854, in *Zhizn' i trudy M. P. Pogodina*, ed. Barsukov 13: 53–54.

24. RGIA, f. 797, op. 24, d. 174, l. 11 (3 letters to the *ober-prokuror* of the Holy Synod about the war in Odessa).

25. Markevich, *Tavricheskaia guberniia*, 12.

26. Baumgart, *The Crimean War*, 116.

27. Innokentii, "Slovo pri Poiavlenii pred Odessoiu flotov nepriatel'skikh," delivered on 9 April 1854, in the Odessa Cathedral, *Sochineniia* 8 (St. Petersburg, 1874): 18.

28. Innokentii, "Slovo pri Poiavlenii pred Odessoiu flotov nepriatel'skikh," 16–17.

29. Innokentii, "Slovo pri Poiavlenii pred Odessoiu flotov nepriatel'skikh," 12.

30. Innokentii, "Slovo pri Poiavlenii pred Odessoiu flotov nepriatel'skikh," 13.

31. See for example the many pamphlets cited at the beginning of this bibliography as well as his collected works. The majority of these published sermons have been gathered into various volumes of Innokentii's collected works. See especially "Slova po sluchaiu obshchestvennykh bedstvii," *Sochineniia*, vol. 8 (St. Petersburg, 1874); "Slova pri poseshchenii pastv'," *Sochineniia*, vol. 2 (St. Petersburg, 1908): 446–86 and, in the same volume, "Slova i rechi k otdel'nym litsam," 543–65.

32. Stephen M. Norris, *A War of Images: Russian Popular Prints, Wartime Culture, and National Identity, 1812–1945* (DeKalb, 2006).

33. RNB, f. 637, d. 941, ll. 1–2 (Innokentii, Ivan Alekseevich Borisov, to Modest Andreevich Korff).

34. RGIA, f. 797, op. 24, d. 174, ll. 1–3.

35. RGIA, f. 797, op. 24, d. 16, ll. 1–3 ob (Communication from Archbishop Innokentii about the enemy located around the city of Odessa).

36. RGIA, f. 797, op. 24, d. 16, ll.1–3 ob.

37. RGIA f. 796, op. 135, d. 719, ll. 2, 2ob (Recognizing Innokentii's war activities); RGIA, f. 797, op. 24, d. 16, ll. 9–9 ob.

38. RGIA, f. 797, op. 24, d. 16, ll . 12–12 ob.

39. RGIA, f. 797, op. 24, d. 16, ll . 17–18 ob.

40. RGIA, f. 797, op. 24, d. 16, l. 25.

41. For a pre-revolutionary treatment of the religious processions established in commemoration of the bombardment, see L. M., *Vospominaniia Arkhiepiskopa Innokentiia (Borisova) v Odesse v pamiat' spaseniia ee ot nashestviia anglo-frantsuzskago flota v 1854–1855* (Odessa, 1907); *Kasperovka Chudotvornaia Ikona Bozhei Materi* (Odessa, 1891); and Ioann Znamenskii, *O Kasperovskoi Ikone Bozhei Materi* (Odessa, 1877).

42. RGIA, f. 796, op. 135, d. 1729, l. 1 (About Archbishop Innokentii visiting his Crimean flock during the Tatar uprising).

43. Innokentii, "Slovo pri poseshchenii pastvy," Karasubazar Cathedral, 17 September 1854, in *Sochineniia* vol. 2 (St. Petersburg, 1908): 239.

44. Innokentii, "Slovo po sluchaiu nashestviia inoplemennikov," St. Alexander Nevsky Sobor, 15 September 1854, in *Sochineniia* vol. 2 (St. Petersburg, 1908): 229, 230.

45. Innokentii, "Slovo po sluchaiu nashestviia inoplemennikov," 230.

46. Innokentii, "Slovo po sluchaiu nashestviia inoplemennikov," 227.

47. Innokentii, "Slovo pri poseshchenii pastvy," 17 September 1854, 241.

48. Innokentii, "Slovo pri poseshchenii pastvy," 239.

49. "Slovo po sluchaiu nashestviia inoplemennikov," 224.

50. "Slovo po sluchaiu nashestviia inoplemennikov," 228.

51. "Slovo po sluchaiu nashestviia inoplemennikov," 223.

52. RGIA, f. 797, op. 24, d. 16, l. 29.

53. The storm eroded trenches around Sevastopol, grounded ships, and sank vessels with medical supplies, food, and ammunition. Although hundreds of men died in the storm, the loss of material goods, such as coats, hats, boots, and gloves, was far more damaging to the British, for it meant that many would perish in the quickly approaching winter. Baumgart, *The Crimean War,* 137–38.

54. Franz Martinovich Dombrovskii, "Buria 2–go noiabria 1854 goda, v Krymu," *OV* 127 (1854); reprinted in *Moskovskie vedomosti* 145 (1854).

55. For the life of St. Stefan the Confessor, Archbishop of Surozh, see "Zhitie Sviatago Stefana Ispovednika, arkhiepiskopa Surozhskago," in *Zhitiia Sviatykh na russkom iazyke izlozhennyia po rukovodstvu Chetikh-minei sv. Dimitriia Rostovskago, s dopolneniiami, ob'iasnitel'nymi primechaniiami, i izobrazheniiami sviatykh* 4 (15 December): 425–31.

56. Innokentii, "Slovo po sluchaiu nashestviia inoplemennikov," St. Alexander Nevsky Sobor, 15 September 1854, in *Sochineniia* vol. 2 (St. Petersburg, 1908): 230; "Slovo pri poseshchenii pastvy," *Sochineniia* vol. 2 (St. Petersburg, 1908): 248.

57. Innokentii, "Slovo pri poseshchenii pastvy," 250–51.

58. Innokentii, "Slovo v den' pamiati sv. Bezsrebrennikov Kozmy i Damiana," *Sochineniia Innokentiia* (1901 ed.), 5: 309.

59. Plokhy, "The City of Glory," 374; Olga Maiorova has expanded upon Plokhy's argument in "Searching for a New Language of Collective Self: The Symbolism of Russian National Belonging during and after the Crimean War," *Ab Imperio* 4 (2006), 187–224.

60. Eduard Totleben, *Défense de Sebastopol. Exposé de la Guerre Souterraine, 1854–1855* (St. Petersburg, 1870).

61. Baumgart, *The Crimean War,* 156.

62. Innokentii, "Slovo pri poseshchenii pastvy," Sevastopol, in the camp, at the church in the northern fortifications, 25 June 1855, in *Sochineniia,* vol. 2 (St. Petersburg, 1908): 257.

63. "Slovo pri poseshchenii pastvy," 25 June 1855, 260.

64. "Slovo pri poseshchenii pastvy," Sevastopol, Nikolaev Sobor, 16 June 1855, in *Sochineniia,* vol. 2 (St. Petersburg, 1908): 262–63.

65. Quoted in Norris, 174.

66. Plokhy, "The City of Glory," 376.

67. Tarle, *Krymskai voina,* 445–48.

68. Captain A. Aslanbegov, "Po povodu zapisok sevastopol'tsa, napechatannykh v 12'u knizhke russkago arkhiva za 1867 g. 'Admiral Stepanovich Nakhimov (biograficheskii ocherk),'" in *Materialy dlia istorii krymskoi voiny i Oborony Sevastopolia. Sbornik izdavaemyi komitetom po ustroistvy sevastopol'skago muzeia,* ed. N. Dubrovin, 5 vols. (St. Petersburg, 1871)1: 210.

69. RGIA, f. 797, op. 24, d. 16, ll. 94–95.

70. Leo Tolstoy, *Sebastopol Sketches,* trans. and with an introduction by David McDuff (New York, 1986), 109. *Sebastopol Sketches* provides an overview of the war in three different sections. Tolstoy dates the middle section, titled "May 1855," as 26 June, the same date Innokentii delivered his famous sermon in Sevastopol.

71. Innokentii, "Slovo po sluchaiu nashestviia inoplemennikov," 231.

72. RGIA, f. 797, op. 24, d. 16, ll. 13–14 ob.

73. RGIA, f. 797, op. 24, d. 16, ll. 30, 30 ob.

74. RGIA, f. 797, op. 24, d. 16, ll. 31, 31 ob.

75. There has been surprisingly little research on the Russian Sisters of Mercy. The most substantial English-language study is: John Shelton Curtiss, "Russian Sisters of Mercy in the Crimea, 1854–1855," *Slavic Review* 25, no. 1 (March 1966): 84–100. For primary accounts, see Aleksandra Krupskaia, *Vospominaniia sestry Krestnovozdvizhenskoi obshchiny* (St. Petersburg, 1861); and Ekaterina M. Bakunina, "Vospominaniia sestry

miloserdiia Krestnovozdvizhenskoi obshchiny," *Vestnik Evropy* 190 (March 1898): 3–6.

76. RGIA, f. 797, op. 24, d. 34, l. 1 (About the appointment of clergy with the sisters caring for the wounded and ill at the war hospitals in Crimea).

77. See his memoirs: N. I. Pirogov, *Sevastopol'skie pis'ma* (St. Petersburg, 1899).

78. RGIA, f. 797, op. 24, d. 34, l. 1.

79. RGIA, f. 797, op. 24, d. 34, ll. 17–21.

80. Baumgart, *The Crimean War,* 138–45.

81. RNB, f. 313, d. 39 (Documents from the correspondence of Archbishop Innokentii of Kherson, 1846–1848, 1857), Monk Innokentii to Archbishop Innokentii, 8 January 1855.

82. See for example, Arkady Stol'pin, "Nochnaia vylazka v Sevastopole," *Sovremennik* 52 (1855): 7, 5–11; and *Materialy dlia istorii krymskoi voiny,* ed. Dubrovin, vol. 2, addendum, p. 46.

83. Quoted in *Materialy dlia istorii krymskoi voiny,* ed. Dubrovin, 5:366.

84. RGIA, f. 796, op. 138, d. 647, ll. 13–13 ob (About the condition of Crimean Sketes after the destruction of the enemy).

85. V. G. Shavshin, *Balaklava* (Simferopol, 1994), 41.

86. RGIA, f. 797, op. 24, d. 16, l. 25 ob.

87. Father Briukhovskii to Archbishop Innokentii, RNB, f. 313, d. 44, ll. 59–61(Documents, letters, reports, articles, and notes from various people to Archbishop Innokentii of Kherson, 1847–1857); Father Briukhovskii to Archbishop Innokentii, RNB f. 313, d. 44, ll. 62–63.

88. RGIA, f. 797, op. 24, d. 16, ll. 54–57.

89. RGIA, f. 796, op. 138, d. 647, ll. 4–5.

90. RGIA, f. 796, op. 138, d. 647, ll. 6–7.

91. RGIA, f. 797, op. 24, d. 16, ll. 82, 82 ob.

92. RGIA, f. 796, op. 135, d. 1729, ll. 2, 2ob.

93. RNB, f. 313, d. 44, l. 72, for the battle of Balaklava, see A. J. Barker, *Vainglorious War* (London, 1971), 150–74; and Tarle, *Krymskaia voina,* 156–54.

94. Father Nikolai to Archbishop Innokentii, 16 October 1854, RNB, f. 313, d. 44, l. 72.

95. Father Nikolai to Archbishop Innokentii, 24 September 1854, RNB, f. 313, d. 44, l. 54.

96. RGIA, f. 796, op. 136, d. 534, ll. 1–2.

97. See Tarle's discussion of the first bombardment of Sevastopol, *Krymskaia voina,* 148–69.

98. RGIA, f. 796, op. 136, d. 534, ll. 1–2 (about the destruction by the enemy of cenoby at Chersonesos and other places).

99. RGIA f. 797, op. 24, d. 16, ll. 113–113 ob.

100. RGIA, f. 797, op. 24, d. 16, l. 41 ob.

101. RGIA, f. 797, op. 24, d. 16, ll. 39–40.

102. RGIA, f. 797, op. 24, d. 16, ll. 88–89 ob and 92, 92 ob.

103. Shavshin, *Balaklava,* 43. For more on Balaklava, see also V. G. Shavshin, "Plenenn' i monastyr'," *Rodina* 3–4 (1995).

104. Most historians consider the bombing of Kinburn, a military target, to be the last significant engagement on the Black Sea. See Baumgart, *The Crimean War,* 164–65. For the diocesan authorities, however, it was Odessa, a city that had great cultural significance.

105. RGIA, f. 797, op. 24, d. 16, ll. 88–89 ob and 99–100 ob.

106. RGIA, f. 796, op. 136, d. 1236, ll. 1–2ob (About the siege of Odessa).

107. M. P. Pogodin, "Konchina Innokentieva," *Venok na mogilu Vysokopreosviashchennago Innokentiia, arkhiepiskopa tavricheskago* (Moscow, 1864), 63–64.

108. RGIA, f. 796, op. 137, d. 408, ll. 2–3 (About permitting Archbishop Innokentii and a few of the clerical peoples in the Kherson Diocese to wear medals for their defense of Sevastopol).

109. "Postavlenie tavricheskago magometanskago dukhovnago pravleniia ot 6–go oktiabria," in *Materialy dlia istorii krymskoi voiny i Oborony Sevastopolia, Sbornik izdavaemyikomitetom po ustroistvu sevastopol'skago muzeia,* ed. N. Dubrovin (St. Petersburg, 1872), 4:17–18.

110. "Proshenie deputatov nogaiskago plemeni, ot 12–go oktiabria," in *Materialy dlia istorii krymskoi voiny i Oborony Sevastopolia. Sbornik, izdavaemyii komitetom po ustroistvu sevastopol'skago muzeia,* ed. N. Dubrovin, (St. Petersburg, 1872), 4:18–19.

111. "Proshenie deputatov nogaiskago plemeni, ot 12–go oktiabria," 18–19.

112. "Proshenie deputatov nogaiskago plemeni, ot 12–go oktiabria," 20.

113. In his article examining Tatar emigration, Markevich cites correspondence between P. I. Keppen and Kh. Kh. Steven (dated in October) that Menshikov ordered the removal of Tatars on the Evpatoria coast inland. And while Menshikov could very well have proposed such an action, I found no evidence of this in archival files. Rather, it appears to have been chiefly Adlerberg who engineered anti-Tatar activities. Markevich, "Pereseleniia Krymskikh Tatar v Turtsiu v sviazi s dvizheniem naseleniia v Krymu," 393.

114. "Adlerberg, Count Nikolai Vladimirovich," *Russkii biograficheskii slovar'* (New York, 1962), vol. 1: 78.

115. V. E. Vozgrin, *Istoricheskie sudby krymskikh tatar* (Moscow, 1992), 324–30.

116. GAARK, f. 26, op. 4, d. 1495, l. 11.

117. GAARK, f. 26, op. 4, d. 1579, l. 4.

118. GAARK, f. 26, op. 4, d. 1605, l. 1 (Tatars giving secrets to the enemy and leaving the borders).

119. GAARK, f. 26, op. 4, d. 1605, l. 3.

120. To be sure, as historians have investigated the Great Reforms and the expansion of the Russian Empire, they have crafted a much more nuanced portrait of Alexander II in recent years. However, the nickname "tsar-liberator" in the traditional biographies nevertheless appears to stick. See for example, Norman Pereira, *Tsar-Liberator: Alexander II of Russia, 1818–1881* (Newtonville, 1983); and W. E. Mosse, *Alexander II and the Modernization of Russia* (London, 1992).

121. GAARK, f. 26, op. 4, d. 1685, l. 65. Although the Tatars declined under Vorontsov, the bureaucrat did subscribe to toleration and often intervened on their behalf. An elderly man when the war broke out, Vorontsov retired from his post at the turn of 1855. See Rhinelander, *Prince Michael S. Vorontsov.*

6: The Legacy of War for Crimean Christianity

1. D. Sokolov, *Progulka po Krymu, s tseliu oznakomit' s nim* (Odessa, 1869), 1.

2. Germogen, Bishop of Pskov, *Tavricheskaia eparkhiia* (St, Petersburg, 1886), 92–94.

3. RNB, f. 313, d. 42, l. 129 (personal fond of Archbishop Innokentii), Prince Vorontsov to Archbishop Innokentii, 12 July 1848.

4. Lebedintsev, "Stoletie tserkovnoi zhizni Kryma," 218–19.

5. The Korsun monastery was formed explicitly for the Old Believer populations relocated to Tauride at the end of the eighteenth century. For more, see: Gosudarstvennyi Arkhiv Avtonomnoi Respubliki Kryma (GAARK), f. 118, op. 1, d. 6165 (Information about the Korsun Mother of God first-class monastery for 1886).

6. Tur, *Krymskie pravoslavnye monastyri,* 56–108.

7. A. A. Pavlovskii, *Putevoditel' po sviatym mestam vostoka* (St. Petersburg, 1903), 645–50; "Pravoslavnye monastyri, skity, i kinovii v eparkhiakh Novorossiiskago kraia i

Bessarabii," *Novorossiiskii kalendar' na 1874* (1873): 114–21.

8. Baumgart, *The Crimean War,* 203–10; see also Baumgart, *The Peace of Paris, 1856: Studies in War, Diplomacy, and Peacemaking,* trans. Ann Pottinger Saab (Oxford, 1981).

9. Baumgart *The Crimean War* ,211–14.

10. Baumgart, *The Crimean War,* 215–16; Curtiss, *Russia's Crimean War,* 470.

11. This number includes the exodus of the Crimean Tatars, which will be discussed below. See Fisher, *The Crimean Tatars,* 89.

12. RGIA, f. 796, op. 138, d. 647, l. 7.

13. Markevich, *Tavricheskaia guberniia,* 214–17.

14. Ibid., 218.

15. Milner, *The Crimea,* 367.

16. These days, "victim" is a loaded word. Since at least the publication of Eric Wolf's *Europe and the People without History* (Berkeley,1982) scholars have been concerned to show that subalterns are not passive recipients of imperial power and within limited spheres can mediate their environments. While this is certainly true—Crews's study provides one excellent example, as do the responses of Tatars described in this chapter—it is also evident that in most cases, subalterns are subject to imperial processes beyond their control, must operate under highly regulated spheres, and undergo decline in some form or another. Thus, it is fair enough to argue that subalterns are victims, even as they are agents.

17. For a Russian reflection on the decline of the Tatars before and during the war, see Eduard Totleben, "O vyselenii tatar iz Kryma v 1860 gody," *Russkaia starina* 78 (1893): 531–50.

18. See G. P. Levitskii, "Pereselenie Tatar' iz Kryma v Turtsiu," *Vestnik Evropy* 5 (1882): 596–639 (here 606–8).

19. "Vyselenie Tatar iz Tavricheskoi gubernii," *Pamiatnaia Kniga* (Simferopol, 1867) 416–33.

20. Ibraim Abdullaev, "Postup' Krestonostsev v Krymu," *Golos Kryma* (24 November 2000): 4.

21. "Vyselenie Tatar iz Tavricheskoi gubernii," 416–33.

22. Tatar immigration to the Ottoman Empire was disastrous. One historian notes that in the course of ten months during a later stage of the emigration from Russia, Tatars died from cholera and malaria, and that out of 1,500 families, only 600 survived. Tatars repeatedly requested return from Russian authorities, but met mixed responses. See B. M. Vol'fson, "Emigratsiia Krymskikh Tatar v 1860 g." *Istoricheskie zapiski* no. 9 (1940), 190–91.

23. GAARK, f. 27, op. 1, d. 7530; I. Abdullaev, "Postup' krestonostsev v Krymu," 4.

24. GAOO, f. 37, op. 1, d. 1790, l. 4 (Founding a diocese in Tauride).

25. GAOO, f. 37, op. 1, d. 1790, ll. 5–7.

26. GAOO, f. 37, op. 1, d. 1790, ll. 13–14.

27. GAOO, f. 37, op. 1, d. 1790, l. 8.

28. Aleksandr Nakropin, "Iz vospominanii o preosviashchennom Innokentii arkhiepiskop khersonskom i tavricheskom," *TEV* 2 (1880): 68–90.

29. A. V. Ishin, "Deiatel'nost' arkhiepiskopa tavricheskogo Guriia (G. P. Karpova)," *Novosti/Zhurnaly* "Istoricheskoe nasledie Kryma" no. 9 (2005), <www.commonuments.crimea-portal.gov.ua/rus/index.php?v=1&tek=89&par=74&l=&art=350>.

30. GAARK f. 118, d. 605, op. l.1, 5–6.

31. RGIA, f. 796, op. 138, d. 647, (About the condition of Crimean Sketes after the ruin of the enemy), ll. 2–4.

32. RGIA, f. 796, op. 138, d. 647 (About the condition of Crimean Sketes after the ruin of the enemy), ll. 8–13.

33. A. S. Glushak, I. A. Antonova, V. F. Filipenko, N. V. Naumova, and S. M. Cherviakov, *Krym khristianskii* (Simferopol, 1996), 91.

34. RGIA, f. 796, op. 138, d. 647, l. 6; GAOO, f. 37, op. 1, d. 1781 (About the conditions of the church and the clergy), l. 11.

35. RGIA, f. 796, op. 138, d. 647, ll. 8–10.

36. RGIA, f. 797, op. 24, 2nd otd., 2 st., d. 16, l. 113 ob, (Communication from Archbishop of Kherson about the location of the enemy around the city of Odessa, and other wartime activities in Crimea).

37. RGIA, f. 796, op. 138, d. 647, ll. 9–10.

38. GAOO, f. 37, op. 1, d. 1781, l. 14.

39. RGIA, f. 796, op. 138, d. 647, ll. 9–10.

40. GAARK, f. 118, op. 1, d. 6192, ll. 51–52.

41. Glushak et al., *Krym khristianskii*, 118.

42. RGIA, f. 796, op. 138, d. 647, l. 12; GAOO, f. 37, op. 1, d. 1781, l. 13.

43. GAARK, f. 118, op. 1, d. 6164, ll. 42–43 (Information about the servitors at the Chersonesos, Katerles, Kiziltash, and Toplov monasteries).

44. GAARK, f. 118, op. 1, d. 671, ll. 9–15 (About returning half the capital of the certificates for the Steamship and Trade Society for the Bakhchisarai skete and cenoby).

45. RGIA, f. 796, op. 138, d. 647 (About the condition of Crimean Sketes after the ruin of the enemy), ll. 14–17.

46. RGIA, f. 796, op. 138, d. 647, ll. 17–20.

47. GAARK, f. 118, op. 1, d. 37a (About the imperial family visiting Crimea).

48. "Poseshchenie Bakhchisaraiskago Uspenskago skita, balaklavskago georgievskago monastyria i khersonskago pervoklasnago monastyria," *Tserkovnaia letopis'* (October 1861): 635.

49. GAARK, f. 118, op. 1, d. 6192, ll. 63–64.

50. Liudmila Iasel'skaia, *Toplovskii sviato-paraskevievskii zhenskii monastyr'* (Simferopol, n.d.), 7–10.

51. GAARK, f. 138, op. 1, d. 22, ll. 40–41, (News of the Toplovski monastery).

52. GAARK, f. 138, op. 1, d. 22, ll. 1–15.

53. GAARK, f. 138, op. 1, d. 18, ll. 196–197 (Turning Cosmas and Damian into a women's monastery).

54. Tur, *Krymskie pravoslavnye monastyri*. 95; GAARK, f. 138, op. 1, d. 41, 38 (Information about the status of and work at the monasteries).

55. For a wonderful analysis of women's monasticism, see Brenda Meehan, *Holy Women of Russia: The Lives of Five Orthodox Women Offer Spiritual Guidance for Today* (Crestwood, 1997).

56. Nepomniashchii, *Zapiski puteshestvennikov i putevoditeli v razvitii istoricheskogo kraevedeniia Kryma*, 74.

57. Mikhail Aleksandrovich Bernov, *Iz Odessy peshkom po Krymu. Pis'ma russkago peshekhoda* (St. Petersburg, 1896).

58. Ibid., 84.

59. Ibid., 162.

60. Ibid., 131. Admirals Vladimir Istomin, Pavel Nakhimov and Vladimir Kornilov died during the siege of Sevastopol; Admiral Mikhail Lazarov died before the war, but is credited with building the Black Sea Navy.

61. Bernov, *Iz Odessy peshkom po Krymu*, 140.

62. K. Zhukov, *Zametki v puti na iuzhnyi bereg Kryma* (St. Petersburg, 1865), 27.

63. Ibid., 30–36.

64. F. V. Livanov, "Khersonesos," in *Putevoditel' po Krymu s istoricheskim opisaniem dostoprimechatel'nostei Kryma* (Moscow, 1875), 1. Each chapter is repaginated.

65. Evgenii Markov, *Ocherki Kryma. Kartiny Krymskoi zhizny, istorii i prirodu,* 4th ed. (St. Petersburg, 1903), 137.

66. "Poseshchenie Bakhchisaraiskogo Uspenskogo skita...," *Strannik* 4.10 (1863): 154–156; G.U. Bakhtin, "Sviatoi kupeli (K 40 letiu Khersonisskogo Sv. Vladimira monastyria)," *Russkii palomnik* (St. Petersburg, 1893): 18, 281–283; 19, 294–295. A. P. Lopukhin, "Iz vospominanii o poezdke Livadiiu," *Tserkovnyi vestnik* 43 (1897): 1401–1414.

67. Murav'ev, *Puteshestvie po Sviatym Mestam russkim,* v, 499. Murav'ev traveled through Crimea in 1847 and 1858.

68. Ibid., 477.

69. GAARK, f. 118, op. 1, d. 6192, (Information about churches, short description about the Dormition skete in Bakhchisarai), l. 31.

70. A. P. Lopukhin, "Iz vospominanii o poezdke Livadiiu," *Tserkovnyi vestnik* 45 (1897): 1366.

71. Pavlovskii, *Putevoditel' po sviatym mestam vostoka,* 645–50.

72. For the importance of Crimea to archaeological study, see Lebedev, *Istoriia otechestvennoi arkheologii.*

73. "Zametka ob ekskursii, sostoiavsheisia posle zakrytia VI Arkheologicheskago s"ezda v Krym," in *Trudy VI Arkheologicheskago s"ezda v Odesse* (1884), ed. D.N. Anuchin, A. S. Uvarov, vol. 4 (Odessa, 1889), LXXVIII–LXXIX.

74. S. B. Filimonov, "Voprosy istorii khristianstva v dokladakh krymskikh kraevedov kontsa XIX–pervoi tretii XX vv.," *Pravoslavnye drevnosti Tavrike. Sbornik materialov po tserkovnoi arkheologii* (Kyiv, 2002), 15–16.

75. Kozelsky, "Ruins into Relics," 668–69.

76. GAARK, f. 118, op. 1, d. 113 (About informing the Odessa Society for History and Antiquities), l. 5.

77. GAARK, f. 118, op. 1, d. 6192, ll. 2–8 (News of the monasteries for 1891).

78. In 1888, the same year as the commemoration of 900 years of Christianity, the Imperial Archaeological Commission displaced the church as the principal supporter of research. Count Alexander Bobrinskii provided a detailed description of the museum and its history in his *Khersones tavricheskii. Istoricheskii ocherk* (St. Petersburg, 1905), 178–83.

79. GAARK, f. 138, op. 1, d. 12, ll. 1–2 (About producing valuables from the excavation at Inkerman).

80. GAARK f. 118, op. 1, d. 6065, (Information about the monasteries, 1868–1870), ll. 670–671.

81. Bert'e-Delagard, *K istorii khristianstva v Krymu.* See also *Ostatki drevnikh sooruzhenii v okresnostiakh Sevastopolia i peshchernye goroda Kryma* (Odessa, 1886).

82. Tur, *Krymskie pravoslavnye monastyri,* 71–72.

83. Germogen, *Tavricheskaia eparkhiia,* 463.

84. Germogen, *Tavricheskaia eparkhiia,* 501.

85. GAARK f. 138, op. 1, d. 15, (About the archaeologist exploiting ruins at Inkerman monastery), ll. 1–4.

86. Quoted and cited from Tur, *Krymskie pravoslavnye monastyri,* 106–7.

87. GAARK, f. 118, op. 1, d. 3250 (About reviewing the Bakhchisarai monastery).

88. GAARK, f. 118, op. 1, d. 3250, ll. 8–10.

89. See for example, Solomon Beim, *Pamiat' o Chufut-Kale* (Odessa, 1862); *Chufut-Kale i karaimy* (St. Petersburg, 1861); "Chufut-Kale i ego pervonachal'nye obitateli," in *Novorossiiskii kalendar'* na 1859 (Odessa, 1858): 431–44.

90. An. Iv. Loginovskii, "O Poslednei poezdke v Krym i poslednikh dniakh zhizni sinodal'nago chlena, preosviashchennago Innokentiia, byvshego arkhiepiskopa Khersonskogo i Tavricheskogo," in *KhEV,* Supplment 5 (1862): 91–92; for more on

Loginovskii, see P. N. S., "Svedeniia o protoierei An. Iv. Loginovskom," *KhEV* 5 (1862): 109–15.

91. Brian Williams notes that the number of migrants at this time was quite small. Williams, *Crimean Tatars: The Diaspora Experience and the Forging of a Nation* (Boston, 2001), 183–90. See also an analysis of return migration: James. H. Meyer, "Immigration, Return, and the Politics of Citizenship: Russian Muslims in the Ottoman Empire, 1860–1914," *International Journal of Middle Eastern Studies* 39 (2007): 15–32.

92. Williams, *Crimean Tatars*, 183–90. Abdureshid Mediev is another Tatar activist whose collected writings have recently been published. See V. Iu. Gankevich, ed., *Abdureshid Mediev. Krymskie pis'ma* (Simferopol, 2005).

93. A. B. Derman, *Delo ob Igumene Parfenii roman-khronika v trekh chastiakh* (Moscow, 1941).

94. Igumen Nikon and Protoierei Nikolai Donenko, *Iugo-vostochnyi Afon Rossiiskoi Imperii Kiziltash* (Simferopol, n.d.), 14. See also Prot. Nikolai Donenko and Liudmila Iasel'skaia, *Kiziltashskii Sviato-Stefano Surozhskii monastyr'* (Simferopol, 2006).

95. Parfenii was canonized in 2001 by the church of Moscow, and the story of his death is repeated in his Life. See "Prepodobnomuchenik Parfenii, igumen Kiziltashkii," Simferopol'skaia i Krymskaia eparkhiia [Diocese of Simferopol and Crimea (official site)] <www.crimea.orthodoxy.su/Chronica/2008-09-04-Parfeniy-Zhitiye.html> (accessed 22 May 2009).

96. Nikon and Donenko, *Iugo-vostochnyi Afon*, 44. It should be noted that the details surrounding Parfenii's murder are highly contested. At the time of writing, a series of articles in *Golos Kryma* by Ibraim Abdullaev challenged Donenko's assertion by arguing that the central conflict existed not between Parfenii and the Tatars, but Parfenii and the diocesan hierarchy. See for example, Ibraim Abdullaev, "Taraktashskaia tragediia," *Golos Kryma* (2 January 2009), <www.goloskrima.com/?p=1399>.

97. Germogen, *Tavricheskaia eparkhiia*, 92–94; an account of the celebration can also be found in *TEV* (1883), no. 9, 10.

98. M. Feofilov, "Istoricheskii ocherk khristianstva v Krymu. Inkermanskaia kinov'ia, Georgievskii monastyr', i Bakhchisaraiskii skit," *TEV* 8 (1899): 605.

99. "Panagiia, ili Uspenskii Bakhchisaraiskii v krymu skit," in *Krymskii Afon*, 12.

100. "Uspenskii skit bliz Bakhchisaraia," *Niva* 26 (1872): 411.

101. GAARK, f. 138, op. 1, d. 3, l. 156 (Tatars at Inkerman).

102. GAARK, f. 118, op. 1, d. 3352, l. 1 (About the Alushta Tatars seizing land from the Cosmas and Damian monastery).

103. GAARK, f. 118, op. 1, d. 3250, ll. 11–12 (Review of Dormition monastery).

104. Edward J. Lazzerini, "Local Accommodation and Resistance to Colonialism in Nineteenth-Century Crimea," *Russia's Orient: Imperial Borderlands and Peoples, 1700–1917* (Bloomington, 1997), 174.

105. Quoted in Press Service of the Russian Society in Crimea, 'Edinaia Rus' "Den' pamiati voinov, pavshikh pri oborone Sevastopolia i v Krymskoi voine, 1853–1856 godov," *Edinaia Rus'* (15 September 2008). <www.edrus.org/content/view/10495/47/>.

106. "O prazdnovanii dnei pamiatii pogibshikh voinov v Krymskoi voine," Edinoe otechestvo (21 September 2008), <www.otechestvo.org.ua/main/20089/2320.htm>. Edinoe Otechestvo (United Fatherland) is a group that formed in response to Pope John Paul II's visit to Ukraine in 2001, and it professes to "speak, to read, to think in the Russian langauge and to worship in the cannonical church of the Moscow Patriarchate." Its mission statement describes the group not as ethnically Russian, but Novorossian (in the historical sense), open to anyone who choses to join the "movement of Orthodox Patriots of Novorossiia." "Edinoe Otechestov, O Nas," <www.otechestvo.org.ua/Links/eo.htm>.

107. Primary documents concerning the deportations have been published in a

series edited by Iuri Biluka and Olga Vlasenko, *Deportovani Krimski Tatari, Bogari, Virmeni, Greki, Nimtsi* (Kyiv, 2004); Rudolf Loewenthal, "The Extinction of the Krimchaks in World War II," *American Slavic and East European Review* 10, no. 2 (April 1951): 130–36.

108. O. A. Gabrielan, S. A. Efimov, V. G. Garuben, A. E. Kislyi, A. V. Mal'gin, A. P. Nikiforov, V. M. Pavlov, V. P. Petrov, *Krymskie Repatriany. Deportatsiia, Vozvrashchenie, i Obustroistvo* (Simferopol, 1998); Ann Sheehy, *The Crimean Tatars, Volga Germans, and Meskhetians: Soviet Treatment of Some National Minorities* (London, 1980).

Epilogue

1. Reverend Andriy Vlasenko, "Pilgrimage to the Crimea," Welcome to Ukraine 2 (1998) <www.iprinet.kiev.ua/wumag/archiv/2_98/pilgrim.htm> (accessed 16 January 2003).

2. Vlasenko, "Pilgrimage to the Crimea."

3. See the diocesan pilgrimage department website: "Palomnichestvo," <www.crimea.orthodoxy.su/index.php?&dv=pilgrimage&ct=routes>.

4. *Krymskii Afon. Sbornik Dukhovno-nravstvennogo prosvesheniia sviato-uspenskogo muzhskogo monastyria* (Bakhchisarai); Kristin M. Romey, "Legacies of a Slavic Pompeii," *Archaeology* 55.6 (November/December 2002): 18–25.

5. The reemergence of religion was facilitated, in some measure, by Gorbachev's reforms. During the second half of the 1980s, the Soviet state relaxed restrictions on religious worship, permitted registration of hundreds of new Orthodox parishes, released religious prisoners, recognized the millenial celebration of Christianity (the baptism of St. Vladimir in 988), and legalized Greek Catholicism. In 1990, the state also passed a law on the Freedom of Religious Conscience, which essentially reversed sixty years of officially sanctioned hostility toward religion. For more, see John Anderson, *Religion, State, and Politics in the Soviet Union and Successor States* (Cambridge, 1994), 137–81; and for Ukraine in particular, see Catherine Wanner, "Missionaries of Faith and Culture: Evangelical Encounters in Ukraine," *Slavic Review* 63, no.4 (2004): 732–55; and *Communities of the Converted: Ukrainians and Global Evangelicalism* (Ithaca, NY, 2007).

6. Frank E. Sysyn, "Politics and Orthodoxy in Independent Ukraine," *Harriman Review* 15, nos. 2/3 (June 2005): 8–19.

7. Irina Borowik, "Orthodoxy Confronting the Collapse of Communism in Post-Soviet Countries," *Social Compass*, 53, no. 2 (2006): 272.

8. Gennadiy Druzhenko, "An Event of 2005 in State-Religion Relations: A Legal Analysis," 20 February 2006, <www.risu.org.ua/eng/religion.and.society/analysis/article;9185/> (accessed 12 November 2006).

9. For the emergence of Islamic movements in the post-Soviet states, see Brian Williams, "Jihad and Ethnicity in Post-Communist Eurasia. On the Trail of Transnational Islamic Holy Warriors in Kashmir, Afghanistan, Central Asia, Chechnya and Kosovo," *Journal of Ethnopolitics* 2, nos. 3–4, March/June (2003): 3–24.

10. Anderson, *Religion, State, and Politics,* 196–98. The Russian Orthodox Church in particular expresses concern over "foreign faiths," which are typically understood as any faith not recognized by Russian law before 1917, as well as Roman Catholicism.

11. Oxana Antic, "The Spread of Modern Cults in the USSR," in *Religious Policy in the Soviet Union*, ed. Sabrina Petra Ramet (Cambridge, 1993), 252–70.

12. Eliot Borenstein, "Articles of Faith: The Media Response to Maria Devi Khristos," *Religion* 25 (1995): 249–66.

13. Victor A. Shnirelman, "Russian Response: Archaeology, Russian Nationalism, and the 'Arctic Homeland,'" in *Selective Remembrances: The Construction, Consecration, and Commemoration of the Past*, ed. Philip Kohl, Mara Kozelsky, and Nachman Ben-Yahuda (Chicago, 2008): 31–70.

14. Antic, "The Spread of Modern Cults," 255.

15. More recently, Jews have also entered the picture, pressing for the restitution of synogogues closed down by the Soviets. For more, see: Department for Jewish Zionist Education, "The CIS Synagogues, Past and Present," <www.jafi.org.il/education/worldwide/synagogues/part2a.html> (accessed 5 November 2006); Vladimir Matveyev, "Trade, Property Restitution on Table as President of Ukraine Visits U.S.," <www.ujc.org/content_display.html?ArticleID=150127> (accessed 5 November 2006); "Decree and Reality: Ukrainian Catholics Say Presidential Order on Property Return," <www.risu.org.ua/eng/kaleidoscope/article;2735/> originally in The Day Kyiv, Ukraine, 15 April 2003 (accessed 5 November 2006).

16. Serhii Plokhy, "Between Moscow and Rome: The Struggle for a Ukrainian Catholic Patriarchate," in *Religion and Nation in Modern Ukraine,* ed. Serhii Plokhy and Frank Sysyn (Edmonton and Toronto, 2003), 146–55.

17. Borowik, "Orthodoxy Confronting the Collapse of Communism in Post-Soviet Countries," 276 n. 1.

18. Anderson notes that in early 1991, western Ukraine had nearly 1,680 registered Greek Catholic parishes compared with approximately 450 Orthodox (UOC-MP) parishes, all within a year after the Greek Catholic Church was legalized. See Anderson, *Religion, State. and Politics,* 189.

19. Irina Borowik, "Between Orthodoxy and Eclecticism: On the Religious Transformations of Russia, Belarus, and Ukraine," *Social Compass* 49, no. 4 (2002): 503.

20. Borowik, "Between Orthodoxy and Eclecticism," 505.

21. Paul D'Anieri, Robert Kravchuk, and Taras Kuzio, *Politics and Society in Ukraine* (Boulder, 1999), 71.

22. Serhii Plokhy, "Church, State, and Nation in Ukraine," in *Religion and Nation in Modern Ukraine,* ed. Serhii Plokhy and Frank Sysyn (Edmonton and Toronto, 2003), 177–78.

23. Many authorities in Ukraine consider the splintered churches to be a chief obstacle to national unity, and so they promote unity between the branches. This does not mean, however, that the state intends to support Orthodoxy as the state religion. D'Anieri, Kravchuk, Kuzio, *Politics and Society in Ukraine,* 82–88.

24. Borowik, "Orthodoxy Confronting the Collapse of Communism in Post-Soviet Countries," 271.

25. Much of the information on religious policy and conflict in post-Soviet Ukraine, including information on sects, comes from Serhii Plokhy. For a good summary of this sect, however, see Iva Barmina and Pavel Sorokin, "White Brotherhood Sect Surviving Second Coming of Maria Devi Christos," initially published in *Argumenty i fakty* (3 October 2001) and on the web, <www.risu.org.ua/eng/major.religions/white.brotherhood/>.

26. Serhii Plokhy, "Kyiv vs. Moscow: The Autocephaolous Movement in Independent Ukraine," in *Religion and Nation in Modern Ukraine,* ed. Serhii Plokhy and Frank Sysyn (Edmonton and Toronto, 2003), 141–43.

27. Plokhy, "Church, State and Nation in Ukraine," 173; see also Anatoly M. Kolodny, Lyudmyla O. Filipovych, and Howard L. Biddulph, *Religion and the Churches in Modern Ukraine. A Collection of Scientific Reports* (Kyiv, 2001).

28. Zoe Knox has analyzed recent church-state relations in Moscow to show that some of the practices of church and state run contrary to official pronouncements. She points to the 1997 law on freedom of conscience and religious association, a law that seems counter-intuitive in privileging the Russian Orthodox Church as the state church while all the while denying such intent. Knox also refers to the Cathedral of Christ the Savior in Moscow, whose rebuilding alarmed many with the speed and state resources made available to assist it, and which now stands symbolically as part of the Orthodox skyline over Russia's capital city, and finally, she points to the amount of

church finances and economic aid received from the state. Zoe Knox, "The Symphonic Ideal: The Moscow Patriarchate's Post-Soviet Leadership," *Europe-Asia Studies* 55, no. 4 (2003): 575.

29. "Old Conflict among Orthodox in Poltava Continues," 10 November 2006, <www.risu.org.ua/eng/news/article;12786/> (accessed 12 November 2006); "UOC-MP Orthodox Bishop of Chernihiv Asks Prosecutor to Help Transfer Church," 9 December 2006, <www.risu.org.ua/eng/news/article;11865/> (accessed 12 November 2006); "Chernivtsi Authorities Intercede in UOC-MP and UOC-KP Orthodox Conflict," 1 January 2006, <www.risu.org.ua/eng/news/article;8702/> (accessed 12 November 2006).

30. Gennadiy Druzhenko, "Ukraine President Stresses Idea of Single National Orthodox Church," <www.risu.org.ua/eng/religion.and.society/analysis/article;9185/> (accessed 12 November 2006); 28 July 2006 <www.risu.org.ua/eng/news/article;11201/> (accessed 11 November 2006); "Autocephalous Orthodox Archbishop, Sobor Representative Discuss Church's Development, Orthodox Unity," 31 May 2005 <www.risu.org.ua/eng/news/article;5570> (accessed 11 November 2006).

31. See for example, Oleg Markelov, "Pod pisan dogovor mezhdu eparkhiei i zapovednikom," *KV*, 18 March 2000, 7.

32. Jane I. Dawson, "Ethnicity, Ideology, and Geopolitics in Crimea," *Communist and Post-Communist Studies*, 30, no. 4 (1997): 427; see also Gwendolyn Sasse, *The Crimea Question: Identity, Transition, and Conflict* (Cambridge, 2007). Sasse's recent book does not address the role of religion in the Crimean transition.

33. Doris Wydra, "The Crimea Conundrum: The Tug of War between Russia and Ukraine on the Questions of Autonomy and Self-Determination," *International Journal on Minority and Group Rights* 10 (2004): 128.

34. Dawson argues that those who voted against Crimean affiliation with Ukraine did so not for any sense of ethnic unity with Russia, but because most Crimeans perceived an economic advantage in keeping a relationship with Russia. Meshkov's failure, in the end, was his playing of the ethnic, rather than the economic, card. Dawson, "Ethnicity, Ideology, and Geopolitics in Crimea," 427–44.

35. Andrei Malgin, *Krymkskii uzel. Ocherki politicheskoi istorii krymskogo poluostrova, 1989–1999* (Crimea, 2000), 10–16.

36. See the series of articles and reader commentary debating the future of the Black Sea fleet in Argumenty i fakty, including Vladimir Svartsevich, "Krym. Otdat Kontsy," 20 December 2006 <www.aif.ru/online/aif/1364/06_03> (accessed 15 January 2007).

37. Tony Halpin, "Georgia: Blockade Threat Risks Escalating Conflict," *The Times*, 14 August 2008 <www.timesonline.co.uk/tol/news/world/europe/article4526577.ece> (accessed 22 August 2008).

38. Viktoriya Karabanova, "Linguistic Tools for Nation-State Building," *Polish Sociological Review* 4 (2003): 417–33.

39. Clifford J. Levy, "Moscow's Mayor Exports Russia's New Nationalism," *New York Times*, 25 October 2008 <www.nytimes.com/2008/10/26/world/europe/26mayor.html?pagewanted=2&_r=1>.

40. Taras Kuzio, "Russian Passports as Moscow's Geopolitical Tool," *Eurasia Daily Monitor* 5, no. 176, 15 September 2008 <www.jamestown.org/single/?no_cache=1&tx_ttnews%5Btt_news%5D=33938>.

41. This paragraph derives from a lengthy description of the program in BBC Monitoring International Reports 2006, "Russian TV Hits Out at Ukraine over Crimea," 19 December 2006.

42. Quoted by BBC Monitoring International Reports 2006, "Russian TV Hits Out at Ukraine over Crimea," 19 December 2006.

43. Varvara Aglamish'ian, "Krym Rossiian ne otdast'" 17 May 2006, *Izvestiia* <www.izvestia.ru/economic/article3092860/>.

44. Maria Rogacheva, "Krym Mozhet Stat' Ukrainskim Kosovo," *Izvestiia*, 25 April 2006 <www.izvestia.ru/world/article3092352/> (accessed 17 December 2006).

45. "Arraid Association Criticizes TV Program on Islamic Extremism in Crimea," 28 April 2006, <www.risu.org.ua/eng/news/article;10022/> (accessed 17 December 2006).

46. The International Committee for Crimea has produced numerous articles about the continuing problems facing Crimean Tatar returnees. For a review of relevant statistics after the Orange Revolution, see Mubeyyin Batu Altan, "Crimean Tatars' Return to Their Ancestral Homeland: The Crimea in Statistics" <www.iccrimea.org/reports/populationstats.html>.

47. "Ukraine lifts ban on Russian TV, sort of . . . ," 25 December 2008 <www.russiatoday.com/features/news/35249>.

48. This is in comparison with 96.5% of Christian organizations for Ukraine as a whole. See Ayder Bulatov, "Interreligious relations in multireligious society: problems and tasks," 1 January 2005 <www.unpo.org/article.php?id=1743> (accessed 14 November 2006).

49. "Number of Religious Organizations as of 1 January 2004, Broken Down according to Regions of Ukraine" <www.risu.org.ua/eng/resources/statistics/reg2004/> (accessed 14 November 2006).

50. Nadezhda V. Proskurina, *Pravoslavnye sviatyni Kryma* (Sevastopol, 1997); see also her later publication, *Palomnichestvo po pravoslavnym sviatyniam Kryma* (Simferopol, 2006); Elena Morozova, *Zemli ulybka, radost' neba* (Yalta, 2006); Anastasia Dmitrieva and Tatiana Dmitrieva, *Iz istorii Khristianstva v Tavride* (Feodosiia, 2005); Iu. M. Mogarichev, A. V. Sazanov, A. K. Shaposhnikov, *Zhitie Ioanna Gotskogo v kontekste istorii Kryma "khazarskogo perioda"* (Simferopol, 2007).

51. See the numerous articles from *KV*, *Krymskaia pravda*, *Golos Kryma*, and other publications that form the basis of this chapter.

52. E. M. Litvinova, *Putevoditel'. Krym. Pravoslavnye sviatyni* (Simferopol, 2005), 304 and 354.

53. Litvinova, *Putevoditel'*, 292 and 146.

54. Aleksandr Mashchenko, "Moliatsia, moliatsia, mozhet, i otmoliat . . ." *KV*, 27 October 1998, 5.

55. "Palomnicheskii Tsentr Simferopol'skoi i Krymskoi eparkhii," *Tavrida pravoslavnaia*, no. 7 (July 1997); "Uroki pravoslavnaia. Po monastyriam i khramom," *KV*, 7 August 1997, 3.

56. Oleg Markelov, "Prik'snovenie k blagodati," *KV*, 18 July 1997, 5.

57. Nadezhda Proskurina, "Palomnichestvo 'Krym Pravoslavnyi,'" *Tavrida pravoslavnaia*, no. 9 (32) (September 1998), 21.

58. "Krymskii Afon 2009," *Tsentr Pravoslavnykh Program "Sofiia,"* <www.palomniksofia.ru/page44>. Sofiia's programs have been linked through the Moscow Patriarchate website. See *Palomnicheskii Tsentr Moskovskogo Patriarkhata* <www.poklonnik.ru/site.xp/053055124049049049048124.html>.

59. Patriarch Aleksii, "Vo vsiu zemliu izyde veshchaniia ikh,' posviashchennoi 2000 letu prishestviia v mir Gospoda i spasitelia nashego Iisusa Khrista," *Tavrida pravoslavnaia*, no. 7 (July 1997).

60. *Krymskii Afon. Sbornik Dukhovno-nravstvennogo prosveshcheniia sviato-uspenskogo muzhskogo monastyria* (Bakhchisarai).

61. Leonid Kravchuk, "Measures for Returning Properties to Religious Organizations," in *Russia and Eurasian Documents, vol. 2, CIS and Successor States, pt. 2, Ukraine*, ed. J. L. Black and David F. Duke (Gulf Breeze, 1993), 180.

62. Leonid Kravchuk, "Measures for Returning Properties to Religious Organizations," 180.

63. Department for Jewish Zionist Education, "The CIS Synagogues, Past and Present" <www.jafi.org.il/education/worldwide/synagogues/part2a.html> (accessed

5 November 2006); Matveyev, "Trade, Property Restitution on Table as President of Ukraine Visits U.S."; "Decree and Reality: Ukrainian Catholics Say Presidential Order on Property Return."

64. For a recent designation as the "Slavic Pompeii," see the article in *Archaeology* by Romey, "Legacies of a Slavic Pompeii," 18–25. References to the Slavic Pompeii extend back into the nineteenth century. Complaints about the futility of drawing comparisons between Pompeii and Chersonesos are quite old as well. See, for example, Bobrinskii, *Khersones-tavricheskii,* 178–79.

65. For an English-language presentation of the preserve's rich excavations, see the joint publication of archaeologists in Chersonesos and at the University of Texas Austin's Institute of Classical Archaeology in Austin Texas and the National Preserve of Tauric Chersonesos, J. C. Carter, and G. R. Mack, ed. *Crimean Chersonesos: City, Chora, Museum, and Environs* (Austin, 2004).

66. Much of this story has been published in Romey's article cited above; other details come from conversations with reserve officials and archaeologists in June of 2006.

67. See Romey, "Legacies of a Slavic Pompei," 23–25.

68. Personal communication, Tatiana Iashaeva, Chersonesos, 30 June 2006.

69. Untitled article posted on the website of the Religious Information Service of Ukraine <www.risu.org.ua/eng/news/article;1274/> (accessed 18 January 2007) and originally published by Evgenia Mussuri, *Kyiv Post,* 2 August 2001.

70. Oleg Markelov, "Pod pisan dogovor mezhdu eparkhiei i zapovednikom," *KV,* 18 March 2000, 7.

71. Liudmila Obukhovskaia, "Komu meshaet monastyr'," *Krymskaia Pravda,* 25 March 2006, 2.

72. Iasel'skaia, *Kosmodamianovskii monastyr'* 32.

73. Obukhovskaia, "Komu meshaet monastyr'," 2.

74. Gennadiy Druzenko, "Building a National Church, a Stumbling Block for the Ukrainian State," 19 February 2006, <www.risu.org.ua/eng/religion.and.society/analysis/article;9188/>.

75. O'Neill, "Constructing Imperial Identity in the Borderland," 163–91.

76. Although I followed this conflict closely in local media during the summer of 2006, my understanding of this conflict (and others) is deeply indebted to repeated conversations with Idil Izmirli, a conflict resolution specialist researching in Crimea. Whereas I watched the news and read local newspapers, Idil Izmirli actively visited sites of conflict and engaged key players in detailed discussions.

77. Adil' Seitbekirov, "Kushchustviia nad pogrebennymi, dobra ne nakhivesh'!" *Golos Kryma,* no. 29 (659), 14 July 2006.

78. RISU is full of stories chronicling the formation of Cossack groups in Crimea, whose racial attitudes it should be clarified, are not representative of all Cossacks. Cossacks are divided between those seeking alliance with Russia (the Don Cossacks) and the Ukrainian Cossacks who pledge loyalty to Ukraine. Carina Korostelina, "The Multiethnic State-building Dilemma: National and Ethnic Minorities' Identities in the Crimea," *National Identities* 5, no. 2 (2003): 141–59.

79. For a digest of news coverage of this event, see <www.iccrimea.org/news/newsdigest6.html>.

80. Abdullaev, "Torg s istoriei ne umesten!"

81. For more on this controversy, see: "Conflict around Dormition Monastery in Bakhchysarai Continues," *Religious Information Service of Ukraine,* 11 July 2002 <www.risu.org.ua/article.php?sid=374&1=en> 16 January 2002; "On Conflict over Lands of Svyato-Uspenskiy Monastery in Bakhchisaray," *Crimean Aspects* (Simferopol), 10 July 2002 <aspects.crimeastar.net/english/comm.php?id=2&nr=070203> (16 January 2002); Anna Vassilyeva, "Ukraine: Muslims Protest against 'Secret' Property Decision," *Keston News Service,* 19 July 2001 <www.keston.org.uk/kns/2001/010719UK.htm>; *"Zincirli*

Medrese Association (Bakhchisaray)," *International Committee for Crimea* (Washington, D.C.) <www.iccrimea.org/ngos/zincirli.html> (16 January 2002).

82. Oleg Markelov, "Do Afona rukoi podat'," *KV,* no. 47, 28 April 2005, 19.

83. "Monastery and Madrassah Dispute in Bakhchysarai," 13 September 2006, <www.risu.org.ua/eng/news/article;11892/> (accessed 25 September 2006); also "Moskal' prosit vlasti Kryma "razrulit" mezhreligioznyi konflict v Bakhchisarai," *Tribuna,* 9 November 2006 <www.risu.org.ua/eng/news/article;10358/> (accessed 19 January 2007).

84. Indris Asanin, "Stroitel'stvo na sviatyniakh (situatsiu sozdal direktor BGIKZ E. Petrov, on dolzhen ee reshat') *Dialog,* no. 23 (16–23 June 2006), 3.

85. Natal'ia Kiseleva, "Slabost' Vlasti i bezzakonie porozhdaiut tatarskii Terrorizm," *Vremia krymskoe,* 22 June 2006, 4.

86. An excellent article on the media hype that fallaciously connects Crimea with Chechnya can be found on the website of the Center of Information and Documentation of Crimean Tatars. See Iulia Tishchenko and Inna Pidluska, "Lobby Conflictology: Crimean Aspect," Research Update #185, 4 September 2000 <www.cidct.org.ua/en/studii/7/4.html> (accessed 17 January 2007); for additional articles see "Crimean Demonstration Against "Islamic Extremism," 28 September 2001, <www.risu.org.ua/eng/news/article;1305/> (accessed 29 January 2007); Arraid Association Criticizes TV Program on Islamic Extremism in Crimea, 28 April 2006, <www.risu.org.ua/eng/news/article;10022/> (accessed 17 January 2007); In the spring of 2006, Ukraine created a special commission to combat "radical extremism" in Crimea that primarily focuses on expelling aliens: "U Krimu bude stvoreno grupu protidii religiinomu ekstremizmu, *proUA,*" 3 April 2006 <ua.proua.com/news/2006/04/03/165239.html> (accessed 19 January 2007).

87. Abdullaev, "Torg s istorii ne umesten!" 1.

88. Aleksei Nezhivoi, "V odnom meste tushim—v drugom zagoraetsia," *KV,* 25 November 2000, 3; "Vozvanie Vysokopreosviashchenneishego Lazaria Mitropolita Simferopol'skogo i Krymskogo pravoslavnoi pastvi i narodim Kryma v sviazi suchastivshimsia sluchaiami oskverneniia khristianskoikh sviatyni," *Krymskie izvestiia,* 2 December 2000; "Uchenye svidetel'stuiut o traditsim ustanovki poklannykh krestov," *Tavrida pravoslavnaia,* no. 5 (11 November 2000).

89. Abdullaev, "Postup' Krestonostsev v Krymu," 4.

90. "Muslim Mufti Gives Conditions for Interreligious Cooperation," 27 January 2003, <www.risu.org.ua/eng/news/article;2054/> (accessed 13 November 2006). The mufti has said that the Crimean Tatars will rejoin the organization if Bishop Klyment of the UOC-KP is also permitted to join, and if the organization will agree that religious symbols do not belong in certain public spaces, a clear reference to the crosses of the summer of 2000. Finally, he has proposed a critical assessment of the Committee on Religious Issues of the Council of Ministers of the Autonomous Republic of Crimea.

91. This comment is a reference to the clash at the marketplace in Bakhchisarai.

92. Shevket Kaibulola, "Net protivostoianiia islama i khristianstva, est' protivostoiianie mezhdu religioznoi tolerantnosteiu i ekstremizmom," *Advet,* nos. 18–19, 11 November 2005, 3.

93. Sasse, *The Crimea Question,* 62.

94. Joan E. Taylor, *Christians and the Holy Places: The Myth of Jewish-Christian Origins* (Oxford, 1993), vii.

95. Bulatov, "Interreligious Relations in Multireligious Society: Problems and Tasks."

96. Mitropolit Simferopol'skii i Krymskii Lazar' i Mufti musul'man Kryma Khadzhi Emirali Ablaiev, "Sovmestnoe Zaiavlenie," 26 February 2004 <www.russk.ru/st.php?idar=408302> (accessed 26 August 2008).

Bibliography

Abbreviations

ITUAK	*Izvestiia Tavricheskoi uchenoi arkhivnoi komissii*
KhEV	*Khersonskie eparkhial'nye vedomosti*
KGV	*Khersonskie gubernskie vedomosti*
KV	*Krymskoe vremia*
MGSY	*Modern Greek Studies Yearbook*
OV	*Odesskii vestnik*
OZ	*Otechestvennyia zapiski*
RS	*Russkaia starina*
TEV	*Tavricheskie eparkhial'nye vedomosti*
ZOOID	*Zapiski Odesskogo obshchestva istorii i drevnostei*

Archival Sources

Gosudarstvennyi Arkhiv Avtonomnoi Respubliki Kryma (GAARK), Crimea:

Fond	26	Kantseliariia Tavricheskogo gubernatora
Fond	118	Tavricheskaia Dukhovnaia Konsistoriia
Fond	13	Simferopol'skoe dukhovnoe pravlenie
Fond	138	Blagochinnyi monastyrei Tavricheskoi Eparkhii
Fond	443	Kosmo-Damianovskii zhenskii monastyr' g. Alushta Tavricheskoi gubernii, 1883–1901
Fond	513	Bakhchisaraiskii skit, gor. Bakhchisarai Tavricheskoi gubernii za 1866–1876

Gosudarstvennyi Arkhiv Odesskogo Oblasti (GAOO), Odessa:

Fond	1	Kantseliariia Novorossii i Bessarabii
Fond	37	Khersonskaia Dukhovnaia Konsistoriia
Fond	167	Perepiska ob uchenoi deiatel'nosti arkhiepiskopa Innokentiia
Fond	207	Khersonskoe Dukhovnoe Upravlenie
Fond	279	Khersonskaia Dukhovnaia Konsistoriia

Rossiiskii Gosudarstvennyi Istoricheskii Arkhiv (RGIA), St. Petersburg:

Fond	796	Kantseliariia Sinoda
Fond	797	Kantseliariia ober-prokurora Sinoda
Fond	835	Plany i fotografii Sinoda
Fond	1661	K. S. Serbinovich

Rossiiskaia Natsional'naia Biblioteka (RNB), St. Petersburg:

Fond	313	Lichnyi arkhivnyi fond Arkhiepiskopa Innokentiia
Fond	531	A. S. Norov
Fond	637	K. G. Repinskii

Selected Works by Archbishop Innokentii

Sochineniia Innokentiia, arkhiepiskopa khersonskago i tavricheskago. 11 vols. St. Petersburg, 1872–1877.
Sochineniia Innokentiia, arkhiepiskopa khersonskago i tavricheskago. 12 vols. St. Petersburg, 1901.
Sochineniia Innokentiia, arkhiepiskopa khersonskago i tavricheskago. 11 vols. St. Petersburg, 1908–1911.
"Novootkrytyi Uspenskii Bakhchisaraiskii skit." *Odesskii vestnik,* nos. 15, 16, 17, and 18 (20, 23, 27 February and 1 March 1852).
O nachale Khristiansvta v Pol'she. Kyiv, 1846.
Piat' slov, skazannykh v Krymu po sluchaiu nashestviia na nego inoplemennikov Innokentiem, arkhiepiskopom khersonskim i tavricheskim. Odessa, 1854.
Poslednie dni zemnoi zhizni Iisusa Khrista. Moscow, 2000.
Rech' proiznesennaia vysokopreosviashchennym Innokentiem, arkhiepiskopom khersonskim i tavricheskim 9-go iiulia 1856-go goda pri osviashchenii goroda Sevastopolia, po ostavlenii ego nepriatelemi, posle molebstvia po semu sluchaiu na sobornoi ploshchad'/ Slovo, skazannoe vysokopreosviashchennym Innokentiem, arkhiepiskopom khersonskim i tavricheskim 8-go iiulia 1856 goda, v Georgievskom Balaklavskom monastyre, pri pervom poseshchenii, po ostavlenii ego nepriateliami. Odessa, 1856.
Slovo, proiznesennoe sinodal'nym chlenom, vysokopreosviashchenneishim Innokentiem, arkhiepiskopom khersonskim i tavricheskim, v voskresenie, 28-go oktiabria, 1856 goda, v Odesskom kafedral'nom sobore. Odessa, 1856.
Slovo, proiznesennoe vysokopreosviashchenneishim Innokentiem, arkhiepiskopom khersonskim i tavricheskim, v Odesskoi Uspenskoi edinovercheskoi tserkvi, po vozrashchenii iz Sevastopolia, iiulia 17-go 1855 goda. Odessa, 1855.
Slovo, skazannoe 26 iiunia 1855g. v Sevastopol'skom Nikolaevskom sobore vo vremia bombardirovaniia sego goroda nepriatelem. Odessa, 1855.
Slovo, skazannoe vysokopreosviashchennym Innokentiem, arkhiepiskopom khersonskim i tavricheskim, v Sevastopole, v lagernoi, chto na severnom ukreplenii, tserkvi, iiunia 25-go, 1855 goda. Odessa, 1855.
Sobranie slov i rechei po sluchaiu nashestviia nepriatel'skogo, proiznesennykh v raznykh mestakh khersonsko-tavricheskoi eparkhii preosviashchennym Innokentiem, arkhiepiskopom khersonskim i tavricheskim. 2 vols. Odessa, 1855–1856.
"Zapiski Innokentiia, arkhiepiskopa khersonskago i tavricheskago, o novouchrezhdennoi epharkhii Rimsko-Katolicheskoi v Khersone." *Russkii arkhiv za 1868* (1869): 416–35.
"Zapiski o vostanovlenii drevnikh sviatykh mest' po goram krymskim." In "Arkhivnye dokumenty, otnosiashchiesia k istorii khersonskago monastyria." *ITUAK* 5 (1888): 81–105.

Other Published Sources

Abdullaev, Ibraim. "Postup' Krestonostsev v Krymu." *Golos Kryma,* no. 48 (24 November 2000).
———. "Torg s istoriei ne umesten!" *Golos Kryma,* no. 28 (7 July 2006).
Abdullaeva, M. A.. "Svyachenyky Parafii grekiv krymu naprikintsi XVIII–na pochatku XXst." In *Podvyzhnyky i Metsenaty: Hretski Pidpryiemtsi Ta Hromadski Diiachi V Ukraini XVII – XIX.* Ed. Valerii Smolii. Kyiv, 2001, 71–75.
Achkinazi, I. V. "Krymchaki." In *Tiurskie narody Kryma. Karaimy, Krymskie Tatary, Krymchaki.* Edited by S. Ia. Kozlov and L. V. Chizhova, 358–93. Moscow: 2003.
———. *Krymchaki. Istoriko-etnograficheskii ocherk.* Simferopol, 2000.

Aglamish'ian, Varvara. "Krym Rossian ne otdast'." 17 May 2006. *Izvestia* <www.izvestia. ru/economic/article3092860>.
Ainalov, D. V. *Pamiatniki khristianskago Khersonesa. Vyp. 1. Razvaliny khramov*. Moscow, 1905.
Aleksii [Ridiger], Patriarch of Moscow and All Russia. "Vo vsiu zemliu izyde veshchaniia ikh, posviashchennoi 2000 letu prishestviia v mir Gospoda i spasitelia nashego Iisusa Khrista." *Tavrida pravoslavnaia*, no. 7 (July 1997).
Allworth, Edward A., ed. *The Tatars of Crimea: Return to the Homeland. Studies and Documents*. 2nd ed. Durham, NC. 1998.
―――. *Tatars of the Crimea: Their Struggle for Survival*. Durham, NC, 1988.
Altan, Mubeyyin Batu. "Crimean Tatars' Return to Their Ancestral Homeland: The Crimea in Statistics" <www.iccrimea.org/reports/populationstats.html>.
Amanton, Victor. *Notices sur les diverses populations du Gouvernement de la Tauride et spécialement de la Crimée. Moeurs et usages des Tatars de la Crimée*. Besançon, 1854.
Amichba, G. A. *Novyi Afon i ego Krestnosti (istoricheskii ocherk)*. Sukhumi, 1988.
"The Ancient Period." National Preserve of Tauric Chersonesos. <www.chersonesos. org/?p=history_ant&l=eng> (accessed 25 May 2005).
Anderson, Benedict. *Imagined Communities: Reflections on the Origin and Spread of Nationalism*. NY, 1991.
Anderson, John. *Religion, State, and Politics in the Soviet Union and Successor States*. Cambridge, U.K., 1994.
Anderson, M. S. *Peter the Great*. London, 1978.
Andrievskii, I. S. "Razvaliny Mangupa." *Odesskii al'manakh na 1840 g*. Odessa, 1839.
Anisomov, E. V. *The Reforms of Peter the Great*. New York, 1993.
Annotirovannyi ukazatel' rukopisnykh fondov GPB. St. Petersburg, 1982.
Antic, Oxana. "The Spread of Modern Cults in the USSR." In *Religious Policy in the Soviet Union*, edited by Sabrina Petra Ramet, 252–70. Cambridge, MA, 1993.
Anuchin, D. N., and A. S. Uvarov, ed. "Zametka ob ekskursii, sostoiavsheisia posle zakrytia VI [shestogo] Arkheologicheskogo s'ezda v Krym." *Trudy VI Arkheologicheskago s'ezda v Odesse* (1884), vol. 4. Odessa, 1889.
Aradzhioni, M. A. *Greki Kryma i priazov'ia istoriia izucheniia i istoriografiia etnicheskoi istorii i kul'tury (88-e gg. XVIII v.–90-e gg. XX v.)*. Simferopol, 1999.
―――. *Hreky Krymu. Istoriia i suchasne stanovyshche, etnokul'turna sytuatsiia ta problemy etnopolitychnoho rozvytku*. Simferopol, 2005.
―――. "Vozvrashchenie v Krym starozhitel'cheskogo khristianskogo naseleniia posle emigratsii 1778." *Materialy po arkheologii, istorii, i etnografii Tavrii*. 8 (2001): 485–501.
Arkas, Z. A. "Drevnosti Irakliiskago Poluostrov," *Zhurnal ministerstva vnutrennikh del* 19 (1847): 91–116.
―――. "Opisanie Irakliiskogo poluostrova i drevnostei ego." *ZOOID* 2 (1848): 245–71.
―――. "Osnovanie skitov okrestnostiakh goroda Sevastopolia vo imia Sv. Ravnoapostol'nogo kniazia Vladimira i Sv. Klimenta, papy Rimskogo, i osviashchenie ikh." *OV* (2 May 1853).
Arkhangels'skii, N. *Innokentii, Arkhiepiskop Khersonskii, kak uchitel' khristianskoi nravnosti (po povodu 40–letiia so dnia ego konchin—27 maia 1857 g.)*. Kazan, 1899.
Arkhiv Kniazia Vorontsova. *Bumagi fel'dmarshala Kniazia Mikhaila Semenovicha Vorontsova*. Moscow, 1891.
"Arraid Association Criticizes TV Program on Islamic Extremism in Crimea." Religious Information Service of Ukraine, 28 April 2006. <www.risu.org.ua/eng/news/article;10022> (accessed 17 December 2006).
Arsenii [sv.] "Vospominaniia o preosviashchennom Innokentii, arkhiepiskop khersonskii i tavricheskii." *KhEV* 5 (1862): 30–62.

"Articles convenus entre les Plenipotentiaires de S. M. L' Empereur et celui de S. S. le Pape à Rome le 22 iuillet/2 août 1847 // Usloviia, podpisannya Upolnomochennymi Ego Imperatorskago E. Sv. Papy v Rime 22 iiulia//3 avgusta 1847." In *Akty i Gramoty o ustroistve i upravlenii Rimsko-Katolicheskoi tserkvi v imperii rossiiskoi*. St. Petersburg, 1849.

Asanin, Indris. "Stroitel'stvo na sviatyniakh (situatsiu sozdal direktor BGIKZ, E. Petrov, on dolzhen ee reshat')." *Dialog*, no. 23 (16–23 June 2006).

Ashik, Anton. *Vosporskoe tsarstvo s ego paleograficheskimi i nadgrobnymi pamiatnikami, raspisnymi vazami, planami, kartami, i vidami*. Odessa, 1848.

Aslanbegov, A. "Po povodu zapisok sevastopol'tsa, napechatannykh v 12'u knizhke russkago arkhiva za 1867 g. 'Admiral Pavel Stepanovich Nakhimov (biograficheskii ocherk).'" *Materialy dlia istorii krymskoi voiny i Oborony Sevastopolia. Sbornik izdavaemyi komitetom po ustroistvy sevastopol'skago muzeia*, edited by N. Dubrovin, 5 vols. St. Petersburg, 1871.

Athanassopoulou, Effie F. "An 'Ancient' Landscape: European Ideals, Archaeology, and Nation Building in Early Modern Greece." *Journal of Modern Greek Studies* 20 (2002): 273–304.

Atlas, D. *Staraia Odessa, ee druz'ia i nedrugi*. Odessa, 1911.

"Autocephalous Orthodox Archbishop, Sobor Representative Discuss Church's Development, Orthodox Unity." Religious Information Service of Ukraine, 31 May 2005. <www.risu.org.ua/eng/news/article;5570/>.

Azarja, Illia. "Sobytia sluzhiviesia v Krymu v karstvovanie Sagin Gireia Chana (perevod iz sovremennoi Evreiski rukopisi)." *Vremennik imperatorskago Moskovskago obshchestva istorii i drevnostei rossiiskikh* 24 (1854): 115.

Bakunina, Ekaterina M. "Vospominaniia sestry miloserdiia Krestnovozdvizhenskoi obshchiny." *Vestnik Evropy* 190, no. 3 (March 1898): 55-105.

Barker, A. J. *Vainglorious War*. London, 1971.

Barnish, S. J. B. "Religio in stagno: Nature, Divinity, and the Christianization of the Countryside in Late Antique Italy." *Journal of Early Christian Studies* 9, no. 3 (2001): 387–402.

Barsov, N. I. *Materialy dlia biografii Innokentiia Borisova, arkhiepiskopa khersonskago i tavricheskago*. St. Petersburg, 1884.

———. *Pis'ma raznykh lits znamenitomu arkhiepiskopu Innokentiiu Borisovu. Materialy dlia istorii Rossii tekushchago stoletiia*. Moscow, 1885.

Barsukov, Nikolai, ed. *Istoriko-politicheskiia pis'ma i zapiski v prodolzhenii k krymskoi voiny, 1853–1856*. St. Petersburg, 1899.

———. *Zhizn' i trudy M. P. Pogodina*. Vol. 3. St. Petersburg, 1899.

Bartenev, Iurii Nikitich. "Zhizn' v Evpatorii." *Russkii arkhiv* 9 (1899): 116–29.

Bassin, Mark. *Imperial Visions: Nationalist Imagination and Geographical Expansion in the Russian Far East, 1840–1865*. Cambridge, 1999.

Batalden, Stephen K. *Catherine II's Greek Prelate: Eugenios Voulgaris in Russia, 1771–1806*. New York, 1982.

Baumgart, Winifred. *The Crimean War, 1853–1856*. London, 1999.

———. *The Peace of Paris, 1856: Studies in War, Diplomacy, and Peacemaking*. Translated by Ann Pottinger Saab. Oxford, 1981.

Bazhova, A. P. "Iz Iugoslavianskikh zemel'—v Rossiiu—." *Voprosy istorii* 2 (1977): 124–37.

Beim, Solomon. "Chufut-Kale i ego pervonachal'nye obitateli." In *Novorossiiskii kalendar'* na 1859 (Odessa, 1858): 431–44.

———. *Chufut-Kale i karaimy*. St. Petersburg, 1861.

———. *Pamiat' o Chufut-Kale*. Odessa, 1862.

Bekirova, Gul'nara. *Krym i krymskie tatary, XIX–XX veka*. Moscow, 2005.

Belov, G. D. *Khersones tavricheskii. Istoriko-arkheologicheskii ocherk*. Leningrad, 1948.

Belov, S. L. *Zhemchuzhina pravoslaviia Kryma. Novyi grad.* Simferopol, 1997.
Bernov, Mikhail Aleksandrovich. *Iz Odessy peshkom po Krymu. Pis'ma russkago peshekhoda.* St. Petersburg, 1896.
Bert'e-Delagard, A. L. *K istorii khristianstva v Krymu. Mnimoe tysiachletie. Vymysel i deistvitel'nost' v istorii Georgievskogo Balaklavskogo monastyria.* Odessa, 1910.
———. *Ostatki drevnikh sooruzhenii v okresnostiakh Sevastopolia i peshchernye goroda Kryma.* Odessa, 1886.
Bhabha, Homi. *The Location of Culture.* London, 1994.
Biluka, Iurii, and Olga Vlasenko. *Deportovani Krimski Tatari, Bolgari, Virmeni, Greki, Nimtsi.* Kyiv, 2004.
Black, J. L., and David F. Duke, eds. "Measures for Returning Properties to Religious Organizations." *Russia and Eurasian Documents.* Vol. 2, *CIS and Successor States.* Pt. 2, *Ukraine.* Gulf Breeze, FL, 1993.
Blagoveshchenskii, N. A. *Afon'. Putevyia vpechatleniia.* St. Petersburg, 1864.
Bobrinskii, Aleksei. *Khersones-Tavricheskii. Istoricheskii ocherk.* St. Petersburg, 1905.
Bobylev, V. S. *Vneshniaia politika Rossii epokhii Petra I.* Moscow, 1990.
Bociurkiw, Bohdan. *The Ukrainian Greek-Catholic Church and the Soviet State (1919–1950).* Edmonton, 1996.
Bode, Maria. "Vospominaniia o preosviashchennom Innokentie arkhiepiskopie khersonskom i tavricheskom." *Strannik* 2, no. 5 (1861): 1–8.
Bollig, Richard J. "The German Catholic Schools in Southern Russia." Catholic University of America Educational Research Monographs, vol. 6, no. 2: 1–29. Washington, D.C., February 1931.
Bolshakoff, Sergius. *Russian Mystics.* London, 1977.
Bonch-Bruevich, V. D. *Materialy k istorii i izuchenii russkogo sektantsva.* St. Petersburg, 1908–1916.
Borenstein, Eliot. "Articles of Faith: The Media Response to Maria Devi Khristos." *Religion* 25 (1995): 249–66.
Borisov, V. N. *Krymskii Afon.* Simferopol, 1995.
Borowik, Irina. "Between Orthodoxy and Eclecticism: On the Religious Transformations of Russia, Belarus, and Ukraine." *Social Compass* 49, no. 4 (2002): 497–508.
———. "Orthodoxy Confronting the Collapse of Communism in Post-Soviet Countries." *Social Compass* 53, no. 2 (2006): 267–78.
Bradley, Joseph. "Subjects into Citizens: Societies, Civil Society, and Autocracy in Tsarist Russia." *American Historical Review* 107, no. 4 (2002): 1094–1123.
Brett, C. E. B. *Towers of Crim Tartary: English and Scottish Architects and Craftsmen in the Crimea, 1762–1853.* Donnington, U.K. 2005.
Breyfogle, Nicholas. *Heretics and Colonizers: Forging Russian Ties in the South Caucasus.* Ithaca, NY, 2005.
Brooks, Jeffrey. *When Russia Learned to Read: Literacy and Popular Literature.* Princeton, 1985.
Brooks, Willis. "Russia's Conquest and Pacification of the Caucasus: Relocation Becomes a Pogrom in the Post-Crimean War Period." *Nationalities Papers* 23, no. 4 (1995): 675–86.
Brower, Daniel R., and Edward J. Lazzerini, eds. *Russia's Orient: Imperial Borderlands and Peoples, 1700–1917.* Bloomington, 1997.
Bruess, Gregory L. *Religion, Identity, and Empire: A Greek Archbishop in the Russia of Catherine the Great.* NY, 1997.
Brun [Braun], F. "(Nekrolog) Mikhail Grigor'evich Paleolog." *ZOOID* 5 (1863): 953–56.
Bulatov, Ayder. "Interreligious Relations in Multireligious Society: Problems and Tasks." <www.unpo.org/article.php?id=1743>.
Bulgakov, Makarii [Metropolitan]. "Biograficheskaia zapiska o preosviashchennom

Innokentie, arkhiepiskop khersonskom i tavricheskom." *Venok na mogilu Vysokopreosviashchennago Innokentiia, arkhiepiskopa tavricheskago*. Moscow, 1864.

———. *Istoriia Russkoi Tserkvi. Kniga pervaia [Book 1], Istoriia khristianstva v rossii do ravnoapostol'nogo kniazia Vladimira kak vvedenie v istoriiu russkoi tserkvi*. Moscow, 1994.

Butkevich, Timofei. *Innokentii Borisov, byvshii arkhiepiskop khersonskii*. St. Petersburg, I. L. Tuzova, 1887.

Carter, Joseph Coleman, and Glenn Randall Mack. *Crimean Chersonesos: City, Chora, Museum, and Environs*. Austin, 2003.

Chapman, John. "Pope St. Clement I." Catholic Encyclopedia. <www.newadvent.org/cathen/04012c.htm>.

Cherniavskii, Leontii. "Balaklavskii Georgievskii Monastyr." *OV*, no. 75 (20 September 1850).

Cherniavsky, Michael. "Holy Russia": A Study in the History of an Idea." *American Historical Review* 63, no. 3 (1958): 617–37.

———. *Tsar and People: Studies in Russian Myths*. New Haven, CN, 1961.

Chetverikov, Sergii [Father]. *Optina Pust'yn. Istoricheskii ocherk i lichnyia vospominania*. Paris, 1926.

———. *Starets Paisii Velichkovskii: His Life, Teachings, and Influence on Orthodox Monasticism*. Translated by Vasily Lickwar and Alexander I. Lisenko. Belmont, MA, 1980.

Chulos, Christopher. *Converting Worlds: Religion and Community in Peasant Russia, 1861–1917*. DeKalb, 2003.

———. "Orthodox Identity at Russian Holy Places." In *The Fall of an Empire, the Birth of a Nation: National Identities in Russia*, edited by Christopher Chulos and Timo Piirainen, 28–50. Helsinki, 2000.

Clay, J. Eugene. "Orthodox Missionaris and 'Orthodox Heretics' in Russia, 1886–1917." In *Of Religion and Empire: Missions, Conversion, and Tolerance in Tsarist Russia*, edited by Robert P. Geraci and Michael Khodarkovsky, 38–69. Ithaca, 2001.

Clowes, Edith W., Samuel D. Kassow, and James L. West, eds. *Between Tsar and People: Educated Society and the Quest for Public Identity in Late Imperial Russia*. Princeton, NJ, 1991.

Comaroff, Jean, and John Comaroff. *Of Revelation and Revolution: Christianity, Colonialism, and Consciousness in South Africa*. Chicago, IL, 1991.

"Conflict Around Dormition Monastery in Bakhchysarai Continues." Religious Information Service of Ukraine, 11 July 2002. <www.risu.org.ua/article.php?sid=374&1=en>.

Crews, Robert. "Empire and the Confessional State: Islam and Religious Politics in Nineteenth-Century Russia." *American Historical Review* 108, no. 1 (2003): 50–83.

———. *For Prophet and Tsar: Islam and Empire in Russia and Central Asia*. Cambridge, MA, 2006.

"Crimean Demonstration against Islamic Extremism." Religious Information Service of Ukraine, 28 September 2001. <www.risu.org.ua/eng/news/article;1305/>.

Cross, S. H., and O. P. Sherbovitz-Wetzor, eds. *The Russian Primary Chronicle, Laurentian Text*. Cambridge, MA, 1953.

Crummey, Robert O. *The Old Believers and the World of Antichrist: The Vyg Community and the Russian State, 1694–1855*. Milwaukee, WI, 1970.

Curtis, M. *A Forgotten Empress*. New York, 1974.

Curtiss, John Shelton. *The Russian Church and the Soviet State, 1917–1950*. Boston, 1953.

———. "Russian Sisters of Mercy in the Crimea, 1854–1855." *Slavic Review* 25, no. 1 (March 1966): 84–100.

———. *Russia's Crimean War*. Durham, NC, 1979.

Danevskii, I. "Ocherk istorii Inkermana." In *Novorossiiskii kalendar' na 1855* (Odessa, 1854): 398–413.

D'Anieri, Paul, Robert Kravchuk, and Taras Kuzio. *Politics and Society in Ukraine*. Boulder, CO, 1999.
Davison, Roderic H. *Essays in Ottoman and Turkish History, 1774–1923: The Impact of the West*. Austin, 1990.
Davydov, Vladimir. *Puteviia zapiski. Vedenniia vo vremia prebyvaniia na Ionicheskikh ostrovakh, v Gretsi, Maloi Azii, i Turtsii v 1835 godu*. 2 vols. St. Petersburg, 1839.
Dawson, Jane I. "Ethnicity, Ideology, and Geopolitics in Crimea." *Communist and Post-Communist Studies* 30, no. 4 (1997): 421–44.
"Decree and Reality: Ukrainian Catholics Say Presidential Order on Property Return [sic]." Religious Information Service of Ukraine, 26 July 2004, <www.risu.org.ua/eng/kaleidoscope/article;2735> originally *The Day*, Kyiv, Ukraine, 15 April 2003.
Demidov, Anatoly [Anatolii]. *Travels in the Crimea; through Hungary, Wallachia, and Moldavia, during the Year 1837*. London, 1853.
"Den' pervyi. Stradanie sviatyikh muchenikov Kosmy i Damiana." In *Zhitiia Sviatykh na russkom iazyke izlozheniia po rukovodstvu Chetikh-minei sv. Dimitriia Rostovskago, s dopolneniiami, ob'iasnitel'nymi primechaniiami, i izobrazheniiami sviatykh* 11 (1 July) (Moscow, 1968–1969): 5–10
Department for Jewish Zionist Education. "The CIS Synagogues, Past and Present." <www.jafi.org.il/education/worldwide/synagogues/part2a.html>.
Derman, A. B. *Delo ob Igumene Parfenie, roman-khronika v trekh chastiakh*. Moscow, 1941.
Dickinson, Sarah. "Russia's First 'Orient': Characterizing the Crimea in 1787." *Kritika: Explorations in Russian and Eurasian History* 3, no. 1 (2002): 3–25.
Dingel'shtedt, N. *Zakavkazskie sektanty v ikh semeinom religioznom bytu*. St. Petersburg, 1885.
Dmitrieva, Anastasiia, and Tat'iana Dmitrieva. *Iz istorii Khristianstva v Tavride*. Feodosiia, 2005.
Dmitrievskii, A. A. *Russkie na Afone. Ocherk zhizni i deiatel'nosti igumena russkago Panteleimonovskago monastyria sviashchenno-arkhimandrita Makariia (Sushkina)*. St. Petersburg, 1895.
Dobroklonskii, A. *Rukovodstvo po istorii russkoi tserkvi. Sinodal'nyi period, 1700–1890*. Moscow, 1893.
Dombrovskii, Fr. "Buria 2-go noiabria 1854 goda, v Krymu." *OV*, no. 127 (1854. Reprinted in *Moskovskie vedomosti* 145 1854).
———. "Feleton. Otkrytie skitskago pustynnozhitel'stva v uspenskoi skala bliz g. Bakhchisaraia." *OV*, no. 74 (13 September 1850).
Donenko, Nikolai, and Liudmila Iasel'skaia. *Kiziltashskii Sviato-Stefano Surozhskii monastyr'*. Simferopol, 2006.
Druzhenko, Gennadiy. "An Event of 2005 in State-Religion Relations: A Legal Analysis." Religious Information Service of Ukraine, 20 February 2006. <www.risu.org.ua/eng/religion.and.society/analysis/article;9185/>.
———. "Building a National Church: A Stumbling Block for the Ukrainian State." Religious Information Service of Ukraine, 19 February 2006, <www.risu.org.ua/eng/religion.and.society/analysis/article;9188>.
Druzhinin, V. G. *Raskol na Donu v kontse XVII veka*. St. Petersburg, 1889.
Druzhinina, E. I. *Severnoe Prichernomor'e v 1775–1800*. Moscow, 1959.
———. *Iuzhnaia Ukraina v 1800–1825*. Moscow, 1970.
———. *Iuzhnaia Ukrainia v period Krizisa Feodalizma, 1825–1860*. Moscow, 1981.
Dubois de Montpereux, Frédéric. *Voyage autour du Caucase, chez les Tscherkesses et les Abkhases, en Colchida, en Georgie, en Arménie, et en Crimée*. Paris, 1843.
Dubrovin, Nikolai F., ed. *Materialy dlia istorii krymskoi voiny i oborony sevastopolia*. 5 vols. St. Petersburg, 1871–1874.
———. *Prisoedinenie Kryma k Rossii*. St. Petersburg, 1885–1889.

Duncan, Peter J. S. *Russian Messianism: Third Rome, Revolution, Communism, and After.* London, 2000.
Duran, James A., Jr. "Catherine II, Potemkin, and Colonization Policy in Southern Russia." *Russian Review* 28, no. 1 (1969): 23–36.
Engelstein, Laura. *Castration and the Heavenly Kingdom: A Russian Folktale.* Ithaca, NY, 1999.
Ershov, S. A. "K probleme predmeta i metodologii tserkovnoi arkheologii." In *Tserkovnaia arkheologiia. Materialy Pervoi Vserossiiskoi konferentsii. Pskov, 20–24 noiabria 1995. Chast' 1, Rasprostranenie khristianstva v vostochnoi evrope,* 17–21. St. Petersburg-Pskov, 1995.
Evgenii [presumed to be Bolkhovitinov], Metropolitan of Kyiv. "O sledakh drevnego grecheskogo goroda Khersona." *Obshchestvo istorii i drevnosti rossiiskikh.* 4, no. 1 (1820): 102–115.
Fedorov, F. A. *Krym s Sevastopolom, Balaklavaiu, i drugimi ego gorodami s opisaniem rek, ozer, gor, i dolin; s ego istroieiu, zhiteliami, ikh pravami, obychaiami, i obrazom zhizni; s trema vidami i planom.* 2nd ed. St. Petersburg, 1854.
Fennell, Nicholas. *The Russians on Athos.* Bern, 2001.
Feofilov, M. "Istoricheskii ocherk khristianstva v Krymu. Inkermanskaia kinov'ia, Georgievskii monastyr' i Bakhchisaraiskii skit." *TEV* 8 (1899).
Filaret [Drozdov], *Metropolitan of Moscow. Sobraniia mnenii i otzyvov Filareta mitropolita moskovskago i kolomenskago. Delam pravoslavnoi tserkvi na vostok.* St. Petersburg, 1886.
Filimonov, S. B. "Voprosy istorii khristianstva v dokladakh krymskikh kraevedov kontsa XIX-pervoi tretii XX vv." *Pravoslavnye drevnosti Tavrike. Sbornik materialov po tserkovnoi arkheologii.* Kyiv, 2002.
Filippenko, V. F. "K istorii Inkermanskogo peshchernogo monastyria (pervyi etap sushchestvovaniia)." *Istoriia i arkheologiia Iugo-Zapadnogo Kryma,* ed. Iu. M. Mogarichev. Simferopol, 1993.
Fisher, Alan. *Crimean Tatars.* Stanford, 1978.
———. "Emigration of Muslims from the Russian Empire in the Years after the Crimean War." *Jahrbücher für Geschichte Osteuropas* 35, no. 3 (1987). 356–71.
———. *The Russian Annexation of Crimea, 1772–1783.* Cambridge, MA, 1970.
———. "Sahin Giray, the Reformer Khan, and the Russian Annexation of Crimea." In *Between Russians, Ottomans, and Turks: Crimea and Crimean Tatars,* edited by Alan Fisher, 106–11. Istanbul, 1998.
Florovsky, Georges. *Ways of Russian Theology.* Edited by Richard S. Haugh. Translated by Robert L. Nichols. Belmont, MA, 1979–1987.
Franklin, Simon, and Jonathon Shepard. *The Emergence of Rus, 750–1200.* NY, 1996.
Frary, Lucien J. "Russia and Independent Greece: Politics, Religion, and Print Culture (1833–1844)." Ph.D. diss., University of Minnesota, December 2003.
Frazee, Charles A. *The Orthodox Church and Independent Greece, 1821–1852.* Cambridge, U.K., 1969.
Freeze, Gregory. "Handmaiden of the State? The Church in Imperial Russia Reconsidered." *Journal of Ecclesiastical Studies* 36 (1985): 82–102.
———. "Institutionalizing Piety: The Church and Popular Religion, 1750–1850." In *Imperial Russia: New Histories for the Empire,* edited by Jane Burbank and David L. Ransel 210-49. Bloomington, 1998.
———. "The Rechristianization of Russia: The Church and Popular Religion, 1750–1850." *Studia Slavica Finlandensia* 7 (1990): 101–36.
———. "Subversive Piety: Religion and the Political Crisis in Late Imperial Russia." *Journal of Modern History* 68 (June 1996): 308–50.
Gabrielian, O. A., S. A. Efimov, V. G. Garubin, et al., *Krymskie repatriany. Deportatsia, vozvrashchenie, i obustroistvo.* Simferopol, 1998.

Gankevich, V. Iu., ed. *Abureshid Mediev. Krymskie pis'ma*. Simferopol, 2005.
———. *Krymskotatarskie medrese. Kurs lektsii*. Simferopol, 2001.
Garkavets, A. N. *Kypchaskie iazyki. Kumanskii i armiano-kypchaksii*. Alma-Ata, 1987.
Garrett, Paul D. *St. Innocent, Apostle to America*. Crestwood, NY, 1979.
Gatrell, Peter. *A Whole Empire Walking: Refugees in Russia during World War One*. Bloomington, 1999.
Gavriil [Rozanov], Archbishop of Kherson-Tauride, "Ostatki Khristianskikh drevnostei v Krymu." *ZOOID* 1 (1844): 320–28.
———. "Pereselenie grekov iz kryma v Azovskiiu guberniiu i osnovanie Gotfiiskoi i Kafiiskoi Eparkhii." *ZOOID* 1 (1844): 196–204.
Gellner, Ernest. *Nations and Nationalism*. Ithaca, NY, 1983.
Geraci, Robert P., and Michael Khodarkovsky. *Of Religion and Empire: Missions, Conversion, and Tolerance in Tsarist Russia*. Ithaca, NY, 2002.
———. *Window on the East: National and Imperial Identities in Late Tsarist Russia*. Ithaca, NY, 2001.
Germogen, Bishop of Pskov. *Tavricheskaia eparkhiia*. Pskov, 1887.
Gertsen, A. G., and Iu. M. Mogarichev. "Salachik—Uspenskii Monastyr'—Chufut-Kale." *Bakhchisaraiskii istoriko-kul'turnyi zapovednik*. Simferopol, 1995.
——— and O. A. Makhneva-Chernets. *Peshchernye goroda Kryma. Putevoditel'*. Simferopol, 1989.
Gillespie, V. Bailey. *The Dynamics of Religious Conversion*. Birmingham, AL, 1991.
Gillet, Lev [Father]. *The Jesus Prayer*. Jordanville, NY, 1987.
Glushak, A. S., I. A. Antonova, V. F. Filipenko, N. V. Naumova, and S. M. Cherviakov. *Krym khristianskii*. Simferopol, 1996.
"God na iuzhnom beregu kryma (1852–1853)." *Dukhovnaia beseda*. 3, no. 5 (1856): 47–72.
Goldfrank, David M. "The Holy Sepulcher and the Origin of the Crimean War." In *The Military and Society in Russia: 1450–1917*, edited by Eric Lohr and Marshall Poe, 491–506. Leiden, 2002.
———. *The Origins of the Crimean War*. NY, 1994.
———. "Policy Traditions and the Menshikov Mission of 1853." In *Imperial Russian Foreign Policy*, edited by Hugh Ragsdale, 119–58. Cambridge, UK, 1993.
Golubinskii, E. ed. *Istoriia russkoi tserkvi*. 2 vols. Moscow, 1901.
Gorodetzsky, Nadezhda. *Saint Tikhon of Zadonsk: Inspirer of Dostoevsky*. NY, 1976.
Gothoni, R. *Paradise within Reach*. Helsinki, 1993.
Greenfeld, Liah. *Nationalism: Five Roads to Modernity*. Cambridge, MA, 1992.
Grigorovich, V. I. *Ocherk uchennogo puteshestviia po evropeiskoi Turtsii*. Kazan, 1848.
Griva, O. A. "Tserkovnaia arkheologiia. Uchenaia distsiplina i uchebnyi predmet." In *Pravoslavnye drevnosti tavriki. Sbornik materialov po tserkovnoi arkheologii*, edited by V. Iu. Iurochkin, 10–14. Kyiv, 2002.
Guthrie, Martha. *A tour, performed in the years 1795–6, through the Taurida, or Crimea, the antient kingdom of Bosphorus, the once-powerful republic of Tauric Kherson, and all the other countries on the north shore of the Euxine ceded to Russia by the Peace of Kainardgi and Jassy*, edited by Matthew Guthrie. London, 1802.
Halpin, Tony. "Georgia: Blockade Threat Risks Escalating Conflict." *The Times*. 14 August 2008. <www.timesonline.co.uk/tol/news/world/europe/article4526577.ece>.
Hamant, Yves, ed. *The Christianization of Ancient Russia*. Paris, 1992.
Harviainen, Tapani. "The Karaites in Eastern Europe and the Crimea." In *Karaite Judaism: A Guide to its History and Literary Sources*, edited by Meira Polliack 633-656. Leiden, 2003.
Hastings, Adrian. *The Construction of Nationhood: Ethnicity, Religion, and Nationalism*. Cambridge, U.K., 1997.

Hefner, Robert W., ed. *Conversion to Christianity: Historical and Anthropological Perspectives on a Great Transformation.* Berkeley, 1993.
Herlihy, Patricia. *Odessa: A History, 1794–1914.* Cambridge, MA, 1986.
Herzen, Alexander. "Gonenie na Krymskikh Tatar." *Kolokol* (December 22, 1861): 973–80.
Hirsch, Francine. *Empire of Nations: Ethnographic Knowledge and the Making of the Soviet Union.* Ithaca, NY, 2005.
Hokanson, Katya. "Pushkin's Captive Crimea: Imperialism in the Fountain of Bakhchisarai." *Russian Subjects: Empire, Nation, and the Culture of the Golden Age,* edited by Monika Greenleaf and Stephen Moeller-Sally, 123–50. Evanston, IL, 1998.
Holderness, Mary. *Notes relating to the manners and customs of the Crim Tatars, written during a four years' residence among that people.* London, 1821.
Hollingsworth, P. *The Hagiography of Kyivan Rus.* Cambridge, MA, 1992.
Holmes, Larry. "Fear No Evil: Schools and Religion in Soviet Russia, 1917–1941." In *Religious Policy in the Soviet Union,* edited by Sabrina Ramet, 125–57. Cambridge, MA, 1993.
Iakov. "Pamiat' i pokhvala kniaziu russkomu Vladimiru." *Khristianskoe chtenie* 2 (1849): 317–29.
Iasel'skaia, Liudmila. "Kosmodamianovskii Monastyr'." Ofitsial'nyi Sait, Simferopol'skaia i Krymskaia Eparkhiia, <orthodox.sf.ukrtel.net/MONASTYR/kosdam.htm>.
———. *Kosmodamianovskii monastyr'.* Simferopol, 1999.
———. *Toplovskii sviato-paraskevievskii zhenskii monastyr'.* Simferopol, n.d..
Iashaeva, T. Iu. *Peshchernyi kompleks v okruge Khersona. Problemy istorii i arkheologii Kryma.* Simferopol, 1994.
Ignat'ev, A. V., ed. *Rossiia i chernomorskie prolivy (XVIII–XX stoletiia).* Moscow, 1999.
Ishin, A. V. "Deiatel'nost' arkhiepiskopa tavricheskogo Guriia (G. P. Karpova)." *Novosti/Zhurnaly.* "Istoricheskoe nasledie Kryma." no. 9 (2005). <www.commonuments.crimea-portal.gov.ua/rus/index.php?v=1&tek=89&par=74&l=&art=350>.
"Istoricheskaia zapiska o sooruzhenii v Khersonis khrama Sv. Ravnoapostl'nago kniazia Vladimira." *ITUAK* 5 (1888): 5–18.
Istoricheskaia zapiska o zhenskom Odesskom s devich'imi monasteryi. Odessa, 1844.
Iurochkin, V. Iu. Ed. "Kratkii Krymskii Paterik." In *Pravoslavnye drevnosti tavriki. Sbornik materialov po tserkovnoi arkheologii.* Kyiv, 2002. 175–78.
Ivanov, Aleksandr. *Vospominaniia o ysokopreosviashchennom Innokentii, arkhiepiskopie khersonskom i tavricheskom.* Pamphlet pubished from no. 23 TEV (1900), Odessa, 1900.
Ivask, George, ed. *Against the Current: Selections from the Novels, Essays, Notes, and Letters of Konstantin Leontiev.* Translated by George Reavey. NY, 1969.
"Izvestie o konchine I. U. Palimpsestova." *TEV* 7 (1 April 1901): 416–17.
Jerris, Randon. "Cult Lines and Hellish Mountains: The Development of Sacred Landscape in the Early Medieval Alps." *Journal of Medieval and Early Modern Studies* 32, no. 1 (Winter 2002): 85–108.
Jobst, Kerstin S. "The Crimea as a Russian Mythical Landscape (18th–20th Century)." In *Mythical Landscapes Then and Now. The Mythification of Landscapes in Search for National Identity,* edited by Judith Peltz and Ruth Büttner, 78–91. Yerevan, 2006.
K materialam dlia istorii osvozhdeniia Bolgarie. Odessa, 1895.
Kabuzan, V. M. *Zaselenie Novorossii (Ekaterinoslavskoi i Khersonskoi Gubernii) v XVIII–pervoi polovine XIX veka (1719–1858).* Moscow, 1976.
Kagan, Frederick W. *The Military Reforms of Nicholas I: The Origins of the Modern Russian Army.* Basingstoke, U.K., 1999.
Kaibulola, Shevket. "Net protivostoianiia islama i khristianstva, est' protivostoianie mezhdu religioznoi tolerantnosti i ekstremizmom." *Advet* (11 November 2005): 18–19.
Kallistos (Ware), Bishop of Diokleia. *The Inner Kingdom.* NY, 2000.

Kane, Eileen M. "Pilgrims, Holy Places, and the Multi-Confessional Empire: Russian Policy toward the Ottoman Empire under Tsar Nicholas, 1825–1855." Ph.D. diss., Princeton University, 2005.

Karabanova, Viktoriya. "Linguistic Tools for Nation-State Building." *Polish Sociological Review*, vol. 4. (2003): 418–33.

Karamzin, Nikolai Mikhailovich. *Istoriia gosudarstva rossiiskogo*. Moscow, 1989.

Karpat, Kemal H. *Ottoman Population, 1830–1914: Demographic and Social Characteristics*. Madison, 1985.

Kasperovka Chudotvornaia Ikona Bozhei Materi. Odessa, 1891.

Katunin, Iu. A. *Iz istorii khristianstva v Krymu. Tavricheskaia eparkhiia, vtoraia polovina XIX–nachalo XX veka*. Simferopol, 1995.

———. *Monastyri Kryma v XIX–XX vekakh, po materialam krymskikh arkhivov*. Simferopol, 2000.

———. *Simferopolskaia Krymskaia eparkhiia v 1950–1964 godakh*. Simferopol, 2004.

Kazanskii, P. "Mysli i chustvovaniia mitropolita Filareta po delu otobraniia litografirovannago perevoda knig vetkhago zaveta." *Pravoslavnoe obozrenie* (January 1878): 106–18.

Kefeli, Agnes. "Constructing an Islamic Identity: The Case of Elyshevo Village in the Nineteenth Century." In *Russia's Orient: Imperial Borderlands and Peoples, 1700–1917*, edited by Daniel R. Brower and Edward J. Lazzerini, 271–91. Bloomington, 1997.

Keppen, P. I. *O drevnostiakh iuzhnogo berega i gor Tavricheskikh*. St. Petersburg, 1837.

———. "O krymskikh peshcherakh." *Russkii zritel'* 5–6 (1828): 132–36.

———. "Opisanie Turkskoi peshchery v Krymu." *Trudy vysochaishie utverzhdennogo Vol'nogo obshchestva liubitelei rossiiskoi slovesnosti* 14 (1821): 220–49.

———. *Spisok izvestneishikh Kurganov v Rossii*. St. Petersburg, 1837.

Khalid, Adeeb. "A review of *Islamization and Native Religion in the Golden Horde* (by Devin DeWeese), *Islamic Historiography and "Bulghar" Identity among the Tatars and Bashkirs of Russia* (by Allen J. Frank), and *L'Islam de Russie* (by Stéphane A. Dudoignon, Dämir Is'haqov, and Räfiq Möhämmätshin)." In *Kritika: Explorations in Russian and Eurasian History* 3, no. 4 (2002): 728–38.

Khanatskii, K. V. *Pamiatnaia kniga Tavricheskoi gubernii*. Simferopol, 1867.

Khomiakov, A. S. *Stikhotvoreniia i dramy*. Leningrad, 1969.

King, A. D. *Colonial Urban Development: Culture, Social Power, and Environment*. London, 1976.

Kinglake, Alexander. *The Invasion of Crimea. Its origin and an account of its progress down to the death of Lord Raglan*. 8 vols. Edinburgh, 1863.

Kipp, Jacob W. "The Grand Duke Konstantin Nikolaevich and the Epoch of the Great Reforms, 1855–1866." Ph.D. diss., Pennsylvania State University, 1970.

Kirimli, Hakan. "Crimean Tatars, Nogays, and Scottish Missionaries: The Story of Katti Giray and Other Baptized Descendents of the Crimean Khans." *Cahiers du Monde russe* 45 (2004): 61–108.

Kiseleva, A. S. "Russkoe naselenie Kryma v kontse XIX v." In *Etnografiia Kryma XIX–XX vv. i sovremennye etnokul'turnye protsessy. Materialy i issledovaniia*, edited by Krymskii respublikanskii kraevedcheskii muzei, Krymskii etnograficheskii muzei, Krymskoe otdelenie instituta vostokovedeniia im. A. E., 60–65. Simferopol, 2002.

Kiseleva, Natal'ia. "Slabost' vlasti i bezzakonie porozhdaut tatarskii Terrorizm." *KV* (22 June 2006).

Kivelson, Valerie A., and Robert H. Greene, eds. *Orthodox Russia: Belief and Practice under the Tsars*. University Park, 2003.

Kizenko, Nadieszda, "The Church-War Memorial at the Shipka Pass, 1880–1903," *MGSY* 16/17 (2000–2001): 243–53.

Klein, Victoria. "Imperial Loyalties and Crimean Identities: The Emergence of Regional Scholarly Societies in Crimea, 1880–1930." Ph.D. diss., Princeton University, not yet completed.

Klippenstein, Lawrence. "Mennonite Pacifism and State Service in Russia: A Case Study in Church-State Relations, 1789–1936." Ph.D. diss., University of Minnesota, 1984.

Kloberdanz, Timothy J. *Thunder on the Steppe. Volga German Folk Life in a Changing Russia.* Lincoln, NE, 1993.

Knight, Nathaniel. "Constructing the Science of Nationality: Ethnography in Mid-nineteenth-century Russia." Ph.D. diss., Columbia University, 1994.

———. "Science, Empire, and Nationality: Ethnography in the Russian Geographical Society, 1845–1855." In *Imperial Russia: New Histories for the Empire*, edited by Jane Burbank and David Ransel, 108–41. Bloomington, 1998.

Knox, Zoe. "The Symphonic Ideal: The Moscow Patriarchate's Post-Soviet Leadership." *Europe-Asia Studies* 55, no. 4 (2003): 575–96.

Kohl, Johann Georg. *St. Petersburg, Moscow, Kharkoff, Riga, Odessa, the German Provinces on the Baltic, the steppes, the Crimea, and the Interior of the Empire.* London, 1842.

Kohl, Philip. "Nationalism and Archaeology: On the Constructions of Nations and the Reconstructions of the Remote Past." *Annual Review of Anthropology* 27 (1998): 223–46.

Kohn, Hans. *Pan-Slavism, Its History and Ideology.* Notre Dame, 1953.

Kohut, Zenon E. *Russian Centralism and Ukrainian Autonomy: Imperial Absorption of the Hetmanate, 1760s–1830s.* Cambridge, MA, 1988.

Kolodny, Anatoly M., Lyudmyla O. Filipovych, and Howard L. Biddulph. *Religion and the Churches in Modern Ukraine. A Collection of Scientific Reports.* Kyiv, 2001.

Korostelina, Carina. "The Multiethnic State-building Dilemma: National and Ethnic Minorities' Identities in the Crimea." *National Identities* 5, no. 2 (2003): 141–59.

"Kosmodamianovskaia kinoviia, v Krymu, i vospominaniia o pervom nastoiateli onoi, igumen Makarii." *TEV* 3 (1882): 133.

Kovalenko, Ivan Mikhailovich. *Dostoprimechatel'nye derev'iia Kryma.* Simferopol, 2004.

———. *Pravoslavia i priroda Kryma.* Simferopol, 2006.

———. *Sviashchennaia priroda Kryma. Ocherki kul'turnogo-prirodookhrannykh traditsii narodov Kryma.* Kyiv, 2001.

Kozelsky, Mara. "Casualties of Conflict: Crimean Tatars during the Crimean War," *Slavic Review* 67, no. 4 (2008): 862–91.

———. "The Challenges of Church Archaeology in Post-Soviet Crimea." In *Selective Remembrances: Archaeology in the Construction, Commemoration, and Consecration of National Pasts,* edited by Phillip L. Kohl, Mara Kozelsky, and Nachman Ben-Yehuda, 71–98. Chicago, 2008.

———. "Ruins into Relics: The Monument to St. Vladimir on the Excavations of Chersonesos, 1827–1857." *Russian Review* 63, no. 4 (2004): 655–72.

Kozlov, S. Ia., and L. V. Chizhova, eds. *Tiurkskie narody Krima. Karaimy, krymskie tatary, krymchaki.* Moscow: Nauka, 2003.

Krupskaia, Aleksandra. *Vospominaniia sestry Krestnovozdvizhenskoi obshchiny.* St. Petersburg, 1861.

Krymskii Afon. Sbornik Dukhovno-nravstvennogo prosveshcheniia sviato-uspenskogo muzhskogo monastyria. Bakhchisarai.

Kutepov, Konstantin. *Sekty khlystov i skoptsov.* Kazan, 1882.

Kutorga, Stepan Semenovich. "Otryvkii iz puteshestvie v Krym, 1833 godu." *Zhurnal ministerstva narodnago prosvieshcheniia* 1 (1834): 81–90.

Kuzio, Taras. "Russian Passports as Moscow's Geopolitical Tool." *Eurasia Daily Monitor*

5, no. 176 (15 September 2008). <www.jamestown.org/single/?no_cache=1&tx_ ttnews%5Btt_news%5D=3938>.

Layton, Susan. *Russian Literature and Empire: Conquest of the Caucasus from Pushkin to Tolstoy*. Cambridge, U.K. 1994.

Lazar' [Shvets], Metropolitan of Simferopol and Crimea and Mufti Emirali Ablaiev. "Sovmestnoe Zaiavlenie." <www.russk.ru/st.php?idar=408302>. 26 February 2004.

Lazzerini, Edward J. "Local Accommodation and Resistance to Colonialism in Nineteenth-Century Crimea." In *Russia's Orient: Imperial Borderlands and Peoples, 1700–1917*, edited by Daniel R. Brower and Edward J. Lazzerini, 169–87. Bloomington, 1997.

Lebedev, G. S. *Istoriia otechestvennoi arkheologii, 1700–1971*. St. Petersburg, 1992.

Lebedintsev, A. "Stoletie tserkovnoi zhizni Kryma, 1783–1883." *ZOOID* 13 (1883): 201–19.

LeDonne, John P. *Ruling Russia: Politics and Administration in the Age of Absolutism, 1762–1796*. Princeton, NJ, 1984.

Lerner, O. M. *Evrei v Novorossiiskom kraiu. Istoricheskie ocherki po dannomi iz arkhiva byvshago Novorossiiskago General-gubernatora*. Odessa, 1901.

"Letopis' Obshchestva." *ZOOID* 1 (1844): 565–80.

Levitskii, Nikandr. *Vysokopreosviashchennyi Innokentii, arkhiepiskop khersonskii i tavricheskii*. Moscow, 1904.

Levy, Clifford J. "Moscow's Mayor Exports Russia's New Nationalism." *New York Times*, 25 October 2008. <www.nytimes.com/2008/10/26/world/europe/26mayor. html?pagewanted=2&_r=1>.

Liber, George. *Soviet Nationality Policy, Urban Growth, and Identity Change in the Ukrainian SSR, 1923–1934*. Cambridge, U.K., 1992.

Lifanov, Viktor. *Nikolaev, 1789–1989. Stranitsy istorii, spravochnik*. Odessa, 1989.

Lincoln, W. Bruce. *In the Vanguard of Reform: Russia's Enlightened Bureaucrats, 1825–1861*. DeKalb, 1982.

———. *Nicholas I, Emperor and Autocrat of All the Russias*. Bloomington, 1978. Reprint, DeKalb, 1989.

———. *Red Victory: A History of the Russian Civil War*. NY, 1989.

Lindenmeyr, Adele. *Poverty Is Not a Vice: Charity, Charity, Society, and the State in Imperial Russia*. Princeton, NJ, 1996.

Lisovoi, N. N. "A. N. Murav'ev i ego kniga Puteshestvie ko sviatym mestam v 1830 godu." Preface Andrei Nikiloevich Murav'ev's, *Puteshestvie ko sviatym mestam v 1830 godu*. Moscow, 2007.

Litvinova, E. M. *Putevoditel'. Krym. Pravoslavnye sviatyni*. Simferopol, 2005.

Livanov, Fedor V. *Istoriia Dukhovnykh Khristian Molokan*. St. Petersburg, 1872.

———. *Putevoditel' po Krymu s istoricheskim opisaniem dostoprimechatel'nostei Kryma*. Moscow, 1875.

Loewenthal, Rudolf. "The Extinction of the Krimchaks in World War II." *American Slavic and East European Review* 10, no. 2 (April 1951): 130–36.

Loginovskii, A. I. "O Poslednei poezdke v Krym i poslednikh dniakh zhizni sinodal'nago chlena, preosviashchennago Innokentiia, byvshego arkhiepiskopa Khersonskogo i Tavricheskogo," in *KhEV*, Supplement 5 (1862): 81–108.

Long, James W. *From Privileged to Dispossessed: The Volga Germans, 1860–1917*. Lincoln, NE, 1988.

M., L. *Vospominaniia Arkhiepiskopa Innokentiia (Borisova) v Odesse v pamiat' spaseniia ee ot nashestviia anglo-frantsuzskago flota v 1854–1855*. Odessa, 1907.

MacKenzie, David. "Serbia and Russia to 1918." *MGSY* 16/17 (2000/2001): 131–44.

Madariaga, Isabel de. *Russia in the Age of Catherine the Great*. New Haven, CN, 1981.

Maiorova, Olga. "War as Peace: The Trope of War in Russian Nationalist Discourse during the Polish Uprising of 1863." *Kritika: Explorations in Russian and Eurasian History* 6, no. 3 (Summer 2005): 501–34.
Maksimovich, Mikhail. "Vospominanie o Tavride. Pis'mo k kniaziu Petru Andreevichu Viazemskomu." *Pis'ma o Kyiv i vospominanie o Tavride*. St. Petersburg, 1871.
Malgin, Andrei. *Krymkskii uzel. Ocherki politicheskoi istorii krymskogo poluostrova, 1989–1999*. Simferopol, 2000.
Manchester, Laurie. *Holy Fathers, Secular Sons: Clergy, Intelligentsia, and the Modern Self in Revolutionary Russia*. DeKalb, 2008.
Marchand, Suzanne L. *Down from Mount Olympus: Archaeology and Philhellenism in Germany, 1750–1970*. Princeton, NJ, 1996.
Markelov, Oleg. "Do Afona rukoi podat'." *KV* 47 (28 April 2005): 19.
———. "Pod pisan dogovor mezhdu eparkhiei i zapovednikom." *KV* (18 March 2000).
———. "Prik'snovenie k blagodati." *KV* (18 July 1997).
Markevich, Arsenii. "Neskol'ko slov o deiatel'nosti v Tavride Innokentiia, arkhiepiskopa khersonskago i tavricheskago." *TEV* 1–2 (1900): 26–43, 95–110.
———. "Pereseleniia krymskikh tatar v Turtseiu v sviazi s dvizhennem naseleniia v Krymu." *Izvestiia Akademii nauk SSSR*, Seriia 8, otdelenie [section] Gumanitarnykh nauk 4–7 (1928): 375–89.
———. *Tavricheskaia guberniia vo vremia krymskoi voiny po arkhivnym materialam*. 1905. Reprint, Simferopol, 1994.
Markov, Evgenii. *Ocherki Kryma. Kartiny Krymskoi zhizny, istorii i prirodu*. 4th ed. St. Petersburg, 1903.
Martin, Janet. *Medieval Russia, 980–1584*. NY, 1996.
Martin, Kingsley. *The Triumph of Lord Palmerston: A Study of Public Opinion in England before the Crimean War*. 1923. Reprint, London, 1963.
Marushchak, Vasilii [Protodiakon]. *Arkhiepiskop Dmitrii (v Skhime Antonii) Abashidze*. Simferopol, 2005.
Mashchenko, Aleksandr. "Moliatsia, moliatsia, mozhet, i otmoliat . . ." *KV* 195 (27 October 1998).
Matejic, Mateja. *The Holy Mount and the Hilandar Monastery*. Columbus, OH, 1983.
"Materialy dlia russkoi istorii pervoi poloviny XIX sloletiia. Pis'ma raznykh lits Arkhiepiskopu Innokentiu Borisovu." *Chteniia v imperatorskom obshchestve istorii i drevnostei Rossiiskikh* 4 (October–December 1884).
Materialy iubileinykh tserkovno-obshchestvennykh konferentsii Simferopol'skoi i Krymskoi eparkhii Ukrainskoi Pravoslavnoi Tserkvi, 1998–2000. Simferopol, 2000.
Matseevich, Lev. *Vysokopreosviashchennyi Innokentii Borisov, arkhiepiskop khersonskii i tavricheskii. Materialy i zametki*. Minneapolis, 1983.
Matveyev, Vladimir. "Trade, Property Restitution on Table as President of Ukraine Visits U.S." <www.ujc.org/content_display.html?ArticleID=150127> (accessed 5 November 2006).
Mawson, Michael Hargreave. *Eyewitness in the Crimea: The Crimean War Letters (1854–1856) of Lt. Col. George Frederick Dallas*. London, 2001.
McReynolds, Louise. *The News under Russia's Old Regime: The Development of the Mass-Circulation Press*. Princeton, NJ, 1991.
Meehan-Waters, Brenda. *Holy Women of Russia: The Lives of Five Orthodox Women Offer Spiritual Guidance for Today*. Crestwood, NY, 1997.
———. "Metropolitan Filaret (Drozdov) and the Reform of Russian Women's Monastic Communities." *Russian Review* 50 (1991): 310–23.
Mendieta, E. A. *Mount Athos, the Garden of the Panaghia*. Translated by M. K. Bruce. Berlin, 1972.
Metcalf, Thomas R. *An Imperial Vision: Indian Architecture and Britain's Raj*. Berkeley, CA, 1989.

Meyer, James H. "Immigration, Return, and the Politics of Citizenship: Russian Muslims in the Ottoman Empire, 1860–1914." *International Journal of Middle Eastern Studies* 39 (2007): 15–32.
Mikaelian, V. A. *Na krymskoi zemle. Istoriia armianskikh poselenii v Krymu.* Erevan, 1974.
Mikhno, Nikolai. "Iz zapisok chinovnika o krymskoi voine." In *Materialy dlia istorii krymskoi voiny i oborony sevastopolia. Sbornik', izdavaemyi komitetom po ustroistvu sevastopol'skago muzeia.* Edited by N. Dubrovin, 3:9–39. St. Petersburg, 1872.
Milianovskii, Feodor. *Pamiatnaia knizhka dlia dukhovenstva Khersonskoi eparkhii.* Odessa, 1902.
Miller, Philip. *Karaite Separatism in Nineteenth-Century Russia: Joseph Solomon Lutski's "Epistle of Israel's Deliverance."* Cincinnati, OH, 1993.
Milner, Thomas [Reverend]. *The Crimea, Its Ancient and Modern History, the Khans, the Sultans, and the Czars. With notices of its scenery and population.* London, 1855.
Mogarichev, Iu. M. *Peshchernye tserkvi Tavriki.* Simferopol, 1997.
———, A. V. Sazanov, and A. K. Shaposhnikov. *Zhitie Ioanna Gotskogo v kontekste istorii Kryma "khazarskogo perioda."* Simferopol, 2007.
Moiseenkova, L. S. "Staroobriadtsy v tavricheskoi gubernii v kontse XVIII–nachale XX v." *Materialy po arkheologii, istorii, i etnografii Tavrii* 5 (1996): 199–212.
"Monastery and Madrassah Dispute in Bakhchysarai." Religious Information Service of Ukraine, 13 September 2006. <www.risu.org.ua/eng/news/article;11892> (accessed 25 September 2006).
Morozova, Elena. *Zemli ulybka, radost' neba.* Yalta, 2006.
"Moskal' prosit vlasti Kryma 'razrulit' mezhreligioznyi konflikt v Bakhchisarai." *Tribuna*. Religious Information Service of Ukraine, 9 November 2006. <www.risu.org.ua/eng/news/article;10358/> (accessed 19 January 2007).
Mostashari, Firouzeh. "Colonial Dilemmas: Russian Policies in the Muslim Caucasus." In *Of Religion and Empire: Missions, Conversion, and Tolerance in Tsarist Russia*, edited by Robert P. Geraci and Michael Khodarkovsky, 229–49. Ithaca, NY, 2001.
Muftiizade, M. M. *Ocherk stoletnei voennoi sluzhby Krymskikh tatar,1784–1904.* Simferopol, 1905.
Murav'ev, Andrei Nikolaevich. *Pis'ma s vostoka 1849–1850 godakh.* St. Petersburg, 1851.
———. *Puteshestvie po Sviatym Mestam russkim.* St. Petersburg, 1888.
Muravev-Apostol, Ivan Matveevich. *Puteshestvie po Tavride v 1820 godu.* St. Petersburg, 1823.
Murzakevich, N. N. "Eparkhial'nye arkhierei Novorossiiskago kraia." *ZOOID* 10 (1875): 297–302.
———. *Istoriia Genuzaskikh poselenii v Krymu.* Odessa, 1837.
———. "Khersonisskaia tserkov sv. Vasiliia (Vladimira)." *ZOOID* 5 (1863): 996–97.
———. "Materialy dlia istorii Novorossiiskoi ierarkhii, Gavriil Rozanov." *KhEV* (1879) supplement: 547–558.
———. "Nekotoriia podrobnosti o tserkvi sv. Ionna Predtechi v Kerchi," *ZOOID* 1 (1844): 625–27.
———. "(Nekrolog) 'Zakharii Andreevich Arkas.'" *ZOOID* 6 (1867): 492–94
———. "Ocherk zaslug sdelannykh naukam svetleishim kniazem Mikhailom Semenovichem Voronstovym." *ZOOID* 4 (1858): 395–413.
———. "Poezdka v Krym 1836." *Zhurnal ministerstva narodnago prosvieshcheniia*, 13 (1837): 625–91.
———. "Svedeniia o nekotorykh pravoslavnykh monastyriakh eparkhii khersonskoi i kishinevskoi." *ZOOID* 2 (1848): 302–29.
Musin, A. [Deacon]. "Arkheologiia Korsunskoi legendy (Arkheologicheskie kommentarii k letopisnoi stat'e 6496 goda i korsunskie drevnosti na Rusi)." In *Pravoslavnye drevnosti Tavriki. Sbornik materialov po tserkovnoi arkheologii,*

edited by V. Iu. Iurochkin, 146–54. Kyiv 2002.

"Muslim Mufti Gives Conditions for Interreligious Cooperation." Religious Information Service of Ukraine, 27 January 2003. <www.risu.org.ua/eng/news/article;2054/> (accessed 13 November 2006).

Nadler, V. K. *Odessa v pervyia epokhi ee sushchestvovaniia*. Odessa, 1893.

Naimark, Norman. *Fires of Hatred: Ethnic Cleansing in Twentieth-Century Europe*. Cambridge, MA, 2001.

Nakropin, Sv. Aleksandr. "Iz vospominanii o preosviashchennom Innokentii Arkhiepiskop Khersonskom i Tavricheskom." *TEV* 2 (1880): 68–90.

Neale, J. M. *Voices from the East: Documents on the Present State and Working of the Oriental Church*. Edited by the Rev. J. M. Neale. London, 1859.

Nepomniashchii, A. A. *Muzeinoe delo v Krymu i ego starateli (XIX–nachalo XX veka). Biobibliograficheskoe issledovanie*. Simferopol, 2000.

———. *Ocherki razvitiia istoricheskogo kraevedeniia Kryma v XIX–nachale XX veka*. Simferopol, 1998.

———. *Razvitie istoricheskogo kraevedeniia v Krymu XIX-nachale XX veka*. Simferopol, 1995).

———. *Zapiski puteshestvennikov i putevoditeli v razvitii istoricheskogo kraevedeniia Kryma (posledniaia tret' XVIII–nachalo XX veka)*. Kyiv, 1999.

Nezhivoi, Aleksei. "V odnom meste tushim—v drugom zagoraetsia." *KV* (25 November 2000): 3.

Nichols, Robert. "The Orthodox Elders (*Startsy*) of Imperial Russia." *MGSY* 1 (1985): 1–30.

Niessen, James P., ed. *Religious Compromise, Political Salvation: The Greek Catholic Church and Nation-building in Eastern Europe*. Pittsburgh, PA, 1992.

Nikon, Igumen, and Nikolai Donenko. *Iugo-vostochnyi Afon Rossiiskoi Imperii Kiziltash*. Simferopol, n.d.

Norris, Stephen. *A War of Images: Russian Popular Prints, Wartime Culture, and National Identity, 1812–1945*. Dekalb, 2006.

Noskova, Nina. *Krymskie bolgary v XIV–nachale XX v. Istoriia i kul'tura*. Simferopol, 2002.

"Number of Religious Organizations as of 1 January 2004, broken down according to regions of Ukraine." Religious Information Service of Ukraine. <www.risu.org.ua/eng/resources/statistics/reg2004/> (accessed 14 November 2006).

"O krymskom istochnik sv. Kosmy i Damian." *OV* 66 (22 August 1851).

"O mestopolozhenii Balaklavskago Georgievskago monastyria v Krymu." *OZ* (1825): 97–104.

"O Viezde iz Odessy preosviashchennago Gavriila." *OV* (5 May 1848).

"Ob otyskanii drevnostei v Khersonise." *ITUAK* 5 (1888): 99–100.

Obolenskii, M. "Skazanie sviashchenika Iakova." *ZOOID* 2.2/3 (1850): 687–692.

Obolensky, Dimitri. "Cherson and the Conversion of Rus': An Anti-revisionist View." *Byzantine and Modern Greek Studies* 13 (1989): 244–56.

"Obozrenie puteshestviia izdatelia otechestvennykh zapisok po Rossii v 1825 godu." *OZ* (1826): 91–117, 440–67.

Obukhovskaia, Liudmila. "Komu meshaet monastyr'." *Krymskaia pravda* (25 March 2006): 2.

Olszamowska-Skowronska, Sophie. "La Correspondance des Papes et des Empereurs de Russie (1814–1878)." *Miscellanea Historiae Pontificiae* 29 (1970).

"On Conflict over Lands of Svyato-Uspenskiy Monastery in Bakhchisaray." *Crimean Aspects* (on-line journal), 10 July 2002 <aspects.crimeastar.net/english/comm.php?id=2&nr=070203>.

O'Neill, Kelly Ann. "Between Subversion and Submission: The Integration of the

Crimean Khanate into the Russian Empire, 1783–1853." Ph.D. diss., Harvard University, 2006.

———. "Constructing Imperial Identity in the Borderland: Architecture, Islam, and the Renovation of the Crimean Landscape." *Ab Imperio* 2 (2006): 163–91.

Orlov-Davydov, Vladimir Petrovich. *Putevye zapiski vedennye vo vremia prebyvaniia na Ionicheskikh ostrovakh, v Gretsii, Maloi Azii, i Turtsii v 1835 godu.* 2 vols. St. Petersburg, 1839–1840.

Otchet Imperatorskoi publichnoi biblioteki za 1887 god. St. Petersburg, 1890.

"Otchet Obshchestva istorii i drevnostei s 14 noiabria 1847 po 14 noiabria 1848 goda." *KGV* 20 (19 May 1849).

[Paleolog] M., G. "Otkrytie glavnago skita Uspenskago, v Krymu bliz Bakhchisaraia." *OV* 70 (1850).

———. "Perechen' sobytii, otnosiashchikhsia k istorii khersonskoi eparkhii." Supplement to [pribavlenie k] *KhEV* 5 (1862).

Palimpsestov, I. U. *Moi vospominaniia ob Innokentii, arkhiepiskop khersonskom.* St. Petersburg, 1888.

———. "Oproverzhenie klevety—otvet na stat'iu ob Innokentii khersonskom v *Russkoi Starine.*" *Strannik* (1861): 1–27.

Pallas, P. S. *Travels through the Southern Provinces of the Russian Empire performed in the years 1793 and 1794 by P. S. Pallas, Councillor of State to the Emperor.* Translated from the German by Francis Blagdon. London, 1803.

"Palomnicheskii Tsentr Simferopol'skoi i Krymskoi eparkhii." *Tavrida pravoslavnaia* 7 (1997).

"Panagiia, ili Uspenskii Bakhchisaraiskii v krymu skit." *Krymskii Afon (Bakhchisaraiskii Uspenskii monastyr' istoricheskhikh opisaniiakh).* Simferopol, 1995.

Parfeny [Peter Ageev]. Igumen. *Skazanie o stranstvovanii i puteshestvii po Rossii, Moldavii, Turtsii i Sviatoi Zemle. Postrizhenika Sviatye Gory Afonskie inoka Parfeniia.* Moscow, 1855.

Parks, Christopher. *Sacred Worlds: An Introduction to Geography and Religion.* London, 1994.

Pavlovskii, A. A. *Putevoditel' po sviatym mestam vostoka.* St. Petersburg, 1903.

———. *Vseobshchii illiustrirovanyi putevoditel' po monastyriam i sviatym mestam rossiiskoi imperii i afonu.* Nizhni Novgorod, 1907. Reprint, NY, 1988.

Petrovskii, S. Sv. *Innokentii Arkhiepiskopa Khersono-Tavricheskii k stoletiu so dnia ego rozhdeniia.* Odessa, 1901.

———. *Sem' Khersonskikh episkopov. Biografii.* Odessa, 1894.

Phillips, E. J. *The Founding of Russia's Navy.* Westport, CN, 1995.

Piatigorskii, Grigorii M. "The Cretan Uprising of 1866–1869 and the Greeks of Odessa." *MGSY* 14/15 (1998/1999): 129–48.

Pidadev, A. V. S. S. Soldatechenko, N. I. Yastreb, and M. Iu. Akhmedzhanov. "O Putiakh issledovanii lichnosti, nauchnogo i dukhovnogo nasledia V. F. Voino-Iasenetskogo doktora Meditsiny, professora-Khirgurga i arkhiepiskopa Luki." In *Materialy iubileinikh tserkovno-obshchestvennykh konferentsii Simferopol'skoi i krymskoi eparkhii Ukrainskoi Pravoslavnoi Tserkvi 1998–2000,* 368–70. Simferopol, 2000.

Pinson, Mark. "Demographic Warfare—an Aspect of Ottoman and Russian Policy, 1854–1866." Ph.D. Diss., Harvard University, 1970.

———. "Russian Policy and the Emigration of the Crimean Tatars to the Ottoman Empire, 1854–1862" (2 parts). In *Güney-Do u Avrupa Ara tırmaları Dergisi* (1972): 37–55 and (1973/74): 101–14.

Pipes, Richard. *Russia under the Old Regime.* NY, 1974.

Pirogov, N. I. *Sevastopol'skie pis'ma.* St. Petersburg, 1899.

Pis'ma A. S. Sturdza k Innokentiiu Arkhiepiskopu Khersonskomu i Tavricheskomu. Odessa, 1894.

"Pis'ma Arkhiepiskopa khersonskago i tavricheskago Innokentiia k Gavriilu, Arkhiepiskopu riazanskomu, 1829–1857." *ZOOID* 14 (1886).
"Pis'ma Arkhiepiskopa khersonskago Innokentiia (Borisova), k Professoru I. M. Bolianskomu." *ZOOID* 13 (1883): 269–71.
Pis'ma Filareta, Mitropolita moskovskago i kolomenskago k vysochaishim osobam i raznym drugim litsam. Tver, 1888.
Pis'ma Innokentiia, Arkhiepiskopa khersonskago i tavricheskago, k raznym litsam. St. Petersburg, 1885.
"Pis'ma Preosviashcheniia Gavriila Rozanova, Pervago v Odesse Arkhiepiskopa Khersonskago k protoiereu Serafimu Antonovichu Serafimovu." *KhEV* (1905) no. 5: 177–79.
"Pis'ma Preosviashchennago Innokentiia k protoiereiu Maksimu Perepelchitsynu," in *KhEV*, supplement (1878): 100–104.
Pis'ma s vostoka k Preosviashchennomu Innokentiiu. St. Petersburg, 1887.
Plokhy, Serhii. *The Cossacks and Religion in Early Modern Ukraine*. Oxford, 2002.
———. "The City of Glory: Sevastopol in Russian Historical Mythology." *Journal of Contemporary History* 35, no. 3 (July 2000): 369–83.
Plokhy, Serhii, and Frank Sysyn, eds. *Religion and Nation in Modern Ukraine*. Edmonton and Toronto, 2003.
Pogodin, M. P. "Konchina Innokentiieva." *Venok na mogilu Vysokopreosviashchennago Innokentiia, arkhiepiskopa tavricheskago*. Moscow, 1864.
Polidorov, Petr [Protoierei]"Preosviashchennyi Polikarp, episkop orlovskii i sievskii (ocherk ego zhizni)." *Strannik* (1870): 239–63.
Polons'ka-Vasylenko, Natalia D. "The Settlement of the Southern Ukraine, 1750–1775." *Annals of the Ukrainian Academy of Arts and Sciences in the United States* 4/5 (1955) (Special Issue).
Poppe, Andrzei. "The Political Background to the Baptism of Rus'. Byzantine-Russia Relations between 986 and 989." *Dumbarton Oaks Papers* 30 (1976): 195–244.
Porfirii [Uspenskii] Archbishop of Chigirin. *Pervoe puteshestvie v afonskie monastyri i skity arkhimandrita, nyne episkopa, Porfiriia Uspenskogo v 1845 godu*. Kazan, 1877, and Moscow, 1880–1881.
Porter, Andrew. "Commerce and Christianity: The Rise and Fall of a Nineteenth-Century Missionary Slogan." *The Historical Journal* 28, no. 3 (1985): 597–621.
Porter, Curtis Hunter. "Mikhail Petrovich Pogodin and the Development of Russian Nationalism, 1800–1856." Ph.D. diss., Vanderbilt University, 1973.
"Poseshchenie Bakhchisaraiskago Uspenskago skita, balaklavskago georgievskago monastyria i khersoneskago pervoklasnago monastyria." *Tserkovnaia letopis'* (October 1861): 634–40.
Pospielovsky, Dimitry. *The Russian Church under the Soviet Regime, 1917–1982*. Crestwood, NY, 1984.
Povest' vremennykh let. The Hague, 1969.
"Pravoslavnye monastyri, skity, i kinovii v eparkhiakh Novorossiiskago kraia i Bessarabii, v eparkhii Tavricheskoi." *Novorossiiskii kalendar' na 1874* (Odessa, 1873): 114–21.
Presniakov, A. E. *Emperor Nicholas I of Russia: The Apogee of Autocracy, 1825–1855*. Edited and translated by Judith C. Zacek. Gulf Breeze, FL, 1974.
"Prepodobnomuchenik Parfenii, igumen Kiziltashkii." Simferopol'skaia i Krymskaia eparkhiia [Diocese of Simferopol and Crimea (official site)] <www.crimea.orthodoxy.su/Chronica/2008-09-04-Parfeniy-Zhitiye.html> (accessed 22 May 2009).
Proskurina, Nadezhda V. "Palomnichestvo 'Krym Pravoslavnyi.'" *Tavrida pravoslavnaia*. 9, no. 32 (September 1998): 21.
———. *Palomnichestvo po pravoslavnym sviatyniam Kryma*. Simferopol, 2006.

———. *Pravoslavnye Sviatyni Kryma*. Sevastopol, 1997.
"Protoierei Gerasim Petrovich Pavskii. Biograficheskii ocherk po novym materialam." *RS* 7, nos. 1–4 (1880), discontinuous pagination.
Protopopov, M. "Uspenskii skit v Krymu bliz Bakhchisaraia." In *Krymskii Afon (Bakhchisaraiskii Uspenskii monastyr' istoricheskikh opisaniiakh)*. Simferopol, 1995.
Prousis, Theophilus. "Aleksandr S. Sturdza: A Russian Conservative Response to the Greek Revolution." *East European Quarterly* 26, no. 3 (1992): 309–12.
———. *Russian-Ottoman Relations in the Levant: The Dashkov Archive*. Minneapolis, MN, 2002.
———. "Russian Philorthodox Relief during the Greek War of Independence." *MGSY* 1 (1985): 31–60.
———. *Russian Society and the Greek Revolution*. DeKalb, 1994.
Prugavin, A. S. *Religioznye otshchepentsy. Ocherki sovremennogo sektanstva*. Moscow, 1906.
Rambo, Lewis R. *Understanding Religious Conversion*. New Haven, CN, 1993.
Ransel, David. *The Politics of Catherinian Russia: The Panin Party*. New Haven, CN, 1975.
Rattue, J. *The Living Stream: Holy Wells in Historical Context*. Woodbridge, U.K., 1995.
Renner, Andreas. "Defining a Russian Nation: Mikhail Katkov and the 'Invention' of National Politics." *Slavonic and East European Review* 81, no. 4 (2003): 659–82.
"Review of the Historiography of Chersonesos according to G. D. Belov." National Preserve of Tauric Chersonesos. <www.chersonesos.org/eng/History/history.sour.htm > (accessed December 15, 2002).
Rhinelander, Anthony L. H. *Prince Michael S. Vorontsov: Viceroy to the Tsar*. Montreal 1990.
Riasanovsky, Nicholas. *Nicholas I and Official Nationality in Russia, 1825–1855*. Berkeley, 1959.
———. *Russia and the West and the Teachings of the Slavophiles*. Cambridge, MA, 52.
Ribas, Aleksandr de. *Staraia Odessa. Istoricheskie ocherki i vospominaniia*. Odessa, 1990.
Robson, Roy R. *Old Believers in Modern Russia*. DeKalb, 1995.
———. *Solovki: The Story of Russia Told through Its Most Remarkable Islands*. New Haven, CN, 2004.
Rogacheva, Maria. "Krym Mozhet Stat' Ukrainskim Kosovo." *Izvestia*. <www.izvestia.ru/world/article3092352/ 25.04.06> (accessed 17 December 2006).
Romey, Kristin M. "Legacies of a Slavic Pompeii." *Archaeology* 55.6 (Nov/Dec 2002): 18–25.
Russkoe Obshchestvo parakhodstva i torgovli. Putevoditel' Russkogo Obshchestva parakhodstva i torgovli na 1912. Odessa, 1912.
Said, Edward W. *Orientalism*. NY, 1979.
"St. Andrew." *Catholic Encyclopedia*. <www.newadvent.org/cathen/01471.htm> (accessed 25 March 2003).
Samodurova, V. V. *Prichernomorskie nemtsy. Ikh vklad v razvitie goroda Odessy i regiona 1803–1917, Bibliograficheskii ukazatel'*. Odessa, 1999.
Sandler, Stephanie. *Distant Pleasures: Alexander Pushkin and the Writing of Exile*. Stanford, 1989.
Sanin, G. A. "Iuzhnaia granitsa Rossii vo 2–i polovine XVII–pervoi polovine XVIII v." *Russian History* 19, nos.1–4 (1992): 433–59.
Saprykin, Sergei J. *Heracleia Pontica and Tauric Chersonesus before Roman Domination: VI–I Centuries B.C*. Amsterdam, 1997.
Sasse, Gwendolyn, *The Crimea Question: Identity, Transition, and Conflict*. Cambridge, MA, 2007.
Saunders, David. *Russia in the Age of Reaction and Reform, 1801–1881*. NY, 1992.
Schmemann, Alexander. *The Historical Road of Eastern Orthodoxy*. Translated by Lydia W. Kesich. NY, 1963.

Schneider, Robert A. *The Ceremonial City: Toulouse Observed, 1738–1780*. Princeton, NJ, 1995.
Schönle, Andreas. "Garden of the Empire: Catherine's Appropriation of the Crimea." *Slavic Review* 60, no. 1 (Spring 2001): 1–23.
Schur, Nathan. *Karaite Encyclopedia*. Frankfurt, 1995.
Seitbekirov, Adil'. "Kushchustviia nad pogrebennymi, dobra ne nakhivesh'!" *Golos Kryma* 29, no. 659 (14 July 2006).
Serafimov, Serafim. "Nekrolog." *ZOOID* 5 (1863): 919–53.
———. "Neskol'ko svedenii ob uchrezhdenii vikariantstva khersonskoi eparkhii v 1852 godu." *KhEV* 19 (1878): 556–67.
———. *Vospominaniia o Preosviashchennom Gavriilie, pervom (v Odessie) arkhiepiskopie khersonskom i tavricheskom, a potom tverskom i kashinskom*. Odessa, 1859.
Shavshin, V. G. *Balaklava*. Simferopol, 1994.
———. *Balaklavskii Georgievskii monastyr'*. Simferopol, 1997.
———. "Plenenn' i monastyr'." *Rodina* 3–4 (1995).
Sheehy, Ann. *The Crimean Tatars, Volga Germans, and Meskhetians: Soviet Treatment of Some National Minorities*. London, 1980.
Shenitz, Helen A. "Father Veniaminov, the Enlightener of Alaska." *American Slavic and East European Review* 18, no. 1 (1959): 57–80.
Sherrard, Philip. *Athos, the Holy Mountain*. London, 1982.
Sheviakova, Daria Petrovna. "Rol' Grecheskogo naseleniia Sevastopolia v vozrozhdenii pravoslaviia v Krymu (kontsa XVIII-nachala XXvv)." *Russkie v istorii Tavridy. Materialy nauchno-prakticheskoi konferentsii*. Ed. V. B. Gaidamaka. Simferopol, 2003).
Shevzov, Vera. "Icons, Miracles, and the Ecclesial Identity of Laity in Late Imperial Russian Orthodoxy." *Church History* 69, no. 3 (2000): 610–31.
———. "Letting the People into Church: Reflections on Orthodoxy and Community in Late Imperial Russia." In *Orthodox Russia: Belief and Practice under the Tsars*, edited by Valerie A. Kivelson and Robert H. Greene, 59–77. University Park, PN, 2003.
———. "Miracle-Working Icons, Laity, and Authority in the Russian Church, 1861–1917." *Russian Review* 58, no. 1 (January 1999): 26–48.
Shiriaev, Grigorii I. *Zapiski o nyneshnem sostoianii russkogo Panteleimonova monastyria na sviatoi gore Afonskoi*. Moscow, 1850.
Shirokorad, A. B. *Russko-Turetskie Voiny, 1676–1918*. Moscow, 2000.
Shishkina, O. P. *Zametki i vospominaniia russkoi puteshestvennitsy po Rossii v 1845 godu*. St. Petersburg, 1848.
Shnirelman, Victor A. "Russian Response: Archaeology, Russian Nationalism, and the 'Arctic Homeland.'" In *Selective Remembrances: The Construction, Consecration, and Commemoration of the Past*, edited by Phil Kohl, Mara Kozelsky, Nachman Ben-Yehuda. Chicago, IL, 2008. 31–70.
Shpalianskii, V. V. "Pravovoe polozhenie evreev v tavricheskoi gubernii v XIX." *Evrei Kryma. Ocherki istorii*. Simferopol, 1997.
Skal'kovskii, Apollon. *Opyt' statisticheskago opisaniia novorossiiskogo kraia. Chast' 1, Geografiia, etnografiia, i narodoschislenie Novorossiiskogo kraia*. Odessa, 1850.
———. *Pervoe tridtsatiletye istorii goroda Odessy, 1793–1823*. Odessa, 1837.
———. "Prostranstvo i narodonaselenie novorossiiskago Kraia, v 1845 godu." In *Novorossiiskii kalendar' na 1849* (Odessa, 1848), 348–79.
Skinner, Barbara. "The Irreparable Church Schism: Russian Orthodox Identity and Its Historical Encounter with Catholicism." In *Polish Encounters, Russian Identity*, edited by David L. Ransel and Bozena Shallcross, 20–36. Bloomington, 2005.
Slezkine, Yuri. *Artic Mirrors: Russia and the Small Peoples of the North*. Ithaca, NY, 1994.
Smith, Anthony D. *Myths and Memories of the Nation*. Oxford, 1999.

Smolich, I. K. *Russkoe monashestvo, 988–1917, zhizn' i uchenie startsev*. Moscow, 1997.
Snow, David, and Richard Machalek. "The Sociology of Conversion." *Annual Review of Sociology* 10 (1984): 167–90.
Sokolov, D. *Progulka po Krymu, s tseliu oznakomit' s nim*. Odessa, 1869.
Spasskii, G. I. *Kniga Bol'shomu chertezhu*. Moscow, 1846.
Speake, Graham. *Mount Athos: Renewal in Paradise*. New Haven, CN, 2002.
Spravochnaia kniga Khersonskoi eparkhii. Odessa, 1906.
Stanley, Brian. "Commerce and Christianity": Providence Theory, the Missionary Movement and the Imperialism of Free Trade, 1842–1860." *The History Journal* 26 (1983): 71–94
Stanton, Leonard J. "Zedergol'm's Life of Elder Leonid of Optina as a Source of Dostoevsky's *The Brothers Karamazov*." *Russian Review* 49 (1990): 443–55.
Stavrou, Theofanis. *Russian Interests in Palestine, 1882–1914*. Thessalonki, 1963.
———. and Peter R. Weisensel. *Russian Travelers to the Christian East from the Twelfth to the Twentieth Century*. Columbus, OH, 1985.
Stein, Howard F. "Russian Nationalism and the Divided Soul of the Westernizers and Slavophiles." *Ethos* 4, no. 4 (1976): 403–38.
Steinberg, Mark. D., and Heather J. Coleman, ed., *Sacred Stories: Religion and Spirituality in Modern Russia*. Bloomington, 2007.
Steinwedel, Charles Robert. "Invisible Threads of Empire: State, Religion, and Ethnicity in Tsarist Bashkiria, 1773–1917." Ph.D. diss., Columbia University, 1999.
Stempkovskii, I. A. "Mysli otnositel'no izyskaniia drevnostei v Novorossiiskom Krae." *OZ* (1827): 41–72.
Stewart, Cecil. *Byzantine Legacy*. London, 1947.
Stol'pin, Arkady. "Nochnaia vylazka v Sevastopole." *Sovremennik* 52 (1855): 5–11.
Strickland, John D. "Remembering Rus in Modern Russia: The Orthodox Church and its Cultural Mission before the Revolutions." *MGSY* 14/15 (1998/1999): 149–67.
Strukov, D. *Drevnie pamiatniki Khristianstva v Tavride*. Moscow, 1876.
Strzheletskii, S. F. *Kleryi Khersonesa tavricheskogo. K istorii drevnego zemledeliia v Krymu*. Simferopol, 1961.
Subtelny, Orest. *Ukraine: A History*. Third ed. Toronto, 2000.
Sumarokov, P. *Dosugi krymskogo sud'i, ili vtoroe puteshestvie v Tavridu*. St. Petersburg, 1803.
Sunderland, Willard. "Peasants on the Move: State Peasant Settlement in Imperial Russia, 1805–1830s." *Russian Review* 52, no. 4 (1993): 472–85.
———. *Taming the Wildfield*. Ithaca, NY, 2004.
Surov, E. G. *Khersones Tavricheskii Lektsii po spetsial'nomu kursu i materialy k seminariu dlia zaochnogo otdeleniia*. Sverdlovsk, 1961.
Svartsevich, Vladimir. "Krym: Otdat Kontsy." *Argumenty i fakty*. December 20, 2006 <www.aif.ru/online/aif/1364/06_03> (accessed 15 January 2007).
Sviatogorets, Serafim/Sergii. "Pis'ma s Afonskoi gory." in *Maiak*, nos. 19, 21, 22, 23, 24 (1845).
———. *Pis'ma sviatogortsa k druz'iam svoim o sviatoi gore Afonskoi*. St. Petersburg, 1850.
Sysyn, Frank E. "Politics and Orthodoxy in Independent Ukraine." *Harriman Review* 15, nos. 2/3 (June 2005): 8–19.
Szczesniak, Boleslaw. *The Russian Revolution and Religion: A Collection of Documents concerning the Suppression of Religion by the Communists, 1917–1925*. Translated, edited, and with an introductory essay by Boleslaw Szczesniak. Notre Dame, 1959.
Tabor, James. "Konstantin Bazili and Russia on the Orthodox East on the Eve of the Crimean War." *MGSY* 20/21 (2004–2005): 43–61
Tarle, E. V. *Krymskaia Voina*. Leningrad, 1950.
Tereshchenko, Artemii. "Ocherki Novorossikago Kraia: Nekotoraia mestnost'. Iuzhnago

Kryma." *Zhurnal ministerstva narodnago prosvieshcheniia* 84.2 (1854): 40.
Tishchenko, Iulia, and Inna Pidluska. "Lobby Conflictology: Crimean Aspect." Research Update #185, 4 September 2000, <www.cidct.org.ua/en/studii/7/4.html> (accessed 17 January 2007).
Titovoi, T. I. [protoierei], and Aleksandr Iakushechkin, eds. *Osnovy Pravoslavnoi kul'tury Kryma*. Simferopol, 2004.
Tolstoi, D. A. *Rimskii katolitsizm v Rossii. Istoricheskoe izsledovanie*. St. Petersburg, 1876.
Tolstoy, Leo. *Sebastopol Sketches*. Translated and introduced by David McDuff. NY, 1986.
Toplovskii Sviato-Paraskevskii zhenskii monastyr'. Simferopol, 2000.
Torzhestvo Pravoslavnykh v Odesse po sluchaiu pereneseniia tela vselenskago i konstantinopol'skago patriarkha Grigoriia iz Odessy v Gretsiu. Odessa, 1871.
Totleben, Eduard. *Défense de Sebastopol. Exposé de la Guerre Souterraine, 1854–1855*. St. Petersburg, 1870.
———. "O vyselenii tatar iz Kryma v 1860 gody." *RS* 78 (1893): 531–50.
Trombley, F. *Hellenic Religion and Christianization, c. 370–529*. Leiden, 1993.
Tsakni, N. *La Russie Sectaire (Sectes Religieuses en Russie)*. Paris, 1888.
"Tserkovno-istoricheskii ocherk osnovaniia v Kherson vikariata i ego zhiznedeiatel'nost' (po povodu ego piatidesiatiletiia, 1853–1903)." *KhEV* 16–21 (1904): 1–128; 1–3 (1905): 129–76.
Tuna, Mustafa Özgür. "Gaspirali v. Il'minskii: Two Identity Projects for the Russian Empire." *Nationalities Papers* 30, no. 2 (2002): 265–89.
Tunkina, Irina V. "The Formation of a Russian Science of Classical Antiquities of Southern Russia in the 18th and early 19th centuries." <www.pontos.dk/publications/books/bss-1-files/BSS1_24_Tunkina.pdf> (accessed 24 May 2009).
Tur, V. G. *Krymskie pravoslavnye monastyri XIX–nachala XX veka. Istoriia. Pravovoe polozhenie*. Simferopol, 1998.
"U Krimu bude stvoreno grupu protidii religiinomu ekstremizmu, proUA." 3 April 2006. <ua.proua.com/news/2006/04/03/165239.html> (accessed 19 January 2007).
"Uchenye svidetel'stuiut o traditsim ustanovki poklannykh krestov." *Tavrida pravoslavnaia* 5 (11 November 2000).
Uehling, Greta Lynn. *Beyond Memory: The Crimean Tatars' Deportation and Return*. NY, 2004.
"Ukraine President Stresses Idea of Single National Orthodox Church." Religious Information Service of Ukraine, 28 July 2006. <www.risu.org.ua/eng/news/article;11201/> (accessed 11 November 2006).
Umanets, A. *Istoricheskie rasskazy o Kryme*. Sevastopol, 1888.
"Uroki Pravoslavnaia. Po Monastyriam i Khramom." *Vrema krymskoe* (7 August 1997), 3.
"Uspenskii Skit bliz Bakhchisaraia." *Niva* 26 (1872): 411.
Vashchenko, V. *Sviatoimennyi' Afon*. Stuttgart, 1962.
Vasileios, Archimandrite of Stavronikita. *Beauty and Hesychia in Athonite Life*. Translated from the Greek by Constantine Kokenes. Montréal, 1996.
Vassilyeva, Anna. "Ukraine: Muslims Protest against 'Secret' Property Decision." Keston News Service (on-line journal), 19 July 2001. <www.keston.org.uk/kns/2001/010719UK.htm> (accessed 24 May 2009).
Vesnin, Serafim. *Sochineniia i pis'ma Sviatogorets, sobranie posle ego smerti*. St. Petersburg, 1858.
Viknovich, V. L. *Karaim Avraam Firkovich. Evreiskie rukopisi, istoriia, puteshestviia*. St. Petersburg, 1997.
Vinogradov, V. N. "The personal responsibility of Emperor Nicholas I for the coming of the Crimean War: An Episode in the Diplomatic Struggle in the Eastern Question." In *Imperial Russian Foreign Policy*, edited by Hugh Ragsdale, 119–58.

Cambridge, U.K. 1993.
Vlasenko, Andriy [The Reverend]. "Pilgrimage to the Crimea." *Welcome to Ukraine* 2 (1998). On-line journal <www.iprinet.kyiv.ua/wumag/archiv/2_98/pilgrim.htm> (accessed 16 January 2003).
Vol'fson, B. M. "Emigratsiia Krymskikh Tatar v 1860 g." *Istoricheskie zapiski*. no. 9 (1940): 186-197.
"Vospominaniia o Preosviashchennom Innokentie, arkhiepiskope khersonskom i tavricheskom." *Severnaiia pchela* no. 177 (1858): 764.
"Vospominaniia o Preosviashchennom Innokentii, arkhiepiskope khersonskom i tavricheskom." *KhEV* 5 (1862): 30-62.
"Vospominanie o pastyrskikh puteshestviakh Preosviashchennago Gavriila, arkhiepiskopa ekaterinoslavskago, khersonskago, i tavricheskago." *KhEV* supplement, part 5 (1861): 336-46.
Vostokov, N. M. "Innokentii, Arkhiepiskop Khersonskii i Tavricheskii," *RS* 21, 23 (1878): 193-204 and 547-572; 367-98; 24 (1879): 651-708.
Vozgrin, V. E. *Istoricheskie sudby Krymskikh tatar*. Moscow, 1992.
Vybornyi, P. M. *Nikolaev*. Odessa, 1973.
"Vysochaishii manifest ot 20 Oktiabria 1853 ob ob'iavlenii voiny Porte," edited by N. Dubrovin, 129-31. In *Materialy dlia istorii krymskoi voiny i Oborony Sevastopolia. Sbornik izdavaemyi komitetom po ustroistvu sevastopol'skago muzeia*. St. Petersburg, 1871.
Walicki, Andrzej. *A History of Russian Thought from the Enlightenment to Marxism*. Stanford, 1979.
Wallace-Hadrill, D. S. *The Greek Patristic View of Nature*. Manchester, 1968.
Walters, Philip. "A Survey of Soviet Religious Policy." In *Religious Policy in the Soviet Union*, edited by Sabrina Ramet, 3-30. Cambridge, MA, 1993.
Wanner, Catherine. *Communities of the Converted: Ukrainians and Global Evangelicalism*. Ithaca, NY, 2007.
———. "Missionaries of Faith and Culture: Evangelical Encounters in Ukraine." *Slavic Review* 63, no. 4 (Winter 2004): 732-55.
Wartenweiler, David. *Civil Society and Academic Debate in Russia, 1905-1914*. Oxford, 1999.
Weeks, Theodore R. "Between Rome and Tsargrad: The Uniate Church in Imperial Russia." In *Of Religion and Empire: Missions, Conversion, and Tolerance in Tsarist Russia*, edited by Robert P. Geraci and Michael Khodarkovsky, 70-91. Ithaca, NY, 2001.
———. *Nation and State in Late Imperial Russia: Nationalism and Russification on the Western Frontier, 1863-1914*. DeKalb, 1996.
Werth, Paul W. *At the Margins of Orthodoxy: Mission, Governance, and Confessional Politics in Russia's Volga-Kama Region, 1827-1905*. Ithaca, NY, 2002.
———. "Orthodoxy as Ascription (and Beyond): Religious Identity on the Edge of the Orthodox Community, 1740-1917." In *Orthodox Russia: Belief and Practice under the Tsars*, edited by Valerie A. Kivelson and Robert H. Greene, 239-53. University Park, PA, 2003.
———. "Subjects for Empire: Orthodox Missions and Imperial Governance in the Volga-Kama Region, 1825-1881." Ph.D. diss., University of Michigan, 1996.
Whittaker, Cynthia H. "The Ideology of Sergei Uvarov: An Interpretive Essay." *Russian Review* 37, no. 2 (1978): 158-76.
———. *The Origins of Modern Russian Education: An Intellectual Biography of Count Sergei Uvarov, 1786-1855*. DeKalb, 1984.
Williams, Brian Glyn. *The Crimean Tatars: The Diaspora Experience and the Forging of a Nation*. Leiden, 2001.
———. "The Deportation and Ethnic Cleansing of the Crimean Tatars." In *Ethnic*

Cleansing in Twentieth-Century Europe, edited by Steven Vardy and Hunt Tooley, 537–58. NY, 2003.

———. "The Hijra and Forced Migration from Nineteenth-Century Russia to the Ottoman Empire: A Critical Analysis of the Great Crimean Tatar Emigration, 1860–1861." *Cahiers du Monde russe* 41, no. 1 (2000): 79–108.

———. "A Homeland Lost: Migration, the Diaspora Experience and the Forging of Crimean Tatar National Identity." Ph.D. diss., University of Wisconsin, 1999.

———. "Jihad and Ethnicity in Post-Communist Eurasia: On the Trail of Trans-national Islamic Holy Warriors in Kashmir, Afghanistan, Central Asia, Chechnya, and Kosovo." *Journal of Ethnopolitics* 2, nos. 3–4 (March/June 2003): 3–24.

Wolff, Larry. *Inventing Eastern Europe: The Map of Civilization on the Mind of the Enlightenment.* Stanford, 1994.

Woodham-Smith, Cecil. *The Reason Why.* London, 1953.

Wortman, Richard. "Ofitsial'naia narodnost' i natsional'nyi mif rossiiskoi monarkhii XIX veka." *Rossiia/Russia* 3 (1999): 233–44.

———. *Scenarios of Power: Myth and Ceremony in the Russian Monarchy.* Princeton, NJ, 1995–2000.

Wrangel, Peter [Baron]. *The Memoirs of Baron Wrangel: The Last Commander in Chief of the Russian National Army.* Translated by Sophie Goulston. London, 1929.

Wydra, Doris. "The Crimea Conundrum: The Tug of War between Russia and Ukraine on the Questions of Autonomy and Self-Determination." *International Journal on Minority and Group Rights* 10 (2004): 111–30.

Wynot, Jennifer. *Keeping the Faith: Russian Orthodox Monasticism in the Soviet Union, 1917–1939.* College Station, TX, 2004.

Zadneprovskaia, T. N. "Tserkovno-arkheologicheskie uchrezhdeniia i ikh rol' v okhrane i izuchenii pamiatnikov tserkovnoi stariny Rossii." In *Tserkovnaia arkheologiia. Materialy Pervoi Vserossiiskoi konferentsii. Pskov, 20–24 noiabria 1995.* Chast' 1, *Rasprostranenie khristianstva v vostochnoi evrope.* 37–40. St. Petersburg–Pskov, 1995.

Zavgorodnii, Z. P. ed., *Khersonu dvesti let, 1778–1978. Sbornik dokumentov i materialov,* Kyiv, 1978.

Zander, Valentine. *St. Seraphim of Sarov.* Translated by Sister Gabriel Anne, s.s.c with an introduction by Father Boris Bobrinskoy. NY, 1975.

Zatko, James J. *Descent in the Darkness: The Destruction of the Roman Catholic Church in Russia, 1917–1923.* Notre Dame, 1965.

Zavadovskii, Aleksandr, "Iz vospominanii o preosviashchennom Innokentie, arkhiepiskopie khersonskom i tavricheskom." *TEV* 2 (1880): 68–82.

Zayas, Alfred M. de. *Nemesis at Potsdam: The Expulsion of the Germans from the East.* Lincoln, NE, 1977.

Zenkovskii, Vasilii Vasil'evich. *A History of Russian Philosophy.* Translated by George L. Kline. London, 1953.

Zenkovsky, Serge A. "The Russian Church Schism: Its Background and Repercussion." *Russian Review* 16, no. 4 (1957): 37–58.

"Zhitie i stradanie sviatogo sviashchennomuchenika Klimenta, papy rimskago." In *Zhitiia Sviatykh na russkom iazyke izlozheniia po rukovodstvu Chetikh-minei sv. Dimitriia Rostovskago, s dopolneniiami, ob'iasnitel'nymi primechaniiami, i izobrazheniiami sviatykh* 3 (25 November), 701–15. Moscow, 1992.

"Zhitie Sviatago Stefana Ispovednika, arkhiepiskopa surozhskago." In *Zhitiia Sviatykh na russkom iazyke izlozhenniia po rukovodstvu Chetikh-minei sv. Dimitriia Rostovskago, s dopolneniiami, ob'iasnitel'nymi primechaniiami i izobrazheniiami sviatykh* 4 (December 15), 425–31. Moscow, 1992.

"Zhizneopisanie vysokopreosviashchennogo Makariia, mitropolita moskovskogo i kolomenskogo." In *Istoriia Russkoi Tserkvi. Kniga pervaia [book 1], Istoriia khris-*

tianstva v rossii do ravnoapostol'nogo kniazia Vladimira kak vvedenie v istoriiu russkoi tserkvi, 11–32. Moscow, 1994.
Zhukov, K. *Zametki v puti na iuzhnyi bereg Kryma*. St. Petersburg, 1865.
"Zincirli Medrese Association (Bakhchisaray)." International Committee for Crimea. <www.iccrimea.org/ngos/zincirli.html> (accessed 16 January 2003).
Znamenski, Andrei A. "Strategies of Survival: Native Encounters with Russian Missionaries in Alaska and Siberia, 1820s–1917." Ph.D. diss., University of Toledo, 1997.
Znamenskii, Ioann. *O Kasperovskoi Ikone Bozh'ei Materi*. Odessa, 1877.
Zorin, Andrei. *Kormia dvuglavogo orla . . . Literatura i gosudarstvennaia ideologiia v Rossii v poslednei treti XVIII–pervoi treti XIX veka*. Moscow, 2001.
———. "Star of the East": The Holy Alliance and European Mysticism." *Kritika: Explorations in Russian and Eurasian History* 4, no. 2 (2003): 313–42.
Zubar, V. M., and S. B. Sorochan. *U istokov Khristianstva v iugo-zapadnoi tavrike. Epokha i vera*. Kyiv, 2005.
Zubov, V. P. *Russkie propovedniki. Ocherki po istorii russkoi propovedi*. Moscow, 2001.
Zuev, V. F. *Vypiska iz puteshestvennikh zapisok Vasil'ia Fedorovicha Zueva, kasaushchikhsia do poluostrova Kryma, 1782 goda. Mesiatseslov istoricheskii i geograficheskii na 1783 god*. St. Petersburg, 1790.

Index

Abkhazia, 81, 123
Ablaiev, Mufti Emirali, 195
Adlerberg, Nikolai Vladimirovich, 147–48, 160, 228n.113
Agathangelos (Typaldos), 71, 76, 119, 120–22
Ageev, Parfeny, 66, 82
Aivazovskii, Ivan, 74
Aleksei, Archbishop Crimea and Simferopol (Rzhanitsyn), 155, 160, 165–66, 170
Aleksii, Patriarch of Russia (Ridiger), 179
Alexander I, 26, 46, 48, 51, 63, 67, 71
Alexander II, 68, 148–49, 152, 159
Alexander III, 183
Alushta, 60, 114–15, 172, 188–89
Amanton, Victor, 4, 70
Anastasia (St.) skete, 85–86, 123, 151, 164, 172–73
Andrew (the Apostle), 6, 55–56, 84, 185
archaeology, 5, 43, 50–54, 59, 165–66, 175; *see also* Korsun
Arkas, Nikolaos Andreevich, 8, 51, 68, 69, 159
Arkas, Zacharias Andreevich, 8, 51–53, 60, 68, 111–12
Armenians, 3, 4, 12, 22–23, 25, 30, 31, 44, 70, 72, 74–75, 78, 105, 155, 174, 183, 193
asceticism, 29, 61–62, 79–87, 109, 161, 164
Azizler, 190

Bakhchisarai, 23, 38–44, 48, 51, 57, 60, 70, 72, 73, 91–92; religious procession, 103–4. *See also* Dormition Monastery
Bakhchisarai State Historical and Cultural Preserve (BGIZ), 192
Balaklava, 8, 49, 53, 60, 159, 185; during Crimean War, 144–45, 148, 151–52, 158; tourism, 159–62, 165; Greek Battalion, 87; St. George Monastery, 69–72, 76, 84, 96, 119–23, 134, 166

Balkan Peninsula, 21, 63, 65, 67
Baranovskii, Aleksei Petrovich, 171
Basil II, Byzantine Emperor, 43
battle of Alma (Sept. 8/20, 1854), 140
battle of Balaklava (Oct. 25/Nov. 6, 1854), 144
battle of Inkerman (Nov. 5/17, 1854), 144
Bazhanov, V. B., 17
Bazili, Konstantin, 64, 65, 76
Beim, Solomon, 169
beratlis, 68–69, 72
Berdiansk: Crimean War, 142, 147; population, 154; sects in, 29–30, 39
Bershatskii, Aleksandr, 29
Berte-Delegarde, A. L., 166
Bessarabia, 4, 22, 31; Crimean War, 152; immigration, 36–37, 154–55
Bizukov Monastery, 121
Black Sea Navy, 37, 52, 68, 110, 120, 135, 163, 173–74, 180–81, 230n.60
Black Sea Society of Steamships and Trade, 159
Blagoveshchenskii, N. A., 80
Bode, Baroness Maria, 59
Briukhovskii, Grigorii, 25, 142–43
Bucharest, 52, 65, 76
Budberg, Aleksander Ivanovich, 123
Bulgakov, G. G., 25
Bulgakov, Makarii. *See* Makarii (Bulgakov) Metropolitan
Burachkov, Platon, 24
Byzantium, 3, 5, 42, 43, 110

Catherine II, 4, 6, 20, 26, 33, 42–46, 49, 54–55, 57, 61, 64–68, 70, 108, 126, 129, 149, 151, 171, 179, 190
Catholicism: adherents in New Russia, 22–23, 30–31, 39, 74, 101, 183, 193; Crimean War, 131; political controversy, 64–66, 81. *See also* Greek Catholic
Caucasus, and missionary activity, 35, 55,

62, 134, 148, 150
charge of the light brigade. *See* battle of Balaklava
Chechnya, 180, 192, 194
Chersonesos, ancient city, 6, 7, 40, 42–46, 49–60, 85–86, 104–6, 118–23, 162, 167, 175; during the Crimean War, 124, 134, 135, 143–44; St. Vladimir monastery, 110–14, 151, 158, 160, 161, 184–88, 193; tourism, 163–65
Chufut Kale, 38, 90, 92, 105–6, 159, 162, 169
Church of the Holy Sepulchre, 64
Clement (St.), 6, 56, 84, 113, 186; church in Crimea, 85, 110, 114, 151
colonists, 23, 27, 36–39, 41, 44, 154–56
Constantine (St. Cassius the Greek, the Wonder-worker of Uglich), 43, 207n.12
Constantinople, 43, 45, 52, 63, 65–66, 71–81, 108, 126, 148, 162, 175
Cosmas and Damian Monastery, 7, 87, 96, 104, 105, 107, 114–19, 122, 123, 136, 151; Tatar pilgrimage (to Savluk Su), 51; women's community, 161, 165, 167; controversy, 172–73, 188
Cossacks, 148, 190–94
Crimean Athos, 85, 104, 109, 176, 185, 186, 220n.28
Cyril (St.), 56, 84, 186

Danubian Principalities, 65, 71, 152
Dashkov, Dmitrii V., 64–65, 212n.15
Davydov, Vladimir, 66, 79, 80
deportation, of Crimean populations, 12, 174, 176, 191
Derman, A. B., 170
dhimmis, 67, 74, 127
Diakovskii, Daniel, 25
Dimitrii, Archbishop (Muretov), 159
Dimitrii of Rostov (St.), 113
Dnepr, 20, 24, 147
Dobychin, Aleksei, 182
Dombrovskii, Franz Martinovich, 104, 135, 210n.64
Dormition Monastery, 7, 44, 70, 71, 85–92, 103–9, 110, 112, 121–24, 158–72, 175, 184, 186, 191; during the Crimean War, 140, 143–44, 151
Dukhobors, 16, 27, 30, 149
Dundas, Admiral James Whitley, 130

Eastern Question, 10; Balkan immigration, and, 67–78; in Crimea, 62–63; Russian attitudes, 63–67
Efimov, Dmitrii Igorovich, 109
Ekaterinoslav, 4, 25, 31, 36, 37, 44
Elijah (St.) skete, 83
Elisavetograd, 27
Enikale, 23, 44, 72, 73
Erasm, Abbot, 171
Eski Kirim. *See* Staryi Krim
Evgenii, Abbot, 59, 158
Evpatoria, 70, 72, 73, 97, 128, 129, 144, 146, 147, 149, 152, 155, 197n.11

Feodoro. *See* Genoese kingdom
Feodosia, 15, 24, 26, 38, 55, 72, 74, 102, 130, 133, 136, 141, 146, 152, 154, 161, 170, 209n.45
Feodosia-Mariupol diocese, 32
Filaret, Metropolitan (Drozdov), 7, 15–18, 32, 80, 126–27, 198n.24
Firkovich, Abraham, 38–39, 106, 169
Flavius, Josephus, 43
Fotisala. *See* Golubinka
Frederick Wilhelm IV, 126

Gaspirali (Gasprinski), Ismail, 10, 12, 17, 170, 191
Gavriil, Archbishop (Rozanov), 15, 17, 19, 24, 26–27, 32, 35, 53–54, 115–16
Genichesk, 133, 157
Genoese kingdom, 113, 169, 221n.56
George (St.) monastery in Balaklava, 49, 70–71, 76, 84, 104–5, 119–23, 151, 160, 163, 165, 166; during the Crimean War, 133, 143–45
George (St.) monastery in Katerles, 151, 158–59
Germans, 3, 4, 24, 29, 36, 72, 155, 174

Index

Germogen, Bishop (Dobronravov), 150, 167, 173
Gerontiia, Abbot, 121, 145
Gett-Dacians, 55–56
Giray, Mengli, 48, 106
Giray, Sahin, 46, 70, 108
Golubinka, 98, 191–92
Golubinskii, Evgenii Evstigneevich, 55
Gorchakov, Mikhail Dmitrii, 137, 138, 141, 146
Goth Alans, 105
Grach, Leonid, 181
Graecophilia, 13, 42–43; *see also* philorthodoxy and phil-hellenism
Greece, 6, 42–43, 47, 62, 64–68, 76–78, 82–86, 175
Greek Catholic Church, 16, 31, 177–78
Greeks, 63, 64, 66, 81–83; ancient, 43, 46–47, 55–56; in Crimea, 3–4, 8, 12–13, 32, 36, 44, 61, 69–78, 87, 119, 122, 153–55, 160–63, 174; in Odessa, 23–24; 51–54, 66–67
Greig, Admiral Samuel, 50, 52
Grigorios V (Patriarch), 63, 71

Hagia, Sofia, 66
Hamelin, Admiral François–Alphonse, 130
haraç, 68, 82
Hare Krishna, 176
hesychasm, 62, 79
Hezb-e Tahrir, 182
Holy Alliance, 128, 212n.4
Holy Synod, 7, 11, 16, 18, 25, 29, 30, 39, 61, 62, 71, 77, 82, 85–88, 109–11, 120, 132, 140, 143, 156–59, 161, 164, 167, 200n.40, 217n.103, 220n.28

Ignatius, Metropolitan, 44, 54, 70
Imperial Archaeological Society, 58, 165
Inkerman Monastery, 7, 53, 56, 84–86, 95, 104–5, 110–14, 118, 123, 161–66, 172, 175, 184; during the Crimean War, 141–44, 151, 158
Iphigenia, 45, 49, 53
Isidor, Exarch of Georgia, 34

Islam, 3, 4, 7, 16, 17, 32, 40, 43, 46, 54, 59, 63, 65, 87, 104, 106, 108, 117, 123–24, 129–30, 134, 146, 150–51, 155–56, 171–82, 192–95
Iuzefovich, Mikhail Vladimorovich, 130

Jehovah's Witnesses, 176
Jemilev, Mustafa, 190
Jews, 3, 4, 8, 12, 15, 16, 22–26, 38–39, 67, 69, 72, 104, 162, 169, 194, 195
John (St.) the Baptist skete, 80, 87, 119, 123

Kaffa. *See* Feodosia
Kapodistrias, Ioannis, 67, 77
Karaim, 22–25, 38–39, 50, 72, 92, 105–6, 157–61, 162, 169, 183
Karasubazar, 72, 73, 133, 141
Kartashev, Anton Vladimorovich, 55
Keppen, Petr Ivanovich, 84
Kerch, 24, 25, 34, 41, 45
Kerch-Enikale, 23, 44, 72, 73, 75, 123, 128, 130, 158, 159
Khazars, 56
Kherson (city), 20
Kherson (province), 4, 15, 17, 21, 26–28, 36, 42, 51, 53, 121, 141, 157
Kherson-Tauride (diocese), 11, 15, 22, 31, 39, 58, 76, 103, 119, 139, 159
Khristos, Abbot, 49
Khrulev, Stepan, 141
Kinburn, 24, 227n.104
Kirimtatar, 16, 17, 35, 38, 76, 105, 161, 181
Kishlav (Bulgarian colony), 74, 154, 161
Kiselev, Pavel, 33
Kiseleva, Natalia, 192–93
Kiziltash, 26, 151, 159, 161, 165, 170–71
Klyment, Bishop (Kushch, UOC-KP), 194, 238n.90
Konstantina (Hermitess), 161
Korff, Modest Andreevich, 131
Korsun, legend of, 6, 7, 42–43, 49, 163, 165
Korsun Monastery (Tauride Old Believer Monastery), 121, 151, 228n.5
Kosovo, 182

268 Index

Kravchuk, Leonid, 178, 186
Kristianovich, Alexander, 165
Krüdener, Juliana von, 212n.4
Kruze, L., 50, 53, 60
Krymchaks. *See* Jews
Kuchma, Leonid, 178–79, 187–88
Kyiv: artifacts, 160, 167; in current events, 174–77, 182–90; Prince Vladimir and, 57, 113
Kyiv-Pecherskaya Lavra, 179
Kyiv Spiritual Academy, 18, 19

Ladinskii, General Lieutenant, 24
Langueron, Alexander, 20
Lazar, Metropolitan (Shvets), 174, 185, 195
Lazarev, Mikhail, 163, 185
Lazzerini, Edward, 173
Litke, Feodor, 158
Livanov, F. V., 163–64
Louis Napoleon, 125
Lviv, 189
Lyall, Robert, 47

Makarii (Bulgakov) Metropolitan, 19, 54–57
Makarii (abbot of Cosmas and Damian), 118
Mangup, 88, 115
Mariupol, 44, 71
Martin (St.), 6, 56, 84, 186
Mejlis, 182, 190
Melitopol, 29, 30, 36, 39, 147, 154
Mennonites, 29, 39, 154
Menshikov, Aleksandr Sergeivich, 130–31, 140, 146–48
Meshkov, Iurii, 180, 194, 239n.34
Methodius (St.), 56, 84, 186
Methodius, Inkerman monk, 167
migration, 5, 12, 13, 38, 62, 74–75, 151–53; Armenian, 43–44, 54–55, 107–8; Bulgarian, 74–78, 151–55; Greek, 43–44, 54–55, 107–8; Tatar, 148–49, 170, 197n.8
missionary activity, 6, 9, 11, 15–17, 27, 29–30, 32; early, 43, 55–56, 64; limitations of, 34–37; Ottoman Empire, 75–76, 81
Mitrofan (St.), 157
Moldavia, 23, 65, 72, 76, 77, 155
Molokan, 16, 27, 29, 30, 39, 154
Montadon, S. N., 84
Mount Athos, 62–63, 65–69, 78–88, 103–4, 109, 119, 149, 175, 184–86, 216n.91,n.99,n.103
Muravev-Apostol, Ivan, 41, 69
Murav'ev, Andrei Nikolaevich, 77, 82, 164
Murzakevich, Nikolai N. 50–51, 111

Nadezhdin, Nikolai Ivanovich, 58
Nakhimov, Pavel Stepanovich, 125, 138–39, 163
NATO, 181–82
Nesselrode, Karl Vasilievech, 76
Nicholas I, 5, 8, 10, 17, 26, 28, 30–32, 49, 54, 64, 70, 71, 82; during Crimean War, 125–26, 148, 152
Nikanor, Abbot, 188–89
Nikitin, Aleksei, 28
Nikolaev, 20, 26, 28, 68, 137
Nogai Tatars, 16, 29, 72, 147, 154
Novy Afon, 62, 81

Odessa, 5, 6–11, 15–21, 25, 28, 31, 35, 39–40, 43, 59, 63, 68, 75–81, 109, 115; during Crimean War, 129–34, 139, 145–46, 157
Odessa Society of History and Antiquity, 20, 50–57, 110–11, 165
Old Believers, 15–17, 26–29, 183
Opochinin, Fedor Petrovich, 220n.28
orientalism, 48–49
Osten-Saken, Dmitrii Erofeevich, 131–32, 145–46
Ottoman Empire, 4, 6, 10, 42, 48, 64–76, 81, 83, 88; during Crimean War, 125–33, 148, 152; immigration, 155

Paissy, Father (Chersonesos), 187–88
Palauzov, Nikolay, 77–78
Palauzov, Spiridon Nikolaevich, 77

Paleolog, Mikhalis, 51, 52
Palimpsestov, Ivan Ustinovich, 19, 59
Pallas, Peter Simon, 41, 46
pan-Slavism, 9–10, 78
Panteleimon Monastery, 80–83
Pantikapeia, 55
Paraskeva, St. Monastery, 151, 161
Parfeny, Abbot, 170–71
Pavsky, G. P., 17
Peace: God's Gift, 194
Perekop, 25, 34, 70–73, 129, 141, 146, 149, 154
Pestel, Vladimir, 25, 147
Petrov, E., 192
philhellenism, 42, 47; *see also* Graecophilia
Philiki Etaireia, 67
Philomousos Etaireia, 67
phil-Orthodoxy, 42, 49, 54
pilgrimage, 12, 44, 46, 63, 66, 74, 78, 81–86, 115, 122, 164, 183–86, 188, 193
Pirogov, Nikolai Ivanovich, 140
Pogodin, Mikhail Petrovich, 19, 58, 126, 130, 145–46
Poland, 19, 178; Poles, 31
Polikarp, Bishop (Radkevich), 63, 86–87, 114, 121
Poltava, 25, 179
population, 3–8, 72–73; exchange 10, 150, 153–55; diversity of, 20–26
Potemkin, Grigorii, 70
property (religious) restitution, 177–79, 186–94
Proskurina, Nadezhda, 183, 185
Protasov, Nikolai, 120, 130, 140–41
Prousis, Theophilus, 10
Pushkin, Alexander, 48
Putin, Vladimir, 188

Reshid Pasha, 67
Riasanovsky, Nicholas, 9
Richelieu Lyceum, 38
Roma, 4, 72
Romanov, Grand Duchess Elena Pavlovna, 140–41
Romanov, Grand Duke Konstantin Nikolaevich, 21, 37, 57, 109

Rossiya-TV, 182
Rulev, V. A., 122

St. Petersburg, 7, 8, 11, 12, 28, 37, 46, 77, 129, 131, 135, 141, 165
St. Petersburg Spiritual Academy, 17, 18
Sakhnovskii, Pavel Ivanov, 25
Salachik, 106
Salvation Army, 176
Savinov, Father Ioann, 141–43
Savluk-Su. *See* Cosmas and Damian
Schlözer, August Ludwig von, 55
Scythians, 55–56, 113
Serbinovich, Konstantin Stepanovich, 220n.28
Sergei Trinity Monastery, 80
Sevastopol, 7, 20, 23–24, 41, 52, 59, 68, 87, 110–14, 123, 181, 185–86; during the Crimean War, 128, 130, 133, 136–41, 144–46, 152, 157–60, 163, 173–74; population of, 70–75
Sevastopol Statistical Committee, 53
Seven Martyrs (of Chersonesos), 56, 186
Skoptsy, 27–30, 39
Simferopol, 3, 11, 12, 21, 23–25, 33, 39–40, 51, 72, 114–15, 133, 141, 147–48, 155–57, 162, 169, 171, 173, 175
Sinope, 125
Slavic Pompeii. *See* Chersonesos
Slavophiles, 9, 126
Sofonia, Archimandrite, 76
Solovets Monastery, 80, 82
Spaso-Preobrazhenskii Skete, 184–85
Spiranda, Constantine, 70–71, 103
starchestvo, 62
Staryi Krym (Eski Kirim), 75, 154
Stefan of Surozh (St.), 84, 136, 184, 186
Stefan of Surozh (St.) Monastery, 159, 161, 165
Stroganov, Aleksandr, 149, 151, 155–57, 160
Sturdza, Alexandru Skarlotovich, 8, 11, 15, 16, 19, 35, 51–52, 76–77
Sudak, 26, 69, 159, 162, 170
Sviatogorets (Sergei/Serafim), 65, 81, 109

Tatars (Crimea), 3–4, 45–51, 70–75, 84, 105–7, 184; Christian tradition and, 104, 108, 114–17, 122–24; during Crimean War, 129, 130, 133, 135, 139, 146–61; population, 22–24, 169–75; post-Soviet return, 180–91; Russian Orthodox Church and, 15–17, 32–36, 40–46, 54–56, 87–88, 191–95

Tatar Tsegany, 72
Tauride Archival Commission, 165
Tauride Society for History, Archaeology and Ethnography, 165
Theodore Studite, 184
Tiraspol, 28, 31, 39
toleration, 4, 15–16, 26, 29, 117, 129, 149, 151–52, 156, 171, 198n.14
Tolstoi, Dmitrii, 25, 39
Tolstoy, Leo, 139
Topla, 151, 161, 162, 168
Toshkov, N. M., 77
Toskhovich, S. D., 77
Totleben, Eduard, 137, 160
Trajan, Roman Emperor, 56, 113
Treaty of Adrianople, 64
Treaty of Bucharest, 65
Treaty of Kutchuk-Kainardji, 65
Treaty of Jassy, 65
Treaty of Paris, 152, 155
Treaty of Unkiar Skelessi, 81
Tsvigun, Marina /Maria Devi Kristos (Maria-Jesus), 177

Ukrainian Autocephalous Orthodox Church [UAOC], 177, 183

Ukrainian (Greek) Catholic Church [UGCC], 177
Ukrainian Orthodox Church of the Kyivan Patriarchate [UOC-KP], 177–79, 183, 194
Ukrainian Orthodox Church of the Moscow Patriarchate [UOC-MP], 177–79, 183, 185, 187, 193
urochishche, 114–18
Uspenskii, Porfirii, 19, 64, 75
Uvarov, Aleksei Sergeevich, 19, 58, 112, 144, 165
Uvarov, Sergei Semenovich, 5, 19, 58, 112

Valaam, 80, 82
Varsofonia, Abbess, 161
Vasilii, Father, 111, 114, 158
Victoria, Queen of England, 125
Vissarian, Archimandrite, 75–76
Vladimir (St.), 6; as founder of Russian state, 51–57, 84; baptism location, 42–45, 49. *See also* Korsun legend
Vladimir (St.) Monastery. *See Chersonesos*
Vorontsov Prince Mikhail Semenovich, 11, 16, 21, 23, 27–30, 32–33, 40, 88, 149–50, 156

Wallachia, 65, 66, 77, 152

Yalta, 23, 25, 129, 142, 148–49, 152, 164
Yanukovich, Victor Prime Minister, 190
Ypsilantis, Alexandros, 52, 67
Yushchenko, Viktor, 179

Zosima, Abbot, 168–69, 173

BX 494 .C75 K69 2010
Kozelsky, Mara.
Christianizing Crimea

NOV 2 3 2009